Women, the State, and Political Liberalization

Women, the State, and Political Liberalization

MIDDLE EASTERN AND NORTH AFRICAN EXPERIENCES

LAURIE A. BRAND

columbia university press

New York

Columbia University Press
Publishers Since 1893
New York   Chichester, West Sussex

Library of Congress Cataloging-in-Publication Data
Brand, Laurie A.
   Women, the state, and political liberalization : Middle Eastern
and North African experience / Laurie A. Brand.
        p.   cm.
   Includes bibliographical references and index.
   ISBN 0-231-11266-1 (cloth). — ISBN 0-231-11267-X (paper)
   1. Women in politics—Morocco. 2. Women—Morocco—Social
conditions. 3. Women in politics—Jordan. 4. Women—Jordan—Social
conditions. 5. Women in politics—Tunisia. 6. Women—Tunisia—
Social conditions. 7. Women in politics—Case studies. 8. Women—
Social conditions—Case studies. 9. Human rights—Case studies.
10. Political development—Case studies. I. Title.
HQ1236.5.M8B73   1998
305.42'095695—dc21
                                                        98-4431
                                                        CIP

Designed by Benjamin Shin Farber

Casebound editions of Columbia University Press books are printed on
permanent and durable acid-free paper.
Printed in the United States of America
c 10 9 8 7 6 5 4 3 2 1
p 10 9 8 7 6 5 4 3 2 1

For Afaf

CONTENTS

List of Abbreviations ix

Preface xiii

Acknowledgments xvii

A Note on the Transliteration xix

Introduction: Women, the State, and Political Liberalization 1

THE **CASES** 27

PART ONE **MOROCCO** 29

1. IN THE REALM OF THE COMMANDER OF THE FAITHFUL 31

2. IN THE SHADOW OF THE *MUDAWWANAH* 46

3. CONFRONTING THE MAKHZEN 69

PART TWO **JORDAN** 93

4. GOD, HOMELAND, KING 95

5. THE STRUGGLE FOR VOICE 120

6. THE STATE RETREATS, THE STATE RETURNS 145

PART THREE **TUNISIA** 175

7. BOURGUIBA AND HIS LEGACY 177

8. CITOYENNES À PART ENTIÈRE? 202

9. THE CHANGING GUISE OF STATE FEMINISM 220

Conclusions 247

Notes 265

Interviews 293

Bibliography 297

Index 307

LIST OF **ABBREVIATIONS**

ADFM: Association Démocratique des Femmes Marocaines

AFTURD: Association des Femmes Tunisiennes pour la Recherche sur le Développement

AMDF: Association Marocaine des Droits de la Femme

AMDH: Association Marocaine des Droits de l'Homme

ATFD: Association Tunisienne des Femmes Démocrates

AWF: Arab Women's Federation

BPWC: Business and Professional Women's Club

CDT::   Confedération Démocratique de Travail

CECF: Club d'Etudes de la Condition des Femmes

CREDIF: Centre de Recherche, d'Etudes, de Documentation, et d'Information sur la Femme

CSE: Commission Syndicale d'Etudes de la Condition de la Femme Travailleur

CSP: Code du Statut Personnel

DII: Democratic Institutions Initiative

FES: Friedrich Ebert Stiftung

FD: Femmes Démocrates

FIS:	Front Islamique du Salut
FLN:	Front de Libération Nationale
GFJW:	General Federation of Jordanian Women
IAF:	Islamic Action Front
JNCW:	Jordanian National Committee for Women
JNWF:	Jordanian National Women's Federation
JWU:	Jordanian Women's Union
KAS:	Konrad Adenauer Stiftung
LMDH:	Ligue Marocaine des Droits de l'Homme
LTDH:	Ligue Tunisienne des Droits de l'Homme
MENA:	Middle East/North Africa
MTI:	Mouvance de la Tendance Islamique
NDI:	National Democratic Institute
NED:	National Endowment for Democracy
NGO:	Non-governmental organization
NHF:	Noor al-Hussein Foundation
NJRC:	New Jordan Research Center
OADP:	Organisation de l'Action Démocratique Populaire
OFI:	Organisation de la Femme Istiqlalienne
OMDH:	Organisation Marocaine des Droits de l'Homme
PCT:	Parti Communiste Tunisien
PI:	Parti Istiqlalien
PPS:	Parti du Progrès et du Socialisme
PSD:	Parti Socialiste Destourien
QAF:	Queen Alia Fund
RCD:	Rassemblement Constitutionel Démocratique
UAF:	Union de l'Action Féminine:
UFT:	Union des Femmes de Tunisie
UGTT:	Union Générale des Travailleurs Tunisiens
UMFT:	Union Musulmane des Femmes de Tunisie
UMT:	Union Marocaine de Travail
UNEM:	Union Nationale Estudiantine Marocaine
UNFM:	Union Nationale des Femmes Marocaines

UNFT:	Union Nationale des Femmes de Tunisie/Union Nationale des Femmes Tunisiennes
USAID:	United States Agency for International Development
USFP:	Union Socialiste des Forces Populaires
USIS:	United States Information Service
WID:	Women in Development
WUJ:	Women's Union in Jordan

PREFACE

By late 1987, a wave of potentially deep-reaching political changes appeared to be underway in the Middle East and North Africa. First, Tunisia's president-for-life, Habib Bourguiba, was ousted after more than thirty years in power. Then even more dramatically, in December 1987 the long-standing episodic civil resistance to Israeli occupation of the West Bank and Gaza crystallized into sustained, and escalating, opposition. Shortly thereafter a number of Arab regimes, manifestly incapable of coping with growing problems of debt, unemployment, and corruption, appeared to begin to give way to successors that promised more political freedoms. Algeria, Jordan, Yemen, and Morocco all witnessed political openings of various types, some more apparently significant than others, but all promising changes that would lessen repression and open the way for greater political participation.

As I watched the unfolding of the political liberalizations in the Arab world, I also began to follow with great interest the "liberalizing" impact of the much more profound economic/cum political transformations that began to sweep Eastern Europe. While each country has had its own experience, several trends emerged. Conservative forces, whether those aligned with the Church or those that were simply reactionary nationalist, began to espouse programs for women that involved a renewed emphasis on motherhood (with restricted if any access to abortion as a corollary) and a woman's "primary duties" in the home. At the same time, the safety nets that the socialist regimes had provided were dismantled or simply disintegrated under the weight of the massive budgetary problems the new market economies were experiencing. Redundant employment in the state sector was being eliminated as well, and women seemed to be bearing the brunt of these cutbacks. Quotas for female representation in people's assemblies, however purely symbolic they may have been, were ended; and women's presence in other political institutions declined markedly. At least in the short to medium term, women appeared to be among the big losers in the much heralded economic and political transformations from communism.

In the Middle East and North Africa, although the processes underway were by no means as "revolutionary" (in the pure sense of the term), nonetheless similar trends appeared. The opening up of the political systems offered, at least initially, the opportunity for a variety of opposition groups to enter the political realm as legal participants. In the Middle East, however, it was not the traditionalists of the Catholic or Orthodox church, but rather those of a particular strain of Islam, often called (inappropriately) for lack of better term "fundamentalists." Such groups entered the political fray with a part of their program aimed at instituting more conservative social policies, among them some which threatened to constrain women's activities and rights. It was as these trends were beginning to become clear in 1991 that this project was initially conceived.

While the political and economic transformations that swept Eastern Europe in 1989–90 continue to unfold, the openings that appeared in the Middle East and North Africa have in virtually all cases been closed. Tunisia's was perhaps the shortest lived, as renewed repression was clear certainly by 1990. Algeria, which in some ways had been the most promising, had, at the time of this writing, fallen into a cycle of low-level civil war between the security forces or civilian villagers and certain Islamist groups. Morocco's 1993 and 1997 elections were disappointments to the opposition, although the associational life that has blossomed since the Gulf war continues to offer hopeful signs. Yemen's amazingly vibrant "cohabitation" degenerated into civil war in the early summer of 1994. And by mid-summer of 1994 fears of popular expressions of opposition to a peace accord with Israel had led the Jordanian government to narrow the margins of freedom of expression in the kingdom.

The question may then arise, why pursue a project on women and political liberalization if the political openings, part of the central problematic of this project, were closed or closing after such short periods? Several responses suggest themselves. The first is that the apparent similarities with the Eastern European cases (as chapter 1 will argue) are too significant to be ignored simply because the transformations were not as thoroughgoing. Exploring possible shared characteristics offers the potential to say something about the significance of culture—Islam as the omnipresent independent variable in Middle East politics—as opposed to structure. Second, it has been suggested by some of the civil society literature that vibrant women's organizations may be the most important precursors to more democratic development. This proposition is worth exploring to determine what such organizations do and how they relate to the state, other political actors, and each other during such periods. Third, trends visible during such periods of limited openings may offer insights into what to expect when the more thoroughgoing changes do come in the Middle East and North Africa.

I am a political scientist, not an anthropologist, but I do believe it is useful for a researcher to situation herself vis-à-vis her study. I am an Arabist, a female, and an American. (I struggled in writing this sentence to determine the priority order of the adjectives, and I am not sure I have it right or that it does not change situationally.) I have never before attempted to write on women, in part because that was not where my intellectual interests lay and, in part because, when it came to the Middle East, the topic seemed like a minefield. When I traveled to Jordan in the summer of 1992, it was on a grant to examine the impact of economic and political liberalization on organized labor. Yet, between writing the proposal and arriving in Jordan, I had found myself drawn to the question of women and political liberalization, in large part because of the developments in Eastern Europe, but also because of what seemed to me similar developments in Jordan during the period of Islamist participation in the cabinet, January–June 1991. I should also say, however, that had it not been for the misogynist policies of the Reagan and Bush administrations aimed at, among other things, legislating away a women's right to choose, I might never have come to view these questions in the same way. Had I not felt my own rights threatened by a gang of sociopolitical reactionaries, I might never have come to the point where such a study was so important to me.

This of course does not make entering this field any less problematic. I am aware that there will be charges that as an outsider (a non-Muslim and non-Arab) I somehow have no right to explore these issues, or am incapable of exploring them objectively. I accept the second charge, but with the understanding that *none* of us is an objective observer or student of *any* event or phenomenon. As for the first, I reject it categorically as insidious and as an indirect attack on academic freedom. If we are qualified to explore only those topics of which we are a part, then our potential contributions as social scientists will be marginal indeed. I would be qualified to write only about middle-class women from the suburbs of Cincinnati who go to Georgetown University, major in French, become interested in Arabic, study Arabic in Cairo . . .

This study has been one of both societal and self-exploration. Never have I had to struggle with questions of cultural relativism, and of what I believe and what I can accept, as I have in conducting this research. I can say that I have not been able to overcome my bias against organized religion (*any* religion) or my implicit distrust of that set of relations called "the state." This does not mean that I refuse to accept the importance of religion and religious values in the countries I have studied or reviewed. I believe one can study and understand societies, and indeed, as I believe I have with the Arab world, come to feel very comfortable and at home in another society, without accepting or adopting all its values. Nor does it mean that I see the state as simply a set of coercive relations that above all else repress. I hope this study shows how complicated and at times contradictory those relations can be.

ACKNOWLEDGMENTS

A comparative study of three countries was a massive undertaking and numerous parties helped to make it possible. First, the Center for International Studies of the School of International Relations of the University of Southern California funded research assistants during the years 1993–94 and 1994–95 who helped me lay the groundwork for this study. I was also the recipient of several grants that enabled me to conduct field research. In chronological order they were: American Center for Oriental Research/United States Information Agency grants for research in Jordan during the summers of 1993 and 1994; a Council of American Overseas Research Centers award for research in Jordan and Morocco during the summer of 1995; a Social Science Research Council grant for field work in Jordan and Tunisia during the fall and winter of 1995; and an American Institute for Maghrib Studies grant for research in Morocco in the spring of 1996. I am most grateful to all of these organizations for the financial support given my project. Special thanks are also due: the American Center for Oriental Research, Amman for assistance and cooperation during my numerous research stints in Jordan; Susan Ossman and the Institut de Recherche sur le Maghreb Contemporain, (IRMC) Rabat; Nabeel Khoury and Fatema-Zohra Salah, USIS, Rabat; La Source, Rabat; Jeanne Mrad and the Centre d'Etudes Maghrebines à Tunis; the Centre National de Documentation, Tunis; Mustafa Hamarneh, director of the Center for Strategic Studies, Jordan University, Amman; Maha Khatib, director of the

UNIFEM office, Amman; and Riccardo Bocco, director, Centre d'Etudes et Recherche sur le Moyen Orient Contemporain (CERMOC), Amman. Each of them offered vital informational and/or logistical support during my field research.

For valuable critiques (in both senses of the word) on various parts of the manuscripts at differents stages in its development I am most grateful to two anonymous readers as well as: Fayez Hammad, Mervet Hatem, Jane Jaquette, Amal Sabbagh, Ann Tickner, Mark Tessler, Greg White, and Ra'eda Zoubi. I would also like to thank Kate Wittenberg of Columbia University Press for supporting this project. Finally, I am indebted to the many Arab women whom I have been privileged to know and call friends over the course of the more than twenty years since my first stay in the region. Without their support and example this book would not and could not have been written.

Laurie A. Brand
Los Angeles, California
September 1997

A Note on Transliteration

As a longtime transliteration purist, I have been confounded by how to deal with North African names. Not only are their vowelling patterns far removed from those of classical Arabic, but also the French rendition of them—the spellings most widely used—removed them even further from anything familiar to those who do their work on the Mashriq or the Gulf. Imposing a standardized classical Arabic transliteration system throughout this manuscript would have turned many North African names into collections of letters virtually unrecognizable to those most familiar with them. Hence, I have opted for a solution which is pragmatic, if not consistent: I have generally replicated names as I found them on (in) books, articles, and business cards. I beg the indulgence of the remaining, and, I suspect dwindling, community of purists.

Women, the State, and Political Liberalization

INTRODUCTION
Women, the State, and Political Liberalization

In 1989, the eyes of the world were fixed on Eastern Europe as the Berlin wall came down, and new leaderships promising greater political economic freedoms gradually took the reins of power. The events in Eastern Europe have been the most recent, and most striking, in what has been called the third wave[1] of transitions from authoritarianism, which began in the 1970s in southern Europe and Latin America.[2] Less noted in the press, but no less significant, by 1989 similar developments had also begun to unfold south and east of the Mediterranean. The first in a series of dramatic developments[3] was the ouster of Tunisia's President Bourguiba in November 1987, followed a month later by the beginning of the Palestinian intifada. Subsequently, a number of Arab regimes, incapable of coping with growing problems of debt, unemployment, and corruption began to give way to successor regimes (or leaderships) that promised economic reforms and greater political freedom.

Although the number of works dealing with Middle East/North Africa (MENA) cases is quite small, a plethora of literature has been produced on the transitions elsewhere. Such issues as timing and sequences of changes, the relationship between economic and political reforms during the transitions, and proper construction of new institutions so as to underpin or reinforce the desired democratic outcome have all been explored.[4] While this literature has examined the pitfalls and the problems, few works fall outside a framework implicitly assuming a relatively—if not equally—positive political outcome for all, with the possible exception of the oppressors of the previous regimes.

Yet history has shown that periods of regime change can be perilous times, even when the change is in the direction of politically more liberal systems. The discourse and many of the actions of the new or "reformed" regimes do promise greater respect for human and civil rights. However, political liberalizations, like other forms of regime or political change, must be understood as having the potential to produce not only winners, but also losers: sectors that are, in one way or another, hurt by or in the course of the transformation. If one moves from the general studies of political transitions to those that focus on or at least consider women, the cases begin to resemble those of the literature on *economic* transitions, for they document a range of ways in which political transitions may pose dangers. Such phenomena as the drop in the number of women legislators in local and national assemblies, changes in labor laws or their implementation at women's expense, and attempts to restrict women's reproductive rights have accompanied most of the "democratic" transitions unfolding in Eastern Europe. In the MENA region, developments in a number of the countries that embarked on liberalization paths also constituted threats to women's status, and in some cases, such as Algeria, their lives.

Evidence of potential or real threats to women inherent in regime change is abundant. If one takes revolutions, the most extreme form of regime change, one finds for example that the French Revolution, while producing the famous "Declaration of the Rights of Man and the Citizen" in August 1789, omitted any reference to the rights of women. Indeed, women's revolutionary activity apparently led the men of the revolution to conclude that the female masses were a force capable of disrupting the state, and eventually to draw "a dividing line between the public and private spheres which women were not allowed to cross." The Napoleonic Civil Code finally inscribed women's inferior status into law.[5] More recently, the Iranian revolution's negative impact on various aspects of women's status, particularly during the Khomeini years, has been widely discussed,[6] while the Taliban's successes in Afghanistan have led to the banning of education for women and girls and women's dismissal from all but a handful of jobs. National liberation struggles offer some similar lessons. Women have participated as fighters, bomb-carriers and leafleteers, only to find, when the dust has settled, that they are to return to their homes, often governed by personal status codes and other laws that are more repressive that those to which they were subject under the colonial regime.[7]

Political liberalizations, although less thorough-going processes than other forms of regime change, including fuller democratic transitions, nonetheless, by definition open the political stage to the free(r) activity of a perhaps unprecedented range of political actors. As Przeworski has argued, they lower "the costs—real or anticipated—of individual expression and collective action."[8] However, such processes are bound by no law of nature or politics to produce only *liberal* groups of actors. Indeed, the crises that trigger the decisions to liberalize (or, in more extreme cases, that undermine the regime) unleash a range of actors, some of them espousing ideologies that seek to regain some of the (often putative) glory or security of the past. Changes in regime bases or in the political system more broadly *often* call into question or threaten some of the political system's basic underlying structures. One common response among national political actors to such threats has been to seek to secure the home front, the family. Constructed in terms of protecting the nation, its values, and its youth, their programs are often directed at reinforcing a woman's traditional role through such means as encouraging her withdrawal from the work force, implementing pro-natalist population policies, and even launching morality campaigns of various sorts which seek to limit women's "exposure" in the public space outside the home.

At the same time, in all but the most carefully managed political liberalizations (those initiated well before pressures from below force more drastic changes), the processes unfold in an atmosphere of regime uncertainty regarding its strength vis-à-vis other political actors. The leadership must determine what the balance of political-economic forces is and how best to respond to it so as to reinforce its position. The search for new allies that may result involves a process of negotiating or bargaining between the leadership/regime and various political actors over programs and goals.[9] During this period, a range of policies may be open to reconsideration, depending upon the political landscape and the nature of the actor(s) with which the power holders may seek to ally.

Hence, explaining the outcome,[10] for both the leadership and various societal sectors, requires first identifying the leadership's/regime's natural allies, given the domestic balance of sociopolitical and economic forces. It also involves determining the issues on which those in power are willing to compromise and the issues which, for the leadership, are above negotiation. Given the preeminent position and power of men in the state/regime and the fact that the transitions often trigger the emergence of parties espousing policies of a defensive, reactionary nature, it is not surprising that "women's issues," so defined by women or the state, may be among the first that the parties to the new political balance seek to use/exploit in political bargaining.[11]

I use a number of basic terms in this study. *Political liberalization* refers to an opening up of the political system in such a way that: more freedom of personal and media expression is allowed; greater numbers and diversity of nongovernmental actors are permitted to operate while those already in existence may expand their field of activities; state coercion in the form of arbitrary arrests, disappearances, and torture are reined in as a new discourse of respect for human rights is adopted; and parliamentary elections are held in an atmosphere that permits freer (if not completely free) competition by a variety of actors representing various parts of the political spectrum. For better or for worse, it is a concept concerned with civil and political, but not generally distributional (economic), rights. 1st (not 2nd) gen.

The concept of *women's status* is more problematic, for it is used in a variety of ways by different authors and has different meanings depending upon context.[12] Because I decided to focus in this study on the national level, changes in women's rights to organize as well as their formal legal status seemed to be key, observable indicators. I pay special attention to such issues as: right and access to contraception and abortion; right and access to education; equality in labor, pension, and criminal legislation; protection against harassment and violence; and role in the so-called public sphere, whether in the labor market or in political life. I have also sought to examine rights not only as they exist according to the law, but also as they are implemented, for there are often wide gaps between text and practice.

It is important to note here that what I consider to be changes constituting progress for women may be viewed quite differently by others, especially some politically, religiously, and/or socially conservative groups, regardless of region. For such groups, for example, expanding women's reproductive rights through providing increased access to birth control, equalizing women's access to divorce, or what this analysis would regard as expanding women's rights to participate in the public arena may well be viewed as indications of decline or moral decay. There is little realm for reconciling these two views, and I am willing to admit to a normative bias in my selection of indicators of improvement or deterioration in women's status. It should be noted, however, that all of the indicators noted above are discussed by important constituent organizations of women's movements in the countries examined. I do not, therefore, feel the approach used here can be labeled simply as "western" and dismissed as inauthentic.

Nevertheless, this is not just a question of what may be called a secularist or nonreligious bias in addressing these issues. The approach also involves a certain elite bias. By this I mean that it has been clear from my own field research over the years as well as from the literature produced by others, that class and region make a difference in how women construct and order their priorities regarding the need for change in their status. For many women, ensuring access to basic services or upgrading the quality of those services would make major contributions to their status. Among what are likely to be the primary concerns of a majority of women are: clean running water in or closer to the home, reliable nearby medical services, improved educational facilities, better working conditions and wages (whether they are concerned that this apply equally to men and women will vary), and more job opportunities, so that overall family economic circumstances improve and young women can stay in school longer.

These are also the concerns that Maxine Molyneux referred to in drawing the distinction between practical and strategic gender interests. Practical gender interests are those that are apparent from the objective conditions women work in and the roles they fill in the gender division of labor. Such interests usually arise in response to an immediate need. They would include such things as easier access to clean water, medical services, adequate housing and nutrition. Strategic gender interests, on the other hand, are those often termed feminist. They are derived "from the analysis of women's subordination and from the formulation of an alternative, more satisfactory set of arrangements to those which exist." Such interests include "removal of institutionalized forms of discrimination, the attainment of political equality, the establishment of freedom of choice over childbearing, and the adoption of adequate measures against male violence and control over women."[13]

It may be useful to think of the practical-strategic gender interests in less dichotomous terms. For example, working women's demands for greater access to childcare facilities or to longer maternity leaves, although they help mitigate certain inequalities, do not necessarily challenge existing structures that oppress women. They may well be understood by many women as partially alleviating a burden which they nonetheless believe is principally theirs to bear. Likewise, while many women may not analyze domestic violence as a structure of oppression, addressing such violence and other forms of abuse may well resonate with women who would not otherwise define themselves as feminists. The point is that while is it important to keep Molyneux's distinction in mind, it should not be overdrawn. Having said that, it does seem clear that it is generally only a part of the elite, broadly defined—middle to upper class women, generally living in urban areas—that is involved in addressing strategic gender concerns, the issues I have chosen to emphasize.

A study of the fate of such concerns during political liberalization requires a focus on the national level. While such an approach clearly has its drawbacks, the rationale for it is clear, for it is at this level that existing laws are amended and new laws are introduced. As Joseph has argued, "[t]he nation-state . . . remains a site of strategic importance to women, as well as minority groups. It is here where these groups gain or lose crucial legal and political protections against other political communities, patriarchies, and religious and secular non-democratic forces. Often women have nowhere other than the state to turn for protection from domestic violence, familial coercion, disriminatory practices . . ."[14]

The next term to clarify is *the state*. It is used here to refer to the network of institutions and relations that exercise governing authority over a particular territory. It is understood to be a complex, not a unitary actor, in which economic, political, and social interests constantly vie for influence on a playing field far from level. Depending upon environmental factors, elements of ethnicity, region, class, and gender may work for or against particular actors or concerns. Because the state is the site of contestations, to survive it must be capable of adaptation and redefinition. Indeed, as will be clear from the case studies that follow, the task of qualifying a state (or a particular leadership) as "women friendly" for example, is by no means a simple proposition. A state or leadership that opens the way to women's participation in the formal labor force or ensures women's rights to contraception is the same set of personalities, relations, and institutions that is the ultimate guardian of structures that oppress women or block reform in other areas.[15]

Finally, I have striven to avoid the use of *modern* and *Westernized*, while, on the other side of the implicit dichotomy (with which I have also done continuous, if not always successful, battle), I have preferred "conservative," to "traditional." "Conservative" is certainly less value-laden, at least in general political discourse. However, perhaps more important, the label "traditional" poses several problems. In societies undergoing rapid and disorienting change, "tradition" may be constructed by the state leadership or oppositional groups to consist of those practices and the values they deem necessary to counter dislocating pressures. Thus, what comes to be canonized as "tradition" is as much a result of political/social selection as natural evolution. Indeed, an emphasis on particular aspects of "tradition" and the ignoring of others can in fact pave the way to "a return" to a radical future; that is, a transformative program the outcome of which bears little resemblance to the past that its proponents often invoke. Hence, to avoid legitimating certain groups' attempts to define what constitutes "tradition" I have tried to avoid this term.[16]

THE NATURE OF POLITICAL LIBERALIZATION

The reasons behind the move to liberalize vary from extreme economic crisis and strong pressures from below (Algeria), to a leadership's desire to maintain power by introducing reforms as a means of preempting the development of more substantial demands for change (Jordan). In addition, external forces, such as defeat in war in the case of Argentina, may exert pressures which, coupled with domestic considerations, may constitute an additional catalyst to liberalize. Political liberalization may involve a regime change (that is, a change in *both* head of state as well as the ruling group) or simply a relinquishment of some power, but the retention of ultimate say by the same ruling group—an outcome generally referred to as a managed liberalization. They may be more gradual, evolutionary processes or be triggered by a single shock. Liberalizations may also be seen as falling along a continuum extending from a limited opening ("decompression," as happened at the beginning of the Brazilian transformation) to a more stark or sudden shift toward democratization, involving real changes in the state, as was the case in several Eastern European countries. Political liberalization does not equal democracy nor does it necessarily lead to it, regardless of the content of state discourse or the promises of the ruling group. Numerous examples across the developing world as well as in Eastern Europe indicate that transitions may stagnate (Romania, until the 1996 elections) or even be reversed (Tunisia).

The reach of the political liberalization will also vary. That is, different sectors will experience the opening to different degrees. Certainly, the more thoroughgoing the liberalization, the closer it comes to a democratic transition, the more likely its impact will be felt by broad sectors of the population. However, as noted above, there are also more limited, or managed liberalizations. In such cases, there is little question that the urban, educated population is most directly affected by the reforms that are introduced; the rural and/or illiterate are much less likely to feel the impact of, for example, greater freedom of the press.

On perhaps the most basic level, political liberalizations involve a move along the subject-citizen spectrum: that is, away from a situation in which men and women are excluded from effective participation and have no means to hold the government accountable (subjectness), toward a system of more meaningful participation and more transparency or accountability in government (citizenness). In authoritarian regimes, the degree to which rights and responsibilities between ruler and ruled are mutual is limited at best. Although one may carry a certain nationality and have the right to vote in elections, the relationship to the government is more often that of subject than citizen.[17] Within this framework, of course, the degree of citizenness or subjectness may be affected by a variety of factors. That is, regardless of where a government falls along the subject-citizen spectrum in its treatment of nationals, there is often further legal and social discrimination based on ethnicity, gender, class, or region of origin.[18] Moreover, as numerous analysts have pointed out, the concept of citizen itself is gendered, constructed in such a way that in virtually all societies women can never be as fully citizen as men. (Military service has long been a means of distinguishing relative citizenness in many societies.)[19] In addition, however, much theorizing about citizenship has taken place in a Western context, which is characterized by an individualism not found in other regions of the world. Joseph has noted that in a Middle East context, for example, such an understanding fails to take account of the numerous states in which subnational group identities and ethnicities in fact structure certain aspects of citizenship.[20] Thus, the term citizenship is used here with the understanding that the bases of its construction and application vary considerably.

WOMEN AND POLITICAL LIBERALIZATION

A wealth of micro-level, country cases and broader theoretical work has been produced on the gendered nature of the state and its policies. Nevertheless, it should be instructive that women as a subject is absent from the general literature on democratic transitions.[21] This is likely due to the continuing allergy that mainstream political science has to gender, for it seems to have no parallel problem discussing labor, the business community, the military, ethnic groups, and other sectors. Even in the literature that has examined the fate of women during transitions, the work has primarily been on the impact of the *economic* transition and focused overwhelmingly on women in Eastern Europe.[22] The body of literature that does seek to understand where women fit into the *political* transitions is either largely descriptive or, in the case of Latin America, interested in showing the role women actually played in the transition and/or in theorizing about the changing feminist component in women's movements during or after liberalizations.[23]

In the literature dealing with the MENA area, much work has been done on women on issues related to nationalism and national struggles, citizenship, patriarchy, and the gendered nature of the state, as well as a range of socioeconomic issues. However, only the work of Mervet Hatem addresses directly the central concern of this work—women and political liberalizations—if from a different perspective. Before examining her conclu-

sions, however, it is useful to review some of the insights from the literature on related topics in the MENA area.

A number of works address the question of women's relationship to the
state during times of crisis or regime change (if not liberalization). For example, Afaf Marsot demonstrates in a study of late eighteenth-century
Egypt that a combination of decentralized and chaotic government in
Egypt created a socioeconomic "space" that allowed elite women a freedom of action that one generally associates with the twentieth century.[24]
She demonstrates that domestic economic and political developments allowed women to acquire property independent of males, and that their
consequent power and wealth actually engendered support for them
among the state religious authorities (*ulama*). Also using Egypt as a case,
Margot Badran has charted the role of (largely elite) women of the Egyptian feminist movement during the period of the nationalist struggle against
the British in the first half of the twentieth century. She shows how women
advanced the nationalist cause while working within the parameters of
Islam.[25] Again, this consideration of women's activities and fates during a
period of challenge and uncertainty (if not real regime change) demonstrates the possibilities for women's taking advantage of and pushing for
further opening of spaces for more meaningful participation.

Julie Peteet has focused on a case involving much greater displacement
and disjuncture: that of the Palestinians.[26] Her work on women in Palestinian refugee camps in Lebanon demonstrates how gender relations are
reconstructed and renegotiated during, not a period of regime change, but
a national liberation struggle carried on outside the homeland and over an
extended period of time. She looks at changes in gender and national consciousness, increasing possibilities for women's activities outside the home,
including involvement in the resistance itself, as well as the structure of
power relations within the resistance organizations. Her work highlights
both the possibilities for, as well as the continuing limits to, altering gender relations during periods of extreme political flux and in the absence of
a central state authority.

Another relevant theme that runs through much of the work on women
in the Middle East is that of the post-independence regimes' use of the so-
called woman question as part of their program to restructure the bases of
political relations and to lay the foundation for more "modern" societies by
breaking the power of certain traditionalist groups.[27] From Turkey and
Tunisia—the most extreme cases of attempts to secularize society—to less
"revolutionary" but nonetheless critical programs of change in the so-
called republican regimes in Egypt, Iraq, and Syria and finally to the socialist program advocated by the Marxists of the People's Democratic Re-

public of Yemen, one may observe various forms of what has been called "state feminism."[28]

State feminism involves policies directed from (as well as generally formulated at) the state leadership level, which aim at mobilizing or channeling women's (re)productive capabilities and coopting them into support for the state through such programs as raising literacy levels, increasing access to the labor market, establishing state-sponsored women's organizations, generally along the lines of the single-party model, and the like. In the cases of Turkey and Tunisia, these attempts were accompanied by the outlawing of certain practices sanctioned by religion, such as polygamy. That many women benefitted from these programs is not in question. That many women were squeezed between the demands of state feminism and of continuing conservative societal practices is also apparent. What needs to be understood, however, is the degree to which state feminist programs were not an end in themselves, but rather served as part of broader statebuilding and/or regime consolidation processes. Women were instruments or tools, and their "liberation" was part of a larger project of reinforcing control within a series of states that continued to be dominated by what are generically referred to as patriarchal structures.[29]

Let us then turn to Hatem's work. In a case study of Egypt, she examines what she terms "the post-1976 neo-liberal system" and its impact on women. She describes the period as one of controlled liberalization that came in response to serious economic and political crises. While admitting that the extent of the political liberalism has been quite limited—one major reason why it was not chosen for consideration in this study—in large part because of the exclusion of Islamists, she notes that "most analysts do not question the gendered accomplishments of the state, because of the belief that secular-liberal regimes . . . are generally favorable to women."[30] Hatem then proceeds to examine and compare the secular discourse of the state with that of the Islamists during this period. She concludes that, despite changes favorable to women in several laws (apportioning additional seats to women in the parliament and introducing some reforms in the personal status law regarding divorce), the practical import of the changes was minimal and that the discourse of the state and that the Islamists, in fact, *converged* on a number of points, thus leaving the definition of women's status based in conservative notions of domesticity and gender difference. The broader conclusion of this work is that while there may be differences on some policy points, in their the basic understanding of women and their role, the Islamists and the liberals do not differ substantially, and hence one should not look for liberalizing regimes to be "women friendly."

means to an end

In a comparative piece examining the experiences of women in Egypt, the Sudan, and Tunisia, Hatem takes the argument a step further and states clearly at the beginning that "[p]olitical liberalization in the Arab world has been characterized by state ambivalence toward women."[31] While one may question on empirical grounds her contention that Egypt "began the regional move toward liberalization" in 1976, nonetheless the argument regarding ambivalence is an important one. She sets the stage for the treatment of her three cases by reminding the reader of the feminist debate regarding how, in the West, "liberal" societies have provided new bases for gender *in*equity, rather than promoting full rights for women. Through brief examinations of the three country cases she concludes that both authoritarian and liberal states are willing to use gender for their own ends. She argues that the "loosening of the state's grip on the gender agenda" in Egypt and the Sudan and the reassertion of state feminism by the Tunisian regime proved to be mixed blessings. In Egypt and the Sudan, reliance on the state was replaced by reliance on outside forces, while in Tunisia the state's use of women in the conflict with Islamists set the women up for possible future backlash.

Hatem's work is the first to point out that so-called liberalizing regimes in the MENA area do not necessarily offer hopeful prospects for women. While the carefully controlled and quite limited liberalizations she examines, especially those of Egypt and the Sudan, cannot be characterized as transitions or regime changes, they are nonetheless consistent with the argument above that periods of political flux, even in an apparently more open direction, may not hold out the opportunities for women that the term liberalization generally brings to mind.

Hatem's point regarding the dubious opportunities that liberalizations offer women is central to the study at hand. However, this study then departs in several ways from the works of Hatem and the other authors noted above. In the first place, it is first and foremost a study about political transitions, what triggers them, but especially how they unfold. Within that framework, it is concerned with the way that women and women's issues are dealt with and play a role in the transitions. It accepts Hatem's argument that the state may well pursue policies of a contradictory nature, but it then seeks to explain the reasons behind the leaderships' choices and the outcomes. To argue that states are gendered, which this analysis does not dispute, in such a way that promotes men's interests (certainly far from a single or coherent set of policies) is a critical starting point, but it does not, in and of itself, explain the differing impact of political transitions on women. Obviously, a broad range of factors shape women's status at any given time and, theoretically, a number of different approaches could have been selected to study women's fate during transitions. This study has used a detailed analysis of three case studies to examine the interactions among various actors political actors—the state, political parties, women's organizations, and the like—to try to explain outcomes during liberalization periods.

Given the limited literature on the liberalizations and on women's place in them in the MENA region, the discussion will now turn to a brief exploration of some of the lessons that emerge from the more extensive literature on liberalizations in Latin America and Eastern Europe. The intention is to draw inferences from these regions' experiences which may serve as guides to the in-depth exploration of the MENA cases in the chapters that follow.

LESSONS FROM EASTERN EUROPE AND LATIN AMERICA

The most striking element in Eastern Europe—and what may render it incomparable to other regions in the eyes of some analysts—is the extent of concomitant political and economic transformation. The turmoil and displacement that have accompanied the transformations in Eastern Europe have no real parallel, as these states have moved from communist authoritarian structures on the political front and from command economy arrangements on the economic front at virtually the same time. A primary focus of many works on the transitions has been the crises triggered by the *economic* transitions.[32] For example, studies have documented marked increases in female unemployment as a result of the dismantling of the state sector, in which women were traditionally overrepresented. This problem has been exacerbated by societal mores which give preference to male employment, particularly in times of economic crisis. Added to the steep rise in unemployment has been the collapse of a number of the social welfare programs of the former communist states—especially in the fields of child care and health. At the same time, prices have risen and shortages have meant even more time spent securing daily supplies—all problems which tend to be borne or "absorbed" by females.

The work that has been done on the *political* fate of women in these countries has generally consisted of reevaluations of the socialist record.[33] One of the most common themes is that of women's "triple burden" under the communists: work outside the home, work inside the home, and childrearing. While the right to work outside the home is generally viewed in the West as basic, for a large number of women living under the communist regimes in Eastern Europe it was hardly seen as liberating. Since work outside the home was performed in the context of an official discourse that downgraded the value of women's burdensome tasks in the home, the idea of liberation defined as involving the right to work outside the home is unappealing to many women in post-communist societies. Just as important, in many women's minds, problems on the job were not seen to be caused by male supervisors, but rather by the state, which was the employer and regulator.[34] Hence, Eastern European women do not tend to view their exploitation as based in gender inequalities. They consider the issue of equality between the sexes as secondary, easily preceded by issues of housing, education, job market access (not generally evaluated in gendered terms), and the like.

Under the communist regimes, any form of political activism had to take place through organizations that were extensions of the state.[35] Since official women's organizations were intended to channel or control women's activism rather than voice grassroots concerns, they inspired little interest among average women. Given the official control and the effective depoliticization of women that communist state policies achieved, there was no organized involvement of women as women in the events which brought down the regimes. Moreover, when these regimes crumbled, the legitimacy of the official women's organizations' crumbled with them. In the immediate aftermath of the fall of the communist regimes—that is, well before the more recent wave of nostalgia for the social safety net and order of the pre-1989 period—any activity around issues that had been supported by the communists was anathema to most. As a result, independent women's organizations were few, and their whole raison d'être appeared suspect—a discredited remnant of an earlier era.

Similarly, women's largely symbolic (as opposed to effective or powerful) representation under the communist regimes served to further delegitimize their post-1989 participation in national or local politics. Seen as mere instruments of the state, women who occupied prominent places in public life under the communists did little to build societal confidence in their ability to play meaningful political roles. The discrediting of the communist states has also affected the way that state social legislation and social welfare provisions have been regarded, including proclamations of commitment to women's liberation and equality. At least initially, virtually all socialist policies were viewed as illegitimate, regardless of their positive elements.[36] Finally, of course, is the continuing demobilization that derives from women's lingering fear of "the political" because of their experiences under the previous regimes. Hence, it should not be surprising that women's post-1989 interest in politics or in a women's movement, both of which are associated with the bitter experiences of the past, is quite limited.

Despite these significant similarities among the Eastern European cases, when one moves to the realm of abortion and reproductive rights, the experiences diverge markedly. While this is only one issue area, it is central in the struggle over who controls women, and hence is an indicator of broader trends regarding women's rights and status. Societal and regime response to the abortion issue in particular can be used to highlight some of the important differences in power configurations or relations in the transitional regimes.

In Romania, for example, a shortage of skilled labor in the 1960s as an intensive drive for modernization or industrialization began, led to a greater focus on women's reproductive role. An antiabortion law was passed in 1966, only to be further tightened by 1986 when Ceaucescu proclaimed the fetus "the socialist property of the whole society," and those women who sought to avoid pregnancies "deserters." Self-induced abortions were punishable by prison sentences and job promotions were linked to women's political obedience, so that unmarried or divorced women could expect not to be promoted. In the 1980s, the legal age of marriage was reduced to 15, and any woman not married by age 25 had to pay a 5 percent tax. Similarly, married couples without children were subject to a higher tax rate.[37]

In comparing the unfolding of the transitions, it is also critical to note that, unlike what transpired elsewhere, the fall of the Ceaucescu regime was swift and bloody, not a gradual process in which the regime gradually retreated and negotiated with contenders for power. In Timosoara, where the revolution began, doctors began performing abortions free of charge just after the town declared itself a free zone. One week later, one of the first decrees of the new provisional government, the self-appointed National Salvation Front, was that of absolute freedom of abortion. This reportedly invested the Front with tremendous popularity as it sought to fill the void left by the exit of Ceaucescu.[38] The intrusiveness and brutality of the previous regime's population policy had been so great that no forces dared to seek to maintain the ban on abortion in the wake of the revolution. It was loathed and discredited along with its author and implementer. Appealing to a reimposition of a ban, whether by the Church or any other group, was virtually unthinkable in the immediate post-Ceaucescu era.

Poland is a polar opposite case, and here it appears that it was the relationship between the two forces that helped bring down the communist government—Solidarity and the Catholic Church, the two most powerful civil society actors prior to and during the transition—that largely explains the outcome.

The elections of June 1989 in Poland were the first free elections in Eastern Europe, and at the time, Poland had a relatively liberal abortion law. To reinforce its position and to pay the Church back for its support over the years, Solidarity adopted the Church's anti-abortion position in the 1989 elections—without consulting its female members. Solidarity's 1981 program had not called for banning abortion. It had merely expressed the hope that improving economic conditions would lead to the end of the need to terminate pregnancies. However, by March 1990, it had endorsed a total ban on abortions, irrespective of economic or health considerations, although the women's section within the union expressed a dissenting opinion. In the spring of 1991, the women's section was dissolved, and the male leadership did not consult the women before endorsing a Senate draft bill banning abortion.[39] Solidarity's position owed not only to its alliance with the Catholic Church and the sexism of the union's male members, but also to the fact that, while women had constituted 50 percent of the union's ranks, they had not filled leadership positions. Indeed, although there had been a mass participation of women in the strike committees in Gdansk in 1980 and in the creation of cells of the then-nascent Solidarity, women's representation among activists and executives actually dropped thereafter.[40]

Although surveys indicated substantial support among the Polish population for women's access to abortion, if with some conditions, the moral authority of the Church, reinforced by its long-standing resistance to communist rule made it very difficult for politicians and journalists to take an openly pro-choice (anti-Church) position.[41] Perhaps just as important, the Church and its supporters were advocating a position that was diametrically opposed to that of the former regime, a fact which must have attracted some support that had little to do with beliefs about abortion per se, and more to do with a broad rejection of the communists. The outcome was the passage in 1991 of a highly restrictive abortion law.

In late March 1992, a group of deputies submitted a bill almost identical to the previous restrictive law, while the women's parliamentary committee submitted one that was much more liberal. Women's presence in the parliament (Sejm) was one problem, as their numbers had declined from a high of 23 percent (1980–85) to only 9 percent in the elections of fall 1991. There was also an absence of grassroots women's movements to take a stand and organize support for continued abortion rights, although the launching of the debate served as a catalyst for the emergence of a small number of groups to protect women's rights. The Communist party women's organizations had developed their own elites, but given the legacy of the past, they were hardly in a position to put themselves forward as representatives of Polish women. [42]

In March 1993, a new and even more restrictive abortion law came into force. However, the tide was about to turn, for the elections of September 1993 removed from power the parties connected with the economic shock that had accompanied the market transformation and brought in their place a coalition of the Democratic Left Alliance and the Peasant Party, both clearly tied to the former communist regime. The Poles appeared simply to want a more human face to and pace of economic transformation. At the same time, however, some analysts argued that the voters sought through the election to humble the Church. Its "moves to consolidate its power—introducing religious instruction into schools, banning abortion—antagonized a growing number of people, particularly Polish women." None of the three parties openly connected with the policy of the Church succeeded in having its candidates elected in 1993. The institution's arrogance along with its close ties to Solidarity, whose former leadership and its inheritors were associated with the hated and disruptive economic reforms, led to the Church's partial discrediting. By 1996, the realignment of forces in the Sejm led to the passage of a new, and less restrictive, abortion law.[43]

The case of Russia falls somewhere in the middle. Perestroika had first opened the way to a surge of "traditional values" among a significant sector of the population, both male and female. This seems only to have increased as the Soviet Union finally crumbled and Russia and the other inheritor states continued the process of political and economic restructuring. Part of what accompanied these developments was the unleashing of a number of socially and politically conservative groups which, in the case of Russia, espoused a nationalism with a strong conservative religious component. The gender dimension in these developments was clear, as economic conditions led these groups to call for women's retreat from the workforce and for a greater focus on family.[44]

In addition, some voices were raised to limit women's access to abortion. In 1992, there was an attempt by a combination of "new-fangled democrats and old-style conservatives" concerned with the falling birthrate in the country to undermine Russia's liberal abortion law. The opponents of abortion rights had (and have) powerful allies in the Russian Orthodox Church and were supported by allies from abroad, especially U.S. anti-choice groups.[45] At the time of this writing, no changes had been introduced into the law. However, these groups' lack of success has not been the result of lobbying by activist women inside or outside government: the introduction of quasi-competitive elections in Russia involved the dismantling of the system of quotas for women's representation and hence led to a decline in the proportion of female deputies from 33 to 16 percent.[46] Indeed, despite the emergence of some new women's groups, since 1991 women's activism has steeply declined.[47] Part of the explanation for the failure of efforts to change the abortion law lies in the role of the Orthodox Church and its relationship to the previous regime. While the Church is certainly a force to be reckoned with in Russia, it did not play the same role in supporting dissidents or in helping to bring down the regime as did the Catholic Church in Poland. In fact it is generally regarded as having been complicit with the communists. Thus, although popular, at the time of the transition it did not enjoy the same legitimacy as its Polish counterpart. However, if one thinks of the previous two cases, it appears that the nature of the transition and the leadership it has produced are also key elements. First, the transition has been more gradual, certainly far more so than in Romania. Second, those who have come to power, primary among them Boris Yeltsin, are former communists turned "democrats," not members of a former anti-communist or opposition party. They owed nothing to the power of the Church and hence were not in a position to have to respond to its priorities. This does not mean that their position on the issues cannot change—indeed, as time passes the leadership seems increasingly interested in cozying up to the Church [48]—but it does give them greater freedom of maneuver on this front. Hence, although the Church and others have raised the abortion issue since the beginning of the transition, their place in the constellation of political forces in the country along with an apparently deeply ingrained belief in the right to abortion inherited from the Soviet period has meant that such challenges have so far come to naught.

Turning to Latin America, one finds tremendous differences in women's participation in and experiences with the transitions. What is striking in contrast to the Eastern European cases is the apparent gains women were able to achieve in several countries, at least during the early period of democratic reconsolidation. Growing economic problems and a population increasingly resistant to continuing brutalization from the military or the state played major roles in forcing these transition. In the case of Argentina, one must add an external element, the 1982 defeat in the Falklands-Malvinas war. Also critical, the transitions were gradual. Indeed, even in the case of Argentina, which represents the most precipitous return of an elected government, it was not until December 1983, a year and a half after the Malvinas debacle, that the civilian Alfonsín administration was installed. Just as crucial, the transitions resulted in clear changes at the top—the ouster of the existing group and the installation of new administrations representing a different political program and form of governance. Thus one is dealing with new regimes that were formed in opposition to, not as a way of shoring up, their predecessors. As a result, distancing one's self from the previous powerholders and defining one's political program in opposition to them was of critical importance. We will return to this point and its direct relationship to women's fate below.

Similar to the experiences in Eastern Europe, in Latin America the role of the Church is crucial to understanding the outcomes. In the case of Brazil, in the 1960s and 1970s, the Catholic Church gradually turned away from the military and toward the poor, and progressive sectors of the institution served as a critical "organizational umbrella for the opposition." Association with the Church accorded the opposition both a kind of moral legitimacy and a form of protection of which a number of women's organizations or women's auxiliaries of other organizations were able to take advantage. While it is true that the religious hierarchy and some of the clergy remained hostile to feminist demands, "nonetheless, the politicization of gender within Church-linked community women's groups provided nascent Brazilian feminism with an extensive mass base unparalleled in most Latin American countries."[49]

In the case of Chile, the Church also provided a kind of support base for the beginning of opposition to the regime, although not to the same extent that it did in Brazil. Assistance generally took the form of aid to those who grouped together to locate disappeared loved ones. The Church also instituted an umbrella organization (The Academy of Christian Humanism) to provide a safe space for alternative research centers, political expression, and the articulation of dissent.[50] This was particularly important in Chile, since it gave legitimacy to the concerns expressed by human rights activists in an atmosphere in which the military regime claimed to be protecting Chilean society from subversion and defending "Christian and Occidental" values. The support of the Church for the human rights activists made it far more difficult for the military to repress them than would have otherwise been the case.[51] The case of Argentina, on the other hand, is quite different, for there the Catholic Church chose to ignore, if not justify, the atrocities of the regime.[52]

Turning to the role of women's organizations, in Chile, for example, with the exception of groups that Augusto Pinochet had established and placed under the leadership of his wife, the major women's organizations were not associated with the state. To the contrary, they sprang to life as a form of protest against state policies and in defense, at least initially, of their families. In all three of these countries, the participation of women in protest activities of various sorts clearly placed women's organizations on the political map of anti-regime activism. Some of these groups (most notably the Madres de la Plaza in Argentina) initially aimed at making the state accountable for their "disappeared" family members. Others were concerned with declining standards of living resulting from economic crises, while still others, especially in the gradual Brazilian transition, pushed for changes in state social and economic policy to benefit women. The fact that they had played such high profile and mobilizational roles meant that these organizations could not be quickly or easily dismissed by the successor regimes.

A final factor that no doubt gave the women's groups' demands more weight as the transitions unfolded was that the traditional image of a woman as sainted mother and wife, keeper of hearth and home, and repository of society's values was part of the discourse of the military authoritarian regimes. This sexism had two major implications for women and the coming transitions. In the first place, it in effect blinded the political leaderships of the authoritarian regimes to the *political* (as opposed to humanitarian or social) character of women's organizing. This no doubt gave women a margin of freedom that other groups did not enjoy. Second, the close association of this discourse with the military regimes meant that when they were forced from power, their approach was discredited with them. This parallels what happened in Eastern Europe, except that given the politics of the ousted regime, the outcome for women in the former communist countries was a retrenchment of rights, not new openings. In these Latin American cases, however, it meant the opening of a greater political space for women's participation and for the expression of those of their demands that challenged existing structures.

These factors—women's prominent participation in bringing down the regime, the support they received from the Church (in Brazil and to a lesser extent in Chile), and the discrediting of the conservative social discourse as a result of its close association with the previous regimes—appear to be of critical importance in explaining the outcomes. First, they meant that the largely male-run political parties needed or would naturally seek to attract the highly visible and mobilized sector that women had become. Second, except in Argentina, women had allies (even if they parted ways when it came to issues like abortion) among what is often the most important bastion of social conservatism outside the state—the religious establishment. Third, the discourse that advocated a reversal of their rights belonged to the program of the discredited regimes. Explaining the outcome as deriving solely from the fact that women had played a notable role in the transitions is insufficient, especially given women's prior historical experiences with national liberation movements. More likely, the mobilized power women's organizations had already demonstrated and therefore had to offer political actors at a time of regime consolidation was too important to be ignored, given the political battles that were being fought to gain electoral advantage.

The result was that in Brazil, for example, when Jose Sarney, the first civilian president in 21 years, took office in 1985, a number of important positive developments for women followed. A National Council on

Women's Rights was created within the Ministry of Justice and a number of activist women, feminists and others, were able to secure a majority of seats on it. From 1985 to 1988 this council intervened in favor of women's rights in areas ranging from agrarian and educational reform to the media. In conjunction with other women, lobbying by this council led to the inclusion of important women's agenda items in the new constitution.[53]

In the case of Chile, shortly after the plebiscite that said "no" to Pinochet, the National Coalition of Women for Democracy was formed to mobilize women and take their agenda to the national political arena for the 1989 elections. As a result, the successful candidate, Patricio Aylwin, made women a key constituency to which he addressed his presidential appeal. Although the results of the elections did not lead to immediate gains, in May 1990 President Aylwin did present legislation to create the SERNAM, the National Women's Service. In the early period after its creation, it undertook numerous networking, informational, and legislative initiatives aimed at improving women's status. While there have been numerous criticisms of SERNAM, and it has not maintained its early dynamism, it nonetheless represents an important achievement. Chile has also seen legislative changes to reform the divorce and labor laws as they apply to women, to reintroduce therapeutic abortion (outlawed under Pinochet), and to address domestic violence.[54]

In Argentina, during the campaign of 1983, in what was expected to be a close battle, women's voting power was recognized and the winner, Raul Alfonsín, "not only raised heretofore dormant demands, but also used women-sensitive language to the point that his closing campaign speech openly criticized machismo." As democratic consolidation proceeded, the record was mixed; for example, there was a debate over the so-called "quota law," an attempt to mandate that 30 percent of the electoral candidates be women. Although the law was finally approved in November 1991, it has never been enforced. On the more positive side of the ledger, under Alfonsín, among a host of institutional developments, a National Women's Agency in the Ministry of Social Action was established, which in turn created a Women's Health and Development Program. In 1986 restrictions on the distribution and use of contraceptives were lifted and the issue of domestic violence, once taboo, was brought out into the open.[55]

To sum up, women in these Latin American countries played visible roles in bringing down the authoritarian regimes and, given the nature of the transition (regime change which discredited the conservatives), and the constellation of political forces, women were able to take advantage of the transition to push for greater consideration of their demands. While the victories have undeniably not been as great as the women had been hoped, and some of the institutions that were established have lost their dynamism or have been coopted over time, women have nevertheless realized some important gains, if within the bounds of a patriarchal state.

THE QUESTION OF CROSS-REGIONAL COMPARISON

My juxtaposition of the experiences of women from three major world regions will no doubt trouble some. For those partisans of cultural explanations, who argue that culture is the driving force in history, the idea of comparing women from three different regions and certainly more than three cultures must seem at very least unsound. Indeed, deriving possible explanations from one region and seeking to confirm or disconfirm their relevance in another may appear heretical, especially when it comes to women, since they always seem to be part of the realm of culture in a way that men are not. Another form of gendering.

Nonetheless, as someone who believes strongly that in-depth study of societies' histories, language(s), and religion(s) are critical to understanding them, I remain unpersuaded that an explanation that works in one society cannot also work elsewhere. At the same time, there is no implicit assumption here. My desire to explore whether apparent lessons from Latin American and Eastern European cases (researched and constructed by specialists on and from these areas) might be replicated in the MENA region derives neither from a belief that culture does not matter nor that women or states are the same all over. Rather, it proceeded from a curiousity about what seemed on the surface to be common patterns—a conclusion that would fly in the face of cultural explanations. I approached this study with the idea that comparability of experiences across regions is an empirical question, which I posed from the position of an agnostic. I will admit, however, to a distaste for the idea of so-called Middle Eastern exceptionalism,[56] and I find it both distressing and disappointing that in comparative studies of women and liberalization, or of questions of economic and political development more broadly, it is always Latin American and Eastern European cases, or Latin American and East Asian cases, that are juxtaposed. Are they inherently more comparable? I remain unconvinced.

The second charge that may be raised is that by daring to compare across regions I am essentializing women, assuming that there must be something unchanging and fixed about them that is reinforced by the suggestion that they can be examined across contexts. (The implication is that comparing women within regions does not—at least necessarily—constitute a similar essentializing exercise.) Such a contention must be countered on several grounds. In the first place, world regions as we have come to know them are constructed entities. For example, taking the existing regional divisions as given, if one writes a study comparing some aspect of Turkey and Bulgaria, or Morocco and Spain, the study is considered cross-regional; however, if it is a comparison of Morocco and Turkey, it is not. This is, quite frankly, absurd. The importance of what is in effect geographic location should not be overemphasized. Second, if one wants to take the essentialist charge based on the grounds of broad comparison to its logical extreme, *any* suggestion of comparison, within or across regions, could be open to the charge of essentializing something or other—the state, women, the economy, the military, and so on. At the same time, it would seem that the tendency to essentialize is just as likely to operate implicitly among those who refuse to push intellectual inquiry beyond the boundaries of our inherited, constructed regions, because such an approach implies that there is something innately (and, implicitly, unchangingly) unifying within them.

A comparative project, like other forms of research, is one which at the most basic level seeks to increase our understanding. There is nothing inherent in it which suggests that by comparing women's experiences across regions at one point in time that the author assumes generalizability of the findings across all time and space. If similarities should be found, they imply neither exact replicas nor a conclusion of unchanging essence. If we cannot engage legitimately in such exercises, then we should simply discard all attempts at theorizing and just stick to strict description of individual events. That does represent one, nonmainstream approach; but it is it not one with which I am comfortable. I began the reading for this project not knowing where it would lead. What I found in the Eastern European and Latin American cases were what appeared to be a number of similar factors at work. My curiosity led me to ask whether comparable forces and processes might be at work in the Middle East and North Africa. My attempts at finding answers lie ahead.

METHODOLOGY AND STRUCTURE OF THIS STUDY

The brief examination of the Eastern European and Latin American experiences suggested that a number of factors may play a role in determining how women, women's issues, and women's organizations will fare during the early stages of political liberalizations:

- the nature of the transition (shock or gradual; initiated from above or forced from below);
- the strength and role(s) of preexisting women's organizations;
- women's role in pushing for the transition;

- the relationship between the previous regime and new regime (complete change or modifications of various elements);
- the relationship between the *ancien régime* and conservative forces, particularly the religious establishment;
- and the balance of political forces as the transition unfolds.

The chapters that follow provide a structured and in-depth examination of the interaction among the state, various political actors, and women activists/organizations during periods of liberalization in three countries: Morocco, Jordan, and Tunisia. The case selection was made based on a number of factors related to both the subject under study and the realities of field research. In the first instance, the selection of three MENA countries was a function of my regional and linguistic expertise and of the gap in coverage of such countries in the literature. When the study was initially conceived, I could have selected a number of countries on the grounds of their having experienced a period of political liberalization. I ruled out Algeria on the grounds of the danger of conducting field research there. I excluded Egypt because, while it has had its liberal or liberalizing periods, none has been terribly broad or sustained and the recent situation can hardly be described as liberal. My decision to explore the role of external factors, including the international climate regarding women's rights, also led to the exclusion of Egypt on the grounds that the brief liberal experiment did not extend into the late 1980s, the period that served as the basis for case selection. While one could also say that Tunisia's liberalization was also short and that the current situation is hardly liberal, the leadership change did come in the late 1980s, and the enthusiasm that the initial period following Bourguiba's departure generated among scholars regarding the possibilities for the emergence of real pluralism seemed to render it a case worth studying. As for Kuwait, the liberalization has been quite limited; Kuwaiti women still have not received the right to vote. Finally, Yemen plunged into civil war in the summer of 1994, the period during which I made my final decision.

For each of the three case countries, there are three chapters: The first chapter in each case country section examines the domestic context, explores the impact of external factors on domestic politics, and details the unfolding of the liberalization. This chapter is intended to provide the reader with the background necessary to understand the reasons behind the liberalization as well as the actors and interests involved. The second chapter in each section offers an overview of the development of organized women's activities and/or national women's movements, followed by an examination of the legal status of women and of changes in laws since the beginning of the liberalization. The second chapters conclude with a discussion of the role of external funders in supporting women's groups. There seems little question that forces at work outside the countries—broader processes of liberalization, emphases on human and women's rights, the availability of funding for the development of nongovernmental organizations (NGOs), the hegemony of neoliberal economic models—may all exert pressures for adaptation and change. In this way, along with the section on external influences on domestic policy in the first chapter, the *international* dimension is examined.

The final chapter in each case section evaluates a number of "critical junctures" in the interaction between women and the state, or between women as political actors on a national level and other actors on the political stage. These junctures are intended to serve as windows on the broader reality of the relationship among the state, women, women's organizations, and the spectrum of other national political actors. Such an approach aims at illustrating two things: first, the possibilities and constraints that women as public or political actors may face during the liberalization; and second, the way that women's organizations and concerns fit into the broader picture of the struggle or bargaining over power that unfolds during these periods. These critical junctures were my selection, but made after extensive background preparation and in consultation with local analysts and activists.

Other foci could have been used to explore the question of women's fate during transitions. Most of these, however, are problematic for one reason or another. For example, some may question the failure to analyze in greater depth statistics in such areas as education, literacy, employment, access to health care, and the like. The reasons are the following. First, while abundant, the accuracy of such numbers is often questionable. Just as important, simply providing statistics on what happens in these areas during the periods under examination says little (without much more information) about the impact of the *political* transition itself, since the numbers for any given year are generally the result of economic, social, health, and other policies that have been in place for some time. Determining what was attributable to policies initiated during the transition would have been quite problematic.

SOURCES

For all three countries, I consulted a variety of sources: The background work on the domestic context and the stories of the liberalization relied chiefly on secondary source material in English, French, and Arabic (although the chapter on Jordan required extensive newspaper archival work as well). The same was true for the sections on the women's movements and on women's legal status prior to liberalization. However, the remaining sections were constructed based on information gathered through interviews (with women and human rights activists, university professors, government officials, and international aid and embassy officials), primary source material gathered from the institutions involved, from newspaper archives, and from participant-observation. The interviews were conducted in Arabic in Jordan and in Arabic or French in North Africa, and generally took place in people's offices or homes. In all but one case, I was the sole interviewer, but in several cases the interviews involved discussions with two women at a time. At no time did I use a tape recorder: I took written notes during the sessions and wrote summaries immediately thereafter. The vast majority of meetings I arranged myself; in a few cases in Morocco and Tunisia I was assisted by others in setting up interviews.

SEVERAL FINAL WORDS

The selection of topic and form of presentation of this study is not meant to imply that periods of political liberalization suddenly lead to the state's recognition of the importance of women. The vast literature on the state shows that it has long had an interest in women—in managing and controlling them—the lack of an explicit policy or institutional structure not withstanding. Indeed, lack of an articulated policy in fact constitutes a policy. Therefore, women's apparent invisibility in the political process (at least on the national and often the municipal and communal levels) in MENA countries should by no means be mistaken for lack of state interest. Indeed, the long period of women's absence from formal public politics in some countries as well as their relatively greater prominence in others may be traced in large part to deliberate policies by the state and by groups or institutions allied with it. In some states, for reasons of domestic economic, political, or social structure, ideology of the ruling group, and/or state legitimacy, women have been continually excluded and attempts to carve out a greater role opposed. (Kuwait and Saudi Arabia fit this model to different degrees.) In others, the same combination of factors has led to the adoption of state feminism, policies that give women more rights and in effect adopt aspects of their "cause" as part of regime's program. (Tunisia, Syria, Egypt, and Iraq serve as examples). The point to bear in mind is that in both sets of cases, despite periodic attempts by women's organizations to redefine the boundaries or raise new issues, the state generally prevailed in marginalizing or excluding those demands that challenged its interests.

Another point also deserves clarification. No pretense is made here of having presented or even of having tried to present the reality of *all* women in the three countries under study. As noted earlier in this chapter, I made a decision early on to study how some "women's issues" are dealt with by the leadership and by a range of formal and informal political actors during periods of political liberalization. While this study does strive to give the reader a sense of the tremendous variety of organizations and activities that have flowered among women, the focus here is on the *national* political battlefield. It is at this level that the decision to liberalize is taken and managed. It is also at this level that it is easiest to catalogue state (and other political actor) *intent.*

The focus in this work on the national level has meant, by necessity, a focus on urban, middle- to upper-middle class women, those who, by virtue of education, resources, and other factors, have direct access to or are most directly affected by national politics. The fact that this study is concerned with the state or national level of politics is not meant to imply that politics of particular relevance to women is limited to this level. To the contrary, power relations and their implications pervade all levels and aspects of life, from the circle of presidential or monarchical advisers through the various levels and hierarchies within the bureaucracy, to the market, and to the level of the family. Change affecting or affected by women can be accomplished at any of these levels, and the process is understood to be interactive.

Some may also argue that the issues on which this study focuses—demands for changing laws and practices that affect women's human, political, civil, social and economic rights—are of little practical concern to women beyond a rather limited urban elite. The point is well-taken. It is most certainly the case that a woman in rural Morocco will be more concerned with the fact that she has to walk five kilometers three times a day to draw water than with national-level discussions of a woman's right to conclude a business contract without her husband's permission. Nevertheless, the undemocratic and seemingly inaccessible political structures and processes that have failed to ensure women's rights in the business realm are often the same as those that have left that rural woman illiterate and deprived of basic services. Hence, although the effect may be indirect and, particularly in more limited liberalizations, far less tangible to the poorer or rural sectors of society, greater accountability of the political system affects all citizens in one way or another, rural or urban, rich or poor, male or female.

It is to explaining how women are affected by liberalizations in these three MENA countries, and why, that the discussion now turns.

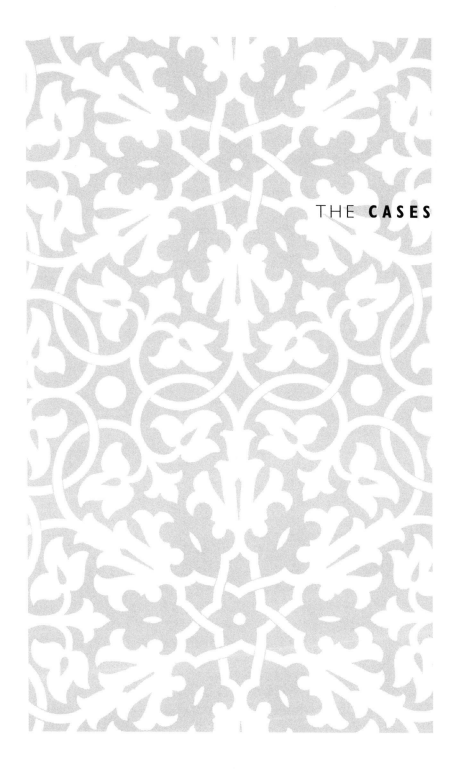

THE **CASES**

PART **ONE**
Morocco

CHAPTER **ONE**
In the Realm of the Commander of the Faithful

Since independence, Morocco has experienced numerous cycles of managed political openings followed by varying degrees of return to repression. As a result, when asked when the most recent liberalization had begun, interviewees for this study suggested a number of starting points. Most traced the beginnings of greater freedom of expression to 1987–88. Others, while not disputing this assessment, nonetheless noted that since 1991 much more progress had been made. However, a few contended that the liberalization could be dated to as early as the mid-1970s. The gradual unfolding of the liberalization will be covered in more detail below. First, however, to set the stage, we turn to a brief, general discussion of the Moroccan political system and economy.

THE MOROCCAN POLITICAL SYSTEM

Morocco's political system is that of a monarchy in which the king both reigns and rules. Although the country has had a parliament since independence, the body has been dominated by conservative, pro-regime parties (in part due to less than free elections over the years) loathe to challenge the status quo. The kingdom does have a long history of opposition party and trade union activity, but most discussions of the Moroccan political system place King Hassan center stage. The contention here is not that an examination of the king can explain all, but that the system is not comprehensible without a discussion of him and his role. "Power is centralized in the monarchy, which sits atop a national political machine. Political parties and unions have little influence in their own right. Rather, they structure interaction among a fragmented elite, most of which benefits from established patterns of machine politics."[1]

There have been a number of key elements in the king's governing formula. One is the role of religion. In the constitution of 1962, the king took for himself the title of *amir al-mu'minin*, commander of the faithful. In so doing, he appropriated responsibility for guiding and pronouncing on matters related to religion. Hassan's claim to have descended from the Prophet Muhammad and his own educational background (law), underscore and, in the eyes of some, reinforce this role. The state apparatus and its attendant patron-client relations, called the *makhzen*, have in turn been supported by the *ulama* (religious scholars), thus further strengthening the conservative nature of the political and social system.

Another key element has been coercion. Morocco has long been the subject of criticism from abroad for its flagrant human rights violations: political abductions and murders; disappearances; torture; arrests and detention for political reasons; deplorable prison conditions; and heavy censorship. In addition, of course, periodic outbreaks of violence, whether led by students, labor unionists, or the disenfranchised of the bidonvilles, belie the contention of regime stability's deriving from the king's religious legitimacy.[2] Also present in the governing formula is what some have described as the complicity of the political parties and the intellectuals. *L'Opinion* editor Khalid Jamai stated quite frankly, "the system continues to work because of our complicity and cynicism."[3] People are afraid to challenge the king, afraid of what might come after him. So they work within the corrupt framework of the "known" out of resignation or out of fear of the unknown.

THE MOROCCAN ECONOMY

Over the past decade and a half the Moroccan economy has been shaped by two major developments: the changes in policy dictated by the imposition of a structural adjustment program and the kingdom's attempts to develop closer ties with the EU. As a group, the EU states account for 40 percent of the kingdom's imports and 50 percent of its exports, and France and Spain are Morocco's two most important trading partners.[4] Hassan has therefore long been interested in expanding trade ties with the EU and in July 1987 applied for full membership. Yet the door to full membership has remained closed. The primary justification has been that Morocco is not a democracy, although the fact that Morocco produces many of the same goods for export as do Portugal, Spain, and Greece has no doubt also been significant as a barrier. Nevertheless, in the meantime, the country has been involved in a variety of negotiations to secure closer economic cooperation with a number of EU member states. The large number of Moroccan expatriates living and working in Europe (and remitting more than $2 billion annually in the last few years) as well as the importance of tourism receipts, a substantial portion of which is from Europeans, (between $1 and $2 billion since 1993) have given the kingdom's ties with Europe even greater importance.[5]

The evolving Moroccan-European relationship must be viewed in the context of the unfolding of economic crisis in the kingdom. Periods of drought in the 1980s and early 1990s have gradually undermined the productivity of agriculture, a sector that continues to employ more than 40 percent of the population. In addition, the drop in the world price of phosphates (of which Morocco is the third largest producer and the largest exporter in the world) in the 1980s severely affected the country's foreign currency reserves. Finally, the war in the Western Sahara, discussed below, which has reportedly cost the country $1 million a day since it was launched in 1975, has been a serious hardship.

As early as 1983, growing external debt in the face of insufficient revenues to service it forced Morocco to seek the assistance of the IMF to reschedule its debt. By 1988 the implementation of reforms led foreign investors to be optimistic, particularly because of new, high growth rates and because of the advantages the kingdom offered as a relocation zone for western industries.[6] However, by 1990, European financial institutions were growing wary of the country's continuingly high debt level and the decline in its foreign exchange holdings. In addition, of course, was the ongoing uncertainty about the Western Sahara as well as the appearance of Eastern European countries as potentially interesting alternative investment outlets.[7]

Despite more than a decade of experience with structural adjustment (and Morocco is generally cited as a success story, at least among Middle East/North Africa countries), external debt servicing continues to take a substantial portion of state revenues, and indeed, the debt has continued to grow. There is no question that one finds in Casablanca and Rabat ample evidence that a slice of Moroccan society has enjoyed tremendous economic success. Unfortunately, they are but a tiny fraction of the population. The rural areas have been devastated by years of drought and inadequate state response, and the manufacturing sector remains fragile, subject to the impact of the international market as well as the whim of investors seeking quick profits. The cost of the ongoing structural adjustment continues to be paid by some of the poorest and least empowered sectors of

Moroccan society. As a result, however, the specter of a sharp increase in immigration owing to deteriorating economic conditions has helped to maintain European interest in developing its trade and aid agreements with the kingdom.[8]

THE ROLE OF EXTERNAL FACTORS

Several external factors have had a major impact on Moroccan domestic politics during this period. The first is its longest-standing unresolved foreign policy issue: the dispute over the Western Sahara. In 1974, when Spain announced its intention to end its colonial presence there, Hassan advanced a claim to the region, and a national consensus developed—even among opposition parties—regarding the "Moroccanness" of the Western Sahara. For those who dissented there were two choices: silence or jail, for no open opposition was tolerated. The most direct impact of this conflict has been on priorities in government spending, in this case in favor of the military. Indirectly, however, the national consensus promoted during this period served to obscure or distract attention from many serious domestic problems, and has been a major source of stagnation in the political system.

Relations with Algeria also figure centrally, both in considerations of the Western Sahara as well as in certain questions of domestic policy. For years, Algeria was the main regional protagonist opposing Morocco's claims to the Western Sahara and provided material and diplomatic support to the Polisario. Even in the realm of political liberalization, the kingdom has been quite concerned with developments in its neighbor's domestic politics, especially the unfolding of Algeria's own political opening and the subsequent descent into civil war. In this regard, the role of Islamists domestically is of direct relevance. While the king has long kept Islamists under at least close surveillance, events in Algeria since 1988 have given the regime further impetus to monitor Islamist activity. In such a climate, official discourse has stressed the kingdom's Islamic heritage, but emphasized that Morocco's is a tolerant Islam and that no individual or group has a monopoly on the interpretation of religion. It seems likely that at least part of the impetus behind Hassan's proposal of constitutional reforms in March 1992, to be discussed below, derived from events in Algeria.

Also relevant to Moroccan-Algerian relations is the role that the Berber question plays in the domestic politics of the two countries. A prominent Moroccan Berber activist in fact traced the revival of a Berber movement in Morocco to developments in Algeria in 1980, the Printemps Kabyle, which led to a popular mobilization there. One of the most interesting products of the political liberalization in Morocco has been the flowering of organizations related to reviving and preserving Berber language and culture.[9] Given the role of the Berbers in resisting the FIS (Front Islamique de Salut) in Algeria and the anti-Islamist (and at times subtly anti-Islamic) content to some Berber discourse in Morocco, the king, if necessary, could use the evolving Berber movement as a way of curbing the growth of Islamist influence in the country.

Finally, on the level of Moroccan-European or Moroccan-U.S. relations, there is the question of human rights, an area in which Hassan has introduced some important changes. A first step came with the licensing of the Organisation Marocaine des Droits de l'Homme (OMDH) in December 1988, on the fortieth anniversary of the publication of the Universal Declaration on Human Rights. A state-sponsored Council on Human Rights was founded in May 1990, followed by a Ministry of Human Rights in 1993. Both developments are, without question, a part of Hassan's drive for greater respectability in Europe and for inclusion in the EU.

THE CYCLES OF POLITICAL LIBERALIZATION

Following a coup attempt in 1971, Hassan dissolved the parliament and responded with further repression when student and other dissent followed. However, in 1974, he initiated what may be called a populist policy which, on the economic front, involved nationalizing certain foreign businesses and property and demanding expanded fishing rights in coastal waters. On the political front, he proclaimed the country's intention to reintegrate the Western Sahara. A year later, not only did he lead the famous Green March of 350,000 Moroccan civilians into the disputed territory, but he also announced his intention to restore democracy. Political prisoners were released, press censorship was eased, and political parties were reinvigorated. Provincial elections were held in 1976 and parliamentary elections in 1977. There were no stunning victories for the opposition, but neither did they complain about the conduct of the elections.[10]

Nonetheless, a series of events led to rising popular discontent and a retreat from this opening: the increasing economic burden caused by the Western Sahara conflict; severe drought; and a drop in the world price of phosphates. Unemployment in the early 1980s was estimated at 30 to 40 percent, and income disparities were wide and growing. Major riots broke out in Casablanca in 1981 in which some 200 youths were killed. When the king postponed parliamentary elections scheduled for 1981, events seemed to have come full circle, as observers were reminded of the clampdown following the 1971 coup attempt.[11]

In 1983, Hassan again postponed parliamentary elections, following another failed coup attempt. Municipal and rural council elections were held, but the serious violations that reportedly characterized them further alienated the public. January 1984 then brought a new round of rioting. Originating in Marrakesh, the disturbances spread among students to Agadir, Safi, and Kasbah-Tadla in the south, Rabat and Meknes in the center, and then on to five cities in the north. Some 150 people were killed in the riots and in their wake between 1,500 and 2,000 people were jailed in a wave of arrests.

The king initially made no concessions; indeed, he responded by threatening the country with further repression. However, shortly thereafter, he resorted to his populist formula again, initiating a union with Libya and allowing elections, which were not marred by excessive interference, to take place. This revival of parliamentary elections marks the beginning of the most recent phase of liberalization which continues, with fits and starts, to the present. It is here then, in the mid-1980s, that this study begins. While the gradual liberalization process that began in the mid-1980s may have had its roots in some of the same pressures and concerns that spurred the king to open the system in 1975, the factors that have shaped it are different or of a different magnitude. Of particular significance has been the role of external factors: the economic demands of structural adjustment and Morocco's attempts to gain greater access to the EU; and the broader international trend of transitions from authoritarian rule in an atmosphere that has increasingly stressed respect for civil and human rights.

Several themes characterize this most recent Moroccan liberalization: human rights; administrative decentralization; the development of associational life; and the continuing stagnation of politics on the national level.

The beginning of the emphasis on human rights during this period may be traced to discussions of political prisoners, especially those arrested during the riots of January 1984. Far from willing to retreat,[12] in July the regime launched a new wave of arrests, this time against Islamists, a group called *al-Shabibah al-Islamiyyah*, which had affirmed its intent to overthrow the monarchy. But the concern with human rights among Moroccans, as well as the daring of several groups to take on the issue, continued in 1986, as the opposition press reported the arrests of extreme leftists and Islamists and denounced them in measured terms. The major opposition parties—the PI (Parti Istiqlalien), USFP (Union Socialiste des Forces Populaires) and PPS (Parti du Progrès et du Socialisme, formerly the Moroccan Communist Party)—all decided to focus on the issue of political prisoners and launched a campaign denouncing torture and calling for the reclassification of some sixty prisoners as political detainees.[13]

The domestic human rights situation then began to have increasingly clear implications for the kingdom's foreign policy. In 1985, Hassan had begun arguing that Morocco should be admitted to the European Community as an appropriate and logical extension of the community's South Mediterranean policy. The kingdom formally applied in July 1987, but was told that the Treaty of Rome stipulated that members were to be both European and full democracies.[14] In February 1988 the European parliament delivered an additional blow by condemning the arbitrary detention of political prisoners and the use of torture.[15] It kept up its pressure in December by urging Hassan to abolish the death penalty and to improve conditions in Moroccan jails.[16]

It was not that Morocco was a stranger to human rights groups: an organization associated with the PI, the Ligue Marocaine des Droits de l'Homme (LMDH) had been established in 1972, and a group that had broken away from the USFP, the Association Marocaine des Droits de l'Homme (AMDF) was founded in 1979. But the LMDH was not particularly active, and many of the more active AMDH's people were leftists and old-time Marxists who were eventually jailed, thus leading to the freezing of AMDH activity. By 1986, a number of people interested in human rights had begun to meet to discuss the need for a new group, but the fight to maintain independence from political parties (particularly the USFP) led the preparatory work to drag on for two years. In 1987 the group finally decided formally to establish itself and requested permission from the authorities to hold a meeting. Permission was granted, but the morning of the meeting (May 29, 1988) the police intervened, saying that while the meeting had not been forbidden, neither would it be allowed to take place.

At that point, pressures began to be brought to bear from both inside and outside the kingdom. Finally, at the end of November, the OMDH was given permission to hold a constitutive meeting on December 10, 1988, coinciding with the fortieth anniversary of the Universal Declaration of Human Rights. The negotiations with the state continued, as the authorities objected to the fact that some of the OMDH leadership had "political pasts." Some changes were made, but the state again attacked the organization by trying to intimidate those without political pasts regarding working with those who had been activists.[17]

In February 1990, a new Amnesty International report charged the government with maltreatment (including torture until death) of prisoners in police custody. These charges were particularly damaging because they came less than a week after the government had given an Amnesty delegation permission to visit the kingdom and meet with Hassan and senior ministers. The publication of the Amnesty report also followed the king's being pressed on the subject of human rights on French television and coincided with the publication (as urged by the Bar Association) by a group of Moroccan associations of a National Charter on Human Rights.[18] Certainly not by coincidence, in May 1990 Hassan established a Human Rights Consultative Council. Officially, the role of the Council members is to inform the king regarding existing cases and to check into conditions in the prisons so that justice can be rendered to all. Although this move, which is but one example of the state's attempting to coopt opposition themes, did temporarily diffuse some pressures, it did not completely satisfy the international community nor the local human rights organizations.[19] The uproar was renewed following the publication in late summer 1990 of *Notre Ami Le Roi*,[20] which made public and broadly available for the first time a cataloguing of many of the regime's most notorious human rights abuses.

In March 1993, just before the parliamentary elections, the Consultative Council on Human Rights acknowledged that there were areas of grave human rights concern in the kingdom. The council had come under criticism, most recently in the annual U.S. State Department Human Rights report, which charged it with being increasingly manipulated by the government. In April, Amnesty International released a new, damning report on the illegal detention of suspects by the security police.[21] Shortly thereafter, the government finally responded to domestic and international pressure to improve human rights by ratifying several international human rights conventions.

Turning to the role of decentralization in the liberalization, in the mid-1980s, the state began to establish regional associations,[22] the announced objective of which was the sociocultural development of their respective regions. The official rationale was that local elites could play a role in improving the efficiency of administrative services by working with the central and local governmental departments involved in the administration of cities. Through their structures and functions, these organizations give local urban elites direct access to centers of power as well as considerable authority in mediating and establishing patron-client relations. They also serve as channels for elite interest aggregation. As such, they compete with the existing parties (and have been denounced by them), but they also have the potential of making the *makhzen*, dominated by rural actors, very uncomfortable.[23] In a related move, communal electoral districts were redrawn by a national commission headed by Driss Basri, minister of the interior and right-hand man to the king. The new plan, which almost doubled the number of communes (from 859 to 1559), was expected both to enlarge and to renew the local political elites.[24]

As for developments within civil society, beginning in the mid-1980s the country witnessed a dramatic increase in the establishment of a variety of organizations. Some worked in traditional development fields, focusing on health and rural conditions, while others moved into less traditional areas such as the creation of small businesses and the further integration of women into the work force. In addition, however, were new associations with political goals, a departure for Morocco, where poltiical parties had long monopolized the field. The OMDH's establishment was discussed above as was the emergence of a number of Berber cultural organizations. A number of women's groups working specifically for changes in the law to make women more fully citizen have also been established.[25] Even taking into account the weakness of some of these groups and the degree to which the state still circumscribes activities, the expansion of associative life in Morocco has been quite remarkable.[26]

Unfortunately, however, the flurry of activity in the associative realm has not been matched by developments at the national governmental level. Following the parliamentary elections of 1984, the opposition parties began to discuss the idea of constructing a national front, with the hope of reasserting themselves in the elections scheduled for 1988. At this point, however, the monarchy was still quite skeptical about the idea of opposition, especially since the parties were more or less clear in their dissatisfaction with the ideological bases of the regime as well as with the principal figures responsible for running the country. The elections were ultimately postponed, with the lack of resolution of the Sahara issue cited as the official reason for the delay.

A dramatic example of growing feelings of frustration came in the spring of 1990, when a new finance law, further cutting state investment and devolving responsibilities for health, education, and infrastructure to the localities, elicited strong criticism from both sides of the aisle. The law led the four major opposition parties to form an alliance on May 14 for only the second time in the history of the Moroccan parliament to raise a censure motion against the government. This was followed by long, impassioned debates, both televised and widely discussed in the press. The motion was ultimately rejected 200 to 82, but the message was clear.[27] Nonetheless, the only real flexibility the regime seemed show at this stage was on the issue of the timing of the next elections, as the king called for yet another referendum to extend the parliamentary term for two more years. Again, the argument was related to developments in the Sahara. The king did not want elections to be held unless the Sahrawis participated, and that required the holding of a referendum in the contested territory itself; any other formula for holding elections would have appeared to be accepting less than full Moroccan sovereignty over the area. The referendum on the postponement passed with a reported 98.83% participation, and with 99.98% voting yes.[28] After that, however, no more extensions of the parliamentary were possible under the constitution. Frustrations with the political stagnation grew.

THE GULF CRISIS AND WAR

As the Gulf War approached, tensions were running high domestically. In mid-December 1990 demonstrations and rioting broke out in Fez during a general strike. The violence then spread to Tangiers, Kenitra, and Meknes. By the end of the second day of rioting, shops, banks, factories, and state buildings had been torched, and light tanks had been deployed throughout the riot-affected areas. While the events began as a trade union affair, the proportions they assumed and the violence they involved revealed dissatisfaction that went well beyond the unions.[29] Because of these disturbances, consultations were opened among the government, the unions, and management, the first such discussions in recent Moroccan history.

Aside from these disturbances, popular ferment at the time was largely manifested in the form of support for Iraq. Hassan was in a difficult position, not only because of his close relations with Saudi Arabia, but also because of the participation of Moroccan troops in the anti-Iraq coalition. The opposition was calling for the troops to be brought home, but their presence in Saudi Arabia was the best guarantor of continued sorely needed Saudi largesse. The pressures were so strong that in early February, Hassan was forced to allow an opposition party-organized pro-Iraq demonstration in Rabat which drew some 300,000 people from across the kingdom. Although Moroccan troop participation in the anti-Iraq coalition was heavily criticized during the demonstration, the king forbade any future calls for troop repatriation because of the harm he claimed it would do to army morale. He made clear that the decision to send troops was part of his royal prerogative, which could not be defied, and thereby placed the issue beyond criticism.[30]

Participation in the coalition enabled the kingdom to maintain its support from the Gulf states, while the limited nature of the involvement limited the domestic damage. Yet, the Gulf War was a major watershed, in large part because of the popular emotion it had elicited and the mobilization, if fleeting, it had triggered. The crisis and war did cause a temporary decline in the importance of domestic cleavages in favor of the horizontal solidary triggered by the invoking of Arabism. However, there were especially urgent socioeconomic problems that needed to be confronted: growing poverty, unemployment, an overburdened educational system, and outmoded legislation in a variety of areas. Hassan evidently did begin to feel that in order to ensure Western financial support he needed to demonstrate flexibility on human rights and opposition demands for reform. As noted above, 1991 was marked by numerous state human rights initiatives, and discussions of human rights and democratization came increasingly to dominate political debates.[31]

In mid-November 1991, the two largest opposition parties, the PI and USFP, looking toward the parliamentary elections scheduled for 1992, announced their intention to form a common front. The 1990 censure motion episode had affirmed the opposition parties' belief that they could in fact work together. Just as important, it led the king to consult with the opposition regarding possible revisions of the constitution. The PI had frequently noted the need for such revisions, arguing that it was not possible to establish a real democracy under the existing document.[32]

The pressures for change grew, while the state's ability (willingness) to resort to traditional levels of repression to enforce the "consensus" was compromised by increased human rights monitoring and criticism from abroad. The result was a political opening in the form of greater freedom of political expression and more respect for human rights.[33] At the same time, however, the rise of the FIS and the January 1992 coup in Algeria likely also had an impact, and on January 31, 1992, Hassan finally announced his intention to reform the constitution. The decision was widely welcomed: legislative elections were due before October 9, so that a new parliament would be in place for the fall session. The king promised that the changes would lead to a better balance between the legislative and executive powers and would guarantee more justice and more efficiency in the authorities' exercise of power.[34]

The king then met with representatives of the opposition parties and included them in a commission of arbitrage, over which he presided, aimed at proposing electoral reforms. Despite their participation, the opposition remained skeptical of the government's motives, although they were assured that the goal was a system which would bring about an eventual rotation of power—*alternance*—between the opposition and the royalist parties.[35] Then, without warning, a trade union problem intervened to threaten the unfolding cooperation. Noubir Amaoui, an outspoken member of the USFP-associated Confédération Democratique de Travail (CDT), gave two interviews within a three-week period in which he directly criticized the monarchy and the regime. He was arrested, tried, and despite support from political parties, unions, and lawyers, was sentenced to two years in prison on April 17.[36]

In part in response to the 'Amaoui affair, the opposition parties refused to participate further in discussions of the electoral law and demanded an independent national commission to organize the elections and oversee their honesty. Hassan refused this, although he realized how important it was not to trigger an opposition party boycott of the elections. On April 29 he announced the creation of two commissions including heads of the political parties: one to examine the electoral laws and the other to look into electoral procedures. The opposition parties presented a list of nineteen points as the basis of their discussions within these two committees. The evolving political party cooperation led on May 18 to the announcement by the PI, USFP, PPS, and l'Organisation de l'Action Démocratique Populaire (OADP), backed by a strong trade union front, of a formalization of their coordination on constitutional and electoral reforms in the framework of a *kutlah wataniyyah*, or national bloc.

As for the *kutlah's* electoral law proposals, the king easily conceded some points while others were more problematic. Hassan had made clear that democracy would come in small doses and that the primary role of the monarchy would be preserved.[37] Indeed, after nearly a month of opposition party clashes with the government over the electoral law, by late May Hassan had turned down a number of their requests: a reduction of the voting age from 21 to 18; the lowering of the minimum age of candidates to 21; and the institution of proportional representation rather than the "first past the post" system. As a result of the king's rejection of their proposals and of the fact that they continued to have only marginal input into the work on constitutional reforms, these parties' MPs boycotted the June 1 parliamentary vote on the government's offer. Ultimately, the opposition parties also decided to withdraw from the national commission set up to prepare for and supervise the voting, a move that led to the postponement of parliamentary elections until April 1993 and then June 1993, thus leaving the country without a functioning parliament for more than a year.

In the meantime, in mid-August the king's proposed constitutional changes were announced. The principal proposal was that the prime minister (rather than the king) would henceforth choose cabinet ministers, who would then have to be approved by the king. The king retained the power to dissolve parliament, but thereafter the declaration of a state of emergency would no longer automatically involve the dissolution of the legislature. Future governments were required to reflect the balance of forces in the parliament and to submit their programs to a confidence vote. The king rejected opposition proposals that all parliamentary representatives be directly elected; a third of the assembly would continue to be drawn from other sources. New laws were to be promulgated a month after being passed by parliament, with royal approval being automatic (rather than requring a signature). A new constitutional council was to be set up whose function was in part to issue binding interpretations of the constitution. Its chairman and four members were to be appointed by the king, with four members nominated by the speaker of the Chamber of Representatives. Finally, the preamble to the revised constitution placed greater emphasis on human rights.[38]

These proposals fell far short of what the opposition had wanted, and a number of splits developed in the *kutlah*. There was fighting within parties, with the leadership in some cases recommending acceptance of the constitutional changes because they were in the right direction, but with the PI and USFP memberships outraged (some because of the Amaoui jailing).[39] The major split, however, came when the PPS departed from its *kutlah* partners, who had decided to boycott the September 4 constitutional referendum, and called for participation with a "yes" vote. The king was furious at the possibility of a boycott by the opposition and, seeking the largest turnout possible, devoted a good portion of an August 20 speech to women and their ongoing drive to change the personal status law (see next two chapters), hoping to mobilize them to participate in the referendum. The outcome of the referendum (a reported 99% in favor) left the regime open to charges of massive fraud, and the palace was outraged. The opposition parties' boycott was viewed as worse than a "no" vote, because they had failed to play the king's political game.[40]

Municipal elections were held only a month later, and the opposition parties, which, with the exception of the OADP did participate, complained again of fraud and corruption. The three largest opposition parties won just 20 percent of the vote. One of the most interesting developments in these elections, however, was the large number of SAP candidates (*sans appartenance politique*—independents) who won. Such an outcome, in a political system in which political parties have traditionally been the only channels through which the regime has been willing to deal with interest articulation, suggests a malaise in the system or a dissatisfaction with representatives of existing political parties.[41]

The long-awaited parliamentary elections were finally held on June 23, 1993. Given the charges that the September 1992 constitutional referendum had been rigged and that the municipal vote a month later was marred by corruption, Hassan was under some pressure to deliver clean(er) elections. While there were charges of vote buying and bribery, in general, reports indicated less corruption in this round. Moreover, two women reached parliament for the first time: one from the PI, one from the USFP. The results were actually quite positive for the four-party opposition: 99 of 222 elected seats. However, with the remaining 111 seats decided by local electoral colleges which tend to be skewed in a royalist direction, in the end, the opposition held only 120 of 333 seats.

Discussions then began regarding opposition participation in the cabinet. Hassan appointed a transition cabinet in mid-November while continuing his negotiations with the opposition parties. The negotiations were rocky, and the palace was upset by its inability to provide even a semblance of wider participation by integrating *kutlah* members into the cabinet. The king offered nineteen minor portfolios, but made clear that *he* would appoint the ministers of finance, foreign affairs, interior, and justice, arguing that the opposition was too inexperienced to be given the positions they were requesting. Much of the tug-of-war resulted from the opposition's desire to oust the powerful Driss Basri from his post as minister of the interior, and the king was simply unwilling to remove his right-hand man and confidant. The one interesting development among the cabinet appointments was the creation of a new post, minister for human rights, filled by Omar Azziman, a founding member of the OMDH.[42]

Not until late March 1995, following a year and half of negotiations, did Hassan finally appoint a new government. Since the opposition—unwilling to be implicated in legitimizing a power structure in which they had no effective input—had continued to reject the terms of inclusion offered by the king, the new cabinet comprised largely loyal conservatives and technocrats, but no *kutlah* members.[43] Basri remained at interior but was stripped of the communications portfolio, which had been his since November 1985. Hence, Hassan's first attempt at establishing the bases of his highly touted *alternance* had failed.

Observers argue that the system cannot continue as it is, that the makhzenian system of governance will eventually be unable to cope with the growing demands of governing an increasingly complex economy and polity. Such predictions seem all the more credible as rumors swirl about the king's ill-health and about the crown prince's insufficient preparation for (and perhaps lack of interest in) taking over his father's duties. In September 1996, a referendum was held that approved the establishment of a bicameral legislative body to replace the unicameral parliament, only two-thirds of whose members had been elected by direct suffrage. This change satisfied one of the longstanding demands of the Moroccan opposition and appeared to move the kingdom one step closer to the *alternance* Hassan indicated he sought. All the more the opposition's dismay, then, when the official results of the parliamentary elections of November 1997 gave the four-party (PI, USFP, PPS, OADP) *kutlah* only 102 of 325 seats, once again rendering the centrist and rightist parties of the regime the majority. Allegations of fraud and other irregularities also marred what was supposed to be a turning point in the role of the opposition parties in governance. Nonetheless, the king followed through with his commitment to *alternance* and on February 4, 1998 tapped USFP leader Abderrahmane Youssoufi to assume the prime ministership and form a government. Negotiations among the various people took more than a month, but the king did not waver in his support for Youssoufi, and on March 14, the first cabinet of *alternance* was announced, with 22 of 41 ministers from the *kutlah*, including two women of the USFP.

CONCLUSIONS

The liberalization in Morocco has unfolded in response to a number of developments. On the domestic side have been the growing pressures for modification of a political system less and less capable of dealing with the demands of an increasingly large and complex society and economy. Such demands have no doubt been strongly influenced by the negative impact of structural adjustment on broad sectors of the kingdom's population. At the same time, however, several external factors have helped to encourage and shape the development of greater freedom of expression and the expansion of the associative movement. One of the most important has been the reinforcement by external actors (state and NGO) of domestic demands for greater respect for human rights. These actors have made clear to the king the possible negative ramifications in the realm of economic aid and economic relations with Europe of continuing disregard for evolving international norms regarding civil and human rights. Another has been regional developments, most importantly, the rise of the FIS in Algeria and the country's subsequent descent into civil war. Algeria's experience heightened the need to end the political stagnation. It also led the regime to continue to proclaim the importance of the country's Islamic values, while at the same time placing substantial restrictions on Islam*ist* organizing and expression. It is in the context of the developing freedom of expression as well as the internal and external pressures mentioned above that a consideration of women's relations with the state during the period of liberalization must be placed.

CHAPTER **TWO**
In the Shadow of the Mudawwanah

A BRIEF HISTORY OF THE WOMEN'S MOVEMENT

The beginnings of a women's movement in Morocco are generally traced to the independence struggle and the signing by Malika al-Fassi (a relative of independence struggle leader Allal al-Fassi) of the Manifeste de l'Indé- pendance. More dramatic, in 1947, Lalla (princess) Aicha, eldest daughter of Mohammed V (the father of Hassan II), became the first Moroccan woman to appear in public with her face unveiled (she wore a white scarf on her head). In effect designated by her father to be the symbol of the emancipation of Moroccan women, she had received her certificate of stud- ies in 1943, having studied along with her sisters at the palace with two French governesses.[1]

The 1940s also witnessed the establishment of a number of women's or- ganizations. The first, Akhwat al-Safa (Sisters of Purity), emerged from within the Partie de la Démocratie et de l'Indépendance (PDI). Then came the founding of women's branches in both the Istiqlal (PI) and Moroccan Communist Party. During the actual independence struggle, sisters and wives of the male activists transported arms hidden in bread, fish, and chil- dren's clothing, carried messages and documents, and distributed tracts and money.[2] In general, however, the women's organizations of the period gave priority to social or charitable work, tended to be directed by men, and gave priority to the demands of the national struggle.[3]

Independence came in 1956 and women's activism began to retreat in the early 1960s. Lalla Aicha's role dwindled, and many of the militants returned to their homes. The princess did continue as the head of a number of charitable organizations and as a representative of Moroccan women on various occasions. But as Daoud says, the transformation was logical: the movement was launched and then, in a very short time, the *daughters* of the king became no more than the *sisters* of the new king, Hassan II, thus completely changing their status and position.[4]

The one exception to the general demobilization of women in the immediate post-independence era was the establishment in 1961 of the UPFM (Union Progressiste des Femmes Marocaines), born out of the pro-government UMT (Union Marocaine de Travail), the only trade union in existence at the time. The UPFM's creation was intended to convince the authorities of the need to overhaul labor and other legislation's treatment of women. In 1961 a number of UPFM sections were constituted across the country. The union held some twenty regional congresses and created a national bureau as well as regional ones. Thereafter, however, its activity declined, the victim of repression by management, the lack of upper level female cadres, and a variety of political battles.[5]

Royal Initiative

Not until 1969 was there a new attempt to establish a women's organization, this time launched by the king himself. On January 8 he called upon local officials to select women known for their competence and their high moral character to form a women's union. He also called upon wealthy families to participate, declaring that it was necessary to overcome men's hesitations.[6] As a result, on May 6, some 300 women gathered in Rabat along with top government dignitaries for the constitutive conference of the Union Nationale des Femmes Marocaines (UNFM). The honorary president was Lalla Aicha, and the actual president another princess, Lalla Fatima Zohra, the wife of the king's cousin Moulay 'Ali, then governor of the Central Bank. The king made clear in his address that it was time to move beyond simple acts of charity and to bring societal problems to the attention of the leadership so that solutions could be initiated. According to Lalla Aicha, the UNFM's role was to see to it that the reforms concerning women remained within the framework of Islam and had the consent of the *ulama*.[7]

The UNFM was recognized as a *utilité publique* and began publishing a journal, *Aicha*, shortly thereafter. The designation of *utilité publique* is important in understanding the development of civil society. Any organization may apply for the designation. If it is received, the petitioning organization is then allowed to engage in fundraising; it is also thereby exempt from certain kinds of taxation and customs duties and can more easily publicize its activities. Over the years, the impression developed that such a designation could be obtained only by organizations whose programs and activities were closely in line with those advocated by the state. This has meant that those organization which directly serve, or at least do not interfere with, the interests of the *makhzen* have been the only ones to be so licensed. It gives them tremendous financial and organizational advantages.[8]

Not surprisingly, given its origins, royal women have been particularly important in the UNFM, not so much in what they actually do but in their visibility and their ability to command support. Yet, the union has never had great social or political weight nor broad appeal among Moroccan women. It has sponsored some social and professional training activities and sends telegrams of support to the state on various occasions. It has also, on occasion, blocked efforts by other organizations to play a greater role among women. A competition of sorts exists between it and the other women's groups, especially those that developed out of the political parties. The competition is not over funding, but over role and program. For example, in July 1976, in the wake of the meeting launching the UN Decade on Women, some 135 participants from across the political spectrum met to create a national commission for women. The project failed because the UNFM refused to renounce the idea that it officially encompassed the entire women's movement.[9]

Women in the Political Parties

During the 1970s, with the exception of the Moroccan Students Federation, the only women's organizations independent of the state were those within the political parties. Yet, given the political repression of the period, they were not in a position to be very active. The Istiqlal, Morocco's oldest political party, was the first to have a women's *section* within it, although its own separate women's *organization* was not established until 1987. It is also the party which, over the years since independence, has had the largest number of women in its leadership bodies. In 1974 its National Council counted nine women out of a total of 410 members and a Central Committee with three women of 60 members; in 1982 the Central Committee had two women of 80 members, and in 1989 two women were finally elected to its 18-member Executive Committee. The party also presented a number of women for seats in local elections in 1976, 1983, and 1992.[10] But, given the Istiqlal's conservatism, the interests of its members have been moderately reformist, not transformist.[11]

The Union Socialiste des Forces Populaires (USFP), which had developed out of the Union Nationale des Forces Populaires (itself an early offshoot of the PI) created a women's committee in 1975. Three women were subsequently elected to the party's administrative committee at its third congress in the late 1970s, while the fourth congress counted seven women of a total of 111 members, and the central committee had for the first time four women among 102 members. Nevertheless, the female base of the party has remained limited and, like the Istiqlal, the recruitment of women generally takes place from within the families of party militants.[12]

The USFP's position on women was that they were a part of a people that was suffering, whose cause the party therefore adopted. Unhealthy and reactionary behavior had to be ended, but without turning Morocco into a permissive society. In addition, in a meeting in 1975 and a conference in 1977, the party called for: a reform of the Personal Status Code or *mudawwanah*; raising the minimum age for marriage; equality of the two sexes with regard to family responsibilities; and equal rights to divorce, if qualified or constrained in order to preserve family equilibrium in conformity with the prescriptions of Islam. Nonetheless, the party did not actively work to achieve these goals.[13] Its approach to the problems of women may be summed up in the 1973 words of then party leader 'Abdallah Ibrahim, who argued that women's struggle was not against men but a unique struggle undertaken by both sexes: there was no difference between men and women, and their joint struggle was to transform the economic, social, and political situation of Morocco.[14]

The position of the the other major opposition party, the PPS, has been that it is only through work that women achieve liberation and that feminism is the result of a subjective antagonism between the two sexes. The PPS calls for equality of wages, facilities for working mothers, and a labor statute for women who work as domestic laborers.[15] In 1985, women from the party decided to establish their own organization, the Association Démocratique des Femmes Marocaines (ADFM) which, although officially independent of the PPS, nonetheless shares a number of key cadres with the party.

Given these attitudes it should not be surprising that the flurry of activity that accompanied the convening of the first international women's conference in Mexico City in 1975 did not immediately translate into any broader mobilization in the country. In the communal elections of November 1976 only 12 of 76 women candidates were elected (out of a total of 42,638 candidates). In the legislative elections of June 1977, none of the eight female candidates was elected, although in the indirect elections that followed, one PI woman was elected from the Chamber of Artisans. Indeed, what seemed to follow was a resurgence of the power of the *ulama*. In January 1979 a conference of the ministers of the Islamic Conference

Organization was held in Fes, and women were forced by the local authorities to wear the veil and the *jallaba*—the long, loose traditional robe worn
by women as an overgarment.

The seventh conference of *ulama* in Oujda shortly thereafter called for
the application of *shari'a*, an end to coeducation and dance at schools, and
the segregation of the sexes on the beach, among other things. The same
year several administrative circulars charged women with obtaining the
authorization of their husband, father, or guardian to obtain a passport.
The year 1979 did witness a renewed discussion of the *mudawwanah* (see
below), but in the end, conservative forces, which viewed any suggestion
of change as an assault on Islam, seemed to have their way, and no changes
were introduced.[16]

The Emergence of a Women's Movement

A number of factors came together in the 1980s to produce, by the decade's
end, a surge of women's activity and organizations. In the political arena,
there was the resumption of political party, union, and associative activity
along with a reexamination by opposition political parties of their programs in the context of the broader socioeconomic changes that had played
a role in triggering the liberalization.[17] As a result, the parties began to
demonstrate a new interest in marginalized social sectors and in questions
related to human rights, women, and youth.[18] The cumulative effect of
long years of waiting for "the revolution" to come and change women's status also played a role. As it became clear that existing organizations could
not deliver, women began to rethink what they could do themselves. By the
1980s, a new consciousness was emerging among some women who began
to see their struggle as parallel, not subordinate or secondary, to the class
struggle. Disillusioned with more formal politics, the women first turned
to social activism;[19] however, their activity gradually was transformed. The
increasing interest in women's condition worldwide also played a role, as
did the declaration of the UN Decade of Women (1975-1985).[20]

The Movement's Constituent Groups

If one examines the timing of the establishment of women's organizations,
one finds that, of 29 in existence in 1989, 16 were founded after 1980.[21] If one
adds those established since 1990, the skewing of the post-1980 period is
even more marked. Most non-Islamist activists trace the revival of women's
activity to a group of women who had been active in the student union
(UNEM) but had broken with it over issues related to the possibility of reform and over the question of women. After leaving the UNEM, they had
helped to form the AMDH and established a women's committee within it.

In 1983, the AMDH's activity was effectively frozen, but the women decided to continue their work in the form of social and cultural clubs in youth centers in Casablanca, Rabat, and Sale. This marked the first time that women's sociopolitical work was not directly under the control of a political party.

In the clubs (which eventually numbered thirteen) the women engaged primarily in educational work: literacy classes (Arabic and French), mathematics, and so on. In addition, there were discussions and seminars on issues related to women and work, health and reproductive issues, family planning, and the like. They also held discussions of the *mudawwanah*. Initially, their work was publicized through a radio program. Thereafter, information about the centers spread by word of mouth, as the women tried to open new clubs in or near popular quarters.[22]

According to former activists, these centers became like second homes. When the young women were not in class, they were there. For three years they operated in this way. Then, the students at one of the clubs in Rabat were called in by the local police to explain what they were doing and what changes in women's status they were advocating. Although the women had tried to reduce the political content of their work, the police insisted that they had gone beyond what a club administered by the Ministry of Youth could sponsor. The police suggested that they try to register themselves as an association, but it was clear that such licensing would not be forthcoming, probably because of the former association of many of the women's with leftist parties.[23] Between 1986 and 1988, all their clubs were closed: by the state; by the women themselves because their cadres graduated and were not replaced; or because of a lack of a longer-term strategy.[24]

However, during this same period, a number of activists began to establish other groups. The first was the ADFM, noted above, an outgrowth of the women's section of the PPS, opened in June 1985. As it grew it used involvement in social projects to support its program of consciousness-raising: professional development; integration of women into income-generating activities like sewing and embroidery; literacy programs; legal and health assistance; seminars and meetings on education, employment, and prostitution; and, for a while, the publication of a periodical entitled *Nisa' al-Maghrib* (Women of the Maghrib). The ADFM soon counted eight branches across Morocco. After four years of operation, in 1989, it held its first conference, which was attended by 400 delegates.[25]

The second organization to be established was that of the PI women (Organisation de la Femme Istiqlalienne, OFI) in February 1987. It then proceeded to organize a series of conferences on such topics as the Moroccan democratic experience, illiteracy, and the Arab Maghrib. The primary demand of these women has been the application of Islamic law and revision of the *mudawwanah* within the framework of the *shariʿa*. The OFI also adopted the demand for greater integration of women into political life as a major theme.[26]

Also in 1987, the Union de l'Action Féminine (UAF) was founded by a group of women who had established the Arabic language feminist magazine *8 Mars* (8 March, International Women's Day) in 1983. Some were associated with the leftist/Arab nationalist OADP, while others were politically independent.[27] The UAF's key figure was and continues to be Latifa Jbabdi, a woman with a long history as a militant who spent two and a half years in prison. In addition to producing the magazine, the women sponsored literacy classes, legal and medical assistance, youth centers and clubs, and so on. The UAF gradually established some fifteen regional sections in Morocco as well as offices in Paris, Toulouse, Aix-en-Provence and Lyon. At its first conference, held in March 1990, it adopted a program of action and a list of demands which included unification of the women's groups in Morocco, effective equality between the sexes, a radical change in the laws, a struggle against patrimonial practices and values, and full citizenship for women.

In the meantime, a number of other women's organizations of a nonpolitical nature were being established. One of the most notable was the Association of Women's Solidarity, established by long-time government social worker Aicha Chenna.[28] Chenna's interest focused on *mères célibataires*, a term that avoids the implication of an unmarried mother (a concept which is not acceptable in Morocco). These are poor women, many former *petites bonnes* (child servants who work in Moroccan homes) who have been abused physically and/or sexually and have become pregnant. Others are young women who have been divorced by their husbands and have no money and no skills. Chenna established her organization to enable the *mères célibataires* to keep their children and to do so without having to resort to prostitution to make a living. The association operates a catering service which offers inexpensive meals to a variety of public and private offices. With the money they earn, the women are expected to rent rooms so that they have a place of their own. The association also has a *crèche*, where the women can leave their children when they go to work. However, the association can accommodate only about 23 women at a time, so they are expected eventually to "graduate" and find jobs elsewhere.

During the same period, on the study/research front, in 1986 a grant from the Konrad Adenauer Foundation to the Faculty of Letters at Muhammad V University (Rabat) enabled a group of researchers that had been active from 1981 to 1983 to resume its work on issues related to the family. This group became known as *Approaches* and was open to male and female researchers, university professors, and others. It produced five works on women and/or the family between 1987 and 1990. In addition to publishing their work, the group held numerous conferences, roundtables, and debates on their research.[29]

It is also worth mentioning some of the publications of the period. In 1986 a new type of magazine, *Kalima*, appeared, published in French. While the magazine had a clear interest in women's issues, this monthly developed a readership that included men as well, as is clear from a perusal of the letters to the editor. It addressed a number of very sensitive issues, including the problem of violence against women and of male prostitution. (The latter topic triggered one of the closures the magazine suffered in its short life.) Many of the articles concerned male-female relations, general family problems, as well as a range of socioeconomic and sociopolitical problems. After two years it was forced to cease publication following an issue devoted almost entirely to a critique of the Moroccan press. This came only seven months after the closure of another high-quality French-language journal/review, *Lamalif*.[30] Published since 1966, it had addressed a range of socioeconomic and political issues, among them women and gender and had managed to survive some of the darkest periods of political repression in Morocco.

Also prominent during this period were the published products of a series of activities organized by well-known writer and sociologist Fatima Mernissi, entitled initially *Femmes 2000*. With support of the German foundation Friedrich Ebert, among others, a series of works on women were published by the Casablanca female publisher Laila Chaouni's Editions Le Fennec. While these are not all academic studies, they are solid contributions to a growing number of works on Moroccan woman. Among the titles are: *Portraits de Femmes*, *Femmes Partagées: Famille-Travail*, *Femmes et Pouvoir*, *La Femme et la Loi au Maroc*, *Femmes et Media*, *Femmes et Politique*, to name only a few. Between 1989 and 1994 Mernissi's group also held numerous writing workshops for women from across North Africa, as well as conferences on women and violence, female leadership, and the associative movement.[31]

The Gulf War as Watershed?

When I posed the question as to whether the Gulf War of 1990–91 had served as a watershed for the invigoration of political activity, a number of my interlocutors answered in the negative. They contended that the war had thrown them into confusion, in part because it had been such a horrible and swift defeat, and in part because it had forced them to truly question what their image of the West was. For those working on human rights and women's rights, issues that are generally perceived as having originated in the West, the contradictions and dilemmas were substantial.

Nevertheless, given the evidence, it seems difficult to ignore the war as a significant marker in domestic politics. For example, it is unlikely that the message of the popular outpouring of anger and frustration manifested in the pro-Iraq demonstration in Rabat in February 1991 was lost on the king. The years of stagnation at the national level had to be overcome and more avenues of popular expression had to be found lest the pent-up energy be turned in more dangerous directions. The burst of civil society activity may also have owed to a sense of growing organizational possibilities which were then reinforced by the increasing availability of funding from foreign institutions eager to jump on the new NGO-promotion bandwagon.

In any case, numerous other women's organizations as well as societies dealing with economic issues, culture, health, and human rights were founded during this period. In April 1994, a center for battered women, where women can receive legal advice and social counseling, was opened in Casablanca. On the research side, a Women's Study Group was established at Mohammed V University in 1992 by English professor Fawzia Ghassasi. The professors meet periodically to discuss research, encourage each other to publish, and stimulate interest in research on women among graduate students. There is also, among the committees of the OMDH, a women's committee, which is quite active, having held a number of discussions and roundtables on such topics as equality between the sexes in Moroccan law and divorce.

In the flurry of activity that accompanied the one million signature campaign to change the *mudawwanah*, discussed in the next chapter, numerous other groups were established. One was the Association Marocaine des Droits des Femmes, a women's offshoot of the AMDH (April 1992). Although at the time of this writing it had no headquarters and very little in the way of resources (all the work is voluntary), it had sponsored a major, full-day workshop on the question of legal protection for women against violence with the assistance of Friedrich Ebert.[32] There is also the Ligue Démocratique des Droits de la Femme, an offshoot of Hizb al-Tali'a (1992), and l'Association Marocaine des Femmes Progressistes (1993). It was not until July 1995 that an independent women's group (Association al-Jusur) finally issued from the ranks of the USFP.

Outside the framework of the official political parties, of course, are the various Islamist groups, which initially opposed the idea of women's participation in politics. The best known of the Islamist groups, Justice and Charity (al-'Adl w-al-Ihsan), led by the famous 'Abd al-Salam Yacine, who lived under house arrest from 1986 to 1996, remains unlicensed. Its members view those political actors that work within the *makhzen* system as corrupt, and they prefer to remain outside this system as the only way of constituting true opposition. Hence, they reject participation in the system by either men or women. Nonetheless, 'Abd al-Salam's daughter Nadia, the unofficial spokesperson of the movement, stated that she had been approached by a number of different groups regarding establishing an Islamist women's organization. She argued that even if one were to accept the principle of participation, any attempt to construct *an* Islamist women's organization would encounter problems because the various groups disagree on a number of matters, religious and political. Small-scale social work projects aimed at alleviating the condition of women do not, in her/their view, bring about change. Women have an important role to play, but perhaps not in the framework of a separate women's organization. For the time being, Justice and Charity's focus remains education and efforts aimed at developing people's faith. [33]

As for those Islamists who may be described as working within the system, the most prominent is the Reform and Renewal Movement (Harakat al-Islah w-al-Tajdid). After repeated unsuccessful attempts to obtain a license, in May 1996 it merged with the center-right Mouvement Populaire Démocratique et Constitutionnel. A women's organizational offshoot of al-Islah w-al-Tajdid was established in 1994. Named Munaththamat Tajdid al-Wa'i al-Nisa'i (The Organization for Renewing Women's Awareness), it was founded by a group of women who wanted to address the terrible problems of Moroccan women—illiteracy, poverty, prostitution, skyrocketing divorce rates. They were not satisfied with the existing women's organizations because of their secular orientation, so they came together with the idea of establishing an organization with Islam as its basis and with the mission of focusing on renewal in the areas of education and culture. The emphasis is on a renewed Islam, not prevaling religious practice, which they argue is based on superstition and a poor understanding of religion. Their primary tools are lectures and seminars on women's and family issues, as well as literacy classes.[34] While they do not rule out more activist kinds of work, they do not regard such activities as within their current capabilities. They situate their efforts in the context of fighting against what they call a westernization assault against Morocco and Islamic society more broadly.[35]

Evaluation

Addressing issues ranging from human rights to art, small business, abandoned children, family relations, health, family planning, and local development, a multitude of women's and other civil society groups developed in the post-1991 period. In general, these organizations work under difficult conditions. Their financial resources are quite limited, there is the *utilité publique* problem, and they do not benefit from the various subventions that political parties do (such as the subsidies party newspapers enjoy). Beyond these considerations, the degree to which their activities are publicized in the press generally is also contingent: if the group is not close to a political party, its activities are likely to languish largely unnoticed.

The women's movement is to a large extent a reflection of both the state of civil society generally and the political map of the country more specifically. On the first point, it is clear that the number of women involved in or directly affected by the women's organizations is quite small. The organizations examined above are limited to the urban areas and, with some exceptions (such as the OFI and the state-sponsored UNFM), generally to Rabat and Casablanca. This means that the rural population is largely left out of the equation. In addition, those who are involved in women's activities tend to be relatively privileged. In a country in which illiteracy is as high as 60 percent (and even higher among women), and much of the population lives in relative if not absolute poverty, there are limits to women's availability and/or ability and/or interest to become involved. There are also apparent limits to the degree to which the more privileged women are capable of bridging the gap between their own socioeconomic situation and that of the broader sectors of the Moroccan population who need their assistance.

Beyond the question of literacy and poverty, of course, is a range of additional problems that limit women's participation in organized activities. Family/societal pressures militate against women's involvement outside the home, unless it happens to be economic activity necessary to support the family. In addition, the combination of work and family responsibilities is tremendous. Unlike men, who can pass entire days in cafés drinking coffee and tea without suffering reproach, women are exposed to charges of "leaving" or "neglecting" their families for other work, for spending too much time outside the home. The question of women's mobility is also critical, for transportation to and from meetings can be a problem, and women's unaccompanied movement at night can be dangerous and is often not accepted by families. Furthermore, women are often socialized into believing that they cannot assume positions of responsibility and therefore are very hesitant to try. They are socialized into not knowing their rights and often intimidated into not exercising them.

Another problem is fragmentation. Despite the relative independence that the women's organizations may enjoy from the political parties from which they emerged, each is clearly identified with a political party, and this makes coordination difficult. The problem is not really one of greatly differing ideological inclinations, but of political or individual rivalries. The state also has an interest in the proliferation of organizations: the more organizations there are, the more difficult coordination is likely to be and therefore the more limited their political impact; and by allowing such organizations to operate, the state can more easily monitor grassroots activism.

In all cases, however, these groups are operating within the system, even if they see themselves in opposition. In effect, they accept the discourse of the *makhzen* and then use it to their best advantage, by pointing out the contradictions between the official line and daily practice.[36] In so doing, they, like others, are obliged to place themselves within the context of Islamic law. Their call is for a revival of *ijtihad* (independent interpretation of religious texts), which they see as the only hope at this stage for modifying what they view as the objectionable impact of *shari'a*.

WOMEN'S LEGAL STATUS PRIOR TO LIBERALIZATION

All of Morocco's post-independence constitutions have stressed the principle of equality between men and women. Article 5 says that "All Moroccans are equal before the law," while article 8 adds that men and women enjoy equally their political and civil rights. Article 12 states that the sexes are equal in exercise of public employment and in the conditions required. However, that equality does not include certain other areas, many of which are critical to women and demonstrate the tremendous gap between the text of the law and the reality of Moroccan life.

The first objection that Moroccan women generally raise is that, while many work outside the home in responsible positions, raising a family and earning money for it, the law continues to treat them as minors. This can be seen in a number of areas of law. For example, the Personal Status Code or *mudawwanah* prohibits a woman from entering into a marriage contract herself: she must have a tutor (*wali*). Moreover, tutorship over a female lasts until she is married (no matter at what age that occurs), so that a 40-year-old unmarried woman must still have a tutor for certain affairs, whereas for a boy the tutor's role ends at puberty.

This minor status is clear in other legislation as well. In the labor code, there is a long list of restrictions on employment that apply to children under age sixteen and to all women. For example, women and children are forbidden to work around specified noxious gases and emissions.[37] One wonders whether to be thankful that women and children are protected from such things, angry that the *state* rather than the individual makes the decision about who can work where, or furious that *anyone* is allowed to work in such conditions. Presumably in these cases, women are excluded for fear that their all-important child-bearing potential may be compromised. Indeed, there are pregnancy and maternity policies that protect women's jobs, and establishments of a certain size (fifty women workers over the age of 15) are required to provide nursing rooms, although the enforcement of such provisions faces many obstacles. In other cases, there are prohibitions about work in areas in which women's morals may be negatively affected (places that are deemed injurious to public morals). The presumption is that women are less able to protect themselves, or that men are better able to resist the corrupting influence of such places. As a book detailing women's status in Moroccan law states:

> Moroccan legislation provides special protection for children under 16 and woman of all ages. These measures are dictated by the physical inferiority of these two categories of workers, by the legislators' concerns that the working woman have the best possible working conditions, given her reproductive role, or by concerns related to the moral order.[38]

However, as one author has noted, at times when the economy is in need of additional manual labor, such concerns can be set aside: in 1928 women were used as laborers in the construction industry and as stevedores at the port of Casablanca. And, for all the proclaimed concern about protecting women, nowhere does the law specifically outlaw salary discrimination, a common practice that clearly harms them.[39]

The penal code also contains discriminatory elements. For example, article 336 stipulates that a woman must obtain the permission of the court in order to join a civil suit against her husband. Article 418 of the penal code states that a man who is the victim of adultery and who as a result commits murder or assault on encountering his wife and her lover benefits from considerations of extenuating circumstances: there is no mention of a parallel right for the wife. Just as damning, a woman who has a child outside of marriage (even if the pregnancy is the result of rape or incest) can be sent to prison for six months (the presumption being that she is a prostitute) and the statute of limitations is five years. Thus, if a woman has a child out of wedlock and tries to register it and no father claims it, she can be arrested. To prove fatherhood according to Moroccan law, the women has to produce twelve witnesses who will testify to the fact that she had sexual relations with the man in question. Abortion is illegal, and a woman who abandons her child (to avoid possible imprisonment) is also liable to be prosecuted.

Described by some as the last bastion of the *shari'a* in the legal codes of most Islamic countries, the Personal Status Code is generally the most impervious to reform. This should not be surprising, since controlling women and the production of children is a necessary part of the societal (patriarchal) order. Moreover, continuing *makhzen* support for such policies reinforces the state's relations with its strongest bases of support: the *ulama* and the rural notables. The version of the *mudawwanah* that was applied until

September 1993 had been drafted by a commission created by Muhammad V and chaired by 'Allal al-Fassi. Its text was released in segments between November 22, 1957 and February 20, 1959. What was produced, not surprisingly, was a law that carefully respected the Malekite tradition, the prevailing Islamic law school in Morocco. Neither society in general, nor the salafists (religious traditionalists) among the ruling elite, were interested in swift or deep changes in women's status or family law. Such change as would occur would take place slowly and within the framework of the *shari'a*. Because al-Fassi tried to amend certain elements, through offering recourse to a judge (which had not been stipulated in existing texts), some women regard him as a hero. Nevertheless, the woman envisaged in the *mudawwanah* is a rich woman who does not work outside the home and whose status is guaranteed by reliance on her family. The poor woman is not really taken into consideration. At the time of its promulgation, wealthy intellectual women seemed unconcerned with key elements of the *mudawwanah*. As Daoud quotes an unidentified bourgeois woman,

> Nous étions des pionnières. Notre dignité, notre émancipation, c'était l'alphabétisation, l'instruction. Tout ne pouvait être que le résultat de l'ignorance. La moudawwana nous apparaissait secondaire.[40]

Yet, there are many elements of the *mudawwanah* to which women object, in addition to the role of the tutor, cited above. For example, a Moroccan Muslim woman may not marry a non-Muslim and a woman/girl may be forced by a judge to marry a suitable partner if there is a fear or suspicion of bad conduct on her part (whereas in general the law says that a woman must give her consent to any marriage contract). The law also states that a woman owes obedience to her husband and his parents, a stipulation that has ramifications for a variety of issues related to the organization and development of family life. The wife also needs her husband's consent to obtain a passport.[41]

The law sanctions polygamy, although the *mudawwanah* insists that it is illegal if there is a concern that the husband cannot treat both/all wives justly. The wife does have the right to stipulate in her marriage contract that her husband not take a second wife and that she be accorded the right to divorce should she so choose; however, in practice, such safeguards are often ignored or contravened. Either spouse may demand a divorce, but the cases in which the woman has a right to divorce are specified and must be requested before a judge, whereas in the case of the male, they are left open. While the law itself states numerous conditions, and there are various kinds of divorces,[42] in practice there are few constraints on the husband's decision and few protections for the woman. The same is true in the realm of compensation for an ex-wife and allowance for children under her care. In general, women do not know their rights, cannot afford to take ex-husbands to court, and often are thwarted either by the process itself or by a system which does nothing to enforce legal judgments against a husband.

The first attempts to change the *mudawwanah* date to 1972, when a royal commission was charged with preparing a draft on the issue. But it was not long before it halted its work.[43] In 1979 two deputies from the Rassemblement National des Independants, (RNI) a royalist or pro-government centrist party, submitted two drafts for changes in the law. The Minister of Justice, acting outside the constitution, decided to turn the issue over to a group of *ulama*. In the end, a proposition regarding a food pension for divorced women was passed, but the other proposals were not even brought to a vote. Other initiatives, such as the proposed creation of 300 personal status tribunals and a project to deal with the problem of the abandonment of illegitimate children, came to naught.[44]

A more thoroughgoing attempt to revise the *mudawwanah* also came in 1979. Written by a royal commission of three magistrates, it suggested many minor changes, as well as a number of major ones. The marriage age was raised for both men and women; the powers of the woman's tutor were further regulated; the husband was required to respect and obey *his* in-laws; the husband would no longer be able to forbid his wife to work if such work served the general or family interest; the right of repudiation of the marriage could be written into the woman's marriage contract; a women's possible grounds for demanding divorce were broadened; and polygamy was placed under the authority of a judge.[45] But the opposition was intense. The *mudawwanah* had acquired a status approaching that of sacred text and the *ulama* and other conservatives bristled at *any* suggestion of change. As with previous attempts, nothing came of these proposals.

CHANGES SINCE LIBERALIZATION

Since the beginning of the liberalization in the mid-1980s, Morocco has signed a number of international conventions that are intended to provide greater legal protection to women of all ages, including in June 1993 the Convention against the Exploitation of Children, the Convention against Torture, and the Convention on the Elimination of All Forms of Discrimination against Women. However, as is the case with other governments, Morocco registered reservations on certain articles, and human rights and women's rights activists continue to press for the elimination of such reservations upon the adoption of these conventions.

There have also been some minor changes in laws. For example, the Finance Law of 1992 exempted women from paying legal fees for cases related to obtaining alimony (*nafaqa*). While this hardly solved the many problems related to the provisions surrounding divorce, it nonetheless was a positive step. Many repudiated women are desperately in need of support for themselves and their children, yet are not in a position to take the ex-husband to court, in part because of the cost. In early 1992 the parliament also shortened from 21 to 15 years the period of service required of women before retirement. While this may be viewed by some as a gain, for others this appears to be a way of getting women out of the work force in order to help solve the growing problem of unemployment.[46]

Besides the changes in the *mudawwanah* (to be discussed in the next chapter), the most significant change in the law came in July 1995, when, at the end of a special session, parliament voted to abrogate an article in the 1913 Law of Engagements and Contracts which forbade married women from concluding commercial contracts without their husbands' consent. This article, a remnant of the Napoleonic Code, was in direct contravention of the constitution, labor legislation, as well as economic rights clearly given to women in the *shari'a*. The change in this law was initiated by USFP and PI deputies. Initially three changes were proposed: (1) that the above-mentioned article be changed; (2) that an article left over from the French protectorate that required a married woman to obtain her husband's permission to open a business (a clear contradiction of Islamic law) be overturned; and (3) that an article requiring a married woman to have a judge's permission to raise a legal suit against her husband be set aside. The second proposal was scheduled to be discussed during the fall 1995 parliamentary session, and the third was yet to be put forward at the time of this writing.

USFP parliamentarian Badia Sqalli explained that it took a great deal of work just to put forward these minor changes. They had to be studied, and then colleagues had to be lobbied and cajoled. An additional obstacle to change is the fact that propositions presented by MPs are considered only after those of the government are addressed. Sqalli did note that she had used the approach of the Beijing conference as a form of pressure, arguing that the proposals were but minor changes and that they would give women something to take with them to Beijing.[47]

Work for the future. A number of legal issues continue to be the focus of women's attention in addition to the desire for further changes to the *mudawwanah*. According to PI MP Latifa Benani-Smires, these include the special demands made of women in order to obtain passports or commercial licenses, the right of a divorced woman with custody of the children to keep the conjugal home, and equality in the penal code.[48] MP Sqalli noted that after the *mudawwanah* reform of 1993, the problem of child custody arose, for, as a result of the changes, a divorced mother now has the choice of never remarrying if she wants to keep the child(ren) (although being a nonremarried divorcée carries a severe social stigma), or remarrying and losing custody. She contended, however, that the most urgent issue was the divorce law. The OMDH has also made a special effort to focus on divorce, holding a special round table on repudiation to which it invited representatives of various women's organizations on March 26, 1994. Even the Islamists are in accord on the need for reform here, since 50 percent of all marriages in Morocco end in divorce. Sqalli clearly feels that further work is needed on a number of issues related to the personal status law, but believes there is better chance for success if they are addressed one at a time.[49]

THE ROLE OF EXTERNAL FUNDERS

One cannot examine the activity of women's organizations in Morocco in any depth and not be struck by the role of external funding organizations—whether governmental, nongovernmental, or international. Several institutions are examined here. The coverage is not exhaustive; the discussion is meant, not to catalogue, but to provide a basis for evaluating the role that external actors may play in shaping the domestic agenda or in influencing the role that women and women's organizations may play.

One indication of the growing importance of foreign funding was the establishment after the Gulf War of a special development unit in the Ministry of Foreign Affairs to oversee, mediate, and coordinate the efforts of external funders and the projects of Moroccan NGOs. Despite one analyst's argument that this was an attempt by the government to control the funding choices or directions of external agencies,[50] a number of women active in NGOs dismissed this contention, arguing that, with only two employees and a very small budget, the office is hardly in a position to make a major impact. This office must be informed of foreign grants and aid, but it is not really in the position to give approval for projects. That type of "censorship" takes place in other ways and at other levels.[51] They also felt it was natural that the government know which foreign institutions are funding what for whom.

Konrad Adenauer Stiftung (KAS).[52] This affiliate of the German Christian Democratic Party began its work in the 1960s, primarily in Latin America, and then expanded into Africa and the Mediterranean area. In Morocco it has had two funding priorities: humanities and social science research, to help nationals study their own country; and economic infrastructure development, especially assisting small and medium-size firms. It is the first function that is relevant to this discussion, because since 1985 KAS has allocated money to Muhammad V University for numerous conferences dealing with issues relating to women, as well as more general methodological seminars for graduate students. It has also supported the publication of a number of studies on women's issues. Officials admit that their budget for such projects is quite small. Yet, while KAS's role may seem minor, it is worth noting that it appears to have been the first foreign institution to sponsor such research. The initial contacts were made by Fatima Mernissi, but have continued through a number of other Moroccan university professors. From this initial set of studies (*Approaches*, noted earlier), eventually a whole series of works on women was generated, some funded by Adenauer, others funded by Friedrich Ebert.

Friedrich Ebert Stiftung (FES).[53] Affiliated with the German Social Democratic Party, this organization's activities were most prominent during the course of the research for this study. Although it was involved in Morocco in the 1980s, its work on women is a post-1990 phenomenon and was described as having proceeded through several steps. The first began with Fatima Mernissi and involved sponsoring the preparation and publication (in cooperation with publisher Laila Chaouni) of a series of books on women's issues mentioned earlier: women and education, women and labor, women and the media, women and politics, and so on. As part of this effort, FES also sponsored a series of writing workshops for women. These books and studies are widely available in bookstores (and research libraries) in Morocco. Although somewhat limited in audience since they are published in French, their very presence in the market has given a great boost to interest in women's issues.

The second stage of FES's work was its support for NGO preparations for the 1995 Beijing conference. It became the primary funder for the Maghrib-wide NGO Collectif 95, an initiative that developed out of the ADFM to include organizations and individuals from Morocco, Tunisia, and Algeria. Their efforts aimed at producing several documents for presentation at the Beijing conference, the most controversial of which was a proposed unified personal status code for the three countries (see next chapter).

The third stage was described by the FES resident representative as the most concrete to date: work with such organizations as the AMDF on concrete proposals for changes in laws that adversely affect women. To that end they sponsored a conference with the AMDF on women and legal protection against violence. The full-day conference (June 24, 1995) produced a series of concrete proposals for amendments and changes to existing personal status, labor, commercial, and penal codes. The proposals were then presented to the press and were also to be submitted to the relevant ministries. Another, related project was being pursued with the LDDF (Ligue Démocratique des Droits de la Femme) regarding the labor law.

Amideast.[54] Amideast, an independent U.S. NGO, has a long history of working in Morocco, and its director, Sue Buret, is a long-term resident of the kingdom. In 1984, with money that had been earmarked by the former Carter administration for human rights projects, Buret, concerned that a program explicitly dealing with human rights would not be permitted in Morocco, put together a program on what she called "legal education." In this context she stressed the importance of choosing an appropriate partner. She decided to work through Fatima Hassar, a woman whom she had known for a long time. Hassar, a member of the PI executive committee who had excellent relations with the palace, was also head of the Moroccan Red Crescent Society (MRCS). Hassar's credentials, as well as the MRCS's humanitarian focus, enabled Amideast to pursue the project. It began by working with the Institut National de la Justice, whose director Buret had known from an earlier Fulbright board association. Through this association she was able to establish a kind of partnership, which over the years sent some forty Moroccans to the Strasbourg Center in France. One indicator of the program's success was the fact that a number of those who participated in this program ultimately became founding members of the OMDH.

Subsequently, from 1986–88, Amideast sponsored a series of eight seminars on legal education, which also had a strong human rights component. It invited government representatives from the ministries of foreign affairs, justice, and the interior as well as the PVOs in existence at the time. The demand to participate in the sessions was far beyond Amideast's expectations. Buret's familiarity with a number of law professors at various Moroccan faculties also enabled her to interest them, within this same context of legal education, in seminars on comparative law. Again, an indicator of Amideast's success was that when the Ministry of Human Rights was established in 1993, many of those who were appointed had been involved in the Amideast project.

The U.S. government. In Morocco the U.S. government has supported democratization through USAID's Democratic Insitutions Initiative (DII), launched in 1991. One target has been the parliament. At the time of this research, it had been proposed that AID provide computer facilities to the parliament to give MPs easier access to information that could be useful in decisionmaking. There have also been a number of USIS and USAID-sponsored international visitor programs which have sent Moroccan legislators to the U.S. to observe national and local elections and/or brought to Morocco Arabophone congressional aides who could explain some of the technical aspects of the U.S. legislative process. This idea has not been without its critics, for some argue that if the parliament itself is not playing a democratic role, there is no reason to strengthen a nondemocratic system. The counterargument has been that any programs that make MPs better legislators are positive contributions.[55]

The other portion of the DII in Morocco has been support for NGOs, especially those working on women's issues and on human rights more broadly. AID has been involved in projects regarding women for some time, but only since about 1993–94 has this been within the framework of the DII. For years, AID worked on women's issues through the two American NGOs in Morocco: Amideast and Catholic Relief Services. With CRS's announced intention to leave Morocco, AID has begun to work directly with some Moroccan NGOs. This has also been possible because of the political liberalization in Morocco and because of the increased domestic focus on NGO development. The objective in working with women's and other NGO's has been to sensitize them and the public to women's issues and to assist some of the NGOs in institution building.[56]

As part of this support, AID has sponsored Moroccan women's participation in local, regional, and international conferences dealing with NGOs, women's issues, preparation for Beijing, and the like. The choice of whom to sponsor and for what projects is made as a result of a close monitoring of the groups and their activities. If a group has good ideas, being small or institutionally underdeveloped has not necessarily been a hindrance to receiving assistance. Sometimes AID approaches the women with ideas, sometimes the opposite occurs.[57]

USIS has also had programs that specifically target women. In July 1993 USIS sent a group of seven women, members of different political parties, to the U.S. as part of an International Visitor (IV) program. This was the first program of its kind from Morocco, and among those who went were Latifa Benani-Smires (the female PIMP) and Amina Lamrini (who ran for parliament from the PPS). Badia Sqalli (the female USFP MP) had been to the U.S. on an earlier IV grant. This thrust has continued, as USIS has made a conscious effort to include more and more women in these programs, some from government and some from NGOs. The USIS facility, Dar Amerika, has also been made available to women to use for gatherings, and USIS itself has sponsored three to four roundtables a year on women's issues.[58]

EVALUATION

There is no question that external agencies are currently, and have been for some time (in the case of Amideast, 10 years), playing a role in funding a range of projects that provide women and women's issues with greater visibility, along with supporting the consolidation of political liberalization.

They have provided money for conferences on women and the law, women and violence, for institutional infrastructure development of NGOs, for development of women's skills and training through participation in regional and international conferences, for addressing taboo issues (such as domestic violence), and for publications and study groups on a variety of issues related to women.

How do actors on the two sides (Moroccan and foreign) see the relationship? All those interviewed were generally positive in their evaluation; however, it is clear that there are tensions. Donors complain about lack of coordination among women's organizations as well as the problem of women who become celebrities and become difficult to work with. There has also been some disappointment with the quality of some of the burgeoning number of studies that have been sponsored.

Perhaps more important, there are concerns that such foreign funding in effect relieves the Moroccan state of some of its responsibilities by providing support to the types of activities that should receive government assistance. On the other hand, direct Moroccan government interference or harassment was not mentioned by any of those interviewed, although at times the state has made its displeasure clear, and the foreign institutions themselves certainly take into consideration the political climate in their decisions to propose or fund projects. In general, however, the state appears not to have the resources to put into such projects and is either indifferent or content to see the initiative taken by an outside agency. The arrangement that such organizations have with the Moroccan government is that they will cooperate only with licensed organizations, and their programs are public, not secret. Representatives of relevant ministries are generally invited. This keeps the relationship clear and aboveboard.

Can one talk about a role of such external funders in setting or altering the domestic agenda? This is a difficult question to answer. During the pre-1990 period, women's organizations often chose their activities on the basis of what previous associations had done rather than on the needs of women and girls.[59] In the post-1990 period, when external funding began to flow, women's groups found their agenda shaped by the projects for which they could secure funding. While these were not projects they did not want to undertake, the funding has often shaped the concentration of efforts in ways that do not necessarily reflect Moroccan priorities. For example, I was told that Fatima Mernissi had approached USIS about funding a center for battered women. They turned her down on the grounds that this did not really fit within their purview. (Mernissi subsequently went to the Germans and obtained the funding she wanted.) NGOs also argue that what they really need is not just project-specific support, which is what the vast majority of this external funding is and the kind the Moroccan government accepts, but more general infrastructural support: assistance in developing general administration and management—skills which are not in abundance, at least among the NGO activists. A bit more disturbing is the missionary zeal in the discourse of some members of the foreign funding community: an excitement and at times a superiority in propagating the "good news" of democratization, women's rights, and economic decentralization.

But does this mean that funders have set or substantially altered the agenda? The answer is a qualified "no." In the first place, these funders did not create the desire on the part of Moroccan women to address the issues in which they are involved. It would be exceedingly unfair to portray women's activity in Morocco as somehow deriving essentially from an external initiative. On the contrary, what had been lacking were sufficient domestic political freedom and financial resources. The desire to militate to change the *mudawwanah*, for example, can be traced to well before the liberalization. Likewise, the most important women's groups, at least to date, were founded during a period that predates external funders' programs focusing on women and democratization. Many of these funders have, on the other hand, long had programs that assisted women in rural development or small income-generating projects, and the like.

That these organizations help to support organizations to keep women's issues in the public eye in a way that they could not without such support is probably beyond question. Many of the conferences, workshops, and publications that have punctuated the liberalization period could not have been realized without external funding, especially since most of these organizations have not been designated *utilités publiques*. But can such Western funding be a liability? A number of interviewees reported that immediately following the Gulf War it was very difficult to take money from any Western funders, although the stigma dissipated quickly. More problematic, human rights and women's rights as they are defined by these Western donors are often viewed as values and movements imported from abroad that are either alien or injurious to indigenous culture(s) and norms. The association of many women's organizations with foreign funding institutions, in addition to their largely secularist message and their generally leftist pasts, makes them particularly vulnerable to charges of being agents of neoimperialism or of betraying indigenous traditions and values. While in an earlier period such charges might not have had great import, they are significant in a period when conservatives, particularly Islamists, see themselves involved in a struggle against imported ideas which they claim pervert indigenous cultural and religious norms. By accepting such external funding, the women do leave themselves open to charges of collusion with the West. However, given the current state of available resources in the country, it is not clear what other options they might have.

In sum, an interactive process is clearly at work: the liberalization has allowed for the establishment and greater activity of women's organizations (and thus for the funding opportunities of which the foreign groups have taken advantage); at the same time the foreign funders reinforce the liberalization process by helping to strengthen organizations and associations that are pressing for greater freedoms and activity for civil society actors. Just as important as the actual funding, however, is the broader international political climate—a climate in which the discourse (if not always the practices) of economic and political liberalization, human rights, and women's rights, has become hegemonic and which rewards those states that pursue projects supporting these norms and punishes or marginalizes those which do not. Thus the activity of these funding organizations must be understood, not only in terms of the domestic context, but also in terms of their relationship to or their role as extensions of a broader set of international movements and institutions. Such activities would likely not have been possible without the liberalization (itself part of one of these broad movements), nor, however, would they have taken on such an importance or found such a resonance deprived of a supportive international environment.

CHAPTER **THREE**
Confronting the Makhzen

The post-1985 political liberalization in Morocco offers a variety of cases that may be used to illustrate the nature of state policy toward or interaction with women and women's issues. I have singled out the cases I discuss below because of some of the different actors and concerns they highlight. They are: the 1992 million signatures campaign to change the Personal Status Code; the 1993 Thabit sex scandal; the 1993 parliamentary campaigns of two women candidates, Amina Lamrini (PPS) and Badia Sqalli (UNSF); and the preparations for the UN Beijing conference.

THE MILLION SIGNATURES CAMPAIGN

In a March 3, 1992 speech Hassan promised constitutional reforms that were to be part of a broader initiative including transparent parliamentary elections and a solution to the Sahara issue. He acknowledged that strikes and a variety of socioeconomic demands were multiplying, but to achieve the goals of his program, he asked the political parties for six months of social peace.[1] This time it was not the parties, the students, or the trade unions, but rather a women's union that was an unexpected source of disruption.

On March 7, the eve of International Women's Day, the UAF launched a petition campaign aimed at changing the Personal Status Code (*mudawwanah*). This was not the first time the UAF had attempted such a campaign: in 1987 it had launched an unsuccessful initiative to put an end to unilateral repudiation by the husband by putting divorce in the hands of a judge.[2] In addition to the general political climate, and the UAF's gradual move toward more action-oriented work, the decision to launch a new campaign had its roots in a UAF-sponsored study day on women, democracy, and civil society. A letter detailing the program's results was sent on March 5 to the president of the parliament and to parliamentary groups and political parties, none of which responded. On March 7, the UAF held a press conference and announced its initiative, publishing its demands the following day in the UAF's magazine *8 Mars*.

The UAF's petition called for the following changes: (1) instituting equality and complementarity between husband and wife in the family; (2) according women, as men, legal competency simply by reaching the legal age of maturity (*sinn al-rushd*); (3) giving women the right to marry without need for a *wali* (tutor) after reaching the age of maturity; (4) placing divorce in the hands of a judge and granting women the same bases as a man for seeking a divorce; (5) stipulating that both spouses have the same rights and obligations in marriage; (6) outlawing polygamy; (7) giving the wife the same right as the husband to guardianship over their children; and (8) establishing work outside the home and education as rights the husband cannot dispute.[3] Although the issue of equal inheritance rights was raised in the initial discussions and appeared in the first set of demands in *8 Mars*, it was not ultimately included in the petition.

The response of the opposition political parties to the petition was very disappointing from the women's perspective. The parties' positions derived from a number of factors: the sensitivity of the issue for *kutlah* coordination as the first parliamentary elections in years approached; the men's general lack of interest in women's issues; and the problem of interparty rivalries. Since the petition campaign was the UAF's initiative, some party activists questioned why they should support an initiative that derived from the OADP (even if the UAF women continue to protest their independence from it).

As UAF president Latifa Jbabdi stated:

we suffered, not only from the state or the Islamists, but also from the political parties. We suffered innumerable pressures to stop the campaign.... I had contacts with the parties, and was attacked more than I ever was by Islamists . . . by the USFP and the Istiqlal. For them, to touch the *mudawwanah* was to touch a taboo which would then create problems."[4]

Hence, even what would have appeared to be their natural constituency, the non-Islamist, opposition parties, were not only unwilling to provide support, but also actively opposed the women on this issue, which they viewed as divisive. Not until the king became involved (see below) did the political parties show any real interest.[5]

Since most activist women were in accord that the *mudawwanah* was retrograde, the UAF decided to work for a united approach to the problem. To that end, it organized a two-day seminar (April 18–19) on the *mudawwanah*. Out of this gathering a "National Committee of Coordination to Change the *Mudawwanah* and to Defend the Rights of Women" was formed in the presence of representatives from a majority of women's organizations and party sections. The meeting decided to call upon specialists and human rights associations to draft proposals for change. It was on this point, however, that the consensus broke down. The UAF wanted to take on the entire *mudawwanah*, or at least many aspects of it, at one time. Other groups felt there would be a better chance of success if they focused on just one issue at a time. But it was the UAF's initiative, and it decided to present a series of demands.[6]

Political party considerations ultimately forced the USFP and OFI women officially to withdraw from coordination with the UAF, although the group was then joined by the Comité de la Femme Ouvrière (newly created in the Union Marocaine de Travail—UMT), women's sections from the newly created Parti de la Renaissance et du Socialisme, as well as by other women labor union activists, researchers, and lawyers. The campaign targeted all democratic forces in the country—men and women—in an effort to reach the goal of collecting one million signatures.[7]

By early April opposition had already appeared among the *ulama* and the Islamist organizations. In the broader division of labor, it has long been state policy to leave matters related to women and the family to the realm of the *ulama*, who have traditionally been very narrow in their interpretation of Islamic law, even though the state has fought Islamist influence in other areas.[8] The initial response came in the Islamist newspaper *Al-Nur*, but it was al-Islah w-al-Tajdid's weekly, *al-Rayah*, which led the attack. In its issue of April 20, 1992, an article by a relatively unknown *'alim* (Islamic scholar) strongly condemned the UAF petition on an number of points (one of which, inheritance, was not part of the final text) and stated that abrogating elements of the *shari'a* was apostasy, a crime punishable by death. The unstated conclusion of such a charge was that the women could then be murdered without retribution. The article further stated that the use of the issue of the *mudawwanah* was not driven entirely by national motives:

> Today more than ever this issue aims at conspiring against Islam to eliminate it, to remove what is left of Islamic law in the Muslim world (Dar al-Islam), and to achieve a complete westernization of the world.

Attacks along the same lines and in the same threatening tone continued in *al-Rayah* as well as in other Islamist papers (especially *al-Sahwah*, but also *al-Huda*, *al-Nur*, and *al-Farqan*) for several weeks.[9] The Islamists also launched their own signature campaign in opposition to that of the UAF, targeting sectors not penetrated by the women's groups, particularly high school women. The final stage in the exchange came on July 6, when *al-Rayah* published a letter from a group of *ulama*. In the letter, which was based on a memorandum they had submitted to the prime minister and the speaker of parliament, they called the campaign part of a larger plot against the Arab and Islamic world, insisted that it was a group of *men* (affiliation or origin not specified) who were in fact directing the women, called the women apostates, and demanded the application of the appropriate judgement, which in Islam, is death.

Neither the Islamist groups' nor the *ulama*'s response addressed the women's core concerns. Their answers were all based on a rejection of the right of *these* women (generally leftists) to interfere in matters related to religion. A high-ranking official of al-Islah w-al-Tajdid explained that the problem was that of a completely different set of reference points. No matter what these women said about *ijtihad* (independent interpetation), given the content and form of their demands, the women were in fact basing their objections and demands on codes and principles from outside an Islamic context. The problem arose when they then tried to artificially situate their demands within the framework of the *shari'a*.[10] The Islamists also argued that they were not inciting to violence, but were merely reminding people of God's judgment in such matters. Indeed, they turned the charge on its head by insisting that it was the women's demands that constituted a form of incitement against Islamic society. They denied that they were opposed to changing the *mudawwanah*, as long as it was within the framework of established religious principles.[11] They insisted that what the UAF women were demanding compromised, rather than expanded, women's rights.[12]

The signature campaign apparently also opened the way for different religious factions—the state *ulama* and the Islamists—to contest power. Several of the early articles in Islamist publications criticized the Moroccan religious establishment for its silence on the issue[13] and for failing to respond to the needs of Muslim society in a changing world.[14] When the official *ulama* did finally respond, not only did both groups coincide in their assessment, but the *ulama* used the Islamist papers to publish their responses. As one analyst observed, given the way the opposition developed, it was worth asking where to draw the line between the *ulama* and the Islamists.[15] This then raises a second point: that the vehemence of the response resulted, not only from a concern with maintaining the "last bastion of Islamic law," but also from a competition between the Islamists and the *ulama* over their political and religious role. Making their voices heard became particularly important for the Islamists given the authorities' continued refusal to license them in the context of the approaching parliamentary elections.[16] It is also possible that part of the reason for the virulence of the response was not just what the women said, but the wide debate they sparked.[17] Had their signature campaign been ignored, it is possible that the controversy would have never erupted.

The women did call upon the state to intervene to stop the incitement to violence against them, but received no response. The AMDH issued a statement, published in the UAF's *8 Mars,*[18] in which it defended the women's initiative on the grounds of freedom of opinion, and noted that there was no textual referent in Moroccan law calling for punishment of anyone who seeking to change the *mudawwanah*. Since the parliament is the responsible legislative authority and the courts are responsible for implementation of the laws, the AMDH called the *alim*'s *fatwa* (religious ruling) an attack on the law, the parliament, and the courts. As for the more mainstream and powerful OMDH, although the UAF fought for it to take a position on the *fatwa*, initially the organization refused, reportedly concerned about creating problems with the Islamists.[19] However, when the OMDH did finally issue its statement three months later, in July, it was quite strong. It stated that the issuing of *fatwa*s pronouncing sanctions against citizens who freely express their opinion within the framework of the law is not only a form of terrorism, but also a transgression of the law and a usurpation of judicial power. The OMDH also reaffirmed its support for reform of the *mudawwanah* and called for a spirit of tolerance and dialogue in discussions of the subject.[20]

In the meantime, the UAF was busy collecting signatures. Work began during Ramadan, and the women therefore held meetings after *iftar* (the meal after the day's fast) to explain the petition. They sponsored seminars and used other gatherings to which they were invited to discuss the issue and collect signatures. Women also went door to door in neighborhoods and to public baths. Not until late summer did the king finally intervene. Since he is the Commander of the Faithful, issues related to Islam are deemed to be properly his prerogative. To a certain extent, then, it was simply an exercising of this role to become involved in addressing a matter (personal status law) which, more than any other body of law, draws heavily on Islamic texts. Second, however, was the issue of the constitutional reforms. It will be recalled from chapter 1 that by this time the parliamentary elections had already been postponed until spring 1993 because the political parties were dissatisfied with proposed changes in the electoral law.[21] In this context, the king was keen to secure broad participation in the upcoming referendum on his proposed amendments (which were released a few weeks later). The women's mobilization and the Islamist response threatened to sidetrack the discussions and take the spotlight off the referendum. Some argued that the king also intervened to save the political parties from having to take a stance so that *kutlah* unity would be preserved and would help ensure broad support for the constitutional changes in the near term. Others contended that with parliamentary elections postponed for only eight months (although municipal elections were scheduled for October) the king did not want the opposition parties to be able to use the women's mobilization to their own advantage. Finally, developments in Algeria, which had just seen its democratic experiment ended abruptly by a military coup that had put an end to Islamist hopes of winning a parliamentary majority, were on everyone's mind.

In such an atmosphere, the women's signature initiative posed both opportunities and challenges to the monarch. The opportunity lay in potentially pleasing a mobilized and politicized group prior to the referendum. The king must also have been interested in how his adoption of the women's campaign would play in Europe (where Moroccan women had succeeded in publicizing the initiative), given the kingdom's continuing desire to enter the EU. Nevertheless, Hassan did not want quarreling over the *mudawwanah* campaign to rupture the *kutlah*, nor did he want to appear to be giving in under pressure. He certainly did not want to alienate the *ulama*, a traditional source of state support, nor allow the controversy that had developed to escalate into violence or confrontations between secularists and Islamists. Finally, he would not have wanted an issue related to religion to have developed a momentum of its own, outside of his control.

Hence, all the key indicators militated in favor of his involvement, but in a demobilizing framework. In a July 29 speech launching voter registration for the municipal elections, he thanked the Moroccan woman for her participation and said he would address her before the elections regarding her place in society. Then in a August 20 speech, Hassan gave priority to the question of women and to the constitutional reform. He acknowledged women's complaints about the *mudawwanah* and its application, but he entreated women not to mix these problems with the constitutional referendum and the electoral campaign, urging them to keep them "outside of politics" to avoid an explosive combination that would risk upsetting the equilibrium of Moroccan society. He called upon the women to address themselves to him directly, to write to the royal cabinet of their concerns. As *Amir al-Mu'minin*, he was the authority who would apply and interpret religion. To calm the concerns of the Islamists and other traditionalists, he promised to consult the *ulama* on the issue.[22] In this way he succeeded in defusing the issue by adopting it himself and by establishing a committee that would have months to deliberate and decide upon recommendations. As one analyst put it, he intervened, not to guide or orient the discussion, but to end it. Once he said "no more," no one dared to continue the discussion, and he thereby deprived the women of the fruits of their remarkable campaign.[23]

Just prior to the referendum, the Ministry of the Interior invited female representatives from the political parties and a number of women from government ministries to meet with the king. The UNFM, which had played no role in the signature campaign, was accorded preeminence: its president was treated as the leader of the group, it was allowed fourteen (one source says twelve) representatives, while the other groups were allowed only one invitee each, and its leaders were responsible for introducing the other invitees to the king.[24] Again in this meeting the king defined the problem as apolitical: "In reality, your problems are of a familial nature. They are numerous. You are not complaining about your political rights, nor about problems related to freedom, but more in the framework of the family."[25]

Once the king became involved and before he placed the issue above discussion, the *mudawwanah* became a subject of interest to the national (official) media, whereas up to that point, only the Islamist papers noted above and the OADP's *Anoual* had given coverage to the petition campaign. Television discussions of reforming the *mudawwanah* allowed the issue to reach an even wider audience. Many men and women had never seen articulate women debate the *ulama* on a religious topic. Hence, the king's involvement also served further to publicize the issue and, indirectly, to educate the public. The conclusion seems to be that many more than the one million signatures hoped for were obtained.

On September 19, 1992, the OMDH called for the inclusion in discussions of revisions of the *mudawwanah* not only those specialized in Islamic law, but also other jurists, as well as specialists in human rights, economics, and sociology.[26] However, the committee assembled by the king was far more conservative than had been envisaged by the OMDH call. It was composed of: two royal advisers, the minister of justice, the minister of *habous* (religious endowments), a member of the Royal Academy, four members of regional councils of *ulama*, four professors of religious sciences, the president of the Islamic university, Qarawin, the secretary-general of the Royal Consultative Council on Human Rights, two high-level magistrates, three professors of law, and one woman (Chbihanna Hamdate) the chargée de mission at the royal cabinet.[27]

Its recommendations were finally announced on September 29, 1993, almost a full year later and shortly before the then-recently elected parliament began its first session. The changes suggested by the council of *ulama* and signed into law by the king were the following. In the section on marriage, a woman who had reached the age of maturity and who was an orphan was allowed to contract her marriage herself (without a *wali*), or could choose her own *wali*. (This seemed very strange to women—that a woman who was an orphan was effectively treated as a major, but that all others continued to require a *wali*.) In addition, the phrase "the woman does not contract her own marriage" was dropped, leaving only "the woman delegates her *wali* to contract the marriage for her." The husband was henceforth required to inform the first wife of his desire to take a second wife, and was required to obtain the permission of a judge for such a marriage. In the section regarding dissolution of the marriage contract, a new provision required the presence of the two parties to register the divorce as well as the permission of the judge to implement the divorce, thus putting some (minor) constraints on unilateral repudiation. In the section on birth and children, the *ulama* designated the father as next in line after the mother for the guardianship of the children and gave the male child upon reaching age 12 and the female upon reaching age 15 the right to decide with which parent s/he chose to live. Tutorship of the boy continues until he reaches the age of maturity and that of the girl until she marries. Tutorship was given to the mother after the father, whereas before, it had gone first to the father and then to the judge or whomever the father designated.[28]

Women activists and others agreed that the changes were a great disappointment given the numerous proposals that had been made. Indeed, in the wake of the announced changes, a number of criticisms were leveled at the handling of the signature campaign. For example, the head of the OFI, Latifa Benani-Smires, one of the two women elected to parliament in 1993, felt that a less confrontational approach should have been followed: given the sensitive nature of the issue, the nature of Moroccan society and the timing, the way should have been paved gradually ahead of time through work to change public opinion.[29]

Why had the UAF women felt compelled to act even in an atmosphere characterized by a resurgence of religious conservativism? While I did not pose this question directly to any of the women, the answer seems clear. First, the king's and political parties' discussions of domestic political reform seemed to open the possibilities for dialogue on questions beyond narrow electoral issues. Second, and more generally, if women continue to wait for "more opportune" moments—moments when *all* variables seem to working in their favor—they may well wait forever. Worse, they may well awaken one morning and find that they have lost rights they thought they had and be forced to engage in a rear-guard action against further assaults. Indeed, the suggestion that women should wait for a more appropriate time (less controversial, for whatever reason) to press their demands sounds like a modification of the national liberation arguments of the 1950s and 1960s or the leftist arguments of the 1960s and 1970s according to which women were supposed to defer to the imperatives of the nationalist or the class struggle. In sum, most of the women interviewed for this study, among them many who worked on the signature campaign or in a parallel activity, felt the effort had been worthwhile, despite the minor legal changes secured, because it demonstrated that the *mudawwanah* was not an immutable, sacred text. Women also pointed out that according to his pronouncements, the king had left the door open to future amendments or changes.

Evaluation

First, the very launching of such a campaign, circulating petitions, and accumulating signatures aimed at changing the law would have been impossible outside of a process of political liberalization. (It was not, however, central to raising the issue for discussion, for that occurred several times in the late 1970s.) Second, the moving force behind the campaign, the UAF, was, itself, established in the early days of the liberalization process. On the other hand, the signature campaign also shows how marginal women and their concerns continue to be at the national level and how few allies they manage to enlist. Most glaring in its absence was the support of the political parties, from which the most active women's organizations have sprung. The liberalization meant that the king was willing to open up greater political space for opposition participation, and they wanted to take advantage of it to the fullest. For the parties that meant not allowing the women's concerns to cause the *kutlah* to flounder. At worst, however, the men were simply acting according to their own deeply held political convictions: either that women's issues needed to be postponed or subordinated to the larger national or class issues, or, as in the case with the PI, that the idea of challenging the *mudawwanah* itself was problematic. Unwilling to sacrifice the potential strength that the *kutlah* provided and unconvinced of a possible offsetting strength to be gained from women as a result of party support for these issues, the parties simply refused to take an active role.

As for the king, the manager of the liberalization, there was a great deal at stake: the constitutional referendum, the support of the *ulama*, the possibilities for a future *alternance* based on a bloc opposition. The number of times the king urged the women not to let the *mudawwanah* become mixed up with political issues (as well as the menacing tone he used *"Iyyaki thumma iyyaki"*—"do not dare") [30] is significant. By adopting the issue himself, the king lifted it above the political fray, saving the parties from having directly to adopt or reject the women's mobilization. By establishing a council, he provided the semblance of serious attention, while at the same time calming the most conservative elements through filling its ranks with traditionalists. In the end, then, the changes had to be accepted by conservatives, and the women could not really reject the amendments since they had been granted them by the king.

THE THABIT AFFAIR

In early February 1993, not quite a year following the launching of the campaign to amend the *mudawwanah*, and only four months before the long-awaited parliamentary elections, Hadj Mohammed Mustapha Thabit, a police commissar for the Ain Sebaa-Hayy Mohammedia area near Casablanca, was arrested after two young women filed a complaint charging him with abduction and rape. The story that gradually emerged was of the commissar's involvement in the rape of some five hundred women (according to his own testimony) over the course of at least 13 years. Sometimes lured by the offer of assistance (in obtaining a passport, for example), sometimes abducted by force, the women were taken to a small apartment where they were assaulted (all recorded on video tape). To those young women who had been virgins prior to the assault, Thabit provided the address of a gynecologist who could "repair the damage" and even issue them a certificate of virginity.

This was the first time that important members of the police bureaucracy—not only Thabit and his immediate group, but also other high-ranking officials in the security and information establishment—had been served up before public opinion.[31] While the official media were silent, the others had an unprecedented field day. Thabit's defense was that he was mentally disturbed, although he also noted, reportedly with pride, that he had never sought medical treatment. The commissar was ultimately sentenced to death, while several of his colleagues were sentenced to lesser terms (life, twenty years, ten years) for their collaboration and cover-up. The entire process from arrest to execution lasted less than two months.

The story raised many questions about the abuse of power in a country where the security services very closely monitor society. While some women were intimidated, shamed, or terrorized into not reporting the violence, evidence of Thabit's crimes was not lacking. For example, he had been police commissar in Beni Mellal, a town about halfway between Marrakesh and Fes, until 1980, when a minor whom he had abused threw herself from a window. Although the local socialist MP denounced the scandal in writing to the ministers of the interior and justice, Thabit was subsequently named director of security in Rabat. Two years later he was promoted to a position in Casablanca, and three years thereafter named to the post in Ain Sebaa, one of the four prefectures in the country's largest city, a position of tremendous power for a man on whom the *makhzen* clearly felt it could depend.[32] In 1990, another young woman had filed a complaint against him, but several of his commissar friends had convinced her to withdraw the charges and then wrote to the state prosecutor that the incident had been a misunderstanding caused by some malicious people.

Thus, one had a case of morals, political corruption, and sexual violence against women. It was a combination that could have given rise to substantial mobilization of women's groups, supported by other broad sectors of society.[33] Yet, it did not trigger the same mobilization as had the *mudawwanah* campaign. Why were the women not able to make use of the Thabit case to revive coordination?

The most broadly based initiative deriving from Thabitgate, as it came to be called, was the publication in early April of a joint communiqué by the women's sections of all the major political parties, the women's unions, women's human rights groups, and women's sections of labor unions. The communiqué made several basic points. First, it argued that the Thabit affair was simply one manifestation of administrative corruption. In the absence of a state of law, this authority had been transformed from an instrument to serve the citizenry into an instrument to observe, control, and subjugate. Second, it insisted that the attempt to portray this as an isolated, individual matter obscured the fact that this was an abuse of power and influence. Third, the large number of women who were victims of Thabit et al. were glaring examples of the exploitation and double oppression that women suffer—as citizens but also as females—given their inferior economic, social and legal rights. Fourth, it called sexual violence one of the ugliest forms of violence against women and their dignity. The women's organizations demanded a comprehensive investigation into all cases of economic and political corruption as well as crimes that touched human rights, inside or outside police stations and prisons.[34] As one analyst points out, the call, not for specific changes in laws, but for a broader examination of corruption, was a major departure from the strategy employed in the *mudawwanah* campaign.[35]

While this communiqué was the one unified women's response, it was not the only attempt by women to become involved in the case as it unfolded. Indeed, one unprecedented move was the attempt by several women's groups to join the case against Thabit as civil plaintiffs. Lawyer 'Aicha Loukhmas and three other UAF members were responsible for filing the request. According to Loukhmas, the union had initially intended to contact the other women's organizations so that through coordination a united plan could be devised. However, in the end the UAF, ADFM, and AMDF all attempted individually to join the case as civil plaintiffs. These requests were ultimately denied, although both the UAF and ADFM stated that they were not surprised by the denial of their requests, given the lack of precedent.[36] In addition, a number of women's groups, along with other political forces, attempted to organize a demonstration, permission for which was denied by the government. In the end there was a sit-in at the Istiqlal headquarters, but nothing more was permitted.[37]

With parliamentary elections only a few months away, the reaction of the political parties focused primarily on those aspects of the case that dealt with political corruption. The PPS made three primary observations: the first concerned the abuse of police power and the need for reform in this department; the second concerned women, noting how common moral and physical violence against women was in Morocco; and the third concerned the extent to which the case demonstrated the crisis of social and political values in the country.[38] The USFP political bureau demanded the resignation of all those who had a political or administrative tie to the Thabit affair and stressed that the scandal offered an opportunity to take legal and administrative measures to protect society from corruption, especially that deriving from positions of authority.[40]

The PI's *L'Opinion* carried a number of articles by editor-in-chief Khalid Jamai which focused on the need for reform in the police force. The OADP's position was that the Thabit affair was worse than a scandal, and that it could not have happened were the political situation not such that authorities were allowed to abuse citizens. It argued that the case against Thabit was not an isolated incident, and cited numerous other examples of assaults against women, extortion and abuse of influence. It further criticized the secrecy of the trial sessions as well as the fact that the entire process compromised Thabit's rights to a fair trial.[40]

The Islamists also weighed in. Many of their points echoed those raised by the secular opposition, as they asked how such practices could continue for so long undetected. They stated clearly that such a case called into question the legitimacy of an apparatus with wide responsibilities for community and national security, but they also held responsible for the corruption broader state policies toward women and the family which, in the name of liberation and equality, had pushed them toward unveiling and mixing with men. The silence of the *ulama* on the issue was criticized (as it had been with regard to the *mudawwanah* campaign). Al-Islah w-al-Tajdid issued an official statement on March 9 which, in addition to indicting the state authorities, blamed an inferior educational system that, it contended, did not prepare people to confront attacks against their honor. It said that such a case raised the issue of the moral decay of citizens generally and of women in particular in the face of material pressures and insisted that such a case showed the need to implement *shari'a*.[41]

Outside the political party opposition, the OMDH also issued a number of statements on the Thabit case. Several weeks into the case it noted a number of irregularities, including: the limited nature of the investigations and the speed with which they took place; the inappropriate role played by the prosecutor, who often spoke without the authorization of the presiding judge, interrupting and sometimes intimidating the defense lawyers; and the court's refusal to call witnesses needed by the lawyers of certain of the accused. All of these elements, according to the OMDH, called into question the fair character of the trial as well as the independence of the judiciary. [42]

The official media were initially silent, until an article was published just before the release of the verdict on March 11 in the official *Le Matin du Sahara*. It insisted that in Morocco, the preeminence of the law was fundamental and that the king, after learning the facts of the case, had immediately moved to begin judicial proceedings against "an employee of the National Security charged with crimes of an extreme gravity." The government action was described as demonstrating that no one was above the law in the country, no matter what their position. The article stressed, however, in describing Thabit's acts as isolated, that his behavior should not in any way reflect on the entire National Security service. In other words, while admitting Moroccans' right to be outraged, the article nonetheless clearly sought to discourage the tendency to generalize from the corruption of this case to the entire state apparatus and regime.

Evaluation

The political sensitivity of the case, as suggested by the regime's official response, and the approach of elections, go a long way toward explaining why mobilization around this issue did not, indeed would not have been allowed to, take a form similar to that of the *mudawwanah* campaign. At base, many of the criticisms leveled during this period called into question the whole makhzenian form of rule.[43] Indeed, the opposition parties sought to frame the case in such a way as to put the political system itself on trial. In any event, it seems certain that the short duration of the trial may be explained by the regime's desire to put an end to such discussions as well as to preempt any possibility that a longer investigation might well implicate more, and higher-ranking, people.

The regime's desire to keep such discussions to a minimum was also no doubt linked to the approach of parliamentary elections. While the king wanted to see the opposition make a respectable showing to provide a basis for his *alternance* proposal, he was not interested in having the opposition pose a real challenge to the royalist majority in the parliament. An extended period of mobilizing around the Thabit case could have been used by the political parties for just such a purpose. The short period of time between arrest and execution helped to keep opportunities to mobilize to a minimum. Although women's groups reacted swiftly, probably energized in part by the mobilization they had achieved during the *mudawwanah* campaign, real lobbying possibilities would probably have required a longer trial.

There is also the shame factor, which may have inhibited women's ability to mobilize around the case. For many, the details of the case were simply too awful or embarrassing even to discuss.[44] Finally, there appears to have been a coordination problem between at least the ADFM and the UAF. These two groups, described by observers as the two most important (in terms of activity and capability) women's groups in Morocco, appear unable to work together. Neither group's discussion of its efforts mentions the other.

Does this mean that the women's actions were totally without effect? Not at all. As a number of the articles written about the case indicate, Thabitgate highlighted the problem of violence against women, a subject that had long been taboo in Moroccan society. Both the UAF and the ADFM mentioned this issue in statements of their evaluation of the import of the case. In the wake of the trial the UAF suggested that a punitive deterrent was not sufficient to put an end to violence against women. What was needed were public awareness and educational campaigns through the media and other institutions.[45]

In a newspaper article, the ADFM's Rabea Naciri made the connection between the *mudawwanah* and violence against women, arguing that the law in fact legitimates such violence: it authorizes the husband as head of the household to hit his wife when she disobeys him; it allows a husband to kill his wife in the case of adultery; it permits him to prevent his wife from traveling, and gives him the right to marry his daughter to someone against her will. The "moral violence" ends up legitimating physical violence. At very least, the Thabit case broke the silence regarding violence.[46]

This is not to imply that the Thabit affair has led to a broad discussion of violence in Moroccan society. It does, however, seem to mark the beginning of a more open discussion in the media of the problem of violence against women. As *Anoual* noted, "this case broke the taboo which surrounded the issue of rape. For the first time we witnessed the newspapers discussing this problem on the first page, whereas in the past it was always a part of the forbidden or shameful issues found in the interior pages."[47]

According to testimonies, it also led to the opening of a number of centers to deal with violence against women. First to do so was the UAF,[48] but subsequently an advice center and hotline was opened in Casablanca under the direction of lawyer and OMDH activist Zineb Miadi in April 1995. There have also been a number of conferences held on the question of violence against women and the legal protection offered to women, such as a major conference held in Casablanca in mid-June 1995, organized by the Association Marocaine des Droits de la Femme (AMDF) and funded by Friedrich Ebert Stiftung.

WOMEN AND THE PARLIAMENTARY ELECTIONS: TWO CANDIDATES

A third case that illustrates women's political potential and possibilities during periods of liberalization may be found in female candidates' experiences during the parliamentary elections of 1993. Below are the stories of two women with long political involvements, each in an opposition party, and each of whom ran in a district in a large city: Amina Lamrini (Rabat) of the PPS (and president of the ADFM), who failed in her election bid; and Badia Sqalli (Casablanca) of the USFP, who is one of only two women who won parliamentary seats in 1993.

Amina Lamrini[49]

Although she had never served in elected public office, Amina Lamrini had a long history as a party activist. In 1975 she was elected to the Central Committee of the PPS. She later rose to membership in the Political Bureau of the party and to the presidency of the ADFM, which developed out of, but which she insists is independent of, the PPS. Lamrini's decision to run for office came as a result of a roundtable held by the ADFM shortly after the launching of the *mudawwanah* campaign with representatives of a variety of organizations. The meeting produced a new group, the Comité National pour la Promotion des Droits Politiques de la Femme, which, among other things, called upon women to become more involved in the political process. She had long called for greater women's participation in the political process. Yet, as she said, "one cannot continue to complain that women never run if you are unwilling to run yourself."

She began her campaign about a month before the elections, even though the official campaign season was only 15 days long. Unlike Badia Sqalli, whose story follows, Lamrini had no problems convincing her party to let her run in a particular district, at least in part because the PPS really did not expect to win any seats. She ran in a middle-class, popular quarter in Rabat where she was not terribly well-known, because she had only recently moved there. She held some 63 meetings in a month, sometimes three or more in one day. The meetings were of various sizes—20, 30, 40, 80 people—and in a variety of settings from homes to public places. In the end, Lamrini lost, having received 7 percent of the vote, which she felt was a respectable showing given that she had inferior financial resources and that the male candidate who won was from the USFP-PI bloc.[50]

Lamrini noted that she was able to draw on her background as an education inspector, as she spent long hours in what she called elementary civics lessons: explaining what the parliament is, how it works, what municipalities are, how elected officials' responsibilities differ, and why people should participate in elections. Often, she said, the entire session would pass without her having explained anything about her own political position. She also mentioned the learning experience the campaign provided. She had known there was poverty in Rabat, but this was the first time she had really seen it. She also learned that changing the *mudawwanah* was far from the immediate concerns of average women; for most, issues like clean water and electricity take precedence. In sum, she felt it was very important that two women won parliamentary seats and that this marked the beginning of a new struggle.

Badia Sqalli[51]

Like Amina Lamrini, Badia Sqalli has had a long history of political party activism, but with the USFP. Unlike Lamrini, Sqalli had previous electoral experience on both a municipal and parliamentary level. In 1976 she was a candidate for municipal elections in Casablanca and lost. She contended that there had been clear government interference against her candidacy, a handicap compounded by the fact that she was running against someone with real financial clout. She did realize, however, as did Lamrini, that the population was not terribly concerned about whether it was a man or a woman who was running. They were most interested in her ideas. For example, she told the story of how, after one campaign meeting, an elderly and bearded man came up to her and said, "May God assist you my daughter. One finds in the river what one does not find in the sea."

After this experience, she ran in the municipal elections of 1983 and won. At the time her party leadership wanted to show its interest in women and women's issues, so they suggested that she become municipal council president. However, she was afraid that people were not yet ready to accept the idea of a woman in such a position. Indeed, in the discussions of the issue, one party member quoted a *hadith* (a saying of or about the Prophet Muhammad) warning against women's assuming positions of political power. She determined that it was wiser to renounce the possible appointment and she served instead as the first vice-president.

Her next experience was in the 1984 legislative elections. She decided to run in the traditionally USFP district of al-Ma'arif, and it therefore took little prodding of the party hierarchy to approve her candidacy. However, she contended that it was clear from certain statements that the authorities did not want a woman to win, but that they hid behind the religious authorities, raising doubts about a woman's abilities and right to legislate. She noted other forms of harassment as well. For example, at gatherings she did not attend, one of her male opponents reportedly cast aspersions on her character because she is not married (she is a widow) and because she smokes. When it came to the actual polling, the examples of state interference were numerous and clear: her observers were barred from the polling places, and the authorities refused to give voting cards to some voters.

In the meantime, as vice-president of the municipal council, she was able to gain valuable experience, and when it came time to choose candidates for the 1993 legislative elections, she was well-known. In the prelude to the campaign, female party members strongly urged the parties to enlist more women candidates. In the end, the results were disappointing: she was one of only two USFP and three female *kutlah* candidates. At the same time, there was a battle in the party regarding in which district she would run. They wanted her to run in a middle- and upper-class area where they thought that a woman would have a better chance to win. This was a dilemma for her, for on the one hand she wanted to be elected, but on the other she wanted to demonstrate that a woman could be elected from a "popular district."[52] At the same time, the Islamists were more developed as a force in 1993 than they had been in 1984, so this increased the challenge as well as the possibility that she might be confronted by them. In the end, the Islamists did not create problems, and only a few people challenged her on religious grounds. This time she was victorious, and she succeeded in keeping her seat in the 1997 parliamentary elections.

Evaluation

Sqalli insisted that, whatever the election, one faces a number of challenges. One must be accepted by men, but one must also succeed in mobilizing women. In 1993, as we have noted, there was a great deal of discussion and publicity around the idea of getting women into parliament, and given the *mudawwanah* campaign and the Thabit affair, women were more mobilized. She also noted, however, that Morocco does not have opinion polling organizations, and so it is not known what it is that makes people vote for one candidate or another. One factor about which there is no doubt is that vote-buying, although against the law, plays an important role, especially in poorer areas. Add to that the fact that the centrist (royalist) parties have more money at their disposal, and seem to use it quite generously around election time, and you have the explanation for a great deal of voting behavior.

Despite her loss, Lamrini considered the experience a successful one. In the first place, she met with hundreds of people, many of them men and many of whom had never before talked politics with a woman or even heard a woman discussing politics. But she did not focus exclusively or even largely on women's issues. She talked about the state budget, unemployment, and agricultural policy. In this way, she felt her efforts had helped to pave the way for other women, by showing men that women can represent them and their interests. Lamrini also noted that the mere presence of women candidates begins to accustom the young to seeing women involved in politics.

Regardless of the 1993 outcome, Sqalli was unsure of the extent to which the authorities may have changed their position regarding female candidates. What is clear, she contended, is that if they do not want someone to be elected, they are capable of interfering to *prevent* it. There was some question in 1993 as to whether the authorities would let women win, especially opposition women. The answer, at least in 1993 and 1997, was obviously "yes." In comparing her legislative election experiences, Sqalli said that the USFP's 1993 *kutlah* alliance with the PI had certainly enhanced her chances of winning. At the same time, the election was more open, and she had gained a great deal of experience in governing. Probably just as important, in 1993 and 1997 the authorities had no reason to oppose her campaign: there was nothing threatening in it, and the idea of opposition parties working with the government had been embraced by both the king and the opposition.

THE BEIJING WOMEN'S CONFERENCE: PREPARATIONS AND IMPACT

The Ministry of Work and Social Affairs was responsible for coordinating the production of the kingdom's national report for the UN Beijing conference. The government's initial plan was to hire a group of experts to write the national report, which they planned to show to NGO representatives who, on the margins of the government committee, were supposed to prepare their own materials for consideration. But the NGO women strongly objected to the idea of consultants putting together a report that would be largely statistical in nature. The various NGOs themselves had been working on numerous topics, and they insisted on playing a major role in writing the report. The outside expert idea was therefore abandoned, and the NGO representatives were included in the process of preparing the national report. In the end, a wide array of women's organizations participated in a number of committees, each of which drafted various sections of the report. For example, Latifa Jbabdi and Fatima Meghnawi of the UAF were responsible for the political report. The fact that there was such broad representation on the government drafting committee was in part a function of the personality of the minister of social affairs, Rafiq Haddaoui, who was highly praised by a number of the women interviewed.[53]

In the end, the women were pleased with the document, probably as much with the process of its drafting as with its content. They admitted that some of the things they had submitted had not been included (Meghnawi mentioned a section on illiteracy); nonetheless, the report was far superior to its predecessors. So much more their dismay, then, when the report was not presented by the government at the Beijing preparatory meeting in Dakkar. Concerned, the women sent letters seeking an explanation from the relevant government offices. They received little in the way of response. Much more disturbing was the fact that the report was not distributed at Beijing either. Again, attempts to solicit explanations were unsuccessful: in some cases they were met with silence, and in others with diversions or lies that the report had been submitted. Only once did one female official, in response to a question regarding the noncirculation, say that this decision had come from higher levels in the government. There may in fact be several factors involved. One interviewee reported they had been told by some UN representatives that some of the very women involved in the drafting process had sabotaged the report.[54]

The failure to present a report was only one very disappointing aspect of Moroccan participation in Beijing. The official delegation was overwhelmingly composed of men, and the women participants were marginalized. The delegation was also disproportionately weighted toward ministry representatives, their clients, and women who had a desire to go to Beijing but who had never been involved in women's activities. Nor did the official delegation make any attempt to interact with the Moroccan NGO delegation. The head of the delegation, Hadi Abu Talib, an adviser to the king, gave a speech at the conference in which he essentially stated that all was well with Moroccan women. Needless to say, the NGO women activists were united in their disappointment with the nature and behavior of the government delegation.

The NGOs had internal problems as well. In preparation for the conference, the UAF had been designated by FEMNET (the African regional organization responsible for coordinating the meeting) as the *point focale* or coordinator for Moroccan NGO preparations. However, the UAF's designation as the *point focale* was not generally acknowledged by other women's NGOs and, indeed, became a contentious issue. Nevertheless, the UAF hosted the first NGO meeting, inviting representatives of all women's organizations as well as representatives of women's sections of political parties, human rights organizations, and unions. It was then agreed that the other NGOs would take turns hosting the meetings, and the UNFM was designated as the next host.[55] However, when the UNFM sent out invitations to the meeting, it did so in *its* name, as if it were its initiative rather than a coordinated effort. A number of women's groups, including the UAF, objected strongly, and some called for ending coordination. One interviewee, who has had long experience with women's issues but who was not directly involved in this episode, related that she had asked UNFM members about the affair and they insisted that it had all been a misunderstanding. My interviewee, however, was convinced otherwise: this had been an attempt by the UNFM to in effect take over *point focale* responsibilities.[56]

A second meeting was finally held, if in a tense atmosphere. A follow-up committee was formed and the UAF then proceeded to distribute forms for women to register for Beijing. They held several subsequent meetings at the UAF headquarters on technical issues and then were preparing for an enlarged meeting at a public place, rather than at the offices of any of the NGOs, given the sensitivities involved. Yet before this enlarged meeting could take place, the UNFM held its own meeting and was able to benefit from wide official media coverage. This was the final blow, as the other organizations sent letters informing the UNFM that they were terminating coordination.[57]

The original committee subsequently tried to relaunch the initiative on the grounds that the lack of coordination was very detrimental, and there was an agreement to try again. Yet it became clear that coordination would be difficult. The UAF made another attempt at the end of October 1994 by calling for a meeting of all the groups that had participated in the coordinating committee, but the atmosphere had been poisoned by what had transpired.[58] All efforts failed, although initiatives to revive coordination continued until almost the last minute: the OFI and OMDH both held meetings in Rabat in mid-August 1995 to put together some kind of joint activity before the conference.[59] In the end, everyone attended separately. The UAF, as part of its solo preparation activities, for example, held a large number of meetings and seminars around the country to raise women's awareness and publicize the conference.[60]

Perhaps the most unusual effort associated with the preparations for Beijing was a trans-Maghribi endeavor. The idea was born as a result of discussions at an October 1991 meeting sponsored by the ADFM entitled "Stratégies de Nairobi pour la Promotion de la Femme: Bilan et Perpectives au Maghreb," the goal of which was to assess what progress Maghribi women had made since the Nairobi conference in 1985. As a result of these discussions, a group of women's associations as well as individuals from Morocco, Tunisia, and Algeria joined to form what was later dubbed the Collectif 95-Maghreb Egalité, whose function was to prepare a serious and credible presence for North African women at the Beijing NGO meetings. The organization was registered in Morocco, and the coordination was directed from Rabat: Morocco's law of associations is far more flexible than those of the other two countries and the political climate offered greater possibilities than that of civil-war torn Algeria or the increasingly police-state Tunisia.

The Collectif was successful in securing substantial funding from a number of key external agencies: FES, UNFP, and UNESCO, as well as lesser amounts from USAID for travel to regional preparatory workshops. However, FES was by far the most important source of support for the four years of research and coordination that went into the preparations. The women decided to work on three reports, to be conducted cross-regionally. The first examined the three countries' ratifications of international conventions concerning women, with a special emphasis on the reservations submitted. The second compared where North African women had been at the time of Nairobi, in terms of health, education, welfare, and labor, with their situation in the early 1990s, as well as in comparison with men's status in the same categories. The third, and boldest, of the documents was a plan for a unified personal status code for the three countries, generally within the framework of Islamic principles, but relying on *ijtihad* to support changes or modifications. Thus, the three documents formed a kind of natural unit, or progression. National teams were assembled to prepare the respective country sections of the report. In addition to presenting these documents at Beijing, the Collectif secured funding from UNESCO for a Parliament of Women from Islamic Countries, intended to debate issues of special concern to these women, presumably primarily issues related to the various personal status codes. They also held a workshop on violence against women and a program of solidarity with the women of Algeria.

Evaluation

One of the clear lessons of the preparations for Beijing is that the combination of a political liberalization that permitted the emergence of a number of new and activist women's groups and a supportive Minister of Work and Social Affairs allowed for the first effective input by Moroccan women into the drafting of a national report. One may also view the government's decision to have such women participate, and on their own terms, as the result of a desire to implicate these women in a state-sponsored project. In such a situation it would seem that both the women and the state drew benefits from the cooperation. At the same time, however, the fact that this report was never submitted at an international conference and that the women have never been given an explanation for its suppression, implies at best bureaucratic lack of coordination or infighting and at worst a decision at a higher level that certain aspects of the report were problematic. The constitution and behavior of the official delegation at Beijing suggests the second explanation is probably closer to the truth. Whether aspects of the report were problematic for "nationalist" reasons or because they would have triggered anger or disquiet among religious elements remains a subject of speculation.

The other major theme illustrated by the Beijing preparations is the continuing negative impact of rivalries among women's organizations (although the experience of the Collectif-95 demonstrated that not only domestic but transnational NGO cooperation is possible). In this case, however, it was not the UAF-ADFM rivalry that was the problem, but rather the unwillingness of the UNFM to cede the limelight to another organization. The UNFM used its superior resources (both financial and media) to try and force itself upon the other NGOs as the de facto *point focale*. Since, apparently, the other NGOs' antipathy for the UNFM is at least equal to what they hold for each other, the outcome was complete lack of coordination among Moroccan NGOs at Beijing. To what extent the UNFM's initiative was suggested or encouraged by official circles is not clear. However, unlike what we shall see in Jordan, where the governmental NGO has an activist and ambitious head in the person of the princess, the UNFM's ability to constrain the activities of the other women's NGOs in Morocco is limited by its own lack of more broadly-based initiatives. The UNFM will not disappear, but it is unlikely to attempt to swallow up all other women's activity in the kingdom.

CONCLUSIONS

There is no question that since 1985, and especially since 1990, the possibilities for women's organizing have increased dramatically and women have taken advantage of the liberalization and perhaps even pushed the boundaries set by the state. The fact that their initiatives have produced less than satisfactory results from their point of view is largely because the changes they sought to one degree or another struck at the very bases of the sociopolitical system. More immediately, they also threatened to trigger the unraveling of political coalitions carefully crafted by male activists to try wrest a small share of power, but without questioning the broader *makhzen* framework.

Hassan certainly saw some opportunities in the mobilization of women in the summer of 1992, as he hoped to coopt them to support his proposed constitutional amendments. In general, however, one may see the king as averse to women's mobilization on both ends of the political spectrum. On the one end are leftist women pushing for greater equality as they define it. While the king must be aware that making minor concessions to them plays well with his Western supporters, he also knows that any changes that would challenge societal practices or Islamic law in Morocco would create resentment and opposition among the *ulama* and other conservatives. On the other end of the spectrum are the Islamists. Making concessions on that front would alienate other influential sectors of Moroccan society and raise the specter of an Algeria or an Iran in the kingdom.

There is no doubt that the regime feels the most comfortable with women's NGO work of an economic development or charitable nature. In the first place, it helps to fill a gap that has widened in the context of economic crisis and the demands of structural adjustment, as the state has been unable or unwilling to maintain the same level of expenditures on social services. On the other hand, these activities are generally not constructed with greater empowerment of women in mind. Such projects tend to ameliorate, but basically reinforce, the status quo. Given the current balance of forces in the country as well as the concern that Algeria continues to elicit, one should not expect women's activities nor state interaction with women to lead to more than changes on the margins. However, given that when Moroccans ponder the possibility of swift change it is usually the military or the Islamists that they see coming to power—neither of which would portend even a marginally more liberal regime for women—the prospect of incremental positive change may be the most hopeful scenario for the near term.

PART **TWO**
Jordan

CHAPTER **FOUR**
God, Homeland, King

The society and politics of Jordan, a small country located strategically in the Eastern Mediterranean between Israel and the Arab world, have been profoundly marked by a series of regional conflicts and crises. The ever-present threat of war is a major reason why, unlike Morocco, where political history since independence has been marked by cycles of opening and repression, pre-1989 Jordan witnessed only two brief political openings. Much of the rest of the explanation for the kingdom's economic and political development may be traced to the policies of its monarch since 1953, Husayn, who has demonstrated a considerable degree of skill both in cultivating external patrons and in riding the waves of regional (and occasionally domestic) turmoil. In part because of the continuing security threats it faced, the Jordanian state that was gradually consolidated under Husayn developed a strong security apparatus and as a corollary was suspicious of attempts at popular organizing. Of the activity that was permitted, most was based on family, clan, or tribal ties, relations which have, both through deliberate action and unintended outcome, developed as basic to power relations in the kingdom. The discussion below and in the next two chapters will explore how such a context shaped the status and place of Jordanian women during periods of repression and liberalization.

Transjordan (later renamed Jordan) was carved out of the territory assigned to Britain as part of the Palestine mandate imposed following World War I. Established to serve imperial interests, the amirate's relatively small administrative bureaucracy was subsidized by the British, who also handled all matters related to defense, finance, and foreign affairs. In no small part due to the Europeans' legacy in the area, regional conflicts or upheavals have regularly buffeted and profoundly affected the kingdom: Arab-Israeli wars in 1948, 1956, 1967, 1973, 1982; civil strife in Jordan in 1970–71; the Palestinian intifada beginning in 1987; the Iran-Iraq war and the Gulf war of 1991; and major influxes of Palestinian refugees in 1948 and 1967, and of those displaced by the invasion of Kuwait in 1990–91.

Jordan is a monarchy in which the king both reigns and rules. The kingdom has long had a functioning parliament, comprising both an upper (appointed) and a lower (elected) house, but with only brief exceptions prior to 1989, the parliament had little more than a rubber stamp function. Political parties were outlawed in 1957, martial law was imposed and political oppositional activity of any sort was forced underground. In the realm of so-called civil society, only professional organizations, such as doctors', engineers', lawyers' and similar unions succeeded, despite state coercion, in maintaining an independent and at times vibrant existence during the martial law regime.[1]

The role of family, clan, and tribal (*'asha'iri*) ties are basic to understanding the kingdom and may be observed on many levels, from everyday interactions in bureaucratic and judicial procedures, to government policy and appointments. Prime ministers are often chosen because of the family or region from which they hail. The cabinet is regularly shuffled as a means of cultivating patronage ties as well as preventing alternative centers of power from developing. Moreover, the composition of any given cabinet is determined, not so much by areas of competence, but rather by a set of political considerations, generally domestic in nature. For example, there must be representation from all parts of the country; there must be at least one Circassian and one Christian;[2] and there are generally several ministers of Palestinian origin.

The balance between Palestinians and Transjordanians (East Bankers), the two major communal groups in the country, has been particularly sensitive over the years and has changed over time. Prior to 1970, there was an attempt to balance representation of Transjordanians and Jordanians of Palestinian origin. While Transjordanians had always been the major recruiting ground for the military, many Palestinians had served in important civil service and ministerial positions. Following the civil war of 1970–71, this began to change, as Transjordanians began to be preferentially recruited into all parts of the military and civilian bureaucracies. Thus, largely excluded from the state, Palestinians came increasingly to form the backbone of the private sector. A division of labor of sorts emerged—Palestinian private sector/ Transjordanian public sector— which has shaped or influenced all Jordan's citizens' understandings of their role and possibilities in the kingdom.

THE JORDANIAN ECONOMY

Although possessing important mineral reserves as well as agricultural land in the north and in the Jordan Valley, Jordan has long relied upon external subsidies to remain solvent. Over the years, for reasons related to the security role the kingdom has filled, Jordan was able to collect substantial "strategic rents" from Great Britain and the U.S. After 1967, and to a greater extent after the conclusion of the peace treaty between Egypt and Israel in 1979, the Arab oil-producing states became the primary aid donors. These rents, combined with state policy toward their use, produced oversized civilian and security bureaucracies as well as an economy dependent upon regular infusions of aid from abroad, rather than domestic productive activity, to finance expansion.

This heavy reliance on external sources of income and employment made the country even more vulnerable than most small economies to the impact of external shocks. To be fair, the shocks that the Jordanian economy has had to endure have been more numerous and serious than those suffered by almost any other small economy: the loss of critical agricultural land and the addition of some 250,000 new refugees as a result of the 1967 war; the regional recession brought on by the Iran-Iraq war and the drop in oil prices; and the gradual termination (well before their expiration date) of Arab states' payments of subsidies promised at the 1979 Baghdad summit. More recently, the 1990–91 Gulf crisis triggered an influx of refugees both Jordanian and foreign, the loss of Iraq as a market, the expulsion of Jordanian expatriates from Kuwait (leading to a drop in remittances and increased strains on domestic services), and the termination of Saudi and Kuwaiti aid.

While the Jordanian economy has shown itself to be amazingly resilient in the face of such crises, it has often been aided by the appearance of new sources of economic assistance to replace those just lost. The kingdom's receipt of high marks from the IMF for progress toward structural adjustment goals along with its participation in the Arab-Israeli peace process have brought debt forgiveness, rescheduling, and additional aid and investment promotion from the West and Japan. Nevertheless, although unemployment, which may have reached 30 percent during the Gulf crisis and war, has dropped, the percentage of Jordanians living below the poverty line has continued to rise, as has the gap between rich and poor.

THE ROLE OF EXTERNAL FACTORS

The previous sections have already alluded to the impact of certain external factors on the kingdom's development. As a result of Jordan's location in the midst of several more powerful (militarily, economically, politically) Arab neighbors, Husayn has had to calculate carefully how his policies will affect his regional relations.[3] The close ties with the West, especially Britain and the United States, begun by Jordan's first king,'Abdallah, and continued by his grandson Husayn, exposed the country to the wrath of some of Jordan's neighbors (notably Egypt, and subsequently Syria and Iraq). All of these relationships, of course, were constructed and realigned in the context of Jordan's place in what was/is the Arab-Israeli conflict. Jordan has the longest border with Israel of any Arab state, and its long sovereignty over the West Bank (1950–1988), as well as its claims to Palestinian loyalty, have meant that Arab-Israeli wars have played a major role in shaping the kingdom's social, economic, and political development. Most recently, the United States' insistence upon progress in the peace process has served as an additional incentive to the kingdom to keep the negotiations moving forward. So, too, however, has been the image of Jordan the king has long cultivated—that of a forward-looking country interested in good ties with the West. Positive reviews from U.S. State Department human rights evaluators as well as high marks from the IMF for moving ahead with structural adjustment are all part of preserving this image and what is assumed will be attendant (financial) interest from the West and Japan.

POLITICAL HISTORY: EARLY LIBERALIZATIONS

Jordan has experienced three identifiable periods of political opening. The first, 1954–57, came shortly after Husayn's assumption of the throne and was precipitated by a number of factors. In the first place, the young monarch was seeking to set his own course, and in so doing often differed with the advisers inherited from his grandfather.[4] In addition, socioeconomic pressures resulting from the incorporation into the kingdom of the West Bank and its refugees (some 900,000, many of whom were destitute and resented the Hashemites, whom they accused of participating in their dispossession) militated economically and administratively for change. Finally, regional ferment owing in part to the Arabs' defeat in the 1948–49 Palestine war and in part to the rise of pan-Arabism also played a role.

In 1955, Husayn faced the first real crisis of his reign, as the announcement of his intention to join a pro-Western defense grouping, the Baghdad Pact, pushed by both Britain and the United States, triggered street demonstrations throughout the kingdom. The army restored order, but the king retreated from his pledge to adhere to the pact. Within this context, political parties, which were never officially licensed, began to operate openly in the kingdom, appealing to both Transjordanians and Jordanians of Palestinian origin. In October 1956, in the wake of Egyptian president Gamal 'Abd al-Nasir's nationalization of the Suez Canal Company, and the surge of Arab nationalist sentiment in the region, the kingdom witnessed its first free elections, which brought in a nationalist government that sought to strengthen Jordan's ties with its Arab neighbors at the expense of its longstanding ties to Britain.

Whatever changes the king may have introduced, the clear differences between his goals and those of his new government eventually led to a crisis. In April 1957 Husayn dismissed his prime minister, Sulayman Nabulsi, who had gone so far as to begin negotiations to open diplomatic relations with the Soviet Union. Shortly thereafter what has been portrayed as an attempted coup against the king was foiled, and martial law was imposed. Dissident elements were rounded up, while political parties were banned and their members imprisoned or exiled. Scores of military officers and civilian officials were dismissed and some were tried by military courts. The government reimposed censorship on the press. The opening was clearly over.

The development of the Palestinian national movement and the founding of the Palestine Liberation Organization (PLO) in 1964 served as the backdrop to the second opening, a decade later. Following the Arab states' defeat in the 1967 war, the Palestinian guerrilla organizations began to attract substantial numbers of followers in the kingdom. The war had weakened the army and security apparatus, just as the regime's loss of legitimacy made it difficult if not impossible to maintain the same tight controls on popular organizing. Thus, the opening of this period was triggered by a defeat in war, loss of territory, and an influx of refugees. The result was a swift and extensive expansion of a variety of organizations, most of them affiliated with one of the Palestinian resistance organizations.

All of this came to an end with the brief war of September 1970 and the eventual expulsion of the Palestinian resistance from the country in July 1971. These events not only marked the end of a period of greater freedom of organizing and expression in the country, although that was certainly severe enough. They also served to reinforce the distinction between native East Bankers, or Transjordanians, and those Jordanian citizens of Palestinian origin.[5] Following the 1974 Rabat Arab League summit's designation of the PLO as the sole legitimate representative of the Palestinian people, the king dissolved the parliament, in which half of the seats represented West Bank (Palestinian) constituencies, contending that were it to continue to function as constituted it would be a violation of the Rabat accord. However, parliamentary elections were also postponed—indefinitely—so as to avoid an electoral legitimation of the 1967 Israeli occupation of the West Bank and its consequent separation from Jordan.

Parliament remained suspended until 1977, when the king assembled what was called a National Consultative Council, empowered to debate issues but not to legislate. While its membership was expanded in 1981 from 60 to 75 in response to rising public dissatisfaction with the lack of public political process in the kingdom, its practical impact was minimal. Therefore, in 1984, again in response to societal pressures, the king recalled the parliament.

There was, however, nothing else of a particularly liberal nature during this period. The country's relations with Syria had been deteriorating, triggering a tightening of security in the country. Student demonstrations at Yarmouk University in 1986 were suppressed bloodily by the military, and the outbreak of the Palestinian uprising in December 1987 led to a further tightening of domestic controls as the regime feared a spillover effect. Exacerbating the situation was the fact that the economy had been suffering from the effects of the regional recession brought on by the Iran-Iraq war and the sharp decline in oil prices.

The value of the Jordanian dinar plummeted in early fall 1988. By the end of January 1989 Jordan, no longer able to service its external debt, was forced to negotiate with the IMF to reschedule its debt repayments. The government accepted a program similar to those agreed to by other countries: cutting domestic spending, including subsidies; curbing domestic demand; encouraging exports; and the like. In mid-April 1989, an announced reduction of subsidies on petroleum and petroleum products triggered rioting that began in Ma'an in the south, and eventually spread to all the major cities of the kingdom with the exception of the capital. The king, who was in the United States at the time, hurried home to address the crisis which, according to Amnesty International, left twelve dead and hundreds wounded and injured.[6]

This then was the backdrop to and the immediate catalyst of the liberalization of 1989. The discussion now moves on to a detailed examination of this most recent and most extensive opening in the kingdom's history. It explores the key issues addressed as well as the changing balance of political forces in the legislature from 1989 through 1995 in order to set the stage for a later analysis of the import of the various discussions and re-alignments on issues of special concern to women. Several themes emerge as key to shaping the period and hence to framing the discussion. First is the power and position of the Islamists (as demonstrated in their positions on confidence votes and the budget, and their participation in the cabinet and in various legislative initiatives). Second is the relationship between the Islamists and other blocs (especially other conservative forces on the one hand, and leftists on the other). Third is the general weakness of parties of the left, including Arab nationalists of various stripes. As the discussion details, issues of special concern to Jordanian women were directly used or affected in the jockeying for power position among these political forces—including the state—during this period of power reconsolidation.

THE UNFOLDING OF THE LIBERALIZATION: 1989–1994

The most immediate product of the April riots was the resignation of long-time prime minister Zayd al-Rifa'i on April 24. A cousin of the king's, Zayd bin Shakir, then Chief of the Royal Court, was tapped to replace Rifa'i on April 27. By late July Husayn had ordered preparations to begin for parliamentary elections, the first in 22 years, scheduled for November. In the meantime a tentative opening began.[7] Political prisoners began to be released, and as the elections approached, the long (and at that time still officially) illegal political parties began to resurface with impunity, although an article of the Jordanian electoral law banning those with political pasts from running for election was not lifted until three weeks prior to the elections. By mid-September, unprecedented public debate had begun about the upcoming voting and the candidates.[8] The major themes of the campaign were the lifting of martial law (in place since 1967), legalizing political parties, relaxing security measures, supporting the Palestinian intifada and fighting corruption. Among the field of candidates were twelve women, a development openly questioned only by some Islamists. However, their reservations regarding women's attempts to enter national political life were greeted with numerous criticisms in the press.[9]

As had been predicted, none of the women candidates won, although the king did subsequently appoint Layla Sharaf, the former Minister of Information (1984–85), to the Senate. Nevertheless, the election did produce a few surprises. In the first place, the turnout was quite low, about 54 percent of registered voters, 37 percent of eligible voters. Skepticism regarding government intentions deterred some, but the complex processes of registering and voting may well have discouraged others. There were also rumors that PLO chief Yasir 'Arafat had urged Jordanians of Palestinian origin not to vote, so as not to provide the Israelis with any evidence for their

"Jordan is Palestine" case. Whether true or not, the Palestinian turnout was even lower than the national average.[10] Thus the overall participation rate was disappointing, although observers were in accord that the elections had been clean.

The second surprise was the success of the Islamists[11], who, in various stripes, took more than 30 of the 80 seats.[12] The reasons for their success were clear. Over the years, the Jordanian regime had allowed them a great degree of freedom of action, if not active encouragement. The Muslim Brotherhood,[13] the oldest and largest group in the Islamist camp, had been recognized as a social organization, and hence was not subject to the same restrictions as political parties, which had been declared illegal in 1957. As a result, it was able to expand its network of mosques as well as social, medical, and educational services, and in the process develop a positive reputation as well as a tangible presence on a popular level. The fact that outside Amman women were among the fundamentalists' strongest base of support is quite telling in this regard.[14] In addition, in contrast to many who had run for parliament, the Islamists generally had no prior governmental experience, no direct association with the corruption that was perceived to have characterized the previous regime. For many average Jordanians there was little reason not to embrace the Islamists' slogan "Islam is the answer."

The question then arose as to whether the regime would allow the Islamist successes to stand.[15] The long years of positive association between the regime and the Ikhwan had laid a foundation for, at worst, loyal opposition. Second, the presence of this large "oppositional" bloc in the parliament seemed to attest to the freedom of the elections and to the legitimacy of the representation they produced.[16] This was a positive step in further defusing the tensions that had led to April 1989 and in reinforcing Jordan's image abroad as a country that was slowly democratizing. The regime opted for inclusion.

Following the elections, on December 4, Mudar Badran was chosen by the king to be prime minister. A former head of the intelligence services, Badran seemed perhaps a strange choice to lead the country's first liberalization government. However, he was known for his good relations with the Ikhwan, cultivated during an earlier (1980–1984) tenure as prime minister when Jordanian support for them, especially their Syrian members, had played a role in the deterioration of relations between Amman and Damascus. At this stage, aside from Western concerns, there was no reason for the government to seek to exclude them, and Badran held discussions with members of the Brotherhood as part of his consultations aimed at forming a government. In the end, their insistence upon receiving the Education portfolio was not acceptable to Badran and, therefore, he ultimately included six independent Islamists, not Ikhwan members, as ministers of justice, labor, health, social affairs, *awqaf*, and a minister of state for government affairs. Just as significant, four ministers from the previous government were retained in their posts—foreign affairs, the interior, finance, and energy and mineral resources—thus limiting the break from the past in the most sensitive areas of policy.[17]

A harsh debate on whether to accord Badran's government confidence preceded the vote which, perhaps surprisingly after all the uproar, Badran won easily, with 65 of 80 votes. Many of the MPs' concerns were addressed in Badran's rebuttal speech; however, demands of the Ikhwan (a 14-point program that began with the demand for the implementation of *shari'a*) figured particularly prominently. The new prime minister stressed the importance of Islam and the fact that it should be reflected in the public information system and in education. Badran also promised to ban alcohol from government functions and public institutions, along with issuing a commitment to repeal the Anti-Communist Law, end martial law within six months, and review the Political Parties Law. In the confidence vote, in addition to the support of the twenty-member Ikhwan bloc, Badran managed to obtain the abstention of six leftists, a success attributed to his responsiveness on the issues of ending martial law and easing restrictions on personal freedoms. Indeed, in these demands, the leftists and Islamists made common cause,[18] although the Islamists were ultimately outmaneuvered by the leftists and other non-Islamists in the vote for speaker of parliament.[19]

With a strong confidence vote behind him, Badran had little difficulty passing the new budget, the greatest challenge after the confidence vote. In the debates, the deputies criticized the policies of the past, especially those that had led Jordan to be so heavily indebted. But in the end, aside from calling upon the government to tackle the economic crisis and in particular unemployment, there were few concrete suggestions, and the budget, drafted by the previous government, passed with 52 MPs (18 of them Islamists) voting in favor.[20]

Badran then began to make good on his promises related to relaxing martial law. Confiscated passports began to be returned, many who had required official permission to travel were allowed to travel freely, and more political prisoners were released. Ministries were also directed to begin rehiring those who had been dismissed over the years for political reasons. On February 15 the national airline, Royal Jordanian, confirmed a ban on alcohol on all flights to Arab and Islamic destinations. Badran's government also began moving to end martial law, the defense laws, the military courts, and the anti-communism law. And, for the first time, demonstrations in support of the Palestinian intifada were permitted. While the progress made was promising, there was resistance to some of these measures from certain politically conservative quarters. The move from martial law required not only a decision to change policy at the top, but also a gradual change in mentality and custom, as well as a reassurance that those whose positions had been an integral part of the martial law regime would not be jeopardized. Such an evolution required time.

In February work began on the National Charter, a document called for by the king and intended to be a supplement to the constitution. Husayn argued that the realities of the new period required a reformulation of state-civil society relations. A royal commission was announced on April 9, headed by former prime minister and former head of the *mukhabarat* Ahmed Obeidat. It comprised sixty members from across the political spectrum, including four women (lawyer Asma Khadr, educator 'Eida Mutlaq, senator Layla Sharaf, and civil servant and columnist Muna Shuqayr), and ten Islamists (including six members of the Muslim Brotherhood). While work proceeded on the document, its completion was delayed by the Gulf crisis. Finally ratified on June 9, 1991, it guaranteed a pluralist political system, but also required acceptance of the Hashemite monarchy, thus depriving the Arab nationalist and leftist parties of one of the traditionally central planks of their program, and thereby removing from discussion what had been a central and contentious issue in the liberalization of the mid-1950s: the question of the legitimacy of Jordan as an entity and of the Hashemites as rulers of it.[21]

In the meantime, with a plurality in parliament, the Islamists began to flex their muscle. In early May 1990 the press reported that the Ministry of the Interior would begin to enforce a ban on male hairdressers. Initially the Ministry denied that such an order existed, but later admitted that it was in keeping with the "general feeling in the country." The issue had evidently been raised in parliament without fanfare and had been referred to the Administrative Committee of the lower house. It had not yet been presented to the full house, which was in recess at the time, yet the Ministry apparently felt compelled to move ahead with implementation. While never officially taking credit for advocating the ban, the Ikhwan did state that they welcomed it because "it increased women's employment chances."[22]

Reaction in the press and among the intelligentsia was strongly negative. Some charged the government with following a policy of appeasement toward the Ikhwan,[23] while a group of women met to plan a strategy to pressure the authorities not to enforce the order, arguing that this was just the first step in a longer term strategy against mixing the sexes.[24] Despite an announced scaling back of the application of the ban, by May 18 the Ministry was forced to rescind it altogether. It is unclear whether the outcome owed to the popular lobbying against the measure or to the fact that a similar attempt in Irbid in 1980 had ultimately been overturned in court. Nevertheless, in the meantime Islamists scored victories on other fronts: in a number of student elections, as well as in municipal elections in Aqaba and Zarqa.

The beginning of the Gulf crisis in August 1990 triggered a huge outpouring of popular emotion in the form of demonstrations, meetings, and rallies—a larger mobilization than had taken place before the elections. This was in part because the liberalization had in effect opened up the space for such mass expressions, but also because, on a major and contentious foreign policy issue, the king had taken a position in keeping with the feelings of most Jordanians. Although the king was actually far more cautious in his pronouncements than the Jordanian people, this did not diminish the domestic support he enjoyed. At the same time, however, the mass mobilization pushed off the agenda issues related to moving the liberalization forward, as everyone's attention was turned toward the Gulf.

The new parliamentary session began in November 1990, in the shadow of the continuing crisis. Its first task was to select the speaker, who would be responsible for guiding house discussions and setting agendas. This time, Islamist 'Abd al-Latif 'Arabiyyat bested Badran ally Sulayman 'Arar for the post (41–28–11). Several factors had produced this outcome. In the first place, the leftists, the so-called Democratic Bloc in parliament, who had not expected a clear victory by 'Arabiyyat in the first round, had cast blank ballots. Second, 'Arabiyyat had benefitted from the votes of all the deputies from his electoral district (Balqa) regardless of political affiliation. In addition, 'Arabiyyat received the support of the powerful Dhuqan Hindawi, a traditional ally of Zayd al-Rifa'i, a Badran nemesis. Thus, a combination of ideological and tribal solidarities, combined with the Ikhwan's support for the government in the previous session and their adoption of policies that could bridge the gap with some nationalists enabled them to win the speaker's post.[25] This changed the face of the government, and negotiations began between Badran and the Islamists over the shape of the next cabinet.

In the meantime, the new budget was presented. Intense debates ensued, with the Islamists arguing for a variety of *shari'a*-related economic policies. Their demands were ultimately scaled down, however, and in the end 22 Islamists voted for the budget, which passed 50–25. Then again, quietly, as had happened with the hairdresser ban, the Legal Committee of the house approved a law changing the formula according to which Miri (state) land could be inherited. Up to this point, women and men had been eligible to inherit equal shares of such land. The new law made such lands subject to *shari'a*, thereby reducing a Muslim woman's share to one-half that of her brother's. The law was proposed and passed by the house so quickly that there was no public reaction until after the fact, when it went to the senate, where it also passed, virtually unchallenged. The Islamists had been joined by a cohort of non-Islamist deputies, including Christians, who reportedly saw nothing detrimental to their interests in a proposal that compromised women's rights.[26]

In early January 1991 an expected cabinet reshuffle was finally announced. This time it was not independent Islamists, but five members of the Muslim Brotherhood who were included in Badran's cabinet: 'Abdallah 'Akaylah, Education; 'Adnan Jaljuli, Health; Majid Khalifeh, Justice; Yusuf al-'Athm, Social Development; and Ibrahim Zayd al-Kilani, Religious Affairs. The inclusion of the Ikhwan in the cabinet was described by observers as reflecting both the group's power and the government's desire to coopt it.[27] The relationship took on particular importance as the clock ticked down to what seemed inevitable armed confrontation between Iraq and the international coalition, for despite its long-standing support from Saudi Arabia, like the rest of society, the Brotherhood was supportive of the king's stance in the crisis.

The Islamist ministers, especially 'Akaylah and al-'Athm proceeded over the next few months to implement a number of policies, including sex segregation of employees in their respective ministries. The details of these initiatives are elaborated upon in chapter 6, but the importance of the uproar the policies triggered should not be underestimated, for it is credited in part with bringing down the Badran government. On June 17, only six months after the cabinet shuffle, Badran resigned and Tahir al-Masri was tapped for the premiership. The appointment of Masri, known as a liberal, was certainly reassuring to a politically and economically significant sector of Amman society which had been alienated by Badran's ministers' controversial policies.

At the same time, however, critical foreign policy considerations were at work. It seemed increasingly likely that a Middle East peace conference was on the horizon, a development the Ikhwan would have been expected to oppose. Masri, a liberal, and the first prime minister in decades to identify himself and be identified by others as a Jordanian of Palestinian origin, was viewed as a natural choice to lead the country at this juncture: only a Palestinian would have the necessary legitimacy to undertake such a step, and no Transjordanian wanted to be in this position, lest he be charged by Palestinians with being a traitor. (Indeed, Foreign Minister 'Abdallah Nsour, from the northern city of Salt, resigned before the October 1991 Madrid conference.) Masri's appointment also made more likely the formation of a joint Palestinian-Jordanian delegation to peace talks, the only form of Palestinian participation that the Americans and Israelis were willing to accept at the time. Finally, Masri's political liberalism enabled him to secure the support of a group of leftist and Arab nationalist deputies known as JANDA (Jordanian Arab National Democratic Assembly) after he promised to work to lift the remaining restrictions on political freedom in the country and not to attempt to infringe on PLO policy.[28]

Hence, from the point of view of both domestic and foreign concerns, the stage was set for at least a reduction, if not an exclusion, of Ikhwan influence from the cabinet. One observer also noted that the support of the Ikhwan for infiltration attempts across the Jordan River had so alienated the king that there was no way he would have allowed them to continue to participate in the cabinet at this point.[29] For their part, in response to the disquiet some of their policy initiatives had triggered during their six months in the cabinet, the Ikhwan complained that the Jordanian political system (a non-Islamic government) had prevented them from achieving many of their goals.[30] They also ultimately declared themselves opposed to participating in the Masri government, unwilling to join a government that intended to participate in a Middle East peace conference. Masri then proceeded to assemble a cabinet described by observers as the most liberal in years. It was a coalition of centrists as well as slightly left- and slightly right-leaning politicians, including several independent Islamists.

Yet the change that many viewed optimistically began shakily. One reason was the coalescing of a new parliamentary group, the thirteen-member Constitutional Bloc, which represented the Transjordanian bureaucratic elite. While it initially took no position on the Masri cabinet, its Transjordanian composition led to fears that it would not support a prime minister of Palestinian origin. The Ikhwan had, not surprisingly, made clear they would withhold confidence. In the end, Masri was able to win the confidence vote, 47–31, having secured all of the votes of the JANDA group, as well as 6 independent Islamists, and 10 members of the Constitutional Bloc. But it was an unstable coalition, the support of whose members derived from expectations that were incompatible in important respects.

The new prime minister first moved to fulfill his promise regarding expanding public freedoms by repealing (through royal decree) on July 7 most of the martial law regulations in force since 1967. This move was greeted with wide public approval. But trouble was brewing as the convening of a peace conference appeared more and more likely. Masri's coalition looked increasingly fragile, and there were rumors of a potential cabinet shuffle to include members of the Constitutional Bloc and release those whose position on the peace process was unclear. By late September, deputies Fakhri Qa'war and Mansour Murad (leftists who under other circumstances should have been natural allies of a Masri government) were calling on the prime minister to resign because of his government's commitment to attend the Madrid conference. On October 4, the cabinet was reshuffled, but hardly in way that promised long life: no members of the Constitutional Bloc were included, and three key Transjordanian members of the lower house were ousted.[31]

At the same time, the Islamists were beginning to feel the brunt of a government offensive aimed at reining in those opposed to the peace process. They insisted that they did not want a disruption of democracy and warned that an attempt to curb democratic freedoms might lead to an Algeria-like situation. While they apparently did not believe that Masri himself was encouraging a violation of freedoms, the Ikhwan did feel that the prime minister was not carefully overseeing the activities of the security services.[32] By early October a contraction in political freedoms was clear, as the regime apparently wanted to take no chances as the country moved closer and closer to the Madrid conference. As a result, when the new cabinet was announced, expressions of no confidence were rampant and calls from deputies for Masri's resignation were raised.

With the peace conference on the horizon, the regular parliamentary session had been postponed and there was no framework within which to raise a no-confidence motion. Nevertheless, shortly after the Madrid conference, parliament began its fall session and a temporary, and in other circumstances unlikely, alliance of Islamist and Constitutional Bloc MPs put forward and won a no-confidence vote. The Islamists' grievances related both to the peace conference and to their recent harassment by the government. Challenging Masri with a no-confidence vote was a way of sending a message to the regime that they were ready to confront it, if not head-on over the peace process.[33] The Constitutional Bloc's opposition derived, not from the government's negotiations with Israel, which this bloc formally supported, but from this powerful constituency's reported alarm with the implications of Masri's Palestinian identity and his alliance with the Jordanian left. "Both factors threatened to undermine the status and influence of the traditionalists in the system, especially when they could not secure a dominant role in Masri's cabinet."[34] These two groups were then joined in their opposition to Masri by leftists who were both opposed to the government's participation in the Madrid conference and unhappy that the development of public freedoms had been curtailed by this "liberal" government.

Once Masri was forced out, the atmosphere changed. The Ikhwan did cooperate with the successor government headed by Zayd bin Shakir,[35] although they did not join the cabinet. Whether they had not wanted to join or simply were not asked is not clear. Bin Shakir's conservatism certainly made him more acceptable to the Ikhwan than Masri; in addition, as the king's cousin he could not be challenged in the way Masri or Badran had been. Bin Shakir also had the advantage of having the Madrid conference behind him. It was no longer the sitting prime minister who was responsible for having taken Jordan to the negotiating table.

Political observers contended that the Constitutional Bloc had also played a crucial role in bringing about a tacit understanding between the government and the Ikhwan: the government would respect and recognize the role of the Ikhwan in exchange for the latter's toning down of its opposition.[36] The fact that the Islamists' candidate, 'Arabiyyat, won the speakership of the house again, was also significant. Given that their large bloc in parliament was not represented in the cabinet, holding the speakership kept them in the fold, preventing them from constituting total opposition.[37] The Ikhwan's MPs were among the 27 deputies who withheld confidence from the bin Shakir government, but both the confidence (46–27) and the budget vote (45–20) were easy victories for the government.

Feeling empowered by the dismissal of Masri and the capturing of the speakership, the Ikhwan returned to its favorite targets. On February 28, 1992 the lower house passed a resolution 34–20–26 recommending a ban on the consumption, sale, and manufacture of alcohol by Muslims. Despite their personal inclinations, many legislators feared taking an opposing position on such a sensitive religious matter. Moreover, the vote simply imposed an obligation on the government to prepare a draft law and present it to the house before the end of the next parliamentary session.[38] The Senate then proceeded to delay any further movement on the issue, but the Islamists had won a moral victory.

In April, as the country awaited the promulgation of the new Political Parties Law, the Islamists (the Ikhwan plus independents) announced the formation of the Islamic Action Front (IAF). Following the promulgation of the new law in late July 1992, a number of groups began to submit applications for licenses. In general the process went smoothly; however, in the cases of a Ba'thist and communist party, initial requests for licensing were denied by the Ministry of the Interior. (The parties appealed the decisions and, after minor changes in name and program, were granted licenses.) On the other hand, the law's requirement that the parties not be extensions of external organizations—a stipulation that could have obstructed the transnational Ikhwan's attempt to register itself in Jordan as the IAF—was not applied in this case, and the IAF was licensed in early December 1992.

In the meantime, there were a number of developments that energized the Islamists. The first was the case of MP Ya'qub Qirrish and the popular MP and engineer Layth Shubaylat. These two Islamists were arrested in September 1992 along with a group of others and charged with illegal possession and transport of weapons and belonging to an illegal organization. While initially the charges of subversion alienated people, as it became clear that at least some state evidence had been manufactured or doctored, popular sympathy turned to the accused. Furthermore, the timing of the arrests—as Shubaylat was heading an anti-corruption campaign that came close to indicting the king's long-time friend and former prime minister Zayd al-Rifa'i—led some to speculate that the entire episode had been fabricated as a way of punishing the MP. Although the two were convicted and sentenced to twenty years at hard labor, a few days later as part of a broad royal pardon, both were amnestied. However, in a November 23 speech the king made clear that Jordan would not tolerate "those elements that seek to impair our country's image and take us back to the past."[39] His message was clear, as he declared his continuing support for pluralism and democracy.

In late November, Islamists won student elections in Irbid and municipal elections in Karak. Although a crack in the Islamist bloc occurred in late December, as independents expressed their dissatisfaction with their representation in the IAF's consultative (*shura*) council, this did not seem to severely damage their influence. In January 1993, the Islamists received a boost with the Israeli expulsion from the occupied Palestinian territories of 415 so-called Hamas (Islamic Resistance Movement) activists to southern Lebanon. The stage was then set for renewed muscle flexing in the parliament.

After the relatively painless passage of the proposed budget for 1993 (by a 58–11 vote, with only a handful of Islamists opposed), the first legislative skirmish of the season came with the vote in the house on an Islamist-sponsored amendment aimed at segregating the sexes in sports and recreational facilities governed by the Ministry of Youth. In late January, the lower house of Parliament passed a draft law (the idea for which had in fact first been introduced in 1992), 34–19, banning the government from licensing recreational centers, sports clubs, and swimming clubs that did not separate men and women. The vote took place when a number of deputies had left for the afternoon, which may explain the vote's success; however, as was the case with the bill on alcohol, some deputies supported the legislation (or absented themselves) so as not appear to be taking a position in opposition to Islamic law. Islamist MPs had already succeeded in requiring the investments of the Civil Defense Martyrs Fund to be accord with *shari'a*.[40]

The Islamists did not fare so well on their next project, which was an attempt to force sex segregation in schools. On March 10, the lower house defeated the proposal, which had come from the Islamist-dominated Education Committee and been endorsed by the Judiciary Committee. Only 16 of the 59 deputies present voted for the bill. One deputy, Faris al-Nabulsi, who had read a statement citing sayings of the Prophet Muhammad which he claimed proved there was no clear call for sex segregation, was nearly physically assaulted by Islamist deputies following the vote. One called him a "promoter of corruption [who sought] to prostitute Jordan." Others shouted similar insults, while one had to be physically restrained. The government position, presented by Deputy Prime Minister and Education Minister Dhuqan Hindawi, opposed the bill, but on the grounds of the economics, not the principle, of the position. Hindawi argued that most Jordanian schools were segregated and that co-education was resorted to only in remote areas where there were insufficient numbers of students to open separate schools for boys and girls. To ban co-education, he claimed, would deny many citizens their constitutional right to an education because the government could not afford to build the additional facilities required by the adoption of such a measure.[41]

By this time it appeared to some observers that the government had been making concessions to the Islamists on social issues as a way of softening their opposition to the peace process.[42] The government was in fact criticized in the press for remaining silent or aloof on the contentious issues of coeducation and mixed swimming pools.[43] At the same time, however, as we have seen, the leftists generally failed to take a strong position in opposition to the Islamists on certain key issues, because their own ranks were in disarray and they were struggling to prevent further marginalization. They did not want to be seen as both bad Muslims and marginalized politicians, yet, virtually anything they said, particularly on issues related to the family or women, would constitute an open challenge to the *shari'a*. Their solution was to keep silent or to side with the Islamists.

By spring 1993, the regime was already planning for the fall 1993 elections and considering ways to diminish the Islamists' influence. The primary goal was to ensure that they would be in no position, whether from parliament or from local governing bodies, to challenge the next stage in the peace process, which many assumed would soon produce a Jordanian-Israeli treaty. In late May the king asked medical doctor and former president of Jordan University 'Abd al-Salam al-Majali to head a new government. Since the parliament was—not coincidentally—not in session, there was no need for a confidence vote. Comprising ministers of different political orientations (except the Brotherhood) the government was presented as temporary, intended to run the country until elections were held. The appointment of Majali, who also headed Jordan's delegation to the peace conference, was a clear reaffirmation of the kingdom's commitment to the peace process. And, although the call was indirect, his mandate also included a reexamination of the electoral law, the goal of which—although denied by the government— was to reduce the numbers of Islamists in parliament.

At a June 10 press conference the king stated that it was still too early to discuss a revision of the Electoral Law, but that any modification would be based on dialogue and democratic principles. Nevertheless, rumors about how the law might be changed began to swirl. One proposal—a quota for women—was widely discussed. The IAF opposed this idea, but also seemed likely to run women candidates were the provision adopted. There was also wide debate of the one-person, one-vote proposal, which would have constituted a simplification of Jordan's electoral law. The Islamists and others had benefitted from the kingdom's multiple-vote per elector system, which lent itself to vote swapping. A one-person, one-vote system threatened to put an end to such deals. The Islamists, quite rightly, saw such a change as intended to cut their power, and threatened to boycott elections if the law were so amended.

By late July, sixteen of the country's political parties had announced their support of the IAF position to boycott elections if parliament was dissolved and the law changed. On August 4 the king dissolved parliament, but announced that elections would be held without electoral modification. Yet two weeks later, he announced his ratification of a temporary amendment of the Electoral Law instituting the one-person, one-vote principle. It was presented as if it were Majali's law, but there was no question that the order had come from the palace. The king had obviously wanted to take no chances that a combination of Islamists, Arab nationalists, and leftists might muster sufficient votes to make passage of such a measure problematic. Despite initial threats, the IAF announced its intention to run candidates after 85 percent of its consultative council members voted in favor of participation in the elections.[44]

Then came the truly unexpected. Without warning, the PLO announced that it had reached a draft peace accord with the Israelis. Husayn was reportedly furious that he had not been consulted before the results of these secret negotiations were announced. His anger was then echoed by Transjordanians, who felt that this was exemplary of PLO (and by extension, general Palestinian) lack of gratitude to and respect for the king and the kingdom over the years. Some argued that if, as a result, Palestinian elections were around the corner, then Jordanian elections should be postponed; otherwise, Jordanians of Palestinian origin might vote in Jordanian elections and then return to Palestine to vote in elections there as well. After wide debate in the kingdom, all indications were that the king had decided to postpone the elections. Yet, at the last minute, to everyone's surprise, he allowed the elections to go ahead as scheduled. But much of the excitement and fanfare that had accompanied the election period in 1989 were absent. Part of the explanation lay in the fact that for several weeks it had been unclear whether elections would be held or not. In addition, at the beginning of the official campaign period, the Ministry of the Interior had issued a ruling—directed primarily at the Islamists—that no rallies could be held in public places. (In Jordan there are very few private spaces large enough for real rallies.) This ban was overturned by the Higher Court of Justice before the elections, but the damage was done.

The electoral outcome was in line with what the regime had sought: a 50 percent reduction in the Islamist presence in parliament. However, trouble within Islamist ranks had also hurt their chances. Problems first arose as it had become clear that, despite the IAF's pretensions to be more than the political party extension of the Muslim Brotherhood, that *was* what it was. Independent Islamists began to desert it, and a major split occurred in late May 1993. Then, some IAF members refused to abide by party discipline and accept the party's choices for candidates in their districts. Some of those not chosen pursued their parliamentary aspirations without official support, thereby diluting the impact of the Islamist vote.

In addition, however, the new law had led, if not to a resurgence then to an increased prominence, of the tribal factor. With only one vote to cast, Transjordanians were unlikely to vote for someone outside their own tribe. And Palestinians, with no vote to lose, were likely to vote for the person who could best deliver to his/her constituency. That meant someone with good connections with the government, usually a Transjordanian.[45] Hence the new parliament was characterized by an increased number of tribal/politically conservative/pro-government deputies. Fewer than a fifth of those elected were Palestinians, and of those, the majority belonged to the Islamic Action Front. The other notable outcome of the elections was that a woman was elected for the first time to the Jordanian parliament: Toujan Faisal, the former broadcaster whose campaign for parliament in 1989 had been marred by Islamist intimidation.[46]

The new parliament comprised four major blocs: the IAF, the National Action Front (the Transjordanian al-'Ahd party), the Jordanian National Front (centrist/liberal), and the Progressive Democratic Alliance (leftists and pan-Arabists). Tahir al-Masri, who had won his parliamentary reelection bid, overwhelmingly defeated the IAF candidate, 'Abdallah 'Akaylah, for the speakership of the House (57–22). The king asked Majali to continue as prime minister and to form a new government, which again included no Islamists, since they had indicated that they would not participate in a government involved in peace talks with the Israelis. Rima Khalaf, who took over the Trade and Industry portfolio, became the first woman to serve as minister in nine years. Also notable about Majali's cabinet was the complete absence of MPs. This was unprecedented and in part explains why the confidence vote was hardly overwhelming (41–29–9). Nevertheless, when it came time for the budget vote only five weeks later, it was won 56–20, with opposition coming from an increasingly common combination of IAF members and leftists.

The Islamists undertook no new legislative initiatives during this period. However, the law on segregating sports facilities was finally sent back to the house after the senate introduced several changes. The senate had deleted the clause stipulating that the Ministry of Youth segregate sexes at public pools, but the house insisted on reintroducing it.[47] However, the deputies did agree that the law would not apply to hotels, public beaches or clubs, since these facilities fell outside the realm of jurisdiction of that ministry. The Islamists had seemed most concerned that the newly booming business of sports clubs be regulated, but also that swimming pools be included. In the end, 37 of 64 deputies present voted for the bill; and, in what was becoming a tradition on such issues, many of the liberal deputies simply absented themselves from the vote.[48]

THE OPENING CLOSES

By late spring 1994, the political liberalization, which had suffered its first major setback in the fall of 1991 prior to Madrid, was grinding to a halt. Renewed, if indirect, restrictions began to be placed on the press, based on the new Press and Publications Law. Jordanian courts at the time had some twenty cases before them, raised by the government and government agencies, against journalists representing a range of publications: *Al-Ahali* (leftist weekly), *Jordan Times* (semi-official), *al-Bilad* (weekly tabloid). The clamp on freedom of expression tightened even further as summer began, and as it suddenly became clear that Jordan soon intended to sign its own peace agreement with Israel. This move also exacerbated Palestinian-Jordanian tensions in the kingdom as Yasir 'Arafat reacted with displeasure to the Jordanian move.

In a related development, in late spring 1994, the government had presented a draft Municipal Councils Law. The draft law called for the dissolution of all municipal councils and the holding of new elections on July 1, 1995. Eight municipal councils were subsequently dissolved and replaced with committees headed by appointed governors. The Islamists felt this law was aimed at them, since the government had chosen to dissolve such councils as that of Zarqa, many of whose members were Islamists.[49]

On June 28, 1994 there was yet another cabinet reshuffle. Majali had come under increasing attack for being too removed from parliament, because of the absence of deputies from his cabinet. Not wanting to risk the development of further parliamentary opposition at this critical juncture, Majali replaced nine ministers with ten (non-Islamist) parliamentarians. Less than a month later, Jordan signed a preliminary peace agreement with Israel. In response, by August 1 the anti-peace treaty content of the Friday sermons of some of the IAF MPs had led three to be detained and summoned to appear in court. The following day, the IAF announced that its deputies would quit the parliament. They quickly withdrew this threat, but on August 10 they called for the formation of a National Islamic Front to oppose normalization of relations with Israel. In the meantime, a number of Islamist deputies were called in by Crown Prince Hassan and lectured to (televised after the fact to the public) regarding how they were expected to behave. The Crown Prince emphasized that their using the mosques as a political forum would not be tolerated. For their part, the IAF MPs reiterated their rejection of the peace process and complained of what they saw as a government crackdown on opposition.[50]

Shock over the suddenness of the move toward peace was clear. Then, in quick succession, additional evidence of normalization appeared: direct phone lines to Israel and the occupied territories, and the king's return to Jordan through Israeli airspace, escorted by Israeli jets. While some were excited and optimistic, many were simply stunned. Among others—Islamists, Arab nationalists, and leftists—the anti-normalization battle cry began to be raised. There was also heated discussion in the parliament, but there was no question, given the balance of forces, that the king would have his way. On October 26 the treaty was signed, and on November 6 the lower house ratified it by a 55–23 vote.

Although Majali had little trouble getting the 1995 budget passed (52–22, with the traditional combination of Islamists and leftists opposed), there was little doubt in December that a cabinet reshuffle was on the horizon.[51] In the event, Majali was dismissed and bin Shakir was brought back. The crown prince met with the Ikhwan on January 3 on the need to keep the lines of communication open, and they expressed their optimism regarding an improvement in relations with the new government. Bin Shakir met their leader, 'Abd al-Majid Dhunaybat, and they appeared amenable to joining the cabinet under certain conditions. But bin Shakir wanted no potential opposition, and therefore the Islamists were excluded from the consultations aimed at forming the government. One analyst argued that the Islamists were losing their support in parliament and among the public at large. The regime, which had been working for such an outcome both directly and indirectly, was therefore not inclined to provide them with an opportunity to regain their strength through government offices and access to state funds.[52] In any case, the new cabinet was sworn in on January 8, 1995. Bin Shakir kept Rima Khalaf (although she was moved to the Ministry of Planning) and added Salwa Damen-Masri as minister of Social Affairs, thus giving the kingdom its first ever two-woman cabinet. The confidence vote was 54–22–1, with those opposed again the IAF and the leftists.

Building upon the October 1994 peace accord and expanding relations with Israel (while distancing Jordan from Iraq) became the clear government priorities. With serious economic stakes involved (debt forgiveness, foreign investment, bilateral aid), the government was not about to take any chances that the peace process might be sabotaged. The king would drag the Jordanian people kicking and screaming, if necessary, although the opportunities for screaming openly were increasingly circumscribed. Such policies would have put it on a collision course with a substantial number of deputies in the 1989 parliament. But the attempts through parliamentary elections and dissolution of municipal councils to cut the Islamists' power on the one hand and to bolster center/right traditionalists on the other had paid off. Whatever popular dissatisfaction might arise, the government (the king) did not have to worry about being challenged significantly from within elected state bodies.

Counting on the July 1995 municipal elections to reassert their strength, the Islamists billed the vote as a referendum on the peace process and appealed to people's dissatisfaction and fears regarding the peace accords. Contrary to their expectations, however, the "anti-peace process referendum" elicited little popular interest. The turnout was low and the Islamists won only 8 mayorships of 259 contested, although among the eight were several important ones, including Madaba, Irbid, and Kerak. Indeed, active or vocal opposition to normalization remained limited, with the most notable example that of the various professional associations that took anti-normalization stands and banned their members from visiting Israel or having professional contacts with Israelis. This angered the king and on more than one occasion he took the professional associations or some of their leaders to task for their involvement in politics. Attempts to organize anti-normalization rallies were also largely quashed.

In January 1996, to put an end to the growing sense of dissatisfaction and to curb corruption, the king announced a White Revolution and appointed a young former minister, 'Abd al-Karim Kabariti, to lead a gov-

ernment charged with cleaning house. Kabariti promised to work to protect public freedoms (a concern of all) and to fight corruption. The group
of ministers finally assembled by the new prime minister left people unim-
pressed at best, although Kabariti himself seemed to generate optimism
and support.[53] Although he included no Islamists in his cabinet, prior to the
confidence vote, the IAF had been making very positive noises about the
40-something prime minister. In the event, he won a sweeping 57–19–2
victory, with two IAF deputies breaking ranks by abstaining and another by
absenting himself from the session, signaling a possible new split in the
Front. During his first 100 days in office, a number of potentially important governmental reforms were begun, but Islamists complained of growing numbers of arrests among their ranks. The general sense of drift continued, as many people, including increasing numbers of Transjordanians,
were more openly expressing dissatisfaction with the economic situation
(which exploded in bread riots in August 1996), the "peace process," the
regime's new anti-Iraq tilt, the seeming omnipresence of the royal family,
and on top of the entire system, the king himself.

CONCLUSIONS

By 1996, the episode of regime transition and reconsolidation following
the events of 1989 had clearly ended. The country had passed from a period of free elections and significant widening of public freedoms to a gradual reassertion of some of the pre-1989 boundaries and practices.

The primary theme of the period is that of the changing fortunes of the
Islamists, as they emerged from the November 1989 elections with more
than a third of the seats in parliament, only to lose nearly half of those seats
by 1993 and by 1995 to have their presence in municipal councils seriously reduced as well. Although the scale of their success in 1989 was evidently not anticipated by the authorities, of all the parties that might have
emerged victorious from these elections, the Islamists had a history of the
closest association with the regime. As a result, from the beginning, the inclination toward inclusion or cooptation was present, although there was
certainly concern that the Islamists not be able to use their weight to work
against policies that were seen as critical to the regime. In the early period
of the liberalization, the possibilities for expression were quite broad, thus
giving the Ikhwan and others a wide margin for activity. Certainly until the
end of Badran's government, and even until the election of the 1993 parliament, this meant that they were able to lobby for a number of laws or
amendments that they saw as critical to their social program, among them,
several notable examples that were or appeared threatening to women. On
the other hand, although the Islamists have actively criticized government

economic policies past and present, at no time have they attempted to organize real opposition to any aspect of the IMF agreement or structural adjustment, nor have they ever asked for any of the *economic* portfolios. Prior to the signing of the Jordan-Israel peace treaty, they seemed to prefer to invest their political capital in the social and educational realms. Tahir al-Masri even contended that the Islamists did not want to win enough to seats to have a majority in parliament because they knew that would not be allowed to push for much of their program.[54]

Because the process of reconsolidation within a more open political framework was still under way, because Jordan is a conservative society, and because of the tremendous support the Islamists appeared to command at the time, following the 1989 elections, it made pragmatic sense to cultivate Islamist support through various forms of inclusion. At the same time, those organized political forces that might otherwise have been expected to counter the Islamists were uninterested in the issues under discussion or too weak openly to challenge the "party of God." In several cases, as we shall see in chapter 6, opposition came from outside the parliament.

Although the Islamists' representation in parliament was not cut until fall 1993, a number of factors began to whittle away at their power, which had reached its zenith with their inclusion in Badran's second cabinet. First and foremost, Jordan's move toward peace negotiations began to close the door on freedom of expression, as reining in the critics of the peace process required reviving some of the martial law practices which had, to that point, been on the decline. It was one thing if Islamists wanted to ban the licensing of new male hairdressers—an issue in which the regime could have had only passing interest. However, as decisionmakers understood it, the kingdom's participation in the peace process was based on a number of domestic, regional, and international imperatives, the most important of which were the presumed economic benefits that would attend achieving a settlement. No political group was going to be allowed to obstruct a key foreign policy initiative of the king's. Coming more than two years after the riots of April, and in the wake of the popular shock that the swift defeat of Iraq had triggered, the legitimacy of the regime was no longer an issue, the population was demoralized, and the balance of political forces in the kingdom was better understood and could therefore be more easily managed.[55]

By marginalizing the Islamists' ability to play the role of partners of the regime, the peace process offered other groups, which were smaller but eager to become or return to the role of central players by demonstrating their loyalty, a chance to (re)assert themselves. At the same time, as a continuation of the king's long-standing, successful strategy of reforming his opponents, the regime undertook a variety of policies—primary among them offering ministerial and other prominent posts—to coopt leftists and Arab-nationalists. Hence, the Islamists were increasingly under a form of national house arrest, and the only other opposition, already seriously weakened by the more general decline of the left and of pan-Arabism, was either coopted or, if it insisted upon opposition to the peace, relegated to the same house arrest as the Islamists. The door was therefore open for the centrists/rightists to return to prominence.

This is not to imply that the situation of public freedoms in Jordan is as it was prior to April 1989. There is no question that there is now greater freedom of expression and movement, just as there are fewer political arrests and detentions. But the level of freedom of expression is not what it was during the summer of 1991, for example. Battles to prevent further encroachment on public freedoms continue, certainly on the margins, sometimes more centrally. But it is as if the regime, which was willing to entertain a variety of suggestions and critiques while it was on life support and in the intensive care ward, has, once recovered, dismissed the vast majority of consulting physicians, and while resigned to some modifications in behavior, nonetheless remains largely unreformed.

It is perhaps ironic, but certainly in keeping with experiences elsewhere, that the period of greatest uncertainty regarding the possible extent or results of the liberalization was also the period of greatest opening. It was during this time that the Islamists' surge and the state's desire to reconsolidate through cultivating their support or at least through not antagonizing them on issues it viewed as secondary, led to some negative developments for women in the legislative realm. In addition, however, one cannot overlook the role of the king, who is very concerned with maintaining Jordan's forward-looking image.[56] His inclinations, combined with the reining in of the Islamists because of the peace process, no doubt also played a key role in forestalling proposals of more conservative changes in the realm of women and the family.

This is in no way to suggest that the king is a feminist: a number of specific examples of the precarious nature of women's rights or the state's dubious policies toward half of its citizens will be provided in chapter 6. First, however, using this presentation as background, the chapter that follows provides a summary of the history of the women's movement, women's legal status, and the role that foreign institutions have played recently in these areas.

CHAPTER **FIVE**
The Struggle for Voice

W hile, as chapter 6 will demonstrate, the post-1989 period has witnessed a notable increase in formal women's activity, women's organizing and lobbying for changes in state policy have a long history. This chapter provides a brief summary of both women's organizing and the evolution of women's legal status in the kingdom to serve as a basis for comparing developments since liberalization (examples of which are covered in detail in chapter 6). The chapter closes with a survey of the involvement of external actors, specifically governmental and NGO funders, in programs related to women's legal status and participation in public (political) life.

THE WOMEN'S MOVEMENT

The first prominent women's activist traces what she calls the renaissance of Jordanian women to the 1940s and the establishment of women's solidarity societies.[1] Founded in 1944, the Women's Social Solidarity Society was presided over by Princess Misbah, the mother of Crown Prince Talal (father of King Husayn). Its goals were limited to caring for children and providing assistance to the poor and needy. She was also named honorary head of the organization founded the next year, the Society of the Jordanian Women's Federation, although the active head was Princess Zayn Sharaf (wife of Talal and mother of Husayn). These organizations differed from their predecessors in that they were concerned with the social condition of Jordanian women, raising their educational level, and improving child health care.[2] The two Jordanian societies combined in 1949 under the name of the Hashemite Jordanian Women's Society, but the joint organization was dissolved in the same year.[3]

In general, women's initiatives during this period involved meetings and seminars aimed at raising women's awareness of health and welfare issues to assist them in attending to their children's needs. However extensive this work was (and that is unclear), the activity was all directed at making women better mothers and at rearing the next generation, not at substantially changing or improving women's socioeconomic or legal position.

The influence of the arrival and incorporation of large numbers of Palestinians who had been active politically against the British Mandate in Palestine prior to 1948 had a major impact on the history and development of the kingdom. While women's activities on other fronts might have been suspect, during this period efforts aimed at addressing the Palestine problem were much more likely to be tolerated and thus served as a focal point around which women might rally to work. On the other hand, the preoccupation with an external issue combined with the rivalries between various political groups led to an ignoring of social developments in Jordan itself.[4]

In 1951 the first Ministry of Social Affairs was founded and among its responsibilities was the supervision of voluntary work as regulated by the Charitable Societies Law (which forbids political activity by its subject organizations). Between 1951 and 1979, more than 340 charitable societies were established throughout the kingdom, only 32 of which engaged solely in "women's" activities. These groups generally comprised wealthy women who, as a way of filling free time, provided assistance to alleviate poverty or to support orphanages and similar institutions. Most of their time was devoted to parties and elaborate meetings, with little energy spent on serious work.[5]

The establishment of the Arab Women's Federation (AWF, *Ittihad al-Mar'ah al-'Arabiyyah*) on June 17, 1954, early in the first period of liberalization, marked a qualitative change in the type of women's organization found in Jordan. As in other Arab countries, in Jordan, women were caught up in the ferment of the 1950s and in helping the displaced Palestinians, so that the atmosphere was one of political activity. At the AWF founding in Amman, attended by more than 100 women, Emily Bisharat, the first female lawyer in Jordan, was elected president. Among the AWF's goals were: fighting illiteracy; raising women's socioeconomic levels; preparing women to exercise their full rights as citizens; and developing bonds of friendship between Arab women and women around the world to improve the situation at home and to strengthen peace. The federation had a fully developed constitution and institutional infrastructure.[6] The degree of the women's involvement in broader national issues was clear from the union's slogan: Equal Rights and Responsibilities, and Full Arab Unity.[7]

Branches of the AWF spread beyond Amman to Irbid, Zarqa, Karak, Salt, and the membership grew to thousands of women. Activity focused on increasing women's political, economic, and social awareness throughout the country. The AWF also demanded a change in the personal status, labor, and electoral laws.[8] Women published and spoke, held conferences and seminars, and participated in numerous Arab and international conferences. In early November 1954, the AWF presented its first memorandum to the prime minister requesting a change in the Electoral Law to give women the right to run for office and to vote in municipal and parliamentary elections. It was supported in this quest by the political parties and professional associations. The government took the matter under advisement and the legal committee in the parliament recommended that an amendment be discussed. However, when the proposed changes were published, they stipulated that only educated women be given the vote, which caused great outrage, since any illiterate male had the right to vote for—and sit in—parliament.

Dissatisfied with this proposed change, the women renewed and repeated their memoranda, meetings, telegrams, and protests to the relevant authorities. A group of illiterate women, excluded from the provisions of the proposed amendment, sent the prime minister a memorandum bearing hundreds of thumbprints (in lieu of signatures)[9]. The AWF then sponsored a Women's Week to discuss the issue of changing the law. Participants, among them representatives of the political parties and popular organizations, agreed on a number of resolutions, which were forwarded to the relevant authorities: equality between men and women in political, representative, and municipal rights; equality in all levels of education; schools for girls in the countryside; improved conditions in rural areas; equality between men and women in employment and salaries; protection of women's rights and avoidance of factionalism and decay of the family.[10]

The women also demanded changes in the personal status law; specifically, the outlawing of arbitrary divorce and polygamy.[11] Such proposals, however, were not given serious attention. In the realm of more broadly acceptable demands and political activity, women were in the forefront of demonstrations in support of Palestine, and against Zionism and the Baghdad Pact, among other issues. In the context of the nationalist surge of the spring of 1956, the federation waged a media campaign demanding that women receive weapons and first aid training. The authorities agreed and officers from the Jordanian army trained female volunteers.

In the meantime, the women continued to send memos each time there was a cabinet reshuffle, and finally the government agreed to reexamine the Electoral Law. In cooperation with other women's societies and with the political parties, the AWF held an historic festival on February 5, 1956, well attended despite the snow. At its conclusion, telegrams were sent to the king, the prime minister, the president of the senate, and the speaker of the lower house about the meeting.[12] Unfortunately, other events at the national level conspired against the federation and its goals. A coup attempt in early April the following year led to a political crackdown which counted the AWF among its casualties.

Thereafter, some of the AWF women continued to work, hold meetings, and send memos to the relevant authorities about changing the law and resuming the dissolved society's activities. But the issue of the franchise would not be raised again until nearly a decade had passed: on April 21, 1966, the king sent a letter to the prime minister on the subject. But political circumstances again intervened to delay action.[13] No swift action was taken and, after the June 1967 defeat, most attention turned to the question of Palestine and the newly occupied territories.

At this point, those interested in political activity, men or women, began to gravitate to the constituent factions of the Palestinian resistance movement, which was based in Jordan until 1970–71. The renewed possibility of political organizing was a direct result of the 1967 war. As was discussed in the previous chapter, the defeat discredited the leadership, the military, and the security services. Shortly thereafter, the Palestinian guerrilla organizations began to take advantage of the consequent political opening to expand their operations.

Their popularity brought new recruits, among them young women primarily, but not exclusively, Palestinians, many from the refugee camps. All of the factions eventually developed their own women's activities. A women's committee emerged in Fateh, the largest resistance organization, but was not acknowledged until 1969[14] and not really activated until 1970. By that time, in addition to its other functions, it operated workshops and vocational training centers. In addition, the General Union of Palestinian Women, founded in 1965 but forbidden to open an official branch in Jordan prior to the 1967 war, also took advantage of the opportunity to offer such facilities as literacy classes, first aid and civil defense instruction, embroidery workshops, and sewing courses. Again, aside from the fact that the women were working in the framework of a political organization, the activities were largely traditional. Very few women were integrated into the decisionmaking frameworks of the resistance organizations. Much of their work ended up resembling that of a women's auxiliary group,[15] although, to be fair, the very fact of going out of the house to a resistance organization office was a major step of liberation for many young women.

The focus on the "national struggle" meant that many other women's concerns were not addressed. As male cadres were wont to argue, women's and other (in their view, less important) issues had to take second place to the national problem lest energies be diverted from that central concern. It was an argument common to third world "revolutionaries," and one that most women accepted, although some only grudgingly. Just as important, the focus on the Palestine question led to a delay in the emergence in Jordan of a national movement concerned primarily with greater democratization in the kingdom.

In September 1970, major violence broke out between the Jordanian army and the Palestinian resistance. By July 1971, the remnants of the resistance had been driven from the country and its institutional infrastructure, including that of the women, had been destroyed or closed down. The lack of preparation socially and intellectually for such developments in Jordanian society led to a multifaceted backlash. One manifestation was on a communal level, as suspicion and enmity between Palestinians and Transjordanians soared. On another level, there was a reaction against what had been viewed as the greater social freedom exercised by resistance members—both men and women. But, of course, the response targeted women and involved a resurgence of "weapons of virtue" and concern with *sharaf* (honor). This was part of a revival of traditional values and practices, most certainly encouraged by the regime, which began to implement an East Banker first policy, intended to recover the conservatism, and rebuild the support for the state that the Palestinian resistance had helped to undermine. All these developments then led to hesitation or reluctance to raise women's issues.[16]

For several years, activist women had limited options: to work with one of the underground parties or with the charitable society of their choice. The first sign of impending change came in a March 5, 1974 letter from the king regarding the franchise for women. The king's letter, which included a royal decree finally amending the Elections Law to give women the vote, came against the backdrop of preparations for the UN Decade for Women, scheduled to begin in 1975. At about the same time, a group of women, many of whom had been active in the AWF, met in anticipation of the UN conference to form a preparatory committee to celebrate the women's year in the name of what they called the National Women's Grouping in Jordan. In addition to their work on the upcoming UN meeting, one of their most important goals was to reestablish a women's federation in the kingdom. As a result of intense activity, on August 13, 1974 the Society of the Women's

Federation in Jordan (WFJ)[17] was licensed by the Ministry of the Interior. On November 17, 1974, the women announced the official establishment of the federation, and two days later the first meeting of its general council elected former AWF head Emily Bisharat president.[18]

The goals of the WFJ were familiar: to raise women's educational and socioeconomic levels; to support women's exercise of their full rights as citizens, workers, and heads of household; to strengthen bonds of friendship and cooperation with Arab and international women's organizations; to represent women in Jordan in international Arab and women's conferences; to support Arab solidarity in the economic, cultural, educational, and social fields; and to support women's effective participation in building the Arab homeland.[19]

In the six years of the WFJ's activity, its membership grew from 100 to some 3,000, with 1,500 in the capital.[20] The federation opened branches in Amman, Irbid, Salt, Zarqa, Madaba, and Aqaba, as well as committees for future branches across the kingdom. Its leadership included women from a broad range of political affiliations, from communists to Fateh, both Palestinians and Transjordanians. The WFJ operated training and literacy centers, and sponsored support services for children, including nurseries. It also briefly published a magazine, al-Ra'idah, until the state publications department closed it without explanation. Among the federation's regular programs were weekly seminars, lectures, story or poetry readings, trips, fundraising dinners, and annual charity bazaars to sell the products of the various training centers.

In the political realm the WFJ demanded the right to participate in discussions of the Labor Law, the right to attend seminars and conferences to offer better presentations on women, whether in the field of education, labor, or political rights, and the adoption of international and Arab resolutions opposing discrimination against women. It also published a number of studies on women and their rights as well as on the Palestine question. While the federation played an active role domestically and internationally, with the parliament inactive there was no opportunity to mobilize women to exercise their newly granted right to vote.[21]

On the surface, the 1979 appointment of the first female cabinet minister in the kingdom's history seemed to mark another important milestone and to bode well for an increasing role for women. Longtime educator In'am al-Mufti was appointed the first head of the newly created Ministry of Social Development. Yet in this case, appearances were deceiving, for a new tendency soon became clear: the desire to incorporate all women's activities into a single organizational framework directly under the control of Mufti's ministry. Shortly after her appointment, she began working to establish a *new* women's union.[22]

In 1980, a meeting was held to which a range of activists was invited so that Jordan's official delegation to the upcoming United Nations Women's Decade meeting in Copenhagen, headed by Mufti, could make a presentation about its activities. At this meeting the idea of a new women's organization was vetted with the presentation of a paper entitled "The Ministry of Social Development—Women's Organizing." The paper spoke of the need to establish specific federations (for rural women, professional women, and so on) and a "General Federation of Jordanian Women" was one of the unions to which the paper referred.[23]

However, it soon became clear that virtually none of these organizations, some of which, including the General Federation, existed only on paper, was in a position to play this role of reaching large numbers of women. So a new idea was generated: to combine the existing women's social societies and agencies with a number of prominent individual women activists as the base of the new union. These activists, none of whom were WFJ members, were then invited to a meeting on September 5, 1981 at which the bylaws of the new federation were proposed. All those who came were considered members by virtue of their attendance, and their attendance was understood to imply their acceptance of this new formula.[24] The General Federation of Jordanian Women (GFJW) was considered operative from that date.

To return to the WFJ's fate, beginning about the time of Mufti's appointment, the state authorities began to harass WFJ delegates to Arab and international conferences, claiming that the federation took positions antagonistic to the kingdom.[25] Rumors began to circulate that the Ministry of the Interior intended to close the WFJ, and finally, on December 18, 1981, the WFJ received a letter from the Ministry dated October 26, 1981 ordering its closure. According to the Charitable Societies Law, the Minister of the Interior was empowered to close any organization if it was demonstrated that it had contravened its constitution; however, a close review of the WFJ's activities revealed that it had committed no such violations. Hence, the real explanation had to lie elsewhere. After discussions between the women and the Minister of the Interior subsequent to the arrival of the closure letter, he scaled down his objections to the WFJ, stating that the problem was in its name, which was similar to that of the new union. The WFJ responded by changing its name to al-Rabitah al-Nisa'iyyah f-il-Urdunn, the Women's League in Jordan, in order to continue its work.[26]

But that was hardly the major issue. More important was the question of jurisdiction and control. An early manifestation of the struggle underway had developed around a WFJ Karak-area dairy project intended to help produce additional income for poor women. When Mufti learned that the dairy project had received approval from the Minister of Labor and a concessional loan from the Industrial Development Bank, she demanded the suspension of the loan on the grounds that her ministry wanted to prepare a study of the area. The relevant authorities complied. The WFJ project was already underway, but ultimately reached a point where the arrival of additional equipment, for which the loan had been requested, was critical. The ministry came under substantial criticism at the time for its position on this issue, but refused to back down. The loan remained "suspended," and as result, the WFJ had to reduce the scale of the project.[27]

In the meantime, the WFJ activists decided to fight the order, and two prominent lawyers took their case on a pro bono basis. The High Court of Justice did look into the case and in fact ruled *against* the Ministry of the Interior. Not surprisingly, however, in the battle of bureaucratic wills during a period of martial law, the Ministry of the Interior succeeded in blocking the implementation of the High Court's ruling.[28] The name change had not saved the federation: the activity of the former WFJ was "frozen."

The effective closure of the WFJ left Jordanian women without an independent, unified institutional framework that was near where they lived, took an interest in their health needs, sought to raise their educational level, and strove to raise consciousness about women's rights. The new federation was of a very different nature. Unlike the WFJ, the GFJW was recognized by only one wing of the General Federation of Arab Women, an indication of the way it was viewed outside Jordan.[29] Inside the kingdom it remained isolated from the vast majority of women.

This isolation was a natural outcome of the federation's internal structure and (lack of) program. In the first place, it depended for members upon societies and clubs subject to the oversight of the Ministry of Social Development. The average member, therefore, had no rights in or obligations to the GFJW, and if one's society ended its membership in the federation, the membership of the individual was also terminated. There was a secondary kind of membership, for individuals; however, this was subject to numerous constraints, such as the requirement that the executive of the federation approve the application for membership. Moreover, at least in the beginning, the GFJW had no regional or branch offices, only one center in Jabal al-Husayn in West Amman, and women had to go there to join. A woman interested in joining would be asked for her telephone number (if she had one) and would then be told she would be called if there was going to be an activity. For many average women, leaving home for a period of several hours and riding a cab or a bus alone are difficult because of responsibilities in the home, social views of women's activity outside the home, and the cost of transportation. A union with no branches and no real organizational structure of its own is not in a position to implement a creative program. In this case, however, that was not a problem: there was no such program.[30]

Before concluding this section mention should be made of one other women's association, the Business and Professional Women's Club (BPWC), which was established in 1976 as a national voluntary organization affiliated with the International Federation of Business and Professional Women. The Amman chapter has been the most active of the club's four branches in the kingdom. With Queen Noor as patron, the BPWC offered two primary services before the liberalization: a legal consultative office for women, which had lawyer trainees available to answer questions; and a small-business counseling office. In November 1990, a new project was added, an information and documentation center for women's studies. In 1993 the BPWC sponsored a series of events, first to register women, then to encourage women to run for office (including providing information on successful electioneering), and then of course to convince women to vote. Although it is impossible to know what impact their campaign had, the final voter turnout was 68 percent of those registered, and women accounted for more than 50 percent of the vote in most electoral districts.[31]

There is no question that over the years, and particularly before the liberalization, during a period when opportunities for such activities were limited, the BPWC had a high profile and sponsored some of the few workshops and seminars for women on aspects of law or business. Its officers were prominent, well-connected women, most of whose business experience resulted from being married to wealthy businessmen, not having run businesses themselves. While the intention of the projects, especially the legal counseling and the production of pamphlets on women and the law, was no doubt noble, observation and interviews indicate that, with some notable exceptions, the elitist composition of the organization kept it removed from the problems of average Jordanian women. The following anecdote is instructive. One of the top BPWC women was responsible for the decision by the state censor in the early 1980s to prevent the publication in Jordan of the book on the women's movement upon which the early part of this chapter's discussion heavily relied. (The book was subsequently published in Beirut.) Her reason: in the introduction there was no mention of or praise for the royal family's role in building Jordan; she had therefore decided not read further.[32]

The BPWC's members have tended to argue that what is required is not so much change in, but proper application of, existing law, thus ignoring the impact of class on women's exercise and knowledge of their rights. Just as serious, a number of unsolicited comments regarding the legal counseling services indicated that, while the counseling was free of charge, the women who went for help were treated rudely and the legal advice offered was inaccurate or unhelpful.[33]

Evaluation

For reasons noted in the previous chapter, civil society in the traditional Western sense has been able to carve out only a very small sphere in Jordan. At the same time, the societal restrictions on women's movement and activity outside the home have placed further constraints on women's participation in what institutions were permitted to operate. Women's work with charitable societies was generally tolerated, although it was easier to register new charitable societies during some periods than during others. The lesson of these experiences seems to be that what the state and the men who run it think of as "women's work" is viewed as apolitical and non-threatening. Indeed, such work reinforces the status quo, an approach that is certainly more acceptable to the upper echelons of the state and society, both men and women.

On the other hand, women's activity that implied the potential development of kingdom-wide structures outside a governmental framework was much more problematic. The success of the AWF may be attributed to the political organizing space that the period of relatively greater freedom (1954–57) allowed. The same may be said of the activities of the unofficial branch of the General Union of Palestinian Women, which operated openly throughout the country between 1967 and 1970. When political crackdowns ended these periods, the women's unions met the same fate as other non-state-sponsored actors (with the exception of the professional associations): closure or destruction. The fate of the WFJ, although related to an intent to centralize control over women's organization, also owed to its more activist program. The whole episode suggests a state apparatus heavily involved in demobilization of women or obstruction of their efforts at independent organizing.

So does the nature of the women involved in the leadership. Over the years "acceptable" women have in effect been designated from above. The women have tended to come from prominent families and few have had experience in serious work on women's issues. Not surprisingly, they have had limited political consciousness and even less understanding of the conditions of everyday life among Jordanian women of less privileged sectors. For them and the small group of women that has surrounded them, GFJW work has enabled them to travel to international conferences, make speeches, attend elaborate parties, and frequently be in the public eye. The BPWC has suffered from many of the same problems, although it has generally been viewed as more active than the GFJW. At the same time, although uninterested in or unable to mobilize women themselves, as we shall see in the next chapter, as political liberalization unfolded, the GFJW leadership fought mobilizing efforts by other women.

The impact of external events should also be noted. As we saw in the previous chapter, the openings of the mid-1950s and late 1960s were inextricably linked to broader regional developments. It also seems likely that had there not been a UN Decade for Women, the WFJ would not have been established, certainly not in 1974. The argument that the kingdom, which likes to portray itself as enlightened, needed a representative of its women to attend the meetings to launch the decade appears sufficient to have led the state to allow the reemergence of a national women's union after the passage of nearly twenty years. That the award of the franchise came during the same period can also likely be explained by the approaching UN meeting and Jordan's position at the time as the only non-Gulf Arab state which had not granted women the vote.

WOMEN'S CIVIL AND LEGAL STATUS

While the franchise on a national and local level is certainly an important right, many other areas must be examined to complete the picture of women's legal status. At the highest level, the Jordanian constitution states that all citizens are equal under the law in terms of rights and obligations. However, while the constitution bars discrimination on the basis of race, language, or religion, there is no explicit ban on discrimination on the basis of sex, and an examination of national legislation reveals some of the bases of women's inferior status.

Education in Jordan became compulsory with the promulgation of the amended 1952 constitution, which insisted upon nine years of schooling. While this was a positive step, it was insufficient. "Compulsory education" simply means the provision of seats. In practice there is no real enforcement regarding attendance, so the decision about a child's education is left to the family, usually the father, who may not value education for a girl, particularly if she may play another, economic role at home. Moreover, some villages do not have a school, and families are unwilling (or unable to afford) to send a female child to a nearby village each day for classes. Attrition continues to be a particularly severe problem for girls. In 1990, although illiteracy among women 15 years of age and older had fallen to 28.1% (10% among males), the proportion of young women holding high school degrees was only 13.4%.[34]

In the realm of citizenship, the law states that all Jordanian men and women are entitled to citizenship, yet only a Jordanian male may automatically pass his citizenship on to his children. A foreign woman who marries a Jordanian is eligible for citizenship after three years if she is an Arab and after five years if not, but there is no provision for a non-Jordanian husband of a Jordanian woman to obtain Jordanian citizenship. Similarly, women and their children may obtain separate passports only with the agreement of the husband/father.

In some other realms, women may appear to be beneficiaries of a particular law. However, a close reading reveals that even the advantages derive from a view of women as primarily dependent upon a male, in need of special protection or expendable from the work force. For example, not only is retirement age for men 60 and for women 55, but widows and widowers have different rights to the pension of a deceased spouse. For a man to receive his wife's pension, he must no longer be working (incapable of work), but for the woman, there is no such condition.[35] Similar themes may be found in the Retirement Law. A man may retire after 20 years of service, a woman after 15. However, a woman who resigns can withdraw what she has put into her pension, but a man cannot. On the other hand, payment of a retirement pension to wives or daughters of a deceased employee stops if they marry, but can begin again if they are widowed or divorced. If they subsequently remarry, the pension stops permanently. If a woman employee receives a pension for her own work, she does not lose it if she marries; however, if she dies, her dependents may continue to receive her pension only if they can demonstrate need and that she was directly responsible for them.[36]

The Labor Law has been singled out for special criticism by women, but from different perspectives. Most basically, the law continues to lack a clear statement regarding wage or employment equality between men and women. Wage discrimination between men and women is rampant in the private sector, and there is no minimum wage. Even in the state sector, which is governed by a series of levels and ranks, women are often discriminated against in promotion policy, which then has wage-level implications. A 1987 survey of the state sector indicated that men received 27.9% more than females of equal education, age, and experience.[37] Women may also be harmed by the fact that many of the services or protections accorded by law to those who work in institutions with five or more employees are not required of the far more numerous smaller establishments.[38] Traditionally, levels of female employment (not including the agricultural sector) have been quite low in Jordan. In 1995, women represented only 15 percent of the formal work force, a much lower percentage than in either Tunisia or Morocco. In addition, unemployment among women has risen from 5.9% in 1972, to 11.7% in 1979 to 30.6% in 1990, and 34% in 1995, substantially higher than the percentage among men.[39]

The Labor Law also forbids women and children to work in certain jobs—there are no comparable provisions for men—just as it rules out certain work hours for both women and children (7 p.m. to 6 a.m.), in the absence of special circumstances. In the field of benefits, prior to the law's amendment in 1995, women were entitled to three weeks of leave before and after childbirth. The three weeks before childbirth were at her discretion, but she was not to work until three weeks after childbirth, and this time was taken at half pay. Any institution with more than thirty female employees was required to have a childcare room for children under age six, but the law gave women no nursing time. Again, many women do not work for large institutions and are therefore not covered by these provisions.[40]

The Civil Status Law is perhaps the most implicitly sexist law. Important parts of this law relate to the "family book" (daftar al-'a'ilah), which is needed for almost all official transactions. Upon marriage, a woman is transferred from her father's daftar to that of her husband. However, if she is divorced or if her husband should leave and take the document, she faces serious difficulties. Without the family book, one cannot vote or be a candidate (conversely, with it, a husband can register the entire family to vote in whatever district he chooses). Without the daftar, women cannot obtain food assistance to which their families are entitled, nor can they register their children in school, university, or for civil service jobs. For a woman who is, through death or divorce, "separated" from a daftar, virtually the only solution is to reregister on the daftar of her father or brother. Sometimes, however, this is not practical (if the family members are living and working overseas) or possible (if the male family member is deceased.)[41]

The Personal Status Law, on the other hand, is the most explicitly sexist. It continues to allow polygamy and arbitrary divorce by the husband. Women, on the other hand, must specifically request a special clause in their marriage contract to obtain the right to divorce, and the law requires men to pay support to divorced wives for only one year. However, the real problem in Jordan is that the few protections that are included in the law are often not respected. This is especially true in the case of arbitrary divorce—women often cannot obtain even the minimal compensation they are due, including support for children—and in inheritance cases, in which women are generally forced by their families to relinquish even their inferior shares to their male relatives.

A presentation of women's status would be incomplete without a discussion of the concept of sharaf or honor. More than in either of the other two countries covered in this study, in Jordan it continues to have serious ramifications for the status of women as full citizens. Maintaining sharaf requires that a woman be a virgin at the time of a first marriage. It also requires that she be faithful during marriage and refrain from involvement in extramarital affairs if she should be widowed or divorced. More generally it demands that she engage in no behavior to which the least hint of impropriety may attend. While it is women's behavior which in the first instance preserves or compromises *sharaf*, nonetheless it is her male family members who are responsible for upholding the family honor: in the event of suspicions of improper behavior, upholding family honor may require that the woman in question be killed.

Such a murder, called an "honor crime," is generally carried out by a young male family member. According to a section of article 340 of the penal code (of 1960), "he who discovers his wife or one of his female relatives committing adultery and kills, wounds or injures one or both of them is exempted from any penalty." Another paragraph states: "he who discovers his wife or one of his female relatives with another in an adulterous situation, and kills wounds or injures one or both of them, benefits from a reduction of penalty." Of course, if the situation is reversed, the woman receives no special consideration. In most cases, those who commit the murders are sentenced to only a few months in jail, and generally serve only a portion of that time. Moreover, families often designate a minor to carry out the murder, expecting that the courts will be even more lenient because of his age. Minors are sent to rehabilitation centers, where they continue their education and learn a profession. At age 18 they are released and have no criminal record.[42] The light sentence is in part due to the fact that the families generally do not file a complaint: when complaints are not filed or are withdrawn, the penalty specified in law is generally cut in half.[43] It is as if in such cases the state simply relinquishes all responsibility for safeguarding the citizen (the woman).

Statistics indicate that the number of honor crimes has in general been increasing. In 1986, 22 honor crimes (of a total of 66 murders) were reported; in 1990, that number was 22 of 82 and in 1993, 33 of 96 murders,[44] while in 1997, 23 were reported. Nevertheless, there are obviously problems in counting such crimes. First, family testimony is accepted at face value. If the family supports the story of the murderer, there is no state investigation of the case. This obtains even in cases where it is shown after the fact that the woman was innocent. For example, in May 1994 a young woman was killed by her family after an anonymous note arrived in the mail saying that the young woman had a boyfriend. Only after she was murdered by her brother was it discovered that the story was untrue and that the letter had been sent by a jealous schoolmate. Just as troubling, those who study these cases believe that many of the so-called honor crimes are in fact economic crimes, committed against female family members with whom there is a dispute about inheritance.[45] A claim that a woman has violated the family honor can then be used a convenient excuse to remove the source of the problem and escape the legal ramifications of murder. It can also be a way of covering up the commission of incest: some of the women murdered in such honor killings had first been raped and impregnated by male family members.

CHANGES SINCE THE LIBERALIZATION

A striking feature of any attempt to change laws in the kingdom, whether for better or for worse, is the length of the process. Drafts first submitted in 1991 or 1992 were often not acted upon until 1994, for example. (Although in some cases, particularly some of the Islamists' proposals, there was deliberate government footdragging.) Hence, only in the last part of the period under study does one begin to see what might be the fruits of many attempts to introduce changes in the law. Another striking feature is the number of women's organizations and committees that, by 1994, were working on reviewing existing legislation and preparing suggestions for changes. The Jordanian Women's Union, the Jordanian National Committee for Women, the Business and Professional Women's Association, the General Federation of Jordanian Women, and the Women's Status Committee of the Jordanian Lawyers Union all were engaged in studies, reviews, workshops, and campaigns aimed at changing discriminatory laws.

As the discussion in the previous chapter highlighted, several legislative initiatives following the 1989 elections gave women reason for pause if not real concern. The first example came in December 1990, when a law was passed making Miri (state) lands subject to Islamic inheritance laws. (Christian churches in Jordan also abide by *shari'a* law in the realm of inheritance.) The previous law, a remnant of Ottoman times, had allowed for equal inheritance of such lands by men and women, regardless of religion. The change meant that a son would now inherit twice as much as a daughter.

While the percentage of the population likely to be negatively affected by the law was small, symbolically the legislation spoke volumes. It passed the house without discussion, deliberately part of a very short bill that did not require additional debate. So low-key was the initiative that Senator Layla Sharaf contended she had had no knowledge of it until it came before the house. Perhaps most alarming was the fact that even those Muslim MPs who did not really support it did not feel it was useful to antagonize the Islamists, who had just done so well at the polls. And as for the Christians, one deputy felt he could not object, since he owed his seat to a pre-election deal with the Islamists; in addition, however, he reportedly felt that it served his interests because he did not want to pass his land along to his daughters. When it the bill came up for vote in the Senate, only two votes were cast against it.[46]

On the other hand, a positive development from the point of view of women was the inclusion in the National Charter of the clause: "Jordanians, men and women, are equal before the law, with no discrimination between them in rights and responsibilities, regardless of race, language or religion." This is stronger than the constitutional clause which merely states that all Jordanians are equal before the law. Shortly after the ratification of the National Charter, in August 1991, Jordan also ratified the UN convention against all forms of discrimination against women (although it had signed it in December 1980). Like other Arab and Islamic countries, however, it registered several reservations regarding passing on nationality to children, movement and freedom of choice of domicile, rights and obligations in marriage and upon its termination, and responsibilities of parents toward children. In other words, it accepted the convention insofar as it did not contradict existing Jordanian law. Jordan also ratified three other international conventions in 1992: the convention regarding political rights for women (1957); the convention regarding the nationality of married women (1957); and the convention regarding minimum marriage age and registering marriage contracts (1964). However, Jordan's ratification of these conventions is not widely known, nor its potential significance understood, so that it is difficult to discern any tangible benefits accruing to Jordanian women as a result.

Another positive change was in the field of health insurance, as in late 1993 the minister of health ordered a change in the law to make children eligible for health insurance through their working mothers. Prior to this amendment, children could be insured only through their fathers, even if their mothers worked and were insured.[47]

More controversial, in May 1994, the Senate ratified a change in the Landlords and Tenants Law to allow a divorced woman or a widow to continue to live with her children in the family's apartment after the divorce or after the death of the husband. The actual proposal was to allow any woman arbitrarily divorced and with custody of her children to keep the rental contract on her home for herself and her children even if the husband ended the lease. The change was to address the problem of divorced women's being thrown out of their homes with their children and having nowhere to go. An amendment to this effect had initially been proposed to the parliament by MP Toujan Faisal the previous February, but had been ignored. Subsequently, Senator Na'ila Rashdan studied the proposal and prepared her own proposal to the senate and submitted it with the support of Minister of Justice Tahir Hikmat.

Initially Rashdan was told that there was insufficient time to address the proposal before the end of the parliamentary session. However, a combination of factors converged to force the issue. This was a project that the GFJW had followed closely, having sent the parliamentarians a report describing the desperate financial situation of divorced or widowed women.[48] Rashdan called for letters from the various women's groups, and although the response was meager—only one letter each from three different groups, including the GFJW, rather than a concerted campaign—it played a positive role. In addition, Umayma Dahhan, recently appointed adviser to the prime minister on women's affairs, contacted Rashdan and pleaded with her to involve Princess Basma (the king's sister) immediately; otherwise, she indicated, the initiative would fail. The princess did ultimately intervene, lobbying senators by phone to vote for the amendment. Rashdan herself also called her senate colleagues to explain why they should vote for the amendment. The debate was evidently quite heated as Senate Rapporteur Ahmad Tarawineh opposed the amendment on the grounds that the landlord should not be affected by such family matters and that the divorced wife should be considered a new tenant, unrelated to the previous renter. Despite all the efforts, including verbal efforts to shame some of the senators to vote in favor, Rashdan's proposition received only 13 votes of the 26 senators present. The tie was broken by the president of the senate, Ahmad al-Lawzi, who voted for the amendment. Apparently much of the opposition to the proposal stemmed from the Jordanians' familiarity with a similar law in Egypt, which accorded the divorced woman the right to *force* the ex-husband from the house. Hence, the senators insisted upon a clause to the effect that the law applied only if the man *chose* to leave the house.[49]

In the realm of labor, a new law was finally passed in 1996. (A draft law had been on the table since the early 1970s.) Among its provisions are some additional benefits for working mothers. For example, it allows a woman employed in an establishment of ten or more workers to have an unpaid year's leave of absence from her job to raise her child. She cannot be terminated beginning with her sixth month of pregnancy or during her maternity leave, and her right to return to this job after that year is guaranteed as long as she has not worked for pay elsewhere during this period. A woman now also has the right to one period each day of no longer than one hour to nurse her newborn during its first year. Moreover, an employer with at least twenty married female employees must provide a nursery for their children under age four—as long as there are at least ten such children. In addition, paid maternity leave was extended to ten weeks.[50] In June 1995, the cabinet approved an amendment to the Civil Service Law granting women ninety days maternity leave instead of sixty.[51]

With regard to more contentious issues, in early 1994 the House referred to the Judiciary Committee a draft law to end the regulations in the passport law that discriminated against women. The draft aimed at giving women the right to acquire passports without the approval of their husbands and at ending the practice of identifying women on passports as the wife, widow, or divorcee of a (former) male partner. Another draft law was concomitantly referred to the same committee to amend the Nationality Law so that Jordanian nationality could be given by women to their children and to foreign husbands. As of this writing no further action had been taken, but this last provision is reportedly unlikely to be passed any time in the near future, in part because of its implications for the Jordanian-Palestinian balance in the country, a sensitive topic. Kabariti's government did, however, promise to study ways to facilitate the ability of foreign husbands of Jordanian women to obtain residence and employment.

In August 1995, as part of discussions of an amended Income Tax Law, a proposal was made to allow a man tax exemptions for multiple wives, not just one as the law then stipulated. Among those most vocally opposed to the amendment was MP Toujan Faisal, whose position was backed by the government. The proposal was defeated, as only 46 deputies were present and only 21 of them voted for the amendment. The Islamist lawmakers had argued that they were protecting women's rights by demanding that men receive tax exemptions for all wives, as well as all children. The Islamists had the support of several leftist and centrist deputies as well. While the Islamists argued that polygamy was an existing part of Jordanian tradition, Faisal contended that it should not be encouraged, and that if a man wanted to take a second wife, he should be able to afford it.[52] Given the state's continuing budget shortages and its relations with the Islamists during this period, it should not be surprising that it opposed such a measure.

Several attempts have been made to draft a new Personal Status Law (see next chapter), but none has been presented to date. More striking have been the efforts by a few persistent men and women to address the issues of domestic violence and honor crimes. One important development was that beginning in 1994 these crimes began to be reported, and with regularity, in the country's English-language daily, the *Jordan Times*. This coverage, along with a concomitant emphasis by the Jordan Women's Union on violence against women, has at very least brought the issue into the open. Honor crimes and violence more broadly are problems in both Palestinian and Transjordanian society, and although they are more often reported among the poor, such crimes transcend class lines. Honor killing is also a crime in which other female family members are generally complicit, whether out of fear for retribution or conviction that the tradition is appropriate. (Although, one should note that it would be difficult to determine when female family members may play a role in trying to prevent such crimes.)

In addition, both the National Strategy on Women (see next chapter) and the national report submitted to the Beijing conference included references to violence against women, a first for Jordan. The National Strategy calls for increasing efforts to raise awareness of manifestations of such violence, and to provide legal and support services to assist the victims. The Beijing report included a breakdown of types of violence against women, and among the categories was "crimes relating to morals," although the report provides no further elaboration on this form of violence, and there is no specific mention of honor crimes. The focus is instead on the question of a woman's being hit or beaten, the explanation for which is given as changing gender roles triggered by broader socioeconomic and cultural transformations, including women's increasing integration into the labor force.[53]

Unfortunately, official circles have (up to the time of this writing) remained largely silent on the issue. One centrist human rights specialist claimed that parliament has never *allowed* the inclusion of honor crimes on its agenda. A number of cabinet ministers in late 1994 did suggest that the system of tribal justice needed to be reviewed: ministers of social development, the interior, and justice all noted the need to put an end to tribal practices such as vengeance killing[54] (not the same as honor crimes) and the Minister of Social Development went so far as to suggest that a conference be held to discuss ways of abolishing such practices. A *Jordan Times* editorial placed blame on the state for indirectly encouraging such practices by either participating in them or ignoring them.[55] Indeed, not until a February 14, 1996 speech at Al al-Bayt University, was the issue of honor crimes addressed by a member of the royal family, Crown Prince Hassan. Hassan discussed the issue and questioned whether these crimes were sanctioned by Islam.[56] The king made his first public statement on the problem in his November 29, 1997 speech from the throne to the newly elected parliament. Implicitly referring to honor crimes, Husayn called such violence against women a "flagrant contradiction of our ongoing calls to preserve human dignity and all human rights."[57] At the time of this writing it remained to be seen if the monarch's exhortations would be translated into concrete legislative initiatives. To date, however, there appears to be no inclination to push for legislation that might begin seriously to address this problem.

The only real institutional response has come from outside official circles. For example, the Jordanian Women's Union began work in 1994 to establish a hot line for women to address complaints of family violence. Another institution, the Violence Free Society, was established in 1995 to deal with the issue of violence against women and children through information campaigns and lectures. Longer-term goals include the establishment of shelters for physically abused women and children which would also offer services to help the abuser, as well as a mobile consultation center where the battered could go to discuss their problems.[58] These are important first steps, but the day still seems distant when a woman's life will be fully protected by the Jordanian state.

Evaluation

This examination of Jordanian legislation reveals several clear themes in the relationship between women and the state. As was clear in the case of Morocco, while some laws apparently are aimed at protecting women, the underlying presumption is often that women are equivalent to minors (indeed, on numerous occasions articles place women and children in the same category). The larger message of these laws, however, is that economic, political, and social control rests with male family members: only men can be recognized as heads of households, regardless of what the reality may be. Numerous aspects of the labor, pension, and social security laws implicitly assume that the woman is being supported by a male and therefore requires neither job nor financial support from the state or her former employer.

In addition to this conclusion, however, as the citizenship law and established practice regarding prosecuting honor crimes indicate, women are not fully citizen in Jordan. Women cannot be considered fully citizen in a country in which they can be killed with relative impunity, on the basis of little or no evidence, on the grounds of suspicion of loss of honor, acts for which male members not only go reproached, but in which they are, in fact, expected to engage.

That said, there have been significant changes in women's legal status since the liberalization. Some working women's lives have been made easier thanks to the changed maternity leave conditions, and some divorced women will not be forced from their homes with their children due to the change in the Tenancy Law. Average Jordanian women are most concerned with how to feed their families and educate their children in increasingly difficult economic circumstances. It would be quite a challenge to convince such women that they should be exercised about the fact that a wealthy woman living in Amman and married to a foreigner cannot give Jordanian citizenship to her children. The concerns are different as is the disposition to challenge the prevailing framework.

Experience of activist women shows that those who are most successful in conveying their message to average women are those who present their arguments within a framework which clearly respects Islam and existing societal structures. However much an outside activist may want to see changes in, for example, the Personal Status Law's articles regarding divorce or inheritance, Jordanian society remains conservative, and more comfortable with the approach of Princess Basma's National Women's Forum (a kingdom-wide women's organization to be discussed in the next chapter), than, for example, with the calls by the Jordanian Women's Union (JWU) for a woman's right to an abortion.

Given the rise of the Islamists, some might argue that the less conservative women should be grateful that their legal situation has not deteriorated further. That, somehow, is of little comfort to a small but growing number of women who have felt their rights threatened as a result of the conservative tide. While this situation is not unique to Jordan, it nonetheless weighs heavily on those women who have an interest in seeing real structural changes in women's status.

ROLE OF EXTERNAL AGENCIES

The global trends of economic and political liberalization have led to a proliferation of NGOs around the world. Predating these trends, however, was a focus by economic development agencies on the role of women, as most large funding agencies, whether public or private sector, developed bureaus or special programs focusing on women in development (WID). The previous chapter attempted to highlight the role of Jordan's external relations in affecting the framework in which the liberalization unfolded. In the same way, one must bear in mind the importance of emerging international norms regarding civil society and women's rights in examining the impact of the liberalization on women. The following examination is meant to be illustrative rather than exhaustive of the trends in project funding, institutional recipients, and impact on national discussions and policy. The focus is on funding that is aimed at national level issues, promoting women's rights and political participation. Hence, although it may well play a direct or indirect political role, assistance aimed at economic development or empowerment is not considered here.

USAID: Like Morocco, Jordan was identified by AID to be part of its Democratic Institutions Initiative. Perhaps the Agency's most significant contribution in Jordan in the realm of women's concerns during this period was its participation in the drafting of the National Strategy for Women, discussed in detail in the next chapter. Shortly after the establishment of the Jordanian National Committee for Women (JNCW), Princess Basma asked USAID to provide a Women in Development (WID) team to work with the committee in preparing a strategy and action plan. "She also asked that they avoid writing yet another report recommending further research on women's status: . . . 'We know about the situation of Jordanian women;

we want ideas of what can be done.' " Following extensive consultations, the WID team prepared a draft of "Issues and Options" for the Committee's consideration. Two sessions were then held. At the first the WID Team offered its findings, and in the second, the Committee presented its own working papers about the proper role and function of the JNCW. Particular concern was raised that the committee not parallel or duplicate existing structures and that it not claim to represent the women of Jordan. Consensus was reached that the JNCW could play a vital role in coordinating between the public and private sectors and in ensuring that women's issues would be addressed at the policy level. It was also agreed that there was a need for the JNCW to help to promote the work of women's groups, to monitor and evaluate progress, and to assist in developing and implementing a national strategy and plan of action to advance women's status.[59]

While it is difficult to determine the exact role of AID in the development of the National Strategy (there are those who say the idea itself originated with AID, while others contend that it simply played a critical support role by assisting with the early stages of its drafting), it does seem likely that without AID's involvement at this early stage, the National Strategy would not have been produced in its present form. What alternative form it might have taken or how the timing of its issuance might have been affected must remain matters of speculation. However, given that these efforts have, through a winding and not always clear path, participated in Princess Basma's assumption of a leadership role and of the establishment of a new, national women's organization, the impact of AID's efforts can certainly be gauged, for better or for worse, as significant.

Amideast:[60] The impetus for Amideast to move away from its more traditional concerns with education and technical training came in the early 1980s with a grant from AID as part of an initiative from the Carter administration to improve human rights. As was the case in Morocco, the decision was made in Jordan that a sensitive issue like human rights could not be addressed directly at that time, so the project was presented as one focused on legal training and education, as a way of addressing many of the concerns related to human rights. The main result of Amideast's effort in this area was the establishment of a judicial institute in 1989.

In the meantime Amideast had moved on to deal with women's rights. At the time, the only group in the country working on such issues was the BPWC. Amideast funded a number of their seminars, publications, and outreach projects. They also supported the BPWC's review of its legal consultative services (then over two years old) with an eye to engaging in preventative work. It also provided a grant for a "what to do if" handbook, initially conceived of as aimed at women, but ultimately produced for both

men and women to help guide them through a series of government bureaucratic procedures and problems. The institution also funded the
Women's Research Center, a body established by more radical women, to
conduct a study of the personal status law.[61]

Then came the DII. While the initial thrust of this project was a needs
assessment for the Jordanian parliament and resulted in AID's procuring of
an electronic voting board for it, there was a women in politics angle as
well. In Jordan this took the form of Amideast's sponsoring of a regional
workshop on women's participation in governance and NGO networking
in April 1994. In this conference women shared experiences in and running
for public office.

Amideast also became involved in early 1996 in the Global Women in
Politics Program, which also has AID funding. Although it was not clear at
the time of this writing exactly which projects would be pursued in Jordan,
the program's goal is full integration of women into the political process: to
"increase awareness, strengthen advocacy, and expand access to positions
and processes; to promote equitable laws, policies and practices; to
strengthen regional capacity to effectively implement and enforce laws,
policies and decisions, and to promote networking that will facilitate the
transfer of ideas, strategies, and resources, and will build regional and international solidarity among women and women's groups."[62]

*National Endowment for Democracy (NED) and the National Democratic In-
stitute (NDI):* NED makes grants through its four core groups, one of which
is NDI, as well as other U.S.-based organizations, to organizations elsewhere in the world "dedicated to promoting the rule of law, fair and open
elections, a free press and the other essentials of a genuinely democratic culture."[63] NDI was established in 1983 "to promote, maintain, and strength-
en democratic institutions in new and emerging democracies." Its programs
focus on technical and training assistance in six areas: political parties, election processes, legislatures, local government, civic organizations, and civil-
military relations. While NED funded a survey in March 1993 on the then-
upcoming parliamentary elections, NDI became involved in programs in
Jordan in December 1993. This followed the Jordanian government's rejection of an NDI "study mission" prior to the November 1993 elections. (The
Jordanians rejected the idea of what they saw as monitors.)

Following these elections, however, a team from NDI went to the kingdom and in discussions with Jordanian politicians and others noted a consensus regarding a need to reexamine the country's Electoral Law, which
had been amended the previous summer. To respond to that need, NDI co-
sponsored a conference on electoral systems around the world in cooperation with an independent Jordanian think tank, the New Jordan Research

Center, which focuses on issues related to civil society and democratization, including projects dealing with women.[64] (It is worth noting that state harassment of NJRC led to its closing just before this conference and for two days the conference's future was unclear.) In addition to sponsoring this conference, NDI gave a small grant to enable NJRC to set up more systematized accounting and management procedures. NED has also helped fund NJRC seminars, workshops, and publications. This support has been critical, since NJRC is a center that has jealously guarded its independence.[65]

Friedrich Ebert Stiftung (FES): Along with NJRC, this German organization sponsored a three-day conference in late May-early June 1994 entitled "Jordan's Democratic Path—Reality and Prospects," which featured one panel on women. The proceedings were eventually published in volumes in both English and Arabic. In early 1996 FES launched a two-year program in conjunction with the Noor al-Hussein Foundation (NHF) entitled "Promoting Women Leadership." A direct response to the Beijing conference, this program aims at building women's political awareness and participatory capabilities. FES also sponsored the publication of a *Who's Who* for both the 1989 and the 1993 parliaments.

Konrad Adenauer Stiftung (KAS): In late September 1993 in cooperation with the GFJW and the Women's University (Amman) and under the auspices of Crown Prince Hassan, KAS sponsored a three-day conference on the "Role of the Jordanian Woman in the Process of Democratization." It was intended to examine various civil society institutions in Jordan and explore what Jordanian women might accomplish through them to better participate in the political process. It was also intended to be a boost for the GFJW, which had been suffering from internal problems for more than three years.[66]

In conjunction with NJRC, in late May 1994 KAS sponsored a five-day workshop on political parties to which representatives from all the political parties were invited. In late December 1995 in Irbid they organized a workshop with the National Committee on Women which aimed at training women in democratic leadership, group work, and problem solving. And in March 1996, along with the Kutba Institute for Human Development, they conducted a three-day workshop in Aqaba focusing on the importance of developing democratic practices within the family.

Friedrich Naumann Stiftung (FNS): In late January 1994 FN, associated with the German Social Democratic Party,, sponsored a one-day seminar entitled "Democracy in Jordan: Concepts and Practice," while in early April 1994 it funded a seminar on political parties. Both were conducted in conjunction with the Jordanian National Society for the Enhancement of Freedom and Democracy. Jointly with the Jordan Environmental Society FN hosted two seminars on the Beijing Women's Conference, one in mid-January 1996 in Amman and the other in early March in Irbid. The gatherings aimed at promoting the role of women and enhancing their participation in sustainable development.

Evaluation

There is no question that the combination of a liberalization process in Jordan and the unfolding of the peace process have brought a great deal of attention and funding from external agencies. Some women believe that the extent of the government's recent interest in women is in fact explained by external NGOs' and other aid agencies' concern with women. NGO grants often have a WID component, so potential recipients must show some semblance of interest if they hope to continue to receive financing. A number of women noted that the availability of money for political programs has in fact led a number of women's and other groups to propose more politically oriented projects. Indeed, in spring 1996, the Noor al-Hussein Foundation, which had not previously been involved in programs related to women in politics, launched its first political training program for women, in large part sparked by the fact that Friedrich Ebert had money for such a program.

While the Germans, Amideast, NDI and others have provided funding to various local NGOs that encourage a more active political role for women, the activities associated with members of the royal family have come to dominate. It will be recalled that at the outset, a concern was raised that the JNCW not duplicate existing structures and not claim to represent the women of Jordan. Its role was to be that of policy coordination. However, activist women now argue that the duplication of roles is clear, that the policy coordination role still is not really operative, and that what has developed out of the JNCW and the preparations for Beijing, the Jordanian National Women's Forum, is in fact an attempt to impose a "representative" structure on the women of Jordan from above. Thus, indirectly, the role of AID, and any other organizations supporting the JNWC (or its mother institution, the Queen Alia Fund for Social Development, also to be discussed in the next chapter) or the Noor al-Husayn Foundation has been to push even further to the margins the country's few, real, serious, and struggling NGOs.

This interaction between state, local civil society actors, and external funders is examined in more detail in the case studies in the next chapter.

CHAPTER **SIX**
The State Retreats, the State Returns

The discussion that follows presents short cases of interactions between women and the state since the liberalization began in 1989. Examples are drawn from elections, the cabinet, the legislature, and women's organizations themselves. No pretension is made here to exhaustive coverage. Nonetheless, the events covered below do illustrate a number of clear trends in the evolution of state and societal policy toward women in the framework of an opening of the political system.

TOUJAN FAISAL: A WOMAN, THE ISLAMISTS, THE COURTS, AND THE KING

When it came time to declare candidacy for the 1989 parliamentary elections, twelve women presented themselves among the hopefuls. While there was speculation (mostly a great deal of doubt) about any of the twelve's chances of winning, the women entered the fray along with their male counterparts. One of the women, Toujan Faisal, a candidate for the Circassian seat in the fifth district (north, outside Amman, including the traditional Circassian areas of Wadi Seer and Na'ur) had worked as a television broadcaster for eighteen years, during which time she had presented a series on women's affairs. She was also known as a writer and columnist who had raised the ire of conservatives on a number of occasions for programs challenging established Islamic or tribal practice.[1] Supported by an array of intellectuals, liberals, Christians and the young, she ran in 1989 as an independent.

The story of interest here concerns an article she wrote prior to officially declaring her candidacy. On September 21 she published a piece in the Arabic daily *al-Ra'y* entitled "They curse us and we elect them" as part of an ongoing debate on women's role in society and their competence in handling national issues. In it Faisal, who is well-versed in Islamic law, criticized "those who hold women to be intellectually deficient and in need of being treated like minors." She claimed that this negative view of women is then covered up by regular proclamations of Islam's having given women all their rights and holding them in a special place of esteem by assigning them the role of mother in the home. Her larger political point was that those who believe in discrimination on any basis cannot be entrusted with a family, an extended household, or a nation. With the franchise, women were in a position to defeat those who in effect denied them their humanity. It was a powerful indictment of both Islamists and other conservatives, but not intended to be a criticism of religion: her references were always to Islamists and not to Islam itself. Two weeks following the appearance of her article, Faisal was visited by "two bearded men" who demanded that she apologize for the article and withdraw from the election or they would take her to court. She refused. [2]

She subsequently received a subpoena to appear in a south Amman *shari'a* court, and learned that an assistant mufti in the armed forces, Shaykh 'Abd al-Rahman 'Ali al-Kurdi and a private in the armed forces, Mu'tasim Faris, had charged her with apostasy. Jordan has no apostasy law, and several *shari'a* courts had refused to accept the case before this court accepted. The suit sought to declare Faisal legally incompetent, dissolve her marriage, reject any repentance should she offer it, deny her all rights, ban her writings, and give immunity to anyone who shed her blood. According to the men's lawyer, the publication of the September 21 article was merely part of the reason for the suit: "people were beginning to listen to her misguided views on Islam because she was given a forum to air her views."[3]

The plaintiffs described the reasons for their outrage with her article in the following terms:

> The defendant had dared to declare her apostasy and ridiculed the Prophet Muhammad's saying which describes women as lacking in mind and religion . . . and considered these sayings as a crime and advocated equality between men and women. . . . She described as contemptuous the instructions to women to be polite and to dress decently and the divine order which stipulates that two women witnesses equal one male witness in court . . . and . . . she called for the domination of the mind rather than the domination of one person over another.[4]

At the time, many activists described the suit as an attempt to "stifle the women's movement in Jordan at a time when women were running in elections for the first time in the kingdom's history." A group of women and other political activists, lawyers, university professors, and journalists submitted a petition to the king denouncing the charges against Faisal as "intellectual and psychological intimidation which will reflect badly on Jordan's image and on the democratic atmosphere for the elections."[5] In a very short time more than 700 signatures were collected.[6] People were also contacted to attend the October 28 court session to show support. So many showed up at the proceedings that the attendees could not all fit into the building.

The day following the hearing, at which the plaintiffs presented their case and as a result of which the judge set a second session for November 9 (the day following the elections), the Jordanian press reported the story and triggered international interest. Journalists scrambled for interviews with Faisal and the case became a *cause célèbre*. It could not have been lost on the king that the first case of apostasy ever raised in the kingdom was coming at a time when Jordan was trying to hold its first democratic elections since the 1950s. The extent to which the regime sought to engage in damage control was demonstrated by a November 1 meeting on the case, and on the Islamists in general, called for by former information minister Layla Sharaf on behalf of a group of prominent Amman activists and personalities. In attendance were the king, Prime Minister Zayd bin Shakir, Crown Prince Hasan, and other ministers and officials. At a press conference that followed, the king "warned against a trend toward extremism" and against those who "exploit religion for political designs."[7]

Both plaintiffs in fact withdrew the case after the Amman *shariʻa* court ruled five days before the elections that the case was beyond its jurisdiction.[8] Shaykh Mahmud Shanqiti based his ruling upon Article 105 of the Constitution, which states that *shariʻa* courts have jurisdiction over cases concerning the personal status of Muslims, blood money, and Muslim religious endowments. Observers viewed the swift decision in the case as stemming from popular indignation and high-level pressure to issue a ruling prior to the elections. Nonetheless, ʻAbdallah Shamaylah, the lawyer for the two plaintiffs, subsequently filed an appeal himself on the grounds that the original lawsuit had been filed on behalf of the "public right."[9] Shamaylah claimed that certain groups in the armed forces had forced the original plaintiffs to withdraw the case. The story continued until February 1990, when a *shariʻa* appeals court found Faisal not guilty of apostasy, although the plaintiff said he planned to file a new lawsuit.

Gallagher notes that it was never clear where the case originated. There were certainly rumors that the mufti of the armed forces, Nuh al-

Qidha, had instigated the case. This is what Toujan Faisal believes, because before the two men called on her, Qidha had reportedly sent a Circassian private, a former classmate of Faisal's, to warn her to withdraw from the elections. Faisal believes that Qidha was acting on behalf of certain wealthy elites, whom she would have targeted for investigation if elected.[10] While difficult to reject out of hand, this seems unlikely, given how little power any single parliamentarian has, and given Qidha's reputation, which we shall examine in more detail in the next section. Some believed that there was Muslim Brotherhood involvement, in order to discredit secularists and mobilize support for their own candidates, but the Ikhwan denied any links to the two plaintiffs and claimed the uproar was hurting their campaigns.

Evaluation

There seems little question that the case was an embarrassment to the king, as it detracted from the campaign period and free elections. Given past experience it is certainly possible that an order was issued from the palace that the series of appeals was to be terminated so that no more international attention would be drawn to the matter. Another key consideration was that the regime was involved in drawing boundaries regarding what kind of activity would be permitted in a new, more open, era in which Islamists had taken one-third of the seats in the parliament. The fact that the Ikhwan stayed out of the fray—whatever their real feelings about Faisal—made it a much easier problem to solve.

Perhaps most important, one should not interpret the treatment of the case as indicative of a special dedication on the part of the palace to the protection of women or women's rights. In the wake of the Faisal case, the crown prince did select a group to study possible changes to the Personal Status Law. But the appointment of such committees has generally been a strategy of adopt and defuse or demobilize rather than adopt and act. That seriously addressing women's concerns was not a primary consideration was clear from the composition of the committee, which initially had no women members. Moreover, in 1993, the same Nuh al-Qidha who was suspected of having been behind the complaint against Faisal was appointed *qadhi al-qudha*, the Jordanian equivalent of a chief justice, by the king. Perhaps this argues against his having been involved in the first place, perhaps it owed to a palace need to placate forces in the army, or in the Ajlun area from which he hailed. Either of the latter two explanations is in keeping with the workings of the Jordanian political system. What the appointment argues against, however, is a regime concerned with further protecting women's rights. Rather, placating, or at least not challenging the forces—tribal, Islamist, or simply socially conservative—upon which the legitimacy of the regime rests has been the most constant feature of palace policy in this regard.

RECONSIDERING THE PERSONAL STATUS LAW

In the wake of the Toujan Faisal row, Crown Prince Hasan assembled a committee composed initially only of religious scholars to review the existing Personal Status Law. When Zulaykha Abu Risha, a prominent feminist and writer, among others, criticized the committee's composition in the press, contending that it should include specialists in other areas as well, the *qadhi al-qudha* at the time, Shaykh Muhaylan, summoned her and four other women to convince them not to worry. Subsequently, one woman, Dr. 'Eida Mutlaq, an educator from the Irbid area, was added to the committee. Muhaylan also requested input from the Business and Professional Women's Club. At the same time, another women's group, the Women's Research Center, of which Abu Risha was a member and which included more committed feminist activists, was officially called upon by a leftist member of parliament to submit another study of the Personal Status Law. Initially, these women had been denied the right even to see the draft.[11]

However, no parliamentary or further government action was taken at the time, perhaps because the legislators were preoccupied with the preparation of martial law-ending legislation. The issue of a new draft of this law resurfaced after the appointment in 1992 of a new chief justice, none other than Nuh Salman al-Qidha, who had been implicated in the Toujan Faisal affair. He was known to be quite conservative, a military man, and made clear some of the changes that he wanted. Again, however, no further action was taken to push the process along, and in the wake of the 1993 elections, he was retired. Given that he was not terribly old (he was brought out of retirement in late 1995 to take the post of Jordanian ambassador to Iran), one can only assume that it was a decision of the palace to replace him (perhaps because of his extreme positions, but I have no solid confirmation of this). In any case, the proposed draft did not offer many serious changes. One positive feature was that it raised the compensation to victims of arbitrary divorce (*talaq ta'assufi*) from one to five years of alimony payments.[12] Another draft was reportedly worked on thereafter, but no one outside the narrow circles of *shari'a* judges seems to have had access to it. And when the government of 'Abd al-Karim Kabariti was formed in early 1996, it was reported that the existing draft would be shelved and that the new government would produce yet another draft, but it did not, nor have its successors.

Evaluation

A shroud of secrecy seems to surround the drafting and redrafting of this law. Women activists speculate that given the socially and religiously sensitive nature of this legislation, the government has no interest in making a draft available for wide public discussion. At the same time, successive prime ministers and governments (as well as the palace) may have preferred to maintain the appearance of working on a new draft, thus placating those who want change, while never actually presenting one, thus avoiding the outcry from both liberal and conservative circles that any proposed changes would be likely to trigger. Some speculate that a deal of sorts may have been struck between the government(s) on the one hand and the religious authorities and Islamists on the other to the effect that reforms may be proposed on the margins of existing laws in other fields, such as labor and pensions, but that no move would be made by the state to force changes in the Personal Status Law.[13] Given the history of the issue as well as the prevailing balance of forces in the country, this appears to be a reasonable conclusion.

THE GENERAL FEDERATION OF JORDANIAN WOMEN

It will be remembered from the previous chapter that the GFJW was established in 1981 to displace the Women's Federation in Jordan and to bring women's activities more closely under the control of the Ministry of Social Affairs. As this organization began to emerge from the martial law period, a controversy arose, in large part as a result of the old guard's trying to maintain its position. The approach of long-overdue elections for the federation's 17-member executive committee polarized women and triggered a contest among the state, the Islamists, and the secular opposition. Elections had been postponed several times in the 1980s, and as the summer of 1990 approached, the existing executive committee had outlasted its legal three-year term by more than a year, having given itself one extension and having received another six-month extension from the ministry. As a result, on June 10, Minister of Social Affairs 'Abd al-Majid Shraydeh appointed a temporary committee to oversee the elections. This caused a huge row, as GFJW members claimed that the minister had no right to make such a decision. Indeed, some committee members blamed Shraydeh for the delay in elections, saying that, in consultation with them, he had postponed the elections for administrative reasons and that he had now appointed a new executive simply to carry out his wishes.[14] The dismissed members of the executive proceeded to file charges against the minister.

The controversy crystallized around a legal/administrative matter. During the term of the then-recently ousted executive, a new set of bylaws had been drawn up that allowed not only for an enormous increase in the federation's membership but also for gerrymandering of a sort. The changes in the bylaws were introduced as a result of the leadership's realization that it had become isolated from Jordanian women. With the liberalization, it now appeared possible and all the more urgent to change the situation. To that end, a decision was made to amend the bylaws to add the possibility of broader, individual membership through a new category of "local committees." Any group of thirty women could form a *lajnah* (committee), and they were often women from a particular quarter who were signed up by several women interested in the union. In this way, the GFJW leadership hoped to attract additional members, including perhaps some from the other, unofficial, women's groups, with the goal of either energizing the federation or perhaps coopting the activists.[15] The executive committee of the union opened the way to such individual membership on February 11, 1990.

The largest number of women who initially took advantage of this change were the members of Rand, the Democratic Women's League, associated with Democratic Front for the Liberation of Palestine. To the dismay of other leftist women, who continued to advocate a boycott of the government-sponsored federation, Rand had been calling since the mid-1980s for a reform of the GFJW to open it up to individual members. Yet, while the leftist women may have been the first to take advantage, beginning in March, women, the majority of whom "looked like they belonged to the Islamic sisterhood," according to one GFJW member,[16] began to show up regularly and in large numbers at the GFJW headquarters with lists and registration fees. The controversy began shortly thereafter.

The uproar that ensued indicated that the changed bylaws were at best complicated and at worst open to contradictory interpretations. Some contended the problem originated with the initial drafters of the changed bylaws, although observers also seemed to agree that the Minister's interpretation of what would become the infamous article 12 regulating voting representation did have clear and deliberate political implications in that it gave unfair representation to certain groups—in this case, Islamist women. According to Shraydeh's interpretation of the new provisions, each social institution, club, and society (no matter how large its membership) was to be represented in the regional councils by two members, while each group of fifty individual members was to be represented by three chosen delegates. The result, according to some, was that individual members were thus overrepresented (since societies generally had more than fifty members), even though they had had very little involvement in the federation's activities up to that time. Ousted members of the executive claimed that Shraydeh had interpreted article 12 "according to his whim."[17]

Shraydeh argued that the ministry had requested federation members to find an acceptable formula for interpreting article 12 for the provincial committees. When such a gathering failed to produce an agreement, he had called for a meeting of delegates to discuss the issue. When differences persisted, the delegates to this meeting agreed to leave the matter of determining a binding ruling to the ministry, after consultation with legal specialists on the interpretation.[18] The former union leadership and their associates were then surprised when the ruling went against them.[19]

The Islamist women claimed that it was only when the minister's interpretation did not meet the liking of the other women that they called foul. The story from the other side was that the "foul call" against the minister had come earlier: that the original executive had been dissolved, not because its term had expired (it had expired more than a year earlier) but because it had refused ministry interference in the union's internal affairs. Thereafter, not only was the executive dissolved, but also members of the former executive who sought to run for high office in the union were banned from ordinary membership. There were also complaints that no one was willing to provide membership figures for the various branches in order to determine who could vote and how many representatives certain associations were due. While this may sound odd, it is quite possible that the level of organization was such that the information was not available. [20]

It was clear from the beginning that this was in part a power struggle between Islamist women and others over control of the union. Leftist women argue that, given the political opening and the union's move to expand membership, they had hoped to forge a national coalition that included centrist and Islamist women. They claim that the Islamist women rejected the coalition idea and instead sought to win complete control of the union at a time when a number of Islamist MPs were calling for women's return to the home, an anti-democratic program.[21] The Islamist women, on the other hand, portrayed their efforts as aimed at thwarting an attempt by a coalition of nonrepresentative leftists and elite women to take control of the union.[22] Given the political climate at the time—the newness of the liberalization experiment and the recent Islamist victories in the elections—the more secular women's fears and the Islamist women's sense of rising fortunes probably ruled out any possibility of compromise even before the fact.

When elections for the executive committee of the Amman chapter were finally held in mid-July, it was—to the surprise of many—not the Islamist women, but a nine-member National Bloc, that won. The leftist (many from Rand) and centrist (pro-government) women had managed to construct an alliance that swept the elections. A record number of women, 228 out of 238 representatives of organizations and individuals, had turned out to vote. However important this victory, the real test, the vote for the national executive committee, still lay ahead.[23]

Shraydeh set the date for the meeting and vote for August 3. On July 28 a seven-member women's delegation met with the speaker of parliament, Sulayman 'Arar, to protest Shraydeh's decision, ask that proportional representation be guaranteed, and request a delay in the elections for the national executive.[24] The most convincing evidence they gave for their demand was that 4,500 women of the various clubs and societies were, according to the current formula, represented by five women, while 1,250 individual members were represented by sixty women. At the same time, the ministry denied the eighty-five (non-Islamist) representatives of the Irbid district's 1,385 individual members the right to participate in the elections, saying that they had not fulfilled the conditions of membership in time,[25] although federation officials denied the charge. The decision was also decried as deliberately favoring Islamist elements, and the Irbid women protested vociferously.[26] Outside those circles directly involved, several members of parliament openly voiced their support for the women and called on the ministry to reconsider.

Several prominent columnists also joined the fray.[27] Ahmad Dabbas criticized the dependence of the union on the ministry and called for severing such ties. Mu'nis al-Razzaz criticized government interference in the union during a period of so-called democracy and called on the union to assert independence from the ministry, even if the consequences, especially the financial ones, would be severe. For their part, Islamist spokespeople argued that the women who had won the Amman elections were willing to declare their victory the result of democracy, but were unwilling to take the next step (national elections), again in the name of democracy: if the leftists/centrists won it was a triumph of democracy, if not, democracy had been violated.[28]

Despite the uproar, the ministry insisted that the elections be held on time, and as a result the non-Islamist women in the capital, as well as the representatives from the governorates, boycotted. Hence attendance at the session included only the sixty Islamist representatives of local committees from the capital. There were protests and even physical altercations outside the voting hall.[29] To no one's surprise, the boycott led to the victory of the Islamist list, headed by Mahdiyyah Zumaylah. The non-Islamist women cried double foul: the ministry had proceeded with the elections, and the nominating and voting processes had been conducted by a show of hands, not by secret ballot, as the bylaws required. Moreover, the boycott by the representatives of the governorates, they argued, meant that the federation had ceased to be a national union. As a result, they decided to take the Ministry of Social Affairs to court.[30] For her part, Zumaylah extended her hand to all those who sought to work for women in Jordan and promised that she would try to be as inclusive as possible.[31] By this time, however, people's attention had turned to the Iraqi invasion of Kuwait, and consideration of all other issues was postponed.

In the meantime, the non-Islamist women awaited the outcome of their court case. In early January 1991, a cabinet shuffle brought a new minister: Yusuf al-'Athm, a Muslim Brother. Later in the month, the GFJW won its appeal to the Higher Court to have the 1990 election results reconsidered. According to the ruling, an interim committee was to take charge of federation business for two months until new elections were held.[32] At this stage, 'Athm's presence made a difference. Rather than implementing the court's decision, he insisted that the existing bylaws were problematic and that they should be reviewed. The differences persisted, and Na'ila Rashdan, lawyer, GFJW and BPWC member, and a woman associated with the Islamists in the GFJW, was asked to write a legal opinion on the problem.[33]

In early May, the non-Islamist GFJW women sent a memo to Prime Minister Badran charging the Ministry of Social Development and the interim executive with delaying the implementation of the court verdict and calling upon him to act to end the dispute. Later in the month, the Higher Court ruled the 1990 election results void and illegal, but 'Athm refused to implement the decision.[34]

In June 1991 Tahir al-Masri was named prime minister and the Ikhwan presence in the cabinet came to an end. The new minister of social affairs, 'Awni Bashir, was none other than the son of former GFJW head Haifa Bashir, who had been president of the union when the problematic articles had been introduced into the bylaws. Not surprisingly, after only a month in office, he assembled a 17-member committee of women of various political affiliations and gave them sixty days to prepare for new elections. He insisted that elections be held according to the existing bylaws, even though in the meantime, an official legal interpretation had ruled that there should be no individual membership in the GFJW.

On October 18, 1991, new elections for the GFJW general congress were held, with elections for the nine-member executive committee to follow. The Islamic Action Committees, Islamic Voluntary Societies, and independents decided to boycott these elections, although under 'Athm's stewardship of the ministry the number of Islamic charitable societies had grown exponentially.[35] In a statement published in the semiofficial daily *al-Dustur*, they announced their decision, arguing that steps taken to prepare for the elections were illegal and had been initiated by a small group that sought to exclude the majority of Jordanian women from participating.

They also complained of a variety of what they contended were electoral irregularities.[36]

These elections, not surprisingly, brought into the leadership a group of non-Islamist women, led by Dr. Haifa Abu Ghazalah, a longtime employee of the Ministry of Education. She had been the choice of the outgoing president (and also, reportedly, of higher powers). The other women who were elected with her were more politicized, like those who had been elected to the Amman council in 1990.[37] But the story does not end here. As a result of what was viewed as yet another unrepresentative outcome as well as the lingering dispute over the bylaws, Na'ila Rashdan filed a suit charging that these election results should also be overturned: a major segment of women (the Islamists) had boycotted, and one particular trend, the leftist women, whom she claimed in no way represented average Jordanian women, had taken control.[38]

The saga dragged on until August 1992, when the Higher Court abolished the regulations regarding individual membership and declared the GFJW executive board illegal. The court ruled that all members had to belong to social organizations that were registered with the Ministry of Social Development.[39] During the period leading up to this decision, the federation's activity had in effect been frozen. In the end, the elections were repeated and Abu Ghazalah won again, in part because of her position as incumbent president and in part because of support she received from above. However, given the termination of the committee form of membership, the leftists who had been voted in with her in 1991 were no longer union members. The result was an executive committee more akin to the pre-1989 formula: a coordinating committee among organizations with no common program. As a result, the final settling of the election and leadership and membership issues did not lead to a reenergizing of the union. The new leadership was almost exclusively Amman-focused, and most seemed more interested in appearing at public functions than in serious work. Stories abound of personal aggrandizement, clientelism, and corruption. In addition, once preparations began for Beijing, Abu Ghazalah was appointed the coordinator of the Arab region for the UN conference and hence spent a great deal of time traveling rather than working on local problems.[40] The near final blow came with the establishment by Princess Basma of the Jordanian National Women's Forum (see below), thus raising questions about the GFJW's future role.

Evaluation

The tortured history of the GFJW is explained in part by political rivalries among various women (particularly the non-Islamists versus the Islamists) but also by the changing composition of subsequent Jordanian governments and, in particular, by the political inclination of the successive ministers of social development. The introduction of the new membership category underlines the fact that until 1989 there was no real interest in individual members, which is quite telling about the GFJW's role and reach. The executive appears to have sought to change the bylaws to check its growing irrelevance and perhaps also to curb or coopt the more politically activist women as the liberalization got underway. What they did not expect, however, was the surge in organized Islamist interest in the GFJW. In the end the strategy backfired, as it led to instability in the leadership and a stagnation of activity on the ground.

The failure of subsequent ministers to resolve the issue owes to their ambivalence or lack of interest as well as the determination by women on both sides of the divide not to accept the status quo. Had Jordan not been in a period of liberalization, it is possible that the issue would simply have been dismissed or that the state would have imposed a new leadership immediately. Thus, the liberalization itself opened the way for a certain amount of contestation and infighting. However, the state's failure to act decisively to resolve the issue in the context of close ministry responsibility for the union indicates both bureaucratic malaise and a continuing lack of interest in seeing women develop effective institutions. In the end, the state's ambivalence toward the federation resulted not only in its being taken over by a leadership that appeared to have little commitment to serious activity, but also, as we shall see below, in its being superseded by a new women's group led directly from (one wing of) the palace.

THE STATE, THE ISLAMISTS AND LEGISLATION

Chapter 4 briefly mentioned several Islamist attempts to issue directives or advocate legislation seen as compromising women's rights. Here the focus is on two Muslim Brotherhood ministers in Mudar Badran's second cabinet, January–June 1991, a period during which the Islamists were still riding high on their 1989 legislative successes.

In 'Abdallah 'Akaylah's first meeting with ministry employees following his appointment as Minister of Education he informed women that he did not want to have them working in sensitive and important places. He also ordered the "cleansing" of the ministry by segregating the sexes, and began firing some of the higher ranking employees and replacing them with Islamists. His "retiring" of fourteen such people was approved by the cabinet, even though at least seven were still productive, and one was a woman, the only female to reach so high a post. 'Akaylah also introduced a series of measures to Islamicize education: he limited the freedom of schools to close on Christian holidays and set the dates for mid-term exams during them, and attempted to ban books deemed incompatible with the kingdom's "moral and religious ethics."[41]

He then moved to ban male sports instructors from working with female students, while his colleagues in parliament submitted a proposal to ban the mixing of the sexes in all educational facilities. None of this, however, elicited any noticeable public reaction. Then on April 30 'Akaylah issued a decision forbidding fathers to attend their daughters' sporting events. The minister argued that the young girls were often scantily clad for such events and that they therefore would not have total freedom to display their skills without embarrassment if males were present. This time, parents reacted swiftly and angrily, forming an ad hoc PTA of sorts. One legislator was approached by a concerned parent for help with drafting a petition protesting the measure, which was then circulated and quickly attracted more than 5,000 signatures.[42] In mid-June, a delegation of parents angry over the minister's decisions met with Badran, insisting upon their right to choose on the issue of mixing of the sexes and rejecting the imposition of the minister's will.[43] Badran resigned only a few days later.

Similar stories are recounted about the Minister of Social Affairs, Yusuf al-'Athm. In the first place, during his brief term in office he allowed the registration of more than fifty Islamic charitable societies, some of which did not meet the legal registration requirements. He reportedly tried to push through seven on his last day in office alone. More troubling, however, were his policies in the ministry itself. He took advantage of the beginning of the Gulf War, as people were upset and distracted, to begin to segregate offices by sex. He also decided to have separate meetings with male and female staff. Yet when he met with female staff, he reportedly did not discuss work-related matters. Instead, he admonished them about their style of dress, telling them they should wear less makeup, that he preferred but would not require Islamic dress, and then requested that they not wear heels that would click as they went up and down the stairs.[44]

He then proceeded to bring women preachers from the Awqaf Ministry to preach to the Muslim women employees; attendance at the weekly sessions was mandatory. The Muslim women were reportedly annoyed with the requirement and complained that the women preachers were deficient in their knowledge of Islam. In the meantime, Christian employees began to feel under siege, as their Muslim colleagues were warned by the minister not to be "contaminated" by them, and subtle forms of pressure were initiated to undermine their position. Al-'Athm also reportedly denied one woman the approval to go abroad based on his concern regarding the poor morals of foreign men and women.[45]

Evaluation

It is difficult to say how important these policies, particularly the uproar created by those of 'Akaylah, were in the decision by the regime to change prime ministers and exclude the Ikhwan from the next cabinet. The importance of the unusual and rapid parental response should not be downplayed given the sector of Amman society—upper and upper middle class—that became involved. Nevertheless, while the king prides himself on the image of Jordan as a moderate and forward-looking country—and the edicts of these two ministers certainly clashed with that image—it seems more likely that foreign policy or security considerations played the primary role in the ouster of the Ikhwan from the cabinet. The prelude to what became the Madrid conference—discussed in chapter 4—and the Ikhwan's likely refusal to support such a meeting seem the most likely explanations for the Ikhwan's fall from grace.

THE ROLE OF PRINCESS BASMA

One of the most significant stories of the period and the counterpart to the decline of the General Federation of Jordanian Women has been the rise in prominence and power of Princess Basma, the king's sister. This section explores two elements of this important development: the establishment of the Jordanian National Committee for Women (JNCW) and the Jordanian preparations for the Beijing Conference.

The Jordanian National Committee for Women

The origins of Princess Basma's interest in women's issues is open to some speculation. What is clear is that until her involvement in 1992 as the patron of efforts to draft the National Strategy for Women, discussed below, the princess had a low profile in the public life of the kingdom. Her most notable involvement was as honorary chairwoman of the Queen 'Alia Fund for Social Development (QAF), which was established in 1977 and which targets developing self-sufficiency, especially among women and particularly in rural areas. If a member of the royal family was to take on a prominent, national role regarding women, however, she was the most obvious candidate, since neither Queen Noor nor Princess Sarvath, the wife of the crown prince, is originally Jordanian. Moreover, in public appearances Basma exudes a warmth and a modesty that have endeared her to many Jordanians.

According to the official account,[46] in September 1991, a delegation from the United Nations Fund for Population suggested the establishment of a national committee on women to work to integrate women more fully into development. As a result, in January 1992 Minister of Planning Ziyad

Fariz (an ally of the Crown Prince, who reportedly has taken a special interest in promoting his sister) and Prime Minister bin Shakir requested that the princess chair such a committee and choose its members. In March 1992, Princess Basma established the Jordanian National Committee for Women (JNCW), a policy forum on women's issues intended to work to improve women's social status and increase their involvement in development, to upgrade their legal status, and to improve their political participation. The JNCW was located within the QAF (officially an NGO) and comprised the ministers of planning, labor, education, and social development *ex officio*, as well as representatives of the civil service bureau, the private sector, the General Federation of Jordanian Women, and women in the public, private, and academic sectors. One of the first tasks set out for the committee was to produce a national strategy for Jordanian women. To that end, USAID was contacted and, as was noted in the previous chapter, a Women in Development (WID) team played an important role in early discussions and proposals for a National Strategy for Women and for an action plan for the JNCW. The AID team submitted its draft proposal in June 1992.

In 1993, a series of four seminars was held by the JNCW, the first for planners and policymakers, but the other three for concerned women in the northern, central, and southern parts of the country to ensure grassroots participation in drafting the National Strategy. Although an attempt was made to include suggestions made at these various meetings, the process was carefully orchestrated from above. For example, at one of the meetings, held in May 1993, it was the ministers who presented papers and who were most clearly directing the intellectual content of the meeting. In this session many women expressed concern regarding the intentions of the JNCW, particularly on the question of what role it would allow for existing women's NGOs. There was also a strong and direct questioning/criticism by Toujan Faisal of the fact that some of the ministers on the committee had been prominent during the martial law era and yet were now involved in project pushing for greater empowerment and involvement of women; why were they now advocating women's causes?[47]

At the final session, a national conference on June 29 presided over by the crown prince, the strategy and recommendations that had been assembled during the meetings in the governorates were distributed, and people were divided into two groups: one to discuss political/legal issues and the other to look at educational and economic issues. When the two groups returned for a plenary session, the presence of the crown prince introduced a formality that made further changes impossible. All the participants were aware that they could not leave that day without having produced a document. Some women objected, saying that the draft could serve as a basis for future work, but not be accepted in its entirety. However, at that point, a deputy (generally described as a leftist) suggested that whoever was in agreement with the document should stand. To have remained seated was not really an option, since it would have been construed as a direct challenge to the princess. The document was adopted.[48]

A number of interviewees made clear that one major problem with the National Strategy and with other work sponsored by Princess Basma is/was that everyone seeks to please her. No one wants to express views they think she may not want to hear, so they simply agree with her.[49] Indeed, when I commented to one of the organizers of the May session (noted above) that Toujan Faisal had been courageous in making her remarks about the ministers' martial law pasts the woman responded, "yes, but it's not proper to speak that way in front of the princess."

The National Strategy was then sent on to the cabinet, which approved it on October 30, 1993, and called upon all relevant bodies to take the steps necessary to implement it. The JNCW then formed a coordination committee comprising several representatives of the main NGOs in Jordan. In addition, several technical committees consisting of a number of specialists and experts were assembled to prepare programs of action in various domains, including action plans for the relevant ministries. In the political domain, one of the key initiatives, begun in 1994, was the appointment of 99 women, recommended by the princess, to municipal and village councils throughout the country. (Such appointments could not have taken place, however, had the government not already, as noted in chapter 4, mandated the dissolution of the legally elected councils as part of its anti-Islamist political program.) The appointments, requested by the princess, were then approved by cabinet decisions.

The women selected for these posts were chosen from existing or recently established "women's committees." Beginning in the 1980s, the QAF had begun to establish community development centers in rural areas to aid rural women in generating income for their families through training, education, and productive projects. Through these centers a series of women's committees was eventually started on the village and governorate level. In 1992, 1,416 women were active in 72 committees, which in turn reached 60,482 women.[50] The women's committees that were involved in the municipal councils effort, however, were something different. They were established in the twelve governorates following the adoption of the National Strategy to promote its goals and to form pressure groups to lobby on women's issues, in addition to their responsibilities in community development in cooperation with the QAF centers. These committees were formed with the cooperation of the governors of the governorates and the Ministry of the Interior, and operate under the umbrella of the JNCW. Government facilities of various sorts have been put at their disposal, especially schools, and a large number of memberships have been solicited among teachers.

The appointment of the 99 women to municipal posts was intended to provide them with training in government service and local issues, to break the women's and the communities' psychological barriers to seeing women in such posts, and therefore to enhance their chances for running in and winning in municipal elections.[51] Following their appointments a number of training workshops were conducted and the JNCW distributed flyers encouraging women to register to vote. In the end, twelve women ran for election: one was elected mayor, in the Ajlun district, and nine others were elected to municipal council posts. Ten, including the one who won the mayorship, had been members of the women's committees.

JNCW activities in other fields have included: the taping of fifty awareness-raising programs on women, family, and the law in conjunction with Jordanian broadcasting; the establishment of nurseries in the Sahab industrial area (south of Amman) to benefit working mothers; the organization of a number of sessions to raise women's awareness of health care issues; and the commissioning of a number of studies on such issues as poverty, female-headed households, and problems of child-rearing.[52]

On December 29, 1995, in a major step, representatives of the women's committees assembled in Amman for a conference founding a new women's organization, the Jordanian National Women's Forum (Tajammu' Lijan al-Mar'ah al-Watani al-Urdunni) (JNWF). The ostensible reason for setting up this forum was to provide the national institutional framework to push forward the National Strategy for Women after the Beijing conference. [53] This structure was intended to tie together all the local committees referred to above. Although it was billed as an NGO and a grassroots effort, with Princess Basma as its head, with logistical and financial support coming from the governorates and ministries, and with its mission the implementation of the government's National Strategy, this was clearly a governmental organization.

In the press coverage of the event, none of the traditional faces from the "women's movement" appeared and none was mentioned. Only passing reference was made to the past role of the general federation in the general framework of the JNWF's intention to continue to work with other women's organizations.[54] The founding of the forum was completely unexpected and literally everyone involved in women's issues—from employees of UN agencies to women activists of various stripes—was taken by surprise. The GFJW and JWU were particularly alarmed and requested meetings with the princess to clarify the nature of their relationship to the new JNWF. The princess reportedly reassured them that the relationship would be one of cooperation, not domination or exclusion, but word was that they were not fully convinced. Whether simply as a means of no longer sharing the limelight with women who owed their positions to people other than her—the patron of the GFJW is Queen Noor—(the most negative interpretation), or out of a desire to in effect "clean house" of those who had been prominent but most active in parties and expensive trips (the most positive construction), or out of a growing desire simply to establish for herself a formal, national women's organization (the most likely explanation), the princess had clearly made her move to take control and begin a new era.[55] The founding congress was charged with looking into the situation of each of the local committees over the next six months in preparation for holding elections.[56]

In a related move, just before the March 8, 1996 celebrations of International Women's day, yet another institution was opened: the Princess Basma Women's Resource Center (PBWRC). Housed within the QAF's Queen Zein al-Sharaf Complex for Development in northwest Amman, the PBWRC is directed by Princess Basma's daughter, Farah Daghestani. Although at the time of this writing it was difficult to ascertain how active the center would be, its goals included: initiating media campaigns to raise public awareness and debate of women's issues; holding seminars and workshops to raise women's awareness; conducting research and collecting information on women in Jordan so as to serve as a national resource center on the subject; and offering cultural, educational, and social activities to women of all ages. It was also intended to provide implementing mechanisms for the Platform of Action, agreed to at Beijing.[57] The center's first formal activity was to serve as a focal point for a week-long program of activities in honor of International Women's Day.

While the atmosphere was hardly ripe for criticism of the royal family, Rand, the Democratic Women's League, probably came close to voicing what many others thought: that the JNWF was an official federation, that it had not been founded at the behest of its committees' reported 15,000 members, and that it therefore constituted blatant interference by the government in the affairs of Jordanian women.[58] On the other hand, Nawal Fa'uri, one of only two women to serve as a member of the IAF *shura* council (its executive body) praised the role of the princess in adopting women's issues on an official level through the National Strategy, the JNCW, and the JNWF. She also referred to the JNWF as the legitimate framework for women's efforts in the kingdom.[59]

The Preparations for Beijing

In early 1992, Princess Basma was designated by the cabinet to serve as the head of Jordan's delegation to Beijing. Certainly by June 1993 it was clear that the discussions surrounding the National Strategy for Women would play an important role in shaping the kingdom's official report to be presented at the conference. As the international conference approached, Basma gradually assumed all the Beijing-related "hats." In addition to heading the official Jordanian preparations, she also chaired the Jordanian committee that coordinated among the NGOs intending to participate. Each country was supposed to have a focal point organization to serve to coordinate NGO preparations for Beijing. However, the princess simply said that it was unnecessary to designate such a focal point, that the national coordinating committee, which was not an NGO but a body housed within the QAF, would carry out this function of establishing liaisons with the various NGOs.[60]

In July 1993 Basma was named an honorary UN ambassador for human resource affairs, and at the end of December she was named by UN Secretary General Boutros-Ghali to membership in the International Advisory Group in preparation for Beijing. At a mid-November 1994 regional preparatory meeting held in Amman under the princess' patronage, she was voted Woman of the Year in appreciation of her efforts. At Beijing itself, she was elected one of six vice-chairs of the conference for the Asian region, a development that received a great deal of play in the Jordanian press.

The Jordanian media highlighted the positive, constructive, yet *moderate* position of their home delegation in the deliberations. Jordan's position was always noted by the princess to be within the framework of the kingdom's traditions and culture, and in keeping with its Islamic heritage, although only one IAF member, Nawal Fa'uri, had been included in the delegation, and there had been no formal participation by IAF women in the preparation of the national report.[61] Shortly after the return from Beijing, the princess held a meeting specifically with IAF MPs to review the outcome of the conference, and the deputies expressed their willingness to cooperate with the JNCW to achieve its goals. She held no such meeting with deputies from other parliamentary blocs or parties. Since then, discussions of the conference have stressed that the decisions of Beijing "promote women and support them in the framework of Islamic teachings, accepted social traditions and mores, and the Jordanian constitution and National Charter."[62]

Evaluation

In the end, the preparations for Beijing served to catapult the princess to a position of prominence and power she had not previously enjoyed. By the end of 1995 with the establishment of the JNWF, she had clearly taken the mantle of leadership of the "women's movement." It remained to be seen whether the hard work promised to improve women's status and legal position would in fact produce concrete results. Certainly the establishment of the PBWRC noted above, as well as, only a week later, the formation of the Jordanian Committee for Non-Governmental Women's Organizations (also to be chaired by the princess) further illustrated her intention to play the premier role in the realm of women's issues in the kingdom. This latter committee was founded to serve as a coordinating body for NGO work in general and had as its first task putting together a working team to revise the National Strategy and to prepare a plan linking the Beijing conference recommendations with the Jordanian National Strategy.[63] In reality, of course, the fact that Jordan's official and NGO delegations were combined is indicative of a broader problem, that of the state's insinuation of itself into what should be civil society activity.

One final important observation regarding the JNWF is that it is heavily Transjordanian, developing out of the QAF centers, the constituent committees of which are based in villages, which are almost exclusively Transjordanian. It is as yet unclear what the practical implications of this development are. It may be an attempt by the regime to try to ease some of the concerns of Transjordanians that the kingdom's future lies with the Palestinians. More likely, it is simply the natural product of the fact that the initiative emerged from the QAF and that the Palestinian refugee camps are serviced by UNRWA (United Relief and Works Agency for Palestine Refugees) and its donor contacts. In any case, the communal dimension is not lost on the women participants.

THE WOMEN'S UNION IN JORDAN

One clear, positive development owing to the political liberalization was the reemergence of the WFJ, under the name of the Jordanian Women's Union (JWU). Its members were generally of a leftist or pan-Arab persuasion, tending toward a more political, if not always feminist, analysis of women's problems in Jordan and therefore less interested in traditional forms of charitable social work. Once it became clear that the GFJW would remain a grouping of societies and not a real women's union, the leftist women who had tried to work within the federation turned their attention to working within the JWU. One source argued that it was the failure of the more politicized, leftist women to take over the GFJW in 1992, after the 1991 elections were overturned, that led them to turn their attention to the JWU and capture the leadership in the 1993 elections.[64]

During the first years of its reinvigoration, the union concentrated on political issues or foreign affairs: collecting donations for the children of the intifada and for the Iraqi people in the wake of the Gulf crisis. However, in April 1993 elections were held and lawyer and activist Asma Khadr was elected president, replacing Da'd Mu'ath, who had been president for nearly twenty years.

Between 1993 and 1995, the union implemented a number of basic reforms, moving toward greater decentralization, establishment of new branches, more democratic forms of interaction, and guarantees for more effective participation of the branches. In 1994, the union counted 3,800 members in the capital alone in addition to branches and centers in Irbid, Zarqa, Madaba, and Ramtha.[65] Two sets of new activities have been particularly notable, as the union has been reenergized. The first aims at changing a variety of laws to promote greater equality between the sexes, and the second concerns family relations and domestic violence. To address the first set of concerns, the union assembled a committee to look into proposals for changes in the Labor Law to enforce equality between men and women, and to accommodate the needs of working mothers.[66] In February 1995 it made public its intention to work to establish a secretaries union in the kingdom as a result of the numerous complaints of exploitation and abuse it had received. In the fall of 1995 the union announced that it planned to offer its premises as a place where divorced parents could visit with their children, to provide an alternative to the existing practice of meetings at police stations. It also began a program to provide free court representation to women, along with the legal advice it had been providing for some time.

In September 1995 the union initiated a campaign to press lawmakers to amend or overturn a series of discriminatory laws. The first target was the Passport Law, which it sought to change so that women would no longer need to obtain their husband's or guardian's permission to obtain a passport. The plan was then that every four months the union would focus on a different law it felt needed amending. Further changes were to be lobbied for in the Nationality Law, the penal code (regarding abortion), the Civil Personal Status Law (to restrict polygamy and arbitrary divorce), the Labor Law, and the Pension Law.[67]

By early 1995 the JWU had opened three legal advice centers, one in each of the two refugee camps of al-Wihdat and al-Baq'a, and the third at the union office in Jebel Husayn. This then complements the second thrust of their work: a campaign to raise awareness regarding the problem of violence against women. To this end they have worked to establish a violence hotline (opened in August 1995 and formally inaugurated in March 1996) and a center that employs counselors who meet with women to advise them of their rights and options.

Although the liberalization enabled the JWU to resume and expand its activities, it has nevertheless encountered some problems. For example, in 1994 a controversy arose between it and the general federation, ostensibly over similarity of name. While the JWU contended that there was no basis for competition, since the GFJW offered membership only to societies and the JWU offered individual membership, the GFJW threatened to take the JWU to court on the grounds that the similarity of name caused confusion. The GFJW did file a complaint with the Ministry of the Interior on these grounds, but the ministry supported the JWU, which had been registered under that name prior to the founding of the GFJW.[68] However, the Ministry of Social Affairs then requested that the JWU either change its name or merge with the GFJW. While the JWU initially refused, contending that they were registered with the Ministry of the Interior, and not the Ministry of Social Affairs, and it should therefore have no jurisdiction over them, in the end there was a name change from Al-Ittihad al-Nisa'i al-Urdunni to Ittihad al-Mar'a al-Urdunniyyah, the Jordanian Woman's Union. Of course, as had been the case in the early 1980s when a name change was forced on these women, the name was not the basic problem. This was a power struggle between the two organizations.

The name change did not end the problem. Khadr claimed that following the initial dispute over the name, the JWU was subjected to a hostile campaign of slander, including charges of embezzlement. In addition, the JWU name change did not lead the GFJW to withdraw its suit. GFJW President Abu Ghazalah continued to contend that the JWU was not really a union and that the name change did not end the confusion. She also questioned the authority of the Ministry of the Interior in such matters. Nevertheless, the JWU ultimately won its case and opened a new headquarters only a few weeks later, inaugurated by the Minister of the Interior.

Also in the late spring of 1994, around the time that the name change problems had begun, the union submitted a change in its bylaws to the Ministry of the Interior. Like other institutions that are not political parties, it is governed by the Charitable Societies Law, which stipulates that these organizations not engage in political work. The text of the changed bylaws included a goal of "raising the awareness among Jordanian women of their role and rights in the social, economic, and political spheres." Objection was raised to the word "political" in this phrase. The JWU leadership had a long discussion with the governor of Amman over this word, trying to convince him that political rights were part of overall human rights and that this did not really aim at achieving political goals, but they were ultimately unsuccessful. [69]

By 1995, as the liberalization was clearly in retreat, it was reported that the final communiqué of the JWU congress in June surprised a number of attendees, who claimed that the positions adopted had been reformulated. The report contended that this had been done under threat of dissolution of the union by the Ministry of the Interior, whose representative was seated at the back of the conference hall.[70] It is also worth noting that the JWU had planned a program called "Beijing in Amman" to coincide with the UN conference. This was to have been a series of activities—lectures, presentations, and discussions—related to what was happening in China. They planned to include presentations of the Jordanian reports, discussions of the working plan submitted to the conference for approval by all women, as well as expositions of relevant UN conventions and presentations by delegations from other countries. The proposed three-day event, September 1–3, was canceled at the last minute. It was unclear whether it had been the victim of the general retreat in freedoms the country had been experiencing or whether the delegation in Beijing had brought pressure to bear at home so as not to lose the limelight.

Evaluation

The JWU's development illustrates a number of the trends noted in the previous examples. In the first place, it is clear that the liberalization opened the door to the energizing of this women's NGO concerned with national political and social issues affecting women. Second, some of the issues it has addressed—domestic violence, abortion, changing the nationality law—were generally not discussed openly before the liberalization. At the same time, however, the possibilities for expanding the union have been limited in part because of competition with the GFJW, but more recently owing to the role and activities of the princess.

CONCLUSIONS

Despite the negatives, there is no question that women's organizations have been able to take great advantage of the political opening. The reinvigoration of the JWU and its concentration on issues that the GFJW would not address is just one example. Its ability to survive the challenge from the GFJW, maintain a high profile, and keep some sensitive issues on the table for public discussion are others. There has also been the growing emphasis on women's involvement in local and national politics, and, no matter whence the initiative, Jordanian society is gradually becoming accustomed to seeing women holding political office. This may be most important at the municipal level, where close interaction with or observation of women candidates may lead to a change in attitudes that the presence of a female deputy in (too far away) Amman cannot.

Moreover, the increasing involvement of women in politics is by no means limited to non-Islamist women. The importance of the female vote to the successes of Islamist candidates in both the 1989 and 1993 elections is widely acknowledged and was noted in chapter 4. The story of the struggle for control of the GFJW was another important episode for Islamist women, even if it ultimately ended in failure. Subsequently, however, some Islamist women with an interest in politics have become members of the IAF, which at the end of 1995 transformed its women's committee into a more powerful "women's section." Two women sit on the IAF's *shura* council and 5 percent of the party membership is female, a percentage they seek to increase. Clear in their goals and well aware of the importance of the female vote to Islamist candidates, these women have also developed a pragmatic approach that allows for alliances with other women's organizations, particularly on issues related to protecting children and the family or on fighting against normalization with Israel, the major field of cooperation at the time of this writing. Depending upon the circumstances surrounding future elections, especially if a quota for women should be introduced into the electoral law, they see a strong possibility of fielding female candidates for parliament.[71]

Another remarkable development of this period is the number of workshops, seminars and conferences devoted either entirely or at least in part to women's issues. While many of these activities have been funded and/or encouraged by foreign NGOs or aid agencies, in many cases they have also been extensions of the activities of existing organizations. Media coverage of women's meetings, whether chaired by the princess or sponsored by one of the major women's organizations, has been prominent and has played a role in sensitizing people to women's concerns.

That said, it is true that the "women's movement" is fragmented. In 1993, Jordan had a few hundred women's associations (not all of which deal with women's issues, of course), five women's organizations that were part of or attached to political parties, and two women's unions. Those women's organizations attached to political parties, like their counterparts else-where, work on women's issues only to the extent that the parties take an interest in them. While some argue that this certainly weakens the "move-ment," it may be unavoidable. Others did not see the existence of a multi-plicity of organizations as in and of itself a weakness. Rather, the weakness derives from the fact that these organizations see themselves as rivals: bick-ering and maneuvering for position are the real problems.[72] There was an attempt in July 1993 to unify women's ranks, but it was called for and or-chestrated by women members of Rand. The five-hour session turned into a shouting match and a free for all.[73] In any case, this situation is not par-ticular to women. It also holds for political parties in general and is proba-bly not unusual after a long period of political repression.

In the realm of state action, a number of women have been appointed to high-level jobs since the liberalization began, but particularly as Beijing ap-proached. The king has appointed several women to the senate: Layla Sharaf (1989, 1993,1994) and Na'ila Rashdan (1993), Rima Khalaf and Subeiha Ma'ani (1997). Both Sharaf and Rashdan played important roles in legislative issues related to women. The prominence of women increased dramatically, however, after the 1993 elections. First, of course, Toujan Faisal was elected to parliament. Shortly thereafter, Prime Minister 'Abd al-Salam al-Majali appointed the first adviser to the prime minister on women's issues, Dr. Umayma Dahhan. In the meantime, Princess Basma had become involved in the National Strategy project, which gave her growing prominence.

Since then, in the cabinet formed in January 1995, Salwa Damen al-Masri was appointed Minister of Social Affairs and Rima Khalaf Minister of Trade and Industry. (She was transferred to Planning in a subsequent cabinet shuffle.) Khalaf's appointment was particularly significant because of the importance of the two ministries she has headed, but also because, unlike what is so frequently the case in Jordan, she was actually qualified professionally to head such ministries. Also notable was the fact that in his early 1996 speech before the parliament presenting his government's pro-gram, the prime minister designate, 'Abd al-Karim Kabariti, stressed that Jordan was bound by the articles of the National Strategy and the resolu-tions of the Beijing conference. This was a clear acknowledgement of the importance of women's issues, the first such reference to women ever by a prime minister.[74] In late May 1996, in another major departure, Kabariti appointed Jordan's first woman judge. It was therefore a disappointment, if not a surprise, that none of the seventeen female candidates in the No-vember 1997 elections was successful, including Toujan Faisal.

Of course, one may also quite rightly argue that the impact of such women is limited and that not all of them have gender concerns among their priorities. One could therefore conclude that these appointments are signs of tokenism rather than early indications of positive changes on the horizon, examples of an embryonic Hashemite state feminism. Indeed, when one considers the emerging role of the princess, such a conclusion may well seem more appropriate than the more optimistic one.

Some observers believe that a planned division of labor is at work, according to which each member of the royal family is made patron (and hence, supervisor or even controller) of a particular sector. In this way, as an increasingly superficial liberalization unfolds, control of various sectors is gradually being taken (back) by the state. The argument is that Princess Basma has been given the "women's movement" portfolio. In this role she must strike a balance between modernization and tradition acceptable to broader regime and societal concerns. One target of her efforts is external funders. Her role in appointing women to municipal council seats and the subsequent efforts of her women's committees to get women elected in July 1995 may be viewed in this context. Some contend that the regime had made a decision that women should be so appointed, since it is good for Jordan's image with the West and with donor agencies to increase women's visibility in public life. The fact that these efforts took place during the immediate prelude to Beijing should also not be forgotten. Some contend that her efforts are also a part of an ongoing process of regime legitimation, and use as an example the fact that meetings of the QAF women's committees have been turned into gatherings in support of the peace process.[75]

While the "division of labor" argument may be appealing in explaining developments in a country in which cooptation of opposition or civil society actors has long been a successful policy, there is also evidence to suggest that developments are not so clearly planned or controlled. A strong argument against such a contention is that policymaking in other areas manifests no such coherence. Moreover, the evidence could just as easily be marshaled to argue that what is going on has less to do with societal control and more to do with ambitions and rivalries among members of the royal family. One indication that the division of labor argument does not hold was an announcement by the NHF in March 1996 that it would hold leadership (political, economic, administrative) training sessions for women. This was really the first NHF (read Queen Noor) attempt to become involved in a realm outside social work, children, and economic development projects, which the "division of labor" argument contends are her "portfolios." Stories of rivalries among the upper tier of royal woman are common. And, the drive for media attention and societal role has only increased in recent years as the next generation of royals (men and women) has begun to come of age and seek the spotlight themselves.

In the women's sphere, the result has been a clear reassertion of state involvement (in the form of the princess) in the women's movement and an increasing marginalization of efforts that fall outside the official framework. This does not coincide neatly with the retreat of the liberalization; it seems to be triggered by the opportunities that Beijing preparations offered. In any case, whether part of a plan or the result of conjunctural factors, the princess' (and to a less prominent extent, the queen's) involvement in women's issues has also led to a growing monopolization of external donor funds by QAF and NHF. Some donors see the patronage of the princess or the queen and assume that by virtue of their positions their respective organizations will have access to the best of personnel, networks, cooperation, and the like, something which others argue is not necessarily the case.

However, even for those who want to work with other, smaller NGOs, there are problems. Despite their NGO designation, the QAF and NHF are, not surprisingly, closely tied to the government. Unlike other organizations with an NGO designation, these royal NGOs (or RONGOs— pun, not of my creation, intended) are not subject to the Laws of Charitable and Voluntary Societies (1966) as are other NGOs, and they cannot be interfered with in the same way (by having elections monitored or results overturned, for example).[76] They do not need permission from the Ministry of Social Development to hold fundraising events or to submit funding proposals to foreign donors (something all other NGOs are required to do), nor are they required to fulfill the same financial reporting requirements as the real NGOs. Moreover, the RONGOs receive money that is part of bilateral (government-to-government) aid packages; regular NGOs do not. In sum, they enjoy all the benefits attending their self-designated (and generally unquestioned) NGO status, while they are subject to none of the controls.

In addition, personnel rotate in and out of them from government ministries and often push potential funders or local NGO applicants in directions that benefit the RONGOs. This is not to say that no funds are available for smaller groups; however, they are increasingly unlikely to be able to compete for large grants. In addition, there have been cases of individual or small NGO efforts that have been quashed or "adopted" by a RONGO: a message was simply conveyed that the proposal would be carried out by the larger organization, and there is not much that can be done to counter a quasi-royal directive. Furthermore, even UN donors' local offices are not in a position to deny a request by a RONGO, since royalty have been known to take their case, always successfully, to UN headquarters and have a funding denial overturned.

On the other hand, while one may criticize the state (princess') increasing control over women's activities in the kingdom, if one takes the example of the preparations for Beijing, one may legitimately ask whether the NGOs in Jordan would have been able to come together and produce a report on their own. Whether the fact that they produced one orchestrated by the state authorities is better than not having produced one at all is another question. Most interviewees note both the positives and negatives of the princess' involvement. She has certainly raised the profile and drawn media and upper-level administration attention to issues that they could otherwise have ignored. She also has the influence to command resources that probably no other woman in the kingdom could. The drawback, however, is that an organization run by a member of the royal family cannot be an NGO in the true sense, if for no other reason than it must be bound by the policy(ies) of the monarchy. While Basma brings a generally enlightened outlook to many issues, her leadership of a national women's movement in the kingdom means that certain topics will not be broached.

Another negative is that the princess has increasingly centered control over women's issues in her QAF and its various extensions. Moreover, a patron-client relationship between the princess and the "activist" women has been established and so people have become afraid or unwilling to do anything without her. They or the princess also reportedly marginalize women who are seen as too strong, and hence, as threatening. Indeed, the departure of Umayma Dahhan from her post as the first adviser to a prime minister on women's affairs after only a few months on the job reportedly owed to pressures from just such women who felt she constituted a threat.[77] In another example, I was told that numerous women had ideas for post-Beijing follow-up. However, because the princess was in charge, no one dared to take the initiative.

Also, interestingly, just as some former male opposition figures appear to be falling over each other to line up for government appointments, so some of the long-time female political activists with an oppositional bent now seem intent upon working with the princess, whether out of conviction that this is the only way to get things done, or because, after having been outside the system so long, the attraction of being an insider is just too great. One of the most notable examples has been Toujan Faisal. Although she railed against various aspects of government policy, she seemed, nevertheless, to have become a favorite of the princess. JWU president (until spring 1997) Asma Khadr had also increasingly been involved in meetings organized by the princess and had served as a legal adviser.

What appears to have developed during the liberalization as well as during the period of "reclosing" is a gradual renegotiation of the boundaries for dealing with issues related to women. While in the early period there were several clashes and certainly some government embarrassment over the behavior of certain ministers and Islamist legislative initiatives related to sex segregation, since 1992 these clashes have all but disappeared. In the first place, the Islamists' presence in the 1993 parliament was only half that of the 1989 parliament. However, the regime (or its government) has also apparently conceded—or made clear its acceptance of Islamist influence in—certain areas. In its semi-official and official organizations dealing with women, the powers that be have been careful to stress that change will be introduced, but only if it is within the framework of society's religious and cultural traditions. The types of legal changes that the JNWF seeks, while significant, are quite modest (improved maternity leave policies are most prominent), and in the social, health, and educational realm, all amendments are presented as strengthening the family (the traditional family) as the basic unit of society. The marking of limits of the types of reforms sought is in effect being exchanged, it appears, for Islamists' refraining from pushing for parts of their program that would, in light of Jordan's modernist image, constitute an embarrassment. The resultant "reformist" program appeals to both the religiously conservative and the more secular, but nonetheless still socially conservative, camps. That includes most of the population.

Indeed, the vast majority of Jordanian women are concerned that issues related to women's rights and their role in society be addressed within a framework that upholds Islam and societal traditions. The percentage of women who feel comfortable with trying to move beyond that framework remains small. Activists who go to villages or refugee camps stress the need to base any discussion with women on Islamic principles; otherwise, women assume that what is being proposed contradicts religion, and will likely reject the ideas presented. This problem is, of course, not limited to Jordanian society. Political liberalization does not necessarily mean social liberalization. And the political liberalization in the kingdom has been in clear retreat since 1994 in any case. Therefore, changes or reforms that imply a restructuring of the existing social order are likely for the foreseeable future to continue to be vigorously resisted by most Jordanians— women and men alike.

PART **THREE**
Tunisia

CHAPTER **SEVEN**
Bourguiba and His Legacy

Tunisia provides two clear examples of political liberalization. The first opening began in the late 1970s and continued, in one form or another, until about 1983. The second began with the coup against Bourguiba in November 1987, and continued until the second half of 1989. The comparison of the two is particularly interesting: while both owed to economic difficulties and political malaise, the first was quite limited and managed, while the second involved a swift overturn of leadership. In both cases, women's organizations and concerns played key roles in the debates and struggles.

THE TUNISIAN POLITICAL SYSTEM

No discussion of modern Tunisia, and certainly none that is concerned with the state's relationship with women, can start without a discussion of the country's president for more than thirty years, Habib Bourguiba. The architect of the Tunisian state embarked after independence in 1956 upon a path of political and social engineering, a transformative project initiated from above that required a careful management of institutions to preempt opposition from below. Bourguiba put in place a vast, centralized state apparatus: a bureaucracy, a single party, and satellite organizations that were subordinate to it. Among such organizations were the UGTT (Union Générale de Travailleurs Tunisiens), the UNAT (Union Nationale d'Agricoles Tunisiens), the UNFT (Union Nationale des Femmes de Tunisie, later renamed the Union Nationale des Femmes Tunisiennes) and UTICA (Union Tunisienne de l'Industrie, du Commerce et de l'Artisanat). There was also a range of sports and charitable groups that did not come under such close control by the state, although most relied on the state for financial support, drew their leadership from the state party, the Parti Socialiste Destourien (PSD), and were subject to close scrutiny.[1]

Bourguiba eliminated progressively, then brutally, all formations that escaped his control. Arrests, interrogations, withdrawals of passports, all "aided" recalcitrants to see the error of their ways. Some were absorbed, others eradicated.[2] While the PSD and its subordinate structures increased their power over time, Bourguiba's most important initial move to consolidate his position had involved breaking the power of traditional centers of influence, particularly those who had supported his primary rivals for power. He neutralized the *fallaghas* (the former anti-French guerrillas), broke the partisans of his opponent and former party secretary-general Ben Youssef, and dethroned the bey.

A primary instrument used to effect change was legislation. Bourguiba modified laws regarding *habous* (religious endowments), reformed education, and unified the legal system so that all Tunisians, regardless of religion, were subject to the state courts. Perhaps best known among his legal innovations, however, was the Code du Statut Personnel (CSP), promulgated beginning in 1956. As in other Arab countries, this law governs issues related to the family: marriage, divorce, guardianship of children, and inheritance. With the CSP, Bourguiba took the bold step of, among other significant changes, abolishing polygamy and making divorce subject to judicial review. Through these policies and then through the formation and expansion of the PSD, Bourguiba in effect created a counter-elite comprising the emerging middle class and relying on at least passive support from women.[3]

The president was careful to locate these changes (through his discourse) within the framework, not of dismissing religion, but of a modernist reading of Islam. Indeed, the reforms contained in the CSP had first been suggested earlier in the century by *Islamist* reformers such as Egypt's Qasim Amin and Tunisia's own Tahar Haddad.[4] Bourguiba was also supported by the mufti at the time, who was willing to accept the modifications, particularly since they were presented as the product of *ijtihad* (independent interpretation), not a break with Islam.[5] Finally, of course, the euphoria that accompanied independence and Bourguiba's considerable personal prestige also played key roles in overcoming what might have otherwise been broader-based opposition to the CSP and the other reforms.

Subsequently, however, Bourguiba became well-known for his secularism and some of his more spectacular violations of Islamic practice (such as drink-

TUNISIA

ing a glass of orange juice on television in 1960 during Ramadan as a way of trying to do away with the fast) or suggesting that Islamic inheritance law should be changed. There is no question that he sought to undermine any independent base of Islamist or traditionalist opposition to his regime. This was in keeping with the general thrust of not eliminating, but rather bringing under state control, all forms of civil society organization. Bourguiba clearly wanted to undercut the religious establishment's ability to obstruct his developmentalist program, just as he sought to take revenge on those conservative factions that had opposed him at the time of independence. To this end, among other measures, Bourguiba replaced the independent Zitouna religious university with a faculty of theology integrated into the University of Tunis, where instructors were chosen from state institutions and nominated by the president. He also made members of the religious hierarchy state employees and ordered that the expenses for the upkeep of mosques and the salaries of preachers be drawn from the state budget.[6]

Nevertheless, while the champion of Tunisian independence may have himself been a secularist, his years in office in no way represent an unrelenting assault against Islam or religion. As noted above, he was always careful to position any suggested changes within a modernist reading of Islam. Indeed, even when he made his (very unsuccessful) anti-fasting appeal in 1960, he did so on the grounds that the country was involved in a *jihad* against poverty and misery and that fasting was not required of those engaged in *jihad*. This is not to minimize the importance of the secularist tradition that Bourguiba engendered in Tunisian society, which continues to be quite deep, at least among the now older generation. It is simply to point out that the record is not without ambiguity on the question of religion.

For example, in 1970, Bourguiba's government, which was regularly cursed by *ulama* of the Arab world for its reformism, sponsored the creation of the Association for Preserving the Qur'an (Association pour la Sauvegarde du Coran) which, at its first congress in 1971, established the objectives of restoring religious practice and promoting the authentic values of Islam. It quickly became a training ground for Islamists. In 1973, the first Tunisian *salon du livre*, organized by the authorities, assisted in distributing the writings of the Egyptian Muslim Brothers, because they were considered antidotes to Marxist literature.[7] Out of these groupings eventually emerged what came to be known as the MTI, Mouvance de la tendance islamique (Islamic Tendency Movement). It gradually began to attract members and by 1979 organized a founding congress to bring together a group of study circles into a more coherent organization.[8] Perhaps the clearest example of the shifting line of the Bourguiba regime vis-à-vis Islamist elements is that of the policies pursued by the moderately liberalizing government of Prime Minister Muhammad Mzali (1980–86). As Minister of Education from 1969 to 1980 almost without interruption, Mzali not only oversaw the Arabization of the teaching of philosophy but also replaced the existing program with a curriculum of Islamic thought from which were excluded all western thinkers associated with the left. It was during Mzali's prime ministership that the MTI came to constitute a major oppositional force, and the prime minister apparently sought to win over some religious conservatives through initiating a number of policies viewed as sympathetic to Islam.

Although women and their "liberation" were the primary target of Islamist and conservative ire over the years, ironically, Bourguiba's program for women was not one that sought fundamentally to undermine traditional family relations. Bourguiba promoted women's equal access to education and to contraception, but he also made clear on a number of occasions that Tunisia's path was not to lead to a westernization of Tunisian women. Indeed, the issuance of the CSP had less (if anything) to do with feminism than with the president's desire to eliminate traditions and practices that he felt obstructed his modernizing program. In other words, Tunisian women were to be educated and capable of controlling their family size but not as part of a project that would undermine their primary role in the home as homemakers and mothers. None of Bourguiba's colleagues remembers that he was particularly concerned with the "women question" before the promulgation of the code.[9] In fact, the president's statements on the role of the liberation of Tunisian women do not represent a coherent single line of argument. What is clear is that he did not envision a Tunisia in which women themselves would make demands for further changes not first proposed by the president. At all times Bourguiba saw himself and himself alone as the liberator of Tunisian women, as the initiator of any and all projects in that domain. If women made any additional demands, they were viewed as ungrateful.[10]

Despite the wavering between or mixing of modernist and conservative elements in Bourguiba's program, religious conservatives viewed him as incorrigibly secularist and saw the CSP not only as the centerpiece of the president's modernization program but also as the symbol of a broader attack against Islam. Islamic family law—which is clear on the division of male and female roles and the centrality of the family—is viewed as the last bastion of *shari'a* in the modern Arab state. Thus, for Islamists, conceding changes in this law involves a weakening of control of women through the family, the central unit in the construction of Islamist society, as well as an assault on the only area of law in which Islamic precepts (if mixed with local custom) continue to hold sway. As a result, in Tunisia, when Islamist elements began to flex their muscle, they aimed first at the CSP. And, although not all non-Islamist men were pleased or satisfied with the rights Bourguiba had given Tunisian women, any questioning of the CSP by the Islamists was understood, by extension, to mean a threat to the broader secularism of Tunisian society. Thus, during periods of liberalization, when the Islamists enjoyed somewhat greater freedom of expression, issues related to women became the lightening rod in attacks against and defenses of laicism in general. This made women the first natural line of defense as well as the first likely victims in any challenge to the state by the Islamists.

THE TUNISIAN ECONOMY

Following independence Tunisia followed an essentially laissez-faire economic policy; however, in 1961, faced with a deteriorating economic situation, the country turned in the direction of a planned economy, with strict import substitution industrialization controls to protect internal markets, a fixed exchange rate and currency regulation. This approach ultimately proved a failure, as it did in many parts of the third world, as inefficiency and corruption plagued state-owned enterprises, and attempts to collectivize the rural areas met with strong peasant resistance. In 1969 the architect of the socialist project, Ahmed Ben Salah, was discredited and Tunisia turned back to a more free-market approach.

The early years of the *infitah*, or economic opening, witnessed tremendous growth. The middle classes in particular, which experienced a notable development under twenty years of Bourguiba's rule, emerged as the base of the regime.[11] Nonetheless, the gap between rich and poor increased as well, and the expansion of the export sector made the country more vulnerable to developments in the international economy. Tunisia found itself in particular jeopardy as the establishment of tariff barriers by its EU partners threatened its interaction with its primary markets. By the early 1980s the boom had ended. The European market had become more and more difficult to penetrate, oil prices fell, drought destroyed harvests, remittances dropped, and employment overseas through migration was no longer able to absorb the excess supply of labor.[12] The country had also been rocked by strikes and violence in 1978 triggered by deteriorating economic conditions. Failure to address the root problems led to further and more extensive rioting and violence in December 1983–January 1984.

By 1986, the economy was in crisis and the government was forced to seek IMF assistance. As a result of a number of factors, including fortuitous ones such as the end of the drought, as well as careful attention to the economy by Bourguiba's successor, Ben 'Ali, the country was able to overcome the crisis and return to a path of economic growth of a sort that once again served to solidify middle-class support for the regime. Tunisia's successes in implementing structural adjustment and in further liberalizing the economy have regularly led international financial institutions to point to it as a model for others to emulate.

THE ROLE OF EXTERNAL ACTORS

In its immediate neighborhood, Tunisia's primary external concerns are its two large and oil/gas wealthy neighbors, Libya and Algeria. Although during the Cold War Tunisia maintained a nonaligned status, its relatively more pro-Western position, combined with its long-standing ties with France, led to periodic ideological, political, territorial, and economic disputes with its neighbors. Its geographic location and alignment posture have traditionally led it to seek good relations with Morocco as a way of balancing the sometimes threatening power of Algiers or Tripoli. Instances of attempts by the Algerian and Libyan regimes to influence or interfere in domestic Tunisian politics are numerous, most notably the Libyan involvement in the Gafsa affair (a 1980 mutiny), and the expulsion of Tunisian workers from Libya in 1985. In the case of Algeria, in early 1988, an FLN (Front de Libération Nationale, the state party in Algeria) representative at the Rassemblement Constitutionnel Démocratique (RCD, the reformed PSD) convention warned Tunisia against a political opening that would include the legalization of the MTI,[13] presumably because such a change could have affected the political game inside Algeria. Ironically, the development and activism of the Front Islamique du Salut (FIS) in Algeria, and the political instability that accompanied its rise, ultimately gave the Tunisian regime an additional reason to clamp down on its own Islamists. The Tunisian regime has continued to cite civil strife in Algeria as an example of what could happen were Ben 'Ali not firm and vigilant in dealing with the Islamists at home.

Outside of its immediate neighborhood, but still within the Arab arena, Tunisia's relations with the Arab Gulf states, especially Saudi Arabia and Kuwait, should be mentioned. Prior to the 1990 Gulf crisis, Tunisia's most important aid donor was Saudi Arabia: it had investments of $275 million, was financing eight projects, and had signed fifteen loan agreements. Kuwaiti aid came next.[14] The negative side effect of these relationships was the greater influence the aid and investment gave these states in Tunisian affairs, both internal and external. While the impact was often subtle, the Arabization of curriculum under Mzali in the 1980s, the increasing tolerance of the regime for the distribution of religious tracts and of an incipient Islamist movement—all of which have had a profound impact on domestic politics—are attributed by some analysts to the relationship between Tunisia and these Gulf states.

Despite the importance to Tunisia of its Arab world ties, over the years, France, the U.S., and the European community have been the country's most important external partners. The U.S. has played an important post-independence role, in no small measure balancing the economic weight of France and in providing military equipment. However, Europe is much closer geographically, and a major theme of Ben 'Ali's foreign policy discourse and activity has been Tunisia's role in the Mediterranean basin. By stressing Tunisia's belonging, not to the Arab world or to Africa, but to the Mediterranean, Ben 'Ali promotes a sense of outwardlookingness.[15] This theme is further reinforced by the emphasis on the country's involvement through numerous conferences and meetings in what is characterized as a dialogue between civilizations in contrast to the extremism or *obscurantisme*—which means, in the North African context, fundamentalism—that has plagued Algeria but that Tunisia has, by implication, managed to tame.

Tunisia's adherence to IMF dictates in reforming the economy has also contributed to the external perception of the country as friendly to investment and serious about economic development. In a November 1995 visit to Tunisia, IMF president Michel Camdessus praised the country for its success with structural adjustment and called it a model of development. Such positive evaluations from powerful international financial institutions are critical to Tunisia's maintaining an image of a country worthy of the attention of international investors. There is no question that Tunisia has been successful in implementing critical economic reforms since 1986, especially since Ben 'Ali came to power. Nonetheless, such high praise from the IMF helps blunt the impact of the reports of Amnesty International (one of which was released only a few weeks before the Camdessus panegyric), which have clearly documented the dark side of the regime's recent development record.

All of these factors—the small size and hence regional vulnerability of Tunisia, its historic and deep ties with Europe and with France in particular, its desire to cultivate an image of tolerance and forwardlookingness, and its need to balance the broader Arab environment—will, in the course of the coming chapters, be shown to have a direct or indirect impact on the course of the liberalization process and its implications for relations between the state and women.

THE LIBERALIZATION STORY ACT I:
THE FIRST OPENING

The first, brief opening of the Tunisian political system actually came in 1970, and it is to this period that one must look for the roots of the opening later in the decade. Primary among the causes of the opening was the failure of the regime's economic policy of collectivism and cooperatives. Perhaps because of the discrediting of the regime that this implied, during this period Bourguiba experienced his first health crisis, apparently depression, and he left for Paris in November 1969 for treatment. The president's seven-month absence somewhat relaxed the grip of the state, and Tunisian society tasted a bit of freedom. After his return, he gave a speech in which he gave the green light to democratization and then assembled a commission to reform the constitution.[16] In these circumstances, the liberal wing of the PSD attempted to press for a further opening of the political system. A war of political factions ensued, with the president's wife, Wasila, taking the part of the liberals in opposition to the newly appointed party loyalist and more hardline prime minister Hedi Nouira.[17] While at first Bourguiba seemed responsive, he subsequently mapped out a strategy to undermine those pushing for a greater opening. Following some "promising debate" at the party congress of 1971, he expelled the leaders of this wing of the party and then proceeded over the next three years to reassert presidential control. This phase was capped by the party's proclamation of him as President for Life in 1975.[18]

During the course of the factional infighting, two new centers of power emerged. The first was Nouira, who continued to rely on the hardline wing of the PSD and managed to bury the projects for constitutional reform proposed by the liberals. The other center was the "palace," i.e., the president's wife and her entourage. Wasila was, by all accounts, a formidable woman and politician who acquired increasing power due to her husband's ill health, his devotion to her, and her own considerable skills. The president's illness in 1969–70 had forced Tunisians to think for the first time of what the post-Bourguiba era might look like. With hindsight it seems at very least ironic that, as early as 1970, power jockeying was taking place on the basis of concern over the "imminent" demise of a man who at this writing (1997), was still alive, if not lucid. However, at the time, the president was 68 years old, and the serious nature of this as well as a series of subsequent crises forced considerations of who might constitute a successor. The maneuvering and intrigues associated with the successor struggle explain a great deal of the economic and political context that led to the liberalization in the late 1970s as well as its contours and characteristics: the major political actors were more absorbed in playing the politics of the succession game than in seriously addressing the country's socioeconomic and political problems.

As was noted above, by the late 1970s the economy was encountering increasing problems, including the impact of domestic regionalism—the preeminence of the coast and the capital over the south—growing unemployment, and stagnation in the agricultural sector. During this period of growing discontent, rather than serving to channel popular feeling, "the PSD continued to become more politically and ideologically monolithic while losing much of its early effectiveness as a vehicle of mass mobilization."[19] As a result, two alternative vehicles emerged to break the blockage.

The first was the UGTT. The UGTT's historic legitimacy from its participation in the independence movement and the broad base of popular support it enjoyed afforded it some protection against state repression, thus leading it to become one of the few institutions from which or in which the regime could be challenged.[20] At the same time, Nouira had a different view of the role of the UGTT than his predecessor. Unlike Ben Salah, whose socialist project had implied a "rigid conception of national unity," Nouira acknowledged the existence of a diversity of interests in Tunisian society. "Not class conflict, but social partners in dialogue was the new model of state-society relations."[21] Hence, part of Nouira's strategy was, within limits, to revive the UGTT.

The second vehicle was the Islamists. It was during this period that what would eventually be formalized (although not legalized) as the MTI began to develop. Its support base was the traditional religious elite, the shaykhs and former students of the Zitouna who found themselves marginalized by the new elite that had been trained in a different curriculum in both European and Tunisian schools. In the 1970s, young activists joined the ranks of this incipient movement as Islam began to emerge as a mobilizing force throughout the region. The would-be activists were encouraged, if not supported, by government policies that targeted what was viewed as the more dangerous left. A journal, *Ma'arifah*, was established, and circles for religious discussion and lessons emerged, first at mosques, then in faculties of theology and from there into the university more broadly.[22] The real energizing force, however, did not come until 1979, with the Iranian revolution.

Some evidence of a liberalizing intent may be detected as early as May 1977, when the Minister of the Interior, Tahar Belkhodja, Wasila's candidate for successor to Nouira, allowed the licensing of the Ligue Tunisienne des Droits de l'Homme (LTDH). This constituted the first break with the state's monopoly on institutions with any kind of political agenda. Belkhodja's liberalism was at least in part a strategy aimed at distinguishing himself and his policies from those of Nouira. A month later, the National Council on Public Liberties was launched following a call from 520 intellectuals and professionals asking the president to allow the emergence of a pluralist democracy.[23]

In this atmosphere, a controversy arose over the growing independence of the UGTT, with Belkhodja pushing for a softer government line on the union and others pressuring Nouira to crack down. The regime first used its traditional arsenal to bring the UGTT into line ("moral suasion, manipulation of elite politicians, appeal to Destourian members of the UGTT").[24] However, when this did not work, following the UGTT general strike in January 1978, Bourguiba called in the army and more direct and bloody measures were used, leaving hundreds dead and wounded.

The country was shocked by the events of January 1978, and their impact on the public at large and the leadership should not be underestimated, for they were seen as resulting from the stagnation of the political system. The most immediate political fallout from the violence was that Wasila's liberals were forced out (Belkhodja was dismissed), although Nouira began to talk about opening up the party to a more diverse range of views through an internal reorganization of the PSD. In tandem, national committees and committees of reflection were to be created to be open to all citizens (not just PSD members), in order to prepare for the next party congress. In the event, the party itself balked, and it became clear that any opening would be limited to a kind of internal democratization: in the 1979 elections, the PSD put up multiple candidates rather than the traditional one for each parliamentary seat.

However, Nouira was on his way out. Bourguiba was unhappy with the way the 1979 party congress, which had seriously discussed the possibility of the party's asserting greater autonomy from the state,[25] was conducted, and the president responded by dismissing three of the prime minister's top supporters. Then came the January 1980 mutiny: a small group of Tunisians trained in Libya took control of the mining town of Gafsa, located in an area largely neglected by the central government. The mutiny, which lasted several days, highlighted the discontent of ignored regions as well as the small country's vulnerability to designs by its larger neighbors. Nouira's health failed shortly thereafter, and in April 1980 Bourguiba chose a new prime minister, Muhammad Mzali, the former minister of education.

Mzali, a long-time party loyalist, was nonetheless an unexpected choice.[26] Like many upper-level Tunisian politicians, he was without a personal constituency or base of support—other than the president. In his first years, he seemed to have no ambitions beyond the prime ministership, although the possibility of his succeeding Bourguiba existed from the very beginning. His major competitor, not surprisingly, was the president's wife. On the question of liberalizing the political system, Wasila and Mzali were in accord. However, the president's wife made clear in a July 28, 1982 interview with *Jeune Afrique* that, contrary to her husband's expressed will—formalized by constitutional amendment in 1976—that his successor be the serving prime minister at the time of his passing, she favored the popular election of a successor. Her argument was that none of the potential successors could command the respect that her husband did without the further legitimation of having won an election. She further clarified that she did not favor Mzali for the job, probably thinking that she could influence elections to produce an outcome more to her liking.[27]

For Mzali, on the other hand, the liberalization was a means of building a record and consolidating power. He began his liberalizing program by bringing into his cabinet a member of the PSD offshoot Mouvement des Démocrates Socialistes (MDS) and several former ministers who had lost their positions in 1977 for opposing the government's hard line against labor.[28] Indeed, it was the UGTT that Mzali first targeted as a possible reserve of support. Some have argued that in so doing he also sought to counter the rising power of the Islamists following the Iranian revolution. Whatever the case, with the PSD largely devoid of energy, Mzali's courting of the UGTT made perfect sense.

At the party congress of 1981 Bourguiba publicly sanctioned the principle of pluralism as long as any new organization worked for the higher good of the country, and rejected fanaticism and violence. This opened the way for the operation of a number of women's groups and for a *limited* experiment in multi-partyism.[29] Outside the realm of political parties, the expansion of civil society continued to be constrained by the requirement that new associations obtain permits from the authorities, and they were rarely forthcoming. In the meantime, as part of his policy of giving the UGTT a greater role by making it the privileged interlocutor of the state, the prime minister began working on concluding an electoral alliance with it. The establishment of a National Front list of candidates from both the PSD and the UGTT was intended both to make the UGTT more of a partner with the government as well as implicate it in government policies. (In fact, the National Front was presented as a creation of the PSD and the UGTT in which the UTICA, UNAT, and UNFT also participated). Thus, contradictory processes or designs were at work: on the one hand Mzali allowed the UGTT to assert its autonomy or independence; yet, immediately thereafter, he courted it as an electoral partner. This not only displeased some UGTT members, who saw in it a betrayal of the hard won autonomy; the newly recognized opposition parties also took exception, for they understood that such an alliance further marginalized their voices.[30]

The UGTT did manage to secure 27 seats in the 1981 elections, but the voting was marred by charges of massive fraud. None of the opposition parties managed to secure the 5 percent of the vote that Bourguiba had set as a requirement for subsequent legalization. The elections were therefore an embarrassment for Mzali, but represented the height of Wasila's power.

Indeed, one source attributed the massive fraud to her directives. Having ensured that there would be no major changes in government as a result of the elections, she was in a position to begin to work with Mzali, or at least not at cross-purposes. This continued until the 1983 elections, by which time Mzali had increased his strength and began to chafe under Wasila's influence and interference.[31]

In the meantime, the Islamists were on the rise. Mzali's position on them and their movement had contradictory elements. On the one hand, as suggested above, it seems that one of Mzali's reasons for courting the UGTT and permitting the open operation of parties other than the PSD derived from a desire to counter the Islamists. Indeed, at one point, Mzali called on all democrats to put aside their differences and form a bloc against intolerance. At the same time, the government in effect tried to occupy the Islamists' space. For example, during Ramadan in 1981, the Minister of the Interior ordered restaurants closed. (Two days later, upon hearing about the order, a furious Bourguiba had the directive rescinded.)[32] Likewise, the MTI's request that it be recognized as a legal political party in 1981 was denied, yet at the same time the state built mosques and established prayer areas in ministries and at the university.[33] The most likely explanation of Mzali's policy appears to be that in order not to allow growing traditionalist sentiment to be exploited solely by the Islamists, he directed certain policies that, while apparently in contradiction to the state's secular image, made the state, or Mzali himself, a kind of competitor with Islamists for the sympathies of traditionalists.

Thus, while the broader socioeconomic crisis had triggered the riots of 1978, the limited political opening of the late 1970s-early 1980s cannot be understood unless one also takes into account the competition within the political class or ruling circles. Liberalization in this case was not so much a survival strategy of the regime as a strategy advocated by certain key political actors intended to reinforce their power and ensure their political future within the existing constellation of forces. Both Wasila and Mzali played liberalization cards to this end. It is for that reason—the liberalization's lack of strong connection to social and political forces in the country and its use as a tactic by individuals, not a commitment by a coherent group—that its boundaries kept shifting.

THE RETREAT OF THE OPENING AND BOURGUIBA'S LAST YEARS

The legalization of the MDS and Mouvement de l' Unité Populaire (MUP) II and the subsequent elections of 1983, to which there was overwhelming, positive popular response, [34] were in fact the high point of Mzali's power and of the opening. Feeling his power in the period leading up to the elections, the prime minister, under the guise of homogeneity and solidarity in the government, began increasingly to eliminate those who could cause problems and replace them with friends and relatives.[35] In general, however, the country continued to drift politically. Frustration was widespread, and Mzali's policy of surrounding himself with supporters led to his increasing isolation.[36] There is no clearer indication of the country's economic and political problems and of the degree to which the prime minister was out of touch than the riots of December 1983–January 1984 after the long-postponed announcement of an increase in bread prices. Rioting broke out in the hinterland (Kasserine) and then spread, first throughout the traditionally marginalized areas, but ultimately to all the major cities. This was not a repetition of the strikes turned violent of January 1978, but something more grave and far-reaching. It brought to an end Mzali's courting of the UGTT, just as it marked the beginning of the end of the period of limited liberalization.

Some 150 people were killed and hundreds more wounded in the violence. In response, Bourguiba rolled back the price increases and the unrest ended, but a new period of repression followed. Numerous MTI members were arrested and MDS meetings were interrupted. The retreat in freedoms also extended to written expression as numerous major magazines—*Jeune Afrique, Réalités, Le Maghreb, al-Mustaqbal*—were closed or banned for extended periods. A number of changes in government structure were also introduced. First, there was a reorganization of the Ministry of the Interior. There were also changes of personnel in the governorates, the creation of four new municipalities, and the reform of existing communal structures. In addition, Mzali had sought broad ministerial changes, but Bourguiba permitted only limited modifications. Following another presidential heart attack in November 1984, the succession issue was reopened,[37] Bourguiba's continuing statements reconfirming Mzali as heir apparent notwithstanding.[38]

Mzali realized his attempt to build a power base with the UGTT had failed, and the attempt to coopt the union was abandoned in favor of a more aggressive policy of undermining UGTT power. On October 30, 1985 the UGTT was finally closed and by the end of the year a number of its leaders had been arrested. On the other hand, Mzali seems not to have abandoned the Islamists quite so quickly, as the summer of 1985 saw the MTI dare openly to call into question some aspects of the CSP. The most likely source of opposition to such a call, the UNFT, was silent in response. Perhaps the silence owed to the fact that it was Mzali's wife, Fathia, who headed the women's organization (and had been at the helm since 1973). In any case, Mzali's record with the Islamists remains controversial. There are those who argue that he saw the Islamists as a potential base of support as his attempts to consolidate the backing of the UGTT failed.[39] He did release MTI leaders Mourou and Ghannouchi in August 1984, thus leading to their de facto recognition.[40] MTI representatives were even received by the prime minister following the autumn 1985 Israeli raid on the PLO headquarters at Hammam al-Shatt. Observers have also charged Mzali with having friendly relations or at least periodic meetings with some Islamist groups, a matter that Bourguiba sought details and explanation of in June 1986, in one of his last meetings with Mzali before his dismissal. Since his fall from grace there have also been charges that he used Ministry of Culture funds to print and distribute Islamist literature, and that small, inexpensive books about various aspects of Islam seemed to find their way into the country in great numbers beginning in 1985.[41]

Mzali's approach to the Islamists may simply have derived from a belief that it was wiser to keep them above ground, where they could be more easily monitored, or that he could coopt substantial numbers by letting them into the game in order to defuse their power (not unlike the policy Ben 'Ali appears to have initiated in the immediate wake of November 7, 1987). Perhaps in response, the MTI did proclaim its attachment to democratic values, identified itself as a political not a religious movement, expressed a willingness to participate in legislative elections, and was represented in and defended by the LTDH.[42] That said, the MTI was never legalized under Mzali, but that may have been due more to the presence of Bourguiba than Mzali's policy preference. In any case, there seems to be little question that Mzali was not a man of particularly strong political convictions. The criticism of the secularists and of many women is that by treating with the Islamists, he encouraged them and provided a context in which the MTI's Mourou could openly call into question the CSP. Following Mzali's dismissal, charges of corruption of various sorts were leveled and he was villainized: even at the time of this research, nearly ten years after he left office, it was clear from my interview experiences that the record of Muhammad and Fathia Mzali remains sensitive and controversial.

In any event by early 1986, Bourguiba seems to have decided that he had had enough of the machinations of the power contenders. Although he reaffirmed his confidence in Mzali at the party congress in spring 1986, rumors began to fly that the prime minister's days were numbered. The first sign that the end was near was Bourguiba's June 23, 1986 decision to close the Ministry of the Family and the Promotion of Women, which had been established and entrusted to Fathia Mzali in November 1983. Only two weeks later, on July 8, the president replaced Mzali with Rachid Sfar, a man not previously discussed as a possible presidential successor. All that remained was for Bourguiba to divorce Wasila, from whom he had been separated since early in the year. Within a few weeks, what had seemed like a closed book on the succession question was reopened with a vengeance. The sense of political drift, but also of anxiety regarding when and how the aging president would finally exit the scene, continued to grow.

LE CHANGEMENT/AL-TAHAWWUL

The contest between Bourguiba and the Islamists became increasingly intractable. Islamist journals were closed, and the MTI leadership arrested and interrogated.[43] Zayn al-'Abdine Ben 'Ali's move against Bourguiba on November 7, 1987, the *changement* or *tahawwul*, as it is called, is generally attributed to the immediate possibility of an Islamist move against the state. A number of Islamists had been convicted of participation in a series of terrorist attacks in July and August and had received what Bourguiba viewed as lenient sentences. Ben 'Ali apparently feared that had the sentences been overturned and the Islamists executed as the president wanted, they would have been viewed as martyrs and might have served to mobilize some of the population against the state. While this may have been the proximate trigger, the state of the economy and the growing political crisis associated with Bourguiba's increasingly unpredictable and irrational style form the broader backdrop.

When thinking about the transition from Bourguiba to Ben 'Ali, it is important to keep in mind that Ben 'Ali had served as director of military security, minister of the interior, and prime minister, assuming the last post only a month before deposing Bourguiba. So it was not apparent that he would have the will or the power to change the system.[44] What was clear was that he needed to consolidate his own position. This required dealing with three main forces: the party (which he had joined only in 1984 and for many members of whose old guard he must have appeared potentially threatening); the Islamists; and the secular opposition. His strategy appears to have been first to defuse the Islamist challenge and to offer hope to the secular opposition as he set to work on a process of revival and renewal in the party. For that he needed a period of relative social calm.

Ben 'Ali took a number of steps immediately following the November 7 removal of Bourguiba which seemed to promise a new beginning for politics in Tunisia and which bought him time with both the Islamist and secular opposition. He abolished the presidency for life and limited the president's tenure to three, five-year terms. Political prisoners began to be released and some exiled politicians began to return home. The state allowed several opposition newspapers to resume publication and the official media began to report opposition party activities. The government also initiated contacts with the opposition parties regarding a new political parties law.

At the same time, Ben 'Ali initiated an Islamization of official discourse. He condemned the extent of his predecessor's secularism and argued that the free expression of religious faith had been compromised. He also began to stress the government's role as defender of Islam and morality. The national radio and television began broadcasting the five daily prayers, the Zitouna University's autonomy was restored, and the president and his entourage began to take advantage of every occasion to demonstrate their attachment to Islam by appearing at mosques on Fridays and days of celebrations, and by making the pilgrimage to Mecca.[45]

Perhaps Ben 'Ali believed he could truly coopt all religious elements by such gestures. More likely, he may have thought that he could coopt at least enough of the pious elements to undermine the Islamists, a repetition of Mzali's early policy toward them. Given the outpouring of apparent support for the Islamist program, it seems likely that he was also trying to determine the relative balance of forces, coopting where possible as he gradually consolidated his position.

Having made initial conciliatory gestures to both Islamists and secularists, Ben 'Ali moved to push through changes in the PSD, where support for his program of reconciliation and renewal was by no means universal. For example in January 1988, the occasion of partial legislative elections triggered demonstrations in which cries of "Long live Bourguiba, down with democracy," could be heard, attributed to some PSD barons who were opposed to the country's new direction. The central committee of the party met in late February, chose a new name, the Rassemblement Constitutionnel Démocratique (RCD), and embarked on a path of renewal. The president took charge of the RCD (a move denounced by the opposition parties) and then proceeded to choose 122 of 200 members of the RCD Central Committee and reduce the number of political bureau members from fifteen to six. In so doing he purged some of the old guard who were staunch defenders of the *ancien régime*.[46] The merging of party and government was a warning of things to come.

In early 1988, following the beginning of the new Islamization of state discourse, a polemical exchange began between Islamists and secularists. The Islamists called for an amendment to the constitution stating that Islam was the state religion. Secularists responded by launching their own petition expressing concerns about making any further concessions to the Islamists. The Islamists then denounced the separation of mosque and state.[47] In the midst of the exchange, in March 1988, the president made his first clear statement on the CSP, the symbol of secularism. On this issue, he insisted, there would be no retreat; however, his position was "the code, but nothing but the code," meaning that women could also expect no further reforms.

Shortly thereafter, a new Political Party Law was announced permitting the establishment of new opposition parties as long as they were not founded on the basis of language, race, ethnicity, or religion. This, of course, continued to exclude the MTI. However, three new parties were founded: the Social Party for Progress (PSP), the Progressive Socialist Assembly (RSP), and the Unitary Democratic Union (UDU). A new electoral code gave opposition parties a role in the distribution and counting of electoral ballots, while financial subsidies were provided to help defray the costs of campaigns. [48]

In the fall of 1988, Ben 'Ali opened a dialogue with opposition politicians, as well as leaders of the main national organizations (labor, employers, farmers, women's unions), with the goal of producing a national pact. While guaranteeing basic freedoms and the right to form political parties, the final document emphasized the consensual nature of Tunisian politics and the country's Arabo-Islamic identity. This last aspect, Ben 'Ali's apparent reaching out to Islamists, certainly altered MTI members' perception of the government.[49] The pact was finally signed on the first anniversary of the *changement* by members of the country's six legal political parties, trade unions, a representative of the still unrecognized MTI, and, of course, the president.

The MTI was, at least officially, doing everything right to render it eligible for legalization, and there had been a number of positive signs from the government (although the official press multiplied its attacks against the Islamists).[50] However, each time the MTI's leaders sought to take part in negotiations with the government aimed at further recognition, new barriers were raised. The state had first demanded that the MTI recognize the validity of the democratic and pluralist game, as well as the specificity of the Tunisian experience, including the CSP. The MTI had accepted these conditions and signed on to the National Pact. They then changed the name of their organization to al-Nahdah to make it more acceptable and in February 1989 applied for a license. During the next four months, al-Nahdah made many positive statements about the regime in hopes of, in addition to recognition, securing the release of its members still in prison, the reinstatement of others in their jobs, approval for the publication of an Islamic newspaper, and the cancellation of the law banning the veil in schools, universities, and government offices.[51]

The state's temporizing with the Islamists should perhaps have been read as an omen for the political system more broadly. The form of the new liberalization was only briefly matched by content, as most observers seem to agree that by the time of the parliamentary elections of April 1989, and certainly by the beginning of 1990, significant political indicators pointed in the direction of a renewed authoritarian swing. Freedom of expression and association were gradually constricted, and members of legal political parties—loyal opposition by most definitions—were increasingly harassed. Accusations of maltreatment and torture, not to mention death while in custody, were widely reported.[52] Just as serious for the long term was that, contrary to the Bourguibist tradition of keeping the military out of politics, Ben 'Ali was gradually insinuating the army into positions of civilian power.[53]

It is worth considering how developments in Algeria may have influenced the Tunisian leadership's approach toward the MTI/al-Nahdah. It was noted above that the FLN representative to the PSD/RCD conference in February 1988 had warned the Tunisians against a political opening that would go beyond the framework of the RCD.[54] However, riots rocked Algeria later that year, and the FLN was forced to initiate its own political opening. Algerian Islamists began to flex their muscle in February 1989, and strikes and demonstrations continued through the spring. The FIS and other parties demanded legalization in the summer, and the Islamist party was finally legalized on September 12. In late fall, the strikes and demonstrations increased as did Islamist violence against women. The effect that this had on Tunisian decisionmakers' thinking is not clear; however, a year later they did deliberately decide to schedule their municipal elections several days ahead of the Algerian municipal elections so as to avoid a spillover effect.

In the meantime, the advance of al-Nahdah, and the government's apparent early willingness to deal with it, had put Tunisian women on the defensive. While the president's March 1988 speech confirming the preservation of the CSP was somewhat reassuring, concerned women did not feel they could be complacent. For example, on April 8, 1988, at an LTDH meeting on "Femme et la Société," the question and answer period deteriorated into a session in which Islamist youth heckled the presenters, until one of them, a lawyer who happened to be four months pregnant, was physically attacked and beaten by one of the attendees who called the woman a heretic as he assaulted her. The fact that the MTI denounced the attack in a communique was of little comfort to women who saw government tolerance for Islamist discourse as creating an environment that encouraged violence against women. Moreover, despite their adherence to the National Pact, during the 1989 electoral campaign some members of al-Nahdah attacked Tunisia's secularism as well as the CSP on the issues of divorce and polygamy. The fact that their meetings attracted large and youthful crowds around the country worried secularist women and men.[55]

Even some members of the government took stands during this period that indicated, if not a sympathy for the Islamists, a clear antagonism toward women. The most notable example occurred during the December 1989 parliamentary discussions of the 1990 budget. During the discussion of the budget for the Ministry of Justice, Deputy Hamza Sa'id called into question Tunisia's laws on polygamy and adoption (the latter of which is permitted in Tunisia but effectively forbidden in Islam), making clear his antagonism toward women. During the discussion of the Ministry of Higher Education's budget, some deputies contended that the increasing feminization of the educational structure was significantly hurting standards. It was suggested that women's work in education should be regulated by law and that women should be forbidden to give birth during the academic year. Another deputy, 'Abd al-Rahman Khalif stated in a newspaper interview that girls should play sports only with other females, thus making clear his preference for sex segregation.[56]

Yet, by this time, the tide had already begun to turn. The 1989 elections, which were legislative and presidential, were a great shock and revelation. In the first place, Ben 'Ali, the only candidate for president, presented himself as the guarantor of both religion and modernity. The powerful electoral machine of the PSD turned RCD, combined with the state's monopoly of information and the meager resources of the opposition parties, allowed the RCD to win all the seats. At the same time, the opposition bitterly complained of electoral abuses. Only al-Nahdah, which had been forced to run its candidates as independents, made a respectable showing, taking as much as 30 percent of the vote in some large industrial and urban areas, especially Tunis. The secular opposition had underestimated the power of both the Islamists and the RCD, while overestimating the president's desire to reform Tunisian political life.[57]

For a year and a half, the new government had aimed at reaching out—within limits—to the more religiously conservative elements in Tunisian society. The 1989 election results showed that while the RCD may have tempered their dissatisfaction, they had not secured their loyalty. Perhaps as shocked by the successes of the Islamists as the secular opposition was with those of the RCD, the state saw in these elections a turning point in its relations with al-Nahdah. The assault against the Islamists began following the 1989 elections, if initially in a measured fashion. For example, on June 8, 1989, al-Nahdah's request for recognition was rejected. In the meantime, the state continued policies aimed at undercutting the Islamists' appeal. A delegate for religious affairs was named for each provincial governor, and the RCD began to organize colloquia at Zitouna. The prime minister inaugurated the first conference of preachers recruited and salaried by the state and charged with disseminating a religious message supporting the state and the president. Such practices reinforced the new president's policy of making the state the sole defender of Islam and protector of the faith.[58]

The Islamists replied in September 1989 by publishing a long list of human rights violations against their cadres. In a bolder move, al-Nahdah attacked the Minister of Education, Muhammad Charfi, the former head of the LTDH, for suggested curricular and textbook reforms. Charfi had also resumed enforcing the law banning the hijab after almost two years of nonenforcement. Such changes made the Islamists furious, and the minister was physically threatened.[59] On October 21, 1989, the president spoke of national reconciliation and dialogue but in his November 7 *changement* anniversary address he made clear that religion and politics were not to be mixed, that there was no place in Tunisia for a religious party, and that Islam was the religion of all, not a subject of competition nor a springboard to power. The only defender of Islam in Tunisia would be the state itself.

A complete rehearsal of all of the twists and turns, carrots and sticks of this period in the relationship between al-Nahdah and the state as well as between the state and the secular opposition is beyond the scope of this presentation. However, expressions of popular discontent exploded in February 1990, triggered by floods in the south. The campuses then witnessed massive sit-ins to which al-Nahdah gave its full support.[60] The strikes continued, making this the worst unrest since Ben 'Ali had come to power, as the authorities resorted to using water cannon, dogs, and tear gas.[61] The June 1990 municipal elections only confirmed the continuing coercive tendencies of the government. Only eighteen independent lists were able to overcome the various hurdles to being placed on the ballot, and some were believed to be RCD lists in disguise.[62] Further marring the balloting were the serious questions raised about the voting lists, since the total was 1.3 million names *fewer* than it had been in 1981.[63] In the event, it was another RCD sweep, as only one list succeeded in beating the RCD (in Chebba, 110 miles south of Tunis).

Only a few months later, Tunisia found itself caught up in the Gulf crisis. Given its desire to preserve its important (financial) relationship with the Gulf states, Tunisia's official position was that it condemned the Iraqi invasion as well as the presence of Western troops in the Gulf. Although the government allowed pro-Iraq demonstrations, the first since Ben 'Ali had come to power, it nonetheless distanced itself from popular reaction as well as the press, which was firmly pro-Iraq. Press confiscations began at the end of August, as two weeklies were banned for publishing articles about Saudi Arabia which were regarded as slanderous. The economic fallout, particularly from the drop in tourism revenues, also hit hard.[64]

On the other hand, relations with the opposition improved somewhat, and it expected something positive from Ben 'Ali in his *changement* anniversary speech. To its surprise, however, his November 7, 1990 message was one of closure, not opening. The president insisted that it was the state that would determine the framework and the climate needed for political competition and dialogue. It was then up to civil society to accept the state's determination and, beyond that, to oppose any actions that ran counter to the (regime-defined) *national* consensus.[65]

At the end of November it was announced that a cell of Islamist terrorists intending to overthrow the state had been rounded up. Al-Nahdah claimed noninvolvement, but arrests of its members followed.[66] As the crackdown on al-Nahdah continued, unease in the opposition ranks grew. On January 12, 1991 the legal opposition parties issued a joint statement declaring their deep concern with "the diminution of political liberties and the trend toward violence." The statement called on the government to lift restrictions on opposition groups, both licensed and unlicensed.[67] In the meantime, al-Nahdah continued to press for legalization.

The point of no return came on March 22, 1991, when Islamists attacked and set fire to an RCD office in Bab Souika, just outside the medina in Tunis. People were outraged by the violence, in which one person was killed and another badly burned. Some 800 people were picked up, including most of the al-Nahdah leadership not in jail or exile, although the group initially denied any responsibility. At the end of the roundups, only three members of its executive committee were left at liberty in Tunis, and they subsequently announced that they were freezing their membership because of the violence. New state claims of discoveries of arms and explosives as well as anti-regime tracts followed, underlining that a full-scale battle was underway.

As Ben 'Ali mounted his final assault against al-Nahdah, he once again reached out to the secular opposition (whose appeal had been severely undermined by Saddam Hussein's humiliating defeat in the Gulf war). He also tried to deflect charges from abroad of torture and other human rights abuses against Islamists. On April 9 the president officially installed a Higher Council on Human Rights and proceeded to create human rights departments in the ministries of foreign affairs, the interior, and justice, as well as in the RCD. On May 1 he announced a revision of the labor code and an increase in salaries to make up for the recent lifting of subsidies on basic items. He assembled a national commission to look into the university crisis and proposed giving subventions ($52,000) and greater media access to each of the legal opposition parties. Opposition papers were also promised some $30,000 each.[68]

Unrest on university campuses broke out again in May and was blamed by the authorities on Islamist student organizations. While the opposition parties implicitly criticized the government's use of force, they continued to place most of the blame on the Islamists. Announcements of new discoveries of Islamist arms caches punctuated the period, and at the end of May, the government announced it had foiled a fundamentalist plot to take power by force. The state struck back with waves of arrests; torture was frequently reported, and death in custody or under mysterious circumstances took on previously unknown proportions.[69] As the offensive continued throughout the summer, the opposition fell in line behind the government, leaving no credible opposition voice. The ferocity of the offensive brought criticism from human rights groups in the country and abroad, leading Amnesty International to send an investigative committee. The Arab Organization for Human Rights called for an end to the climate of political violence in the country. The severity of the anti-Islamist campaign reportedly left the population traumatized.[70]

At the same time, attention was focused on Algeria and the coming parliamentary elections there. Once the FIS was declared illegal, the elections suspended, and first-round results overturned, the disquiet about Islamists in Tunisia diminished somewhat, although it is not clear there were many Islamists left above ground to repress after the assault of the previous months. But this did not mean that a new opening might be around the corner; indeed, political life in the country had been crushed. The only opposition of any consequence had been pulverized while the legal opposition parties were victims of their continuing weakness in the face of the RCD machine, the cooptation of their best and brightest, and their complicity of sorts in the suppression of al-Nahdah.

On the other hand, the state increased its support for the expansion of what one might call apolitical associative life. The official line was that civil society organizations were not only an example of the new pluralism in post-Bourguiba Tunisia, but also that such organizations constituted a critical shield against the forces of obscurantism (i.e., the Islamists). The focus by international aid and development agencies on decentralization and NGOs has no doubt also played a role in the government's decisions to allow the proliferation of such organizations. The state has also provided subsidies to defray the operating costs of such groups, whose number a 1992 study put at well over 5,000.[71]

But one must keep in mind that these organizations operate within the same political context that was detailed above. The state's provision of subsidies is neither systematic nor institutionalized. Moreover, official circles encourage RCD loyalists to join such groups as a way of controlling their activities. Occasionally the regime has resorted to creating a duplicate union (as was the case with Human Rights League) to "dilute and countervail the influence of the original." When none of these strategies works, coercion is always available. "To the extent that the regime fosters associational life it is because the regime sees associations as 'transmission belts' for its own policies."[72]

CONCLUSIONS

Although the two openings examined above had somewhat different proximate triggers, both came in response to gathering crises. As a result, Mzali, within the framework of the continuing Bourguibist regime, and Ben 'Ali, as he tried to chart a new course after retiring the aging president, experimented with alternative bases of support. In both cases, the Islamists were part of the experiment, as each leader sought to deal with them or perhaps include them in a way that marked a departure, in the case of Mzali, and arguably a break in the case of Ben 'Ali, with the approach Bourguiba had used.

While Mzali apparently sought to engage the Islamists in some sort of dialogue from the beginning, his first target in his effort to consolidate power was the UGTT. When that experiment failed, he turned more openly toward the Islamists, allowing them more freedom of action. Ben 'Ali's approach was a bit different, no doubt because he had retired Bourguiba, but also because he was a man from the military-security apparatus. While his personal commitment to secularism is unclear, he was certainly intent from the beginning on reintroducing so-called Arabo-Islamic values into state discourse. Whether the goal was to test the waters, draw out the Islamists to see their true strength, coopt whom he could by lessening the most objectionable aspects of Bourguiba's secularism, or all of the above is not clear.

Whatever the case, the fact that the Islamists were seen as potential bases of support or that parts of their discourse were tolerated or even adopted meant that secularist women felt and were threatened. The concern was greater with the arrival of Ben 'Ali precisely because he needed to break with the Bourguibist legacy—in which women were heavily invested and implicated—in order to consolidate his own power.

EPILOGUE

This is not the end of the story of government interaction with Islamists or with the secular opposition. It is, however, the end of the final chapter of the limited liberalization following the *changement*. By early fall 1992, the regime claimed that al-Nahdah had been crushed, although efforts were still underway to silence its leaders in exile.[73]

In January 1993, Ben 'Ali announced changes to the electoral code to ensure that the opposition would be represented (although the changes also ensured that the RCD would win an overall majority). At the beginning of 1994, in preparation for coming presidential and parliamentary elections, yet another electoral reform was announced setting aside twenty seats (of 163) for opposition parties, based on the proportion of the total vote they received. In a daring move, LTDH activist Moncef Marzouki tried to run against Ben 'Ali but, along with another candidate, was thwarted by a constitutional obstacle. Nonetheless, Marzouki's attempted candidacy proved very embarrassing to the president: the Tunisian press was forbidden to report it and foreign journalists were warned against noting it. During the campaign itself, the opposition parties were subsidized by the government and accorded air time on radio and television. While there were some complaints of irregularities, the April 1 elections were generally held to be a great improvement over 1989 in terms of proper procedure and constituted a clear success for the RCD and Ben 'Ali.

The history of the last few years is one of periodic and largely symbolic gestures in the direction of political opening, but any attempt to take advantage of the purported openings generally leads to harassment or jail. The government wants the trappings of pluralism, but does not want, and indeed as of fall 1995 would no longer tolerate, expressions of anything less than full support. At the time of this writing, human rights abuses continue, if not at the same level as 1991–92, and the press is all but dead. Discussions of decentralization are largely a window dressing intended to so impress outside agencies that they will overlook the high levels of coercion applied. The strong performance of the Tunisian economy, an IMF structural adjustment success story, has also seduced outside agencies.

Many Tunisians view the regime as development-oriented, and the presence of a large middle class, with consumer tastes it can now indulge, has certainly contributed to the regime's staying power. There is a sense that, at least in the realm of the economy, the country is moving forward. Further contributing to popular support for (or lack of active opposition to) the regime has been the Tunisian state's involvement in welfare and development activities, functions that, as a result of state financial incapacity and bureaucratic malaise, the Islamists have taken over in such countries as Egypt and Algeria. Perhaps its most notable effort in this regard has been the establishment of the National Solidarity Fund, 2626, which is used to finance projects in poorer or neglected areas (*manatiq al-dhill* or *zones d'ombres*). Although there is a real drive for rural development, there are also projects in all the governorates especially aimed at the Islamists' tradition-al targets: housing and youth employment. Ben 'Ali's machine may be re-pressive and corrupt, but is not sclerotic.[74]

The relative homogeneity of Tunisian society reduces the number of po-tential societal fault lines and may also militate for greater stability. Proba-bly more important has been the regime's utilization of the fear Islamists engender among the liberal opposition to legitimate its control of power and its rejection of more open political contestation. Whether Islamists continue to pose a threat to Tunisia is an open question, but what seems to be a matter of consensus among a majority of Tunisians is that Ben 'Ali's as-sault against the Islamists saved the country from going the way of Algeria and that any political moves that might allow the Islamists to resurface are simply not worth the risk. It remains to be seen how long the Islamist threat and the specter of Algeria can be used by the regime to legitimate its au-thoritarian reality thinly veiled with *faux* pluralism.

CHAPTER **EIGHT**
Citoyennes à Part Entière?

W hen asked in which Arab or Islamic country women's legal status is most advanced, Arab women are virtually unanimous in naming Tunisia. The discussion of women's rights in this chapter makes clear that such an evaluation is to a large extent true, thanks primarily to the promulgation of the Code du Statut Personnel (CSP) in 1956. However, the process by which Tunisian women have secured and maintained their rights has less to do with a broad-based and activist women's movement (which has never existed) than to decisions from above intended to promote a socioeconomic program or consolidate control. In Tunisia a clear program on and for women has long been an explicit part of state policy.

A BRIEF HISTORY OF THE WOMEN'S MOVEMENT

The first women's organization formally established in Tunisia was the Union Musulmane des Femmes de Tunisie (UMFT), established in 1936 and primarily concerned with women's education. (While It was followed by the establishment of a women's section in the Association des Jeunes Musulmans in 1944 and by the Club de la Jeune Fille Tunisienne in 1954, the UMFT has remained the most important of the three.) Its members, although of a religious orientation, shared many of the ideas of the famous Islamic jurist and reformer Tahar Haddad. His book, *Notre Femme dans la Loi et dans la Société*, which appeared in 1930, was the first Tunisian tract to deal seriously with the renewal of Islamic law and, in particular, to call for the abolition of polygamy and for the institution of judicial divorce.

The next major women's organization to emerge was the Union des Femmes de Tunisie (UFT) (and subsequently the affiliated Union des Jeunes Filles de Tunisie), founded by women from the Tunisian Communist Party (PCT), who placed more emphasis on social issues and labor organizing. The membership, including most of the leadership, especially outside of Tunis, was largely European.[1] However, as time passed, the PCT took on an increasingly nationalist cast. As a result many of the French women left, so that the UFT membership became increasingly Tunisian. At the same time, the UFT further developed its social program and then moved on to support the victims of the anti-colonial struggle. Its numerous activities notwithstanding, its presence and work remained marginal due to the class background of its members and the ethnicity of its founders.[2]

The national movement devoted no attention to women's issues nor did it carry out a serious examination of the condition of women until late in its development.[3] As in other anti-colonial struggles, to the extent that "the woman question" was considered, it was viewed by many as better postponed until after liberation. If anything, men of various ideological stripes sought to control the women's groups. (According to testimony, Bourguiba attended most of the UMFT meetings to coordinate national resistance.)[4] Once independence was achieved, however, the new state began the process of harnessing popular activity. A new women's organization, the UNFT (Union Nationale des Femmes de Tunisie), was established in 1958 through a fusion of the women's cells of Bourguiba's Neo-Destour party and the UMFT. Yet Bechira Ben Mrad, the woman who had served as president of the UMFT for twenty years, was in effect pushed out, humiliated by being offered an undistinguished place in the new union. Similarly, between 1956 and 1959, UFT activities, contacts, and demonstrations diminished. Authorizations for activities were not granted, and the police controlled even the least action. UFT leaders were arrested and interrogated, and, in some cases, their passports were taken away.

The UFT members were then faced with the dilemma of whether to integrate into the UNFT or to boycott it. In the euphoric atmosphere following the liberation, the hopes people had for the new Tunisian state created a reconciliation in the context of a common national project. This spirit led many women to join the UNFT. In general, however, they were quickly disappointed by the rigidity of the organization and its decision-making structure.[5] The UFT applied in vain to register with the post-independence government, although it managed to continue its activities until about 1963. One of its last battles was over securing the franchise for Tunisian women.[6] By the early 1960s, the UFT (as well as the PCT) were closed.

Concomitant with the early process of unifying women's activity within one structure was Bourguiba's promulgation of a series of laws, most part of the CSP, aimed at upgrading women's status. It should be stressed that his policies on women were but one part of a broader strategy by which he sought to set Tunisia on the road to "modernization." Bourguiba came to refer to himself (and others to him) as the Liberator of Tunisian Women, proclaiming proudly that he had spared Tunisian women from having to join these battles themselves. However, by freeing them from subjection to a range of archaic practices, he established his own tutelage over them. Women's subordination to Bourguiba was clear in his behavior at the UNFT congresses, which he opened with speeches containing his directives, all of which subsequently were incorporated into the union's action plans.[7]

The UNFT was only one of the constituent structures of Bourguiba's one-party state, a monolithic entity that attempted, through a series of these subordinate institutions, to channel (and control) popular political participation. Most fundamentally, membership in the UNFT required prior membership in the PSD. Beyond that, the most basic UNFT structure was that of sections, with local and regional delegations respectively above them. The UNFT also had a youth branch, *al-Shabibah al-Tunisiyyah*, membership in which was open to those 14–25, but which had virtually no appeal among university-age women. A national council brought the UNFT regional delegates together for periodic meetings, but the union was capped by an executive committee, each member of which headed a functional committee such as administration, finance, or rules. Regional and local delegates were not so much elected from the base as selected by the leadership. Likewise, all activities were determined by directives from above. This heavy centralization of activity and top-down approach to decisionmaking meant that the UNFT was controlled by a small group of women who were also PSD faithful, close to the president.[8] The union's president was regularly a member of the National Assembly and, later, of the Political Bureau of the PSD.

While the UNFT regularly underlined the areas in which women still lagged behind men or suffered discrimination, the union almost never initiated proposals for concrete changes. Its primary task was to implement state policy. Thus, it must be seen as complicit in endorsing the policies regarding and the pressures upon Tunisian women.[9] Some of its more notable campaigns came in the 1960s against visits and offerings to marabouts (saints), and against the increase in dowry levels, both of which were considered contrary to the socialist goals of post-independence Tunisia.[10]

There was also a major literacy campaign in the 1960s and, beginning in 1973, a campaign to address the condition of rural women.[11]

The UNFT was also the state's designated mechanism to engender awareness among women of Bourguiba's projects and expectations.[12] The primary goal of state policy (and, therefore, the UNFT's approach) toward women was to achieve a "proper balance" between women's efficient participation in the economic life of the country and a healthy and harmonious family life.[13] In Bourguiba's view, the maintenance of the strength of the family (traditional family) unit was key to social harmony, and a basis of progress. Education was central and work outside the home was also fundamental, but were not to interfere with a woman's primary role in the home.[14] The rights she had been given were to enable her better to fulfill her responsibilities toward her family and by extension toward society and the state.

Even bearing in mind the negative aspects of this kind of state feminism, one should not underestimate the importance of the reforms Bourguiba introduced. In the mid-1990s, most Arab/Muslim women continue to be exposed to the problems that Bourguiba's reforms of forty years ago addressed, especially the questions of judicial review of divorce and polygamy. Had other Arab or Islamic states followed suit by issuing similar reforms, the perception may not have been the same. But they did not, and whatever one may say today about Bourguiba's goals or the need for additional reforms of the CSP, a number of Bourguiba's reforms have had a very positive long-term impact.

Nevertheless, admiration for Bourguiba did not necessarily translate into joining the UNFT; indeed, women tended to join for reasons related to ambition—belonging to the party and the union could only be viewed positively by the relevant powers—or because of the services the union offered. A typical UNFT member was a woman of middle class or more modest means. (Upper class Tunisian women generally had little desire to be involved in political work.)[15] Hence, the tie between the UNFT and its "troupes" was largely based on clientelism, established in the framework of assistance campaigns among poor women who generally saw the union as little more than a department charged with popular assistance.[16] Chater's 1992 study provides a sample of opinions of the UNFT. Women's evaluations range from charging the union with complete absence from meaningful social work, to admitting to having joined it because it facilitated job-related contacts with local authorities.[17] In addition, however, one of the negative consequences of the UNFT's devotion to the party and the state's program of modernization was that the leadership, who were themselves in effect dictated to by the state, then projected their own lack of power onto those who were less empowered than they. If one reads the charters adopted at the first three UNFT congresses, one has the sense that the union was addressing itself to handicapped and immature youngsters in whom it had to instill an awareness of obligations.[18] Having said that, there is no question of the reach of the UNFT. Its offices were to be found throughout the country. According to official statistics (which should be viewed with some skepticism) from some 13,881 in 1960, its ranks grew to 38,821 in 1969, fell to 26,008 in 1972, but climbed to 57,000 in 1980 and 70,000 in 1984.[19]

The union did pass through several distinct phases, and it is worth reviewing them briefly. In 1970, under its president since 1958, Radhia Haddad (a niece of the president's and his choice to run the union), the UNFT initiated a campaign to introduce additional changes into the CSP. Haddad, although neither feminist nor revolutionary, nonetheless saw room for ameliorating the CSP. Yet, despite her close relationship to the president, he quickly quashed her efforts. And this was only the beginning of Bourguiba's problems with Haddad, for in 1971, she was among those members of the liberal wing of the PSD who opposed him on the question of his designation (rather than party election) of the members of the PSD's political bureau. The defeat of this liberalizing attempt within the party meant her ouster from it and, as a result, the termination of her term as president of the UNFT on March 8, 1972. More serious, her passport was withdrawn, her parliamentary immunity was lifted, and she was prosecuted, fined, and given a suspended sentence.[20]

After a brief interregnum, in 1973 Fathia Mzali, PSD party activist and wife of then Minister of Education Muhammad Mzali, became UNFT president, a post she held until 1986. A woman of great energy as well as ambition, respected by some, resented by others,[21] Mzali developed the organization into her own fiefdom. Although different accounts credit both Haddad and Mzali for attempts at invigorating the union—Haddad in 1970 and Mzali beginning in 1975—[22] in 1978, Mzali admitted that the union had at least one major problem: "We still do not know if the UNFT is supposed to be primarily involved in politics or economics, if it is supposed to defend the rights of women or if it should devote itself solely to social work."[23]

During her tenure, especially after the energizing effect of the 1975 UN Conference on Women, Mzali did make a number of suggestions for policy initiatives. In general terms, the union began to call upon women to become more involved. UNFT activists also participated in discussions of the sixth development plan, with the goal of introducing into it a plan of action dedicated to women. The union then began to show greater and greater interest in organizing national, regional, and international seminars and meetings as well as in publishing studies on the condition of Tunisian women.[24]

It also launched discussions aimed at securing more governmental leadership positions for UNFT activists. For example, in 1979, in order to increase female representation in parliament, the UNFT proposed an amendment to the electoral law to provide for a quota of seats for women. In 1982 Mzali recommended that a ministry be created to take charge of the "women question."[25] In 1983, in an attempt to attract women to whom the UNFT had not generally appealed (intellectuals), Mzali announced the founding of what were called *rabitat* (leagues, *alliances*, in French). Each *rabitah* focused on a particular profession, such as legal careers, education, and the like, and one did not need to be a member of the UNFT or the PSD to join. While not overwhelming successes, they did serve to capture the imagination and interest of some intelligent and energetic women.

In November 1983, Bourguiba named Mzali to the cabinet: she was the first woman to serve as a minister, and was charged with founding and developing a completely new ministry, that of the Family and the Promotion of Women. However, Mzali did not step down as head of the UNFT following her cabinet appointment, and the whole incident only further underlined the lack of separation among the state, party, and national organizations. Her appointment as minister, not surprisingly, did nothing to invigorate the UNFT. If anything, it led to further stagnation as she became more and more involved in activities outside it.

In the meantime, however, the beginnings of an independent women's grouping had already begun to take root. Generally educators and intellectuals of a leftist bent, these women began to meet in small but growing sessions in late 1978. Because they coalesced during the first liberalization period, the story of their development is one of the cases considered in the next chapter.

WOMEN IN TUNISIAN LAW

The discussion below divides the development of Tunisian women's status into several stages: the institution of the CSP in 1956 along with several other pieces of early legislation; the revision of the CSP in 1981; and the revision of the CSP and other legislation related to women in 1993. These sections review and analyze the actual revisions. The next chapter analyzes the changes of 1981 and 1993 against the backdrop of their relationship to the liberalization process.

As noted above, Tunisia is best known for the CSP promulgated beginning on August 13, 1956, which came to be celebrated as Women's Day in the republic. Originally applicable only to Muslims, it was extended to all

Tunisians the following month, thereby putting an end to religious jurisdiction over certain legal matters. In the first place, the Code set a minimum marriage age for men and women: 20 and 17 years respectively. Below these ages, special authorization is needed from the court. Second is the stipulation that a woman cannot be married except with her consent, thus ending the right of a woman's guardian/tutor to force her to marry against her will. In addition, a woman who has reached the age of majority, 17 years, need not have a guardian represent her at her marriage. Previously, a woman was a minor until married (no matter at what age that occurred) and had to have a male guardian represent her at the writing of her marriage contract. Perhaps most notable, polygamy is forbidden and is punishable by a fine and imprisonment, according to the CSP.

Just as important, divorce, which in some Islamic countries can (or at least at the time could be) accomplished by a simple formula of repudiation (with or without the woman's knowledge), was made more difficult as the CSP made divorce a matter to be administered by the courts. According to the CSP, a divorce cannot be granted until there have been attempts at reconciliation. Moreover, there are three kinds of divorce: by mutual consent; divorce for cause, which can be demanded by either partner, and for reasons specified in the CSP (which are not equal for men and women, although there is a great degree of judicial discretion); and *divorce abusif*—for which one need not give reasons specified in law and for which both partners have the same right to file. Nonetheless, some judges continue to have difficulty accepting the idea that a woman may initiate a divorce and, therefore, in practice, it remains more difficult for a woman than a man to do so.[26]

The Code also gave women full legal capacity in the realm of contracts, something they had not had before. Nonetheless, two of these articles were in contradiction with other laws: article 803 which forbids a married woman to engage her services without her husband's permission and permits him to void a contract; and article 1481, which restricts a woman's disposition of her belongings. Perhaps the most objectionable part of the CSP in the view of women activists was that the husband was required to pay a dowry to the woman and take care of her material needs in exchange for her duty to manage the house obediently and submissively. There are also unequal requirements regarding cohabitation: the woman is required to live with her husband, but the husband is obliged only to provide material support.[27] Nevertheless, the positive elements of the CSP should be clear. Through these changes, a woman was given greater sovereignty over herself and her future, and the institution of the family was strengthened by removing from a woman's concerns the threat that her husband might take another wife or divorce her unilaterally.

Another revolutionary part of Tunisian law affecting women concerns the state's support for voluntary family planning. A family planning program was instituted in 1961, and the importation and selling of contraceptives was legalized. Moreover, having large families was discouraged by the termination of family allocations for children born after the fourth child. Beginning in 1970 a "contraception prize" was awarded each year to the governorate that had converted the largest number of women to contraceptive use. From a level of 7.7 children in 1966, the fertility level dropped to 5.8 in 1975 and 3.34 in 1991, the lowest in the Islamic world. By 1990, 55 percent of women were using contraceptives.[28] Even more revolutionary, and again setting Tunisia well apart from other Arab and Islamic countries, abortion was legalized (with certain conditions) in 1965 and was made completely legal in 1973 at the same time that the National Office of Family Planning, charged with increasing the diffusion of contraceptives, was created.

Education was another key part of Bourguiba's modernizing program. Women in Tunisia have the right to an education, even if school texts continue to depict women in negative or traditional ways. The proportion of girls in primary education facilities was 51 percent in 1975 (with boys at 77 percent) and 82 percent in 1994 (versus 88 percent for boys). As for enrollment in secondary school, the proportions were 32.4 percent in 1975 and 47.2 percent in 1993. The main problem continues to be dropout rates for girls in the 10–14 age group, especially in rural areas. In 1966, illiteracy stood at 53.9 percent among males and 82.4 percent among females. In 1989, the rates had dropped to 26.4 percent and 48.3 percent, respectively.[29]

The right to work has also been critical.[30] The proportion of women in the active (formal) workforce jumped from 6.2 percent in 1966 to 19.5 percent in 1989 (having reached a high of 21.7 percent in 1984). Despite the rise in percentages, however, unemployment among women has also grown markedly, from 11 percent in 1984 to 20.9 percent in 1989. In terms of sectors, women are concentrated in agriculture (as seasonal, day, or family workers), administration and services, and industrial manufacturing establishments (especially textiles and leather).[31] According to the law, women have the right to work without discrimination in access or salary, except in the cases of certain jobs which are off-limits as a way of "protecting" them. (This protection, however, as we have seen in the cases of Jordan and Morocco, puts women in a category of physically and morally inferior beings.) Women's rights to maternity leave also have positive and negative aspects, for while the law protects their jobs, it also stresses their role as mothers and, at least implicitly, casts aspersions on the seriousness or importance of their participation in the work force. The law continues implicitly to support the idea that women are expected to carry out their work functions in a way that does not interfere with their primary duties, those of wife and mother.[32]

As for other legislation, although in principle the marriage of a Tunisian woman with a non-Muslim is not forbidden, in practice it is, and in this respect Tunisian practice conforms to that of other Arab states. The problem may be overcome by the man's conversion; however, while this was once a mere formality, it has become more difficult with the imposition of a probationary stage during which the potential convert must take an exam to test his knowledge of Islam. Discrimination is also clear in the realm of nationality law. It is much easier for the wife of Tunisian man to become Tunisian than for the husband of a Tunisian woman to do so. In addition, and not surprisingly, before the 1993 amendments to the CSP, a Tunisian woman could not give her nationality to her children, unless they were born in Tunisia of a non-Tunisian father or if the father was unknown. A child born abroad had to wait until s/he came of age and then make a special request. If there was no opposition, nationality was granted by presidential decree.[33]

In the case of the criminal code regarding adultery, a man who catches his wife in the act and murders her (or her partner) is subject to only five years of prison. There is no similar provision for a wife who finds her husband in such a situation and acts in the same way. In 1968 the law was changed to make both partners equally liable to be prosecuted for adultery. Prior to this, only the woman could be prosecuted.[34]

In the field of entitlements, both working men and women have a right to social security. However, if both spouses are eligible, the family allocation is given to the father. As for retirement, since 1988, women who have three children under the age of 20 or one child with a severe handicap have the right to pension on demand. Prior to that, the law stipulated that women with three children under the age of 15 could benefit from a proportional pension if they had 15 years of service, with the retirement pension delayed until the age of 50. Again, while perhaps a positive change in one sense, as Chamari argues, all of these "laws of protection," considered as positive discriminatory measures, have served to create a category of problematic workers, costly for the employers, one consequence of which are recruitment policies that discriminate against women.[35]

Inheritance, one of the most sensitive areas of law because of the clarity regarding it in the *shari'a*, is an area left largely untouched by the CSP. It did, nonetheless, include one important change for women: if the deceased has no living male children, then the female children, not the paternal uncles, receive the entire inheritance. Bourguiba clearly wanted to move farther on this issue. In 1974, saying that he had one last goal to achieve before considering his mission complete, the president attempted to change the *shari'a*-based inheritance law according to which a daughter receives one-half the share her brother does. But the opposition he encountered was so great, including within the party and among his own entourage, that he relented.[36]

Finally, in the realm of political rights, since 1957 Tunisia women have had the right to vote, just as they enjoy the right to run for election at all levels of government. Indeed, the Tunisian constitution defines all citizens as equal, although it does not specifically bar discrimination on the basis of sex. Tunisian women have pushed for such a change, but the response has always been at best silence: for the state to proclaim explicitly that men and women are equal before the law would call into question the clear definition of different roles for the two sexes that is both implicit and explicit in Islamic law. This is a battle that the Tunisian authorities appear uninterested in joining. Moreover, average Tunisian women, unpoliticized and nonfeminist, are most concerned with their gains in the areas of education, work and contraception.

It should be stressed, in conclusion, that no matter how advanced legislation may be, it is valuable only insofar as it is applied. Tunisian women have been fortunate to live under a set of legal codes that have promoted a number of rights that women elsewhere in the Arab and Islamic world still do not enjoy. Nonetheless, the law is applied in the context of a social system underpinned by a family structure in which women continue to be viewed and treated as unequal or dependent. This de facto inferior status is the basis of much of the discriminatory treatment they continue to suffer.[37]

CHANGES IN THE CSP: 1981

In November 1980, having learned of the difficult financial situation of some widowed and divorced women, and apparently moved by their stories, Bourguiba called for the first time for a review of the CSP with an eye to making it more equitable, especially in the area of divorce.[38] After study over a period of months by a group of jurists and other specialists, recommendations were made, and in February 1981 the CSP was revised. Several important changes in the area of divorce were introduced. For example, the new provisions gave women the choice between two different systems of compensation: a single payment determined by a judge or a single payment followed by monthly installments based on the woman's previous standard of living. Second, a system resembling that of community property was introduced to respond to the fact that while more and more women were working outside the home and contributing to the costs of running and furnishing the home, they were often left with nothing at the time of the divorce since immovable property was traditionally registered in the name of the man. While progressive in orientation, both these new provisions triggered criticism as being too favorable to women. In addition, because of existing prejudices, judges have made clear their dislike for the second compensation option[39] and, therefore, generally have not imposed a level of alimony payments that would enable a woman to take care of herself. Some argued that the problem lay, not with the provisions of the existing law, but with judicial interpretation. Therefore, rather than changing the law into one that in effect crystallized the characterization of women as weak or as victims, a campaign should have been initiated to change judges' attitudes.[40] In any event, despite Bourguiba's good intentions, divorce continues to place a heavy economic burden on women.[41]

Another important change concerned the question of guardianship over children in the case of divorce. Prior to 1981, guardianship was shared by the ex-spouses, whereas the new law gave primacy to the best interest of the child. This has generally meant that the mother is named guardian; but she may lose this status if she remarries, a provision that does not apply to the father. This law also required the ex-wife to choose a place of residence near the ex-husband or else lose her guardianship, thus limiting her freedom of movement.[42]

THE CHANGES OF 1993[43]

The political background to the introduction of the most recent set of CSP changes will be discussed in more detail in the next chapter. Here only a brief summary of the content of the changes is necessary. In early 1992, Ben 'Ali assembled a commission to review women's legal status. It submitted its report on August 13, Tunisia's Women's Day, and the changes were finally entered into law in 1993. Among the new provisions were the following. As concerned gifts exchanged by an engaged couple, the principle of reciprocity was introduced, so that in the event of the termination of the engagement, each has the right to have his/her presents returned. The same is true in the case of the dissolution of a marriage before its consummation. The idea of reciprocity was further developed in the section on spousal obligations. While the code continues to call the husband the head of the household, the language requiring a wife to obey her husband was replaced with the principle of mutual assistance in running the household, and educating and raising children. The code also added the requirement that a minor's *mother* and not just his/her tutor consent in order for him/her to marry. The amendments further stipulated the establishment of a new fund to guarantee a food allowance to divorced women and their children.

And, in the field of nationality, a Tunisian woman married to a non-Tunisian now has the right to give her child (born outside Tunisia) Tunisian nationality if the father is in agreement.

In the case of the Labor Law, in which special conditions for salary had been set applying to both women and children (and thus placing them in the same category), the reference to women was removed. In addition, violation of the principle of nondiscrimination in employment was made subject to punishment. In the penal code, a husband who murders his wife after catching her in the act of adultery no longer benefits from special considerations limiting his punishment to five years. On the other hand, in the case of assault, a new provision was added to the effect that if the guilty party is a relative (*ascendant*) or spouse of the victim, the victim's withdrawal of the complaint terminates the prosecution/case. Such possibilities often work against women, as family pressure can be brought to bear to force women (or minors) to withdraw suits against older or more powerful (generally male) relatives.

Finally, less striking and earlier in Ben 'Ali's presidency, in the realm of education, in 1989 the *école de base* (6 to 16 years) was instituted, along with a number of social measures intended to reduce inequality in education, especially in rural areas, and to force parents to put their children in school. As a result, women's presence in all three levels of education has increased. This reform also changed some of the curricular programs and instruction manuals in which new values (liberty, equality, citizenship, responsibility) as well as a more positive image of women were presented.[44]

In sum, there is no question that the introduction of the CSP in 1956 has had a deep and positive impact on the status of Tunisian women. The provisions regarding divorce and polygamy are the two most important ones and those most often cited by Tunisian women as having made a difference in their sense of rights and empowerment. So have the state's emphasis on education for women and upon the right to work outside the home (if within limits), two other aspects of Bourguiba's (and Ben 'Ali's) policies. Having said that, the basic "package" of women's rights came as a result of initiatives from above. Hence, there is a sense that the president is both liberator and the guarantor of women's rights. The fact that the policies did not come in response to broad or systematic organizing from within women's ranks has three serious implications. The first is that Tunisian women have not, by and large, felt responsible for fighting for their rights and hence many simply take them for granted (or at least they did until the Islamist challenge of the late 1980s). The second is that because the rights were granted without struggle and because the state has itself worked to circumscribe civil society organizing, women's rights and status are subject to the changing considerations of the leadership. Third, there is a feeling among many Tunisians, men and women, that women have already received all their rights and that there is little or nothing left to fight for. Thus, while the CSP has clearly empowered women within certain spheres, the continuing dependence upon the good will or interests of the state undermines this liberation in a broader sense. Average Tunisian women are not concerned with pushing the boundaries of the political/civil empowerment; they seem more interested in the social and economic rights they have already gained.

THE ROLE OF EXTERNAL FUNDERS

Before turning to the case examples of relations between Tunisian women and the state in the next chapter, we conclude here with an examination of the role of external funders. Foreign aid and development institutions have been involved in a variety of Tunisian programs, including projects dealing with women, for many years. Projects dealing with rural women, women and development, and women and the environment, although important, are not a central concern of this study. We are interested here in determining which agencies have played a role in supporting projects that may have enabled women and women's organizations to take advantage of political openings through pushing for changes in laws or in expanding the realm of their activities. A number of foreign institutions, both governmental and nongovernmental, have been in a position to play such a role. An attempt was made to cover some of the institutions that were examined in Morocco and Jordan, in order to put the extent of activity in context. While some of these organizations (USAID, Friedrich Naumann) were active in Tunisia during the period of the first liberalization, the focus by such organizations on women's rights and political participation, and in particular their emphasis on supporting NGO's developed only during the second liberalization period. Notable in their absence here are summaries of activities of a variety of UN organizations—FAO, UNDP, UNFPA, and UNICEF—that played a significant role in helping Tunisian women's groups to prepare for the Beijing conference, whether through assisting in information dissemination, networking, organizing pre-conference activities, or funding participation. They are not included here because, outside the pre-Beijing activity, they have generally not been involved in funding activities that may be viewed as political or activist in nature.

USAID: Although USAID had long had a presence in Tunisia and was in fact involved in supporting family planning efforts in earlier decades, in the 1990s the focus of its work in the women sector shifted. Tunisia was one of the countries designated by USAID as a DII country in 1991. The funding for this initiative was initially appropriated for three years and was then renewed for a fourth. Several interviewees expressed concerns about the aims, coherence, or appropriateness of the programs' component projects, but that is properly the subject of a broader critique. One thrust of the program was to aid women's NGO's in the target countries.

USAID was well-acquainted with the UNFT and indeed had previous experience with some of its top people, such as Faiza Kefi (who became president in 1993), from her time at the Ministry of Planning. They also regarded the UNFT as the most important player among the women's organizations.[45] In the early 1990s, the UNFT was in search of additional funding and went to AID for possible support. However, the DII required working with NGOs. The UNFT had recently changed its relationship with the PSD-turned RCD from one of complete subsumption to that of having "privileged ties." The opportunity to obtain funding from USAID led the UNFT to put together the required documentation to be officially classified as an NGO. Once that had been accomplished, it was then eligible for AID monies. Indeed, AID became the UNFT's most important funder.[46]

Among the first projects for which it received AID support was an updated *Guide Juridique* for Tunisian women (an earlier version of which AID had funded in the 1980s). In 1992, AID provided the funding for studies including an opinion poll on women's status and a project monitoring women's image in the media. The results of both of these studies were included in an impressive volume published by the UNFT in 1995 entitled *L'image de la Femme dans la Société Tunisienne*. AID also sponsored three seminars on "Democracy and Environment," each of which brought together women municipal counselors, UNFT members, and independent women from particular regions. AID also funded an extensive documentation program for UNFT to enable it to organize and classify its archives.[47]

The most high-profile and ambitious project aimed at awareness-raising among women in preparation for the 1995 municipal elections. The first part of the project involved was the production and broadcast of television commercials, or public service announcements, which linked women's role in the home to their civic role and which encouraged both men and women to vote. The second part involved twenty regional conferences throughout the country on three different topics: women and the city; being a candidate; and voting for women.[48]

As part of the Beijing-related activities, AID provided funding to Rihana, a network of ten women's NGOs working on coordinated participation in the UN conference. AID support enabled Rihana representatives to attend the preparatory conference in Dakkar in November 1994, as well as a number of meetings in Tunisia to educate people regarding the Plan of Action and the position of Tunisian NGOs on it. AID also enabled Rihana to produce a video on its member organizations, two posters, and a brochure on women's associations in Tunisia, all for Beijing, and it financed five Rihana members' trips to Beijing.[49]

Finally, AID funded two publications by the impressive CREDIF (Centre de Recherche, Etudes, Documentation, et Information sur la Femme), a research center founded by the state: *The Legal Status of Tunisian Women: 1993 Reforms* and *La Femme Tunisienne en Chiffres*. However, in summer 1995 AID closed its country operations in Tunisia. It is not clear which organization(s), if any, will step in to fill the gap.

AMIDEAST:[50] One of the requirements attached to some of the AID DII funds mentioned above was that the money be channeled through an American NGO, if possible. As the only American NGO operating in Tunisia, therefore, Amideast found itself in the middle of this initiative. Since one of the foci was women's rights, Amideast consulted with a women's study group, Association des Femmes Tunisiennes pour la Recherche sur le Développement (AFTURD, see next chapter) about producing brochures on various aspects of women's rights—in marriage, work, and divorce. It appears that the project was almost complete when the 1993 changes in the CSP were announced, and the brochures had to be changed. At the time of this research (fall 1995), the project funding had been exhausted, but the brochure had not yet been produced.

As for other activities, Amideast organized a six-country forum in Amman in 1994 aimed at increasing women's involvement in the political process and in establishing transnational networking. The Tunis office selected and sponsored three women to participate in the meeting: one from AFTURD, one from the independent women's union ATFD (Association Tunisienne des Femmes Démocrates), and another, a parliamentarian from the Bizerte UNFT cell. The project seemed successful, but foundered on the question of post-conference networking. Tunisia still did not enjoy an extensive computer presence, and the Internet, access to which was highly restricted, was viewed with suspicion, not just by the government, but by many average Tunisians as well. Hence, the most efficient method of remaining in regular contact was not available to Tunisian women.

Part of the DII also targeted human rights. Apparently without knowing about the availability of such funds, the LTDH approached the United States Information Service in spring 1995 with a proposal for funding the purchase of a variety of basic infrastructure that its office lacked: phone, bookshelves, chairs, a photocopy machine, a fax, brochures, even rent. It also requested funds to produce a video on human rights. The decision regarding the proposal was made by the embassy democracy working group, which did appropriate some funds for a brochure, for a cassette on human rights for children, and for a video on human rights for adults, but the equipment requests were turned down. Instead nearly half the funds (some $80,000) were designated to send a group of LTDH members to the United States for a special International Visitor program. As an organization under siege by the state and one that relies on members' contributions to remain open, the LTDH was reportedly less than enthused about the allocation decision.

FRIEDRICH NAUMANN STIFTUNG:[51] This development organization associated with the German Social Democratic Party has been active in Tunisia since the mid-1960s. Its primary activities in the country in the 1990s have been with women and the media. In the case of women, its primary partner is CREDIF. In the case of the media, its partner is also governmental, the Centre Africain pour le Perfectionnement des Journalistes Communicateurs. While in recent years Naumann has funded some activities of the Association Tunisienne des Femmes Démocrates (ATFD) in general it has not chosen to work with NGOs.

The fact that Naumann, which has a policy preference for working with NGOs, has most often chosen governmental partners in Tunisia, is explained by several factors. One is the absorptive and administrative capacities of the NGOs. Often they are too small and have few concrete ideas about what they want to accomplish. Government organizations, on the other hand, at least in Tunisia, know what they want and are capable of absorbing the assistance. Just as important is the question of the political climate. One event Naumann had scheduled with the ATFD was not held because the hotel canceled the room, presumably owing to state pressures. Such things happen periodically in Tunisia, especially to those NGOs which try to sponsor activities of a political nature.

AGENCE CANADIENNE DU DÉVELOPPEMENT INTERNATIONALE (ACDI):[52] The Canadians do not have any projects that deal specifically with women; however, since 1991 Canadian development policy has attempted to ensure that women are adequately represented among those served by its projects. The ACDI does not have any directly political programs nor any dealing with human rights. It was their evaluation at the time of this research that the atmosphere in the country was not appropriate for such activities. They do have a long history with the ATFD and have financed the ATFD's violence hotline and violence advice center. They also funded the participation of one ATFD member in the Beijing conference. However, their most important or showpiece funding project is CREDIF, which was slated for renewal in 1996. This money is part of a bilateral Tunisian-Canadian agreement that specifies CREDIF as the recipient, but allows the research organization a great deal of flexibility in its use of the money.

Evaluation

There is no question that Tunisia in some ways offers a very fertile climate for external support of women's activities. But the question is, which women's activities and to what end? There is little problem promoting women in development projects: the state has constructed its image as enlightened (if respectful of tradition) and developmentalist. The problem arises when one tries to formulate programs that would further empower women. This is a project that the Tunisian state has, with only brief intervals, appropriated to itself. It has defined the parameters of citizenship and of women's contribution. As Tunisian society moved into the second half of the 1990s, the realm for the exercise of meaningful citizenship—by men or women—had perhaps never been smaller. In such an atmosphere, it is virtually impossible for external funders to play a significant role in supporting women's efforts to shape the state's agenda toward them, or toward anything else, for that matter. An activist, repressive state leaves little or no room for such activity.

Through the brief review above, one cannot but be struck by the lack of any meaningful political opening in the country and the degree to which this has constrained, if not straitjacketed, the activities of this selection of aid agencies. The contrast with the possibilities for involvement in Morocco or Jordan should be striking. Human rights education and women's consciousness raising regarding their legal rights have been possible only on the margins in Tunisia of the 1990s. In Morocco and Jordan such programs were in effect the precursors of greater state flexibility on and civil society involvement in these issues. Not so in Tunisia.

One of the problems, clearly, is the weakness of NGOs. Although theoretically they are supposed to be more flexible than government organizations, on the other hand, particularly in developing world contexts, they suffer from institutional and personnel weaknesses (they may in fact be only one or a handful of people). This is a particular problem in a country like Tunisia, which for so long insisted upon a monopoly on "civil society activity" by state corporatist formations such as the UNFT. The preexisting weakness on the one hand, combined with the continuing authoritarian nature of the regime on the other, make it very difficult for NGOs with anything resembling a political program (like the ATFD) to grow stronger.

Some organizations are established simply because funding is available for a particular purpose and because organizations, such as the European Union, will give money only to NGOs. They are not really grassroots organizations in the traditional sense, arising from local initiative and need, and, therefore, may have only short existences. More dangerous than the fly-by-night phenomenon, however, is the growth of governmental NGOs, reminiscent of the RONGOs in Jordan: organizations that are closely affiliated with the government in terms of funding or personnel, but that carry out the kinds of grassroots activities associated with NGOs.[53] Indeed, the emergence of organizations such as CREDIF or the reclassification of others such as the UNFT as an NGO are only two Tunisian examples of what is a much broader phenomenon in states in which the appearance and the "financial attraction" power of an NGO is created against the backdrop of little or no desire on the part of the state to relinquish power.

Finally, while donors clearly prefer working with some of the NGOs, beyond the question of absorptive capacity is the question of reach. It is undeniable that if one wants to reach a large number of Tunisian women, the organization that has the structure and cadres in place is the UNFT. Indeed, some women argue that like it or not, these are the women who count, the ones who will make a difference if, indeed, anyone can. One finds women who have joined the UNFT or decided to work with it precisely for this reason: the only way change can come in the present atmosphere is by working with the government. By trying to work outside, one is doomed to marginality at best, suppression at worst. This applies to external funders as well, who generally are not interested in spending their money on projects of highly limited impact. Of course, there are those who argue that by working with an organization as closely associated with the state as is the UNFT, the external funder is really hurting women and that it is better to stay outside or stay away.[54] The jury remains out and the debate will continue over whether by funding projects that strengthen an organization like the UNFT, the foreign aid agencies may in fact be laying the foundations for a future empowerment of women or are in fact helping to further consolidate and reinforce an authoritarian regime—a direct contradiction of their espoused goal of promoting civil and human rights.

CHAPTER **NINE**
The Changing Guise of State Feminism

Τ he two periods of political liberalization explored in chapter 7
offer numerous examples of interaction between women and
the state that have implications for women's rights and status. I
have selected several cases from each period for examination below. We
begin with the first liberalization period and a consideration of: the emergence of an autonomous women's "movement"; the atrophying of the
UNFT; the 1981 changes in the CSP; the 1983 appointment of women
ministers for the first time in Tunisia's history and the establishment of the
Ministry of the Family and Promotion of Women; and MTI's challenge to
the CSP. The second half of the chapter will discuss several cases drawn
from the post-*changement* period: the interaction among women, Islamists,
and the state; the revival of the UNFT; the licensing of the ATFD; and a
final section on women and the state as liberalization ended.

THE FIRST LIBERALIZATION

The Emergence of an Autonomous Women's Movement

By 1975, Bourguiba's modernizing program, including the CSP, had been
in place for nearly twenty years. Women's labor force participation was
19.1 percent, up from 6.2 percent in 1966;[1] and as a result of universal education, literacy among women had risen to 32.1 percent, up from 17.6
percent at the time of independence.[2] Finally, the availability of family

planning support since the early 1960s had given women much greater control over their fertility. Thus, the first generation of women to have been born and reached maturity under the CSP had, in effect, arrived by the late 1970s. The development of a lobby for further changes in women's status required the emergence of a new generation of women who viewed the CSP, not as a gift to be accepted without question, but as a cornerstone on which further building could take place.

In 1978 a group of independent, although generally leftist women co-alesced into a study group at the well-known Tahar Haddad Club, a cultural institution located inside the medina of Tunis. It was controlled by the Ministry of Cultural Affairs, but was also supervised, not surprisingly, by women from the UNFT. The establishment of the Club d'Etudes de la Condition des Femmes (CECF) was seen as daring at the time, because it appeared as a challenge to the UNFT, which, to date, had enjoyed a monopoly on women's organizing. Among its goals, the club sought to make Tunisian women aware of their continuing oppression despite the formal rights they enjoyed, to aid them in recognizing their intellectual capacities and the role they could therefore play in the country's economic and cultural development, and to demonstrate that the women's struggle needed to be situated, not vis-à-vis men, but vis-à-vis the social structures that permitted the concentration and the maintenance of power in men's hands.[3]

One critical event in the evolution of CECF women was a meeting entitled "La femme dans les sociétés européennes et maghrebines," sponsored by the local authorities in Tabarka in the summer of 1979. Because the gathering was not held in Tunis, there were greater opportunities for expression; and this was the first time Tunisian women outside official institutions discussed their situation in terms other than simple praise for Bourguiba. The significance of the event, however, derived from how the women were treated during and after the meeting. In the first place, the local authorities changed a number of the names of panels and presentations to less controversial ones, and during discussions the women were repeatedly criticized in an aggressive and often vulgar fashion. Then, upon their return to Tunis they began to hear rumors about their purportedly illicit behavior during the meeting. The women were shocked and for some it constituted a turning point, as they were then determined to continue under the auspices of the CECF the discussions that had been so rudely and crudely silenced at Tabarka.[4]

Beginning in October 1979, the women began to meet every Saturday for discussions. They eventually decided to form committees to examine different issues such as "women and the family" or "women and culture," or "women and history." After a while, however, the meetings became plenary, rather than committee, sessions.[5] Beyond the issues of their own internal functioning and organization, the women also faced the question of their relationship to broader society. They held debates, showed films, and sponsored exhibitions of paintings, books, and posters in addition to their closed, club discussions. They also introduced and eventually managed to have March 8 broadly accepted as women's day in Tunis, thus affirming their international ties and distancing themselves from the state's August 13 celebration. The activity for which they are perhaps best known was a petition they circulated against a Ministry of Interior order that women secure written permission from their father or husband whenever they left the country. In the end the order was revoked.[6]

> [G]iven the domination by the PSD over public institutions and the domination by the extreme left in other arenas, the women's club Tahar Haddad was really the only democratic place in all of Tunisia, the only place where people could actually get up and express different ideas, and still meet the following week to continue the discussion. It was something truly exceptional. . . .[7]

But tensions gradually developed in the group, partly but not exclusively between those who wanted the Club to be simply a place where women could meet and discuss issues and those who thought that this work should then serve as a point of departure for more directed political activity. This was true even for the issue of the CSP: after passionate debate the majority refused to agree to hold a discussion of revising the CSP even in a closed session, much less have a more public event.[8] External factors also began to take their toll. Members began to be pressured by men in various ways and mocked for participating in CECF activities. The studies and discussions also increasingly confronted the women with difficult existential and identity issues, including their definition of and identification with feminism, which reportedly led to an increasing number of divorces. The women continued to meet into 1982, working in small groups. Eventually, however, the tensions between members led to serious divisions and the club lost its momentum.[9]

To recount the next episode in the development of an autonomous Tunisian women's movement, one must backtrack for a moment. At a CECF meeting on March 8, 1980, the idea of constituting a women's labor union committee was discussed. A series of meetings to specify the contours of this committee followed. Again, however, there were internal political problems: the constitution of such a group was opposed by many female (not to mention male) labor activists on the grounds that it divided the working class along gender lines. To assuage these concerns, as well as those of the UNFT that this would be a competing organization, the committee that was founded was constituted as a study bureau.[10] The establishment of the Commission Syndicale d'Etudes de la Condition de la Femme Travailleur (CSE) was finally announced by the Secretary General of the UGTT, Taieb Baccouche, on March 8, 1982.[11] Most of its members were university and high school instructors, many were CECF members, and it began to gather momentum as the CECF was losing steam. To address UGTT and UNFT concerns about who would control it and what it would do, it was located within the organizational framework of the Bureau National d'Etudes of the UGTT.

The CSE was charged with a variety of tasks: sensitizing the structures and union members to workers' problems; reinforcing women's participation in union life; pinpointing specific problems regarding women's participation, studying them, and proposing solutions; and making the public aware of these problems. Many of the women were not happy with these limits but accepted them since the formation of the group allowed them to realize at least some of their aspirations. The first meetings had about sixty attendees—all women, even though the CSE was constituted as a mixed organization.[12]

Again questions related to program and goals arose. The women debated whether they should focus on women and ensuring their job security or take on the misogynous nature of the labor union itself and confront the state.[13] Over a three-year period the CSE organized a number of seminars on problems particular to women workers. For example, thanks to its efforts a report on the condition of female workers and on their specific demands—the protection of the right of women to work and the struggle against the forms of exploitation to which they were subject—was adopted by the 16th national congress of the UGTT, in 1984. In general, however, the commission was not successful in gaining the ear and attention of the UGTT leadership, which saw the CSE as a recourse for women workers and hence a counterweight to its power[14]—a threat rather than an asset. On a lower level, some UGTT cadres refused to cooperate with the CSE by obstructing its contacts with other women workers, and the UGTT Centrale's monthly *Echaab* refused to publish the texts of the commission's studies.[15]

At the same time, the CSE found itself enmeshed in broader UGTT politics and concerns: demands for greater autonomy, the intensification of labor union demands in the 1970s,[16] and Mzali's efforts to coopt the UGTT through the formation of the National Front. Since the PSD was beginning to perceive the UGTT as a competitor, it should not be surprising that the UNFT, which had begun a campaign against the independent women's movement, took particular aim at the CSE.[17] In any case, owing to both internal UGTT problems and external challenges, the commission was dismantled at the end of 1985 following the UGTT's closure.

Meanwhile, the independent women came to the realization that their "mobilizing structures"—the two study groups—did not permit political expression and public demonstration of their positions. Therefore, another informal group emerged, which included some of the same women. Called the Femmes Démocrates (FD), its first public activity was a demonstration in 1982 in response to the General Union of Palestinian Women's call for solidarity in the face of the Israeli invasion of Lebanon.[18] Beginning in 1983, the FD decided to have regular meetings to discuss a variety of issues. One of the first topics broached was whether they should consider joining the UNFT. It was decided that until the FD constituted a more structured or formal group, the question was premature.[19]

The FD reappeared in public after the 1984 bread riots. Hundreds had been arrested, and in the trials that followed some were condemned to death. In response, the FD published a declaration charging the government with responsibility for the demonstrations and denouncing the irregularities in the trials that followed. They were also the first to call clearly for the abolition of the death penalty.[20] Yet their activities continued to be reactive and spontaneous. Finally, the decision to publish a bilingual journal, *Nissa*, gave them the focus they had lacked. They applied for permission to publish in July 1984 and received it the following November.

Focus did not mean consensus, however. From the first issue, the women faced the dilemma of how to position themselves vis-à-vis the CSP. As one activist noted,

> [t]he Personal Status Code was then being attacked by the Islamists, but at the same time it was strongly defended by the government. There was no question, of course, of allying ourselves with the Islamists, but we didn't want to sound like a mouthpiece for the government either. Yet if we argued too strongly for progressive changes in the CSP, the journal might be confiscated by the authorities. . . .[21]

There were no easy answers to these issues and they continued to disagree over which questions they could or should address, in what way, and how to make such decisions.

The journal also suffered from financial problems. The start-up capital had come from the founders, as each contributed fifty Tunisian dinars.[22] But they were never able to sell enough copies to make the journal a break-even venture. Nor did they benefit from the financial assistance that the

Ministry of Culture had offered to other cultural journals: the Ministry routinely bought only 10 copies of *Nissa*, whereas it typically bought 1,000 copies of other journals. Nor did the women benefit from the government subsidy for paper, although one activist stated that this may have been the fault of the journal.[23]

Its last issue (number 7) appeared on the occasion of International Women's Day 1987.[24] During its brief life, *Nissa* had contributed to a movement of opinion aimed at promoting just and satisfying relations between the sexes. It had treated such issues as rape and the death penalty, the rights of children and the right to life, the campaign against the CSP, coeducation and mixing of the sexes, feminism, and labor union activism. There is no question in the mind of activists that in their experience with the journal they had benefitted from a certain openness under the Mzali government.[25] In the end, however, as we have seen with the study groups, that was not enough: "We were, throughout the whole experience of *Nissa*, unable to resolve our different points of view about the relationship between women's issues and broader issues. . . . We, and I speak about all of us, just didn't have the minimum tolerance necessary for other points of view."[26] Internal problems and dissent, not state coercion, appear to have been the most important immediate factors in the journal's demise, although the backdrop of an authoritarian state played a key structural role.

Not until 1986 was a distinct women's association established (although it was not formally granted its "visa" until 1989): AFTURD, l'Association des Femmes Tunisiennes pour la Recherche sur le Développement, which began as a local section of the Association Africaine pour la Recherche sur le Développement, based in Senegal. This, again, was a research-oriented organization, the objective of which was to conduct studies on the integration of women into the economic and social development process.[27]

EVALUATION

There seems little question that the opening of the early 1980s played a critical role in allowing for the operation of the various women's groups described above. In my interviews, women referred to these years as the golden age in comparison with the situation in the 1990s. However, the UNFT monopoly on women's activity made it much more difficult for the independent women to organize anything other than study groups. Hence, the coercive nature of the state played a key role in shaping what sort of groups might operate and how extensive their activities might be. At the same time, however, the Tunisian women activists are quite frank in their autocritiques, as they realize that their inability to reach a consensus on certain issues or on how to proceed also hampered their efforts.

The Atrophying of the Union Nationale des Femmes Tunisiennes (UNFT)

This development, like the others, has its roots in the general fossilization of the PSD and the broader crisis in the Tunisian political system. By 1980, there appears to have been little life left in the union, independent of the role some of its members played in various PSD and governmental structures. In other words, while it continued to play a role in the development of certain women's political careers, its service function had been seriously neglected. Given that it had been imposed from above as opposed to having been demanded from below, and given the paternalistic attitude Bourguiba and his regime had toward women and the UNFT, it was largely viewed as an organization intended to implement policy formulated from above and to reflect the glory of the Liberator of Tunisian Women.

Fathia Mzali did initiate the founding of a Committee on Women's Labor, which was intended to conduct research into the low levels of female labor force participation. There was also some discussion of focusing on the special problems and needs of women who emigrated abroad.[28] However, neither of these initiatives seems to have produced much in the way of results. Little concrete information about union activities is available for this period aside from the union's journal, *Al-Mar'ah*. From this journal the personality cult of Mzali is clear. By the mid-1980s, the journal was appearing infrequently and contained summaries of international or Arab regional conferences that the union hosted or attended rather than articles on UNFT activities.[29]

The most important development of the period was the establishment of the *alliances* or *rabitat*. Some of the *alliance* women did in fact prepare studies for and participate in discussions of draft laws,[30] but the *alliance* initiative was likely a defensive response to the beginnings of more open activism among the women who ultimately came together as the FD. Indeed, the fact that the UNFT had been allowed to lose its original dynamism did not mean that it (read, its president) was willing to cede territory it assumed to be its own without a fight. There is certainly enough evidence of UNFT displeasure with the emerging independent activity to support this contention. It was the UNFT that insisted the CSE be called a "study" club, that it be contained within the UGTT, and that it not be allowed to take on a life as a competing women's *political* organization.

Mzali's dismissal from her ministership as part of the events surrounding her husband's political demise led to her replacement for only a few months by UNFT treasurer Chehrezade Chaouche. At that time, newspaper stories began to appear that decried the UNFT's deterioration. The union was described as having become an official club for the socially prominent[31] which had allowed the union's literacy and professional training facilities, located largely in the rural areas, to languish. There were also several commentaries regarding the need to review *Al-Mar'ah* and to change its format to one that was more relevant to average women. These criticisms must be understood, of course, in the context of the permissibility of attacking the record of Mrs. Mzali, who had been dismissed and discredited, not as examples of freedom of expression. By this time the political opening was clearly over.

The UNFT Congress held in October 1986 elected a new president, Fatima Duweik, a member of the PSD Central Committee and a parliamentary deputy who had effectively left the union along with a number of other activists during the last years of Mzali's presidency. The press then changed its tone: it began to praise the new leadership, claiming that the problem of excessive bureaucratization had been overcome and that ideas and demands from the masses of women were now being received.[32] In fact, however, the changes were negligible. Indeed, despite her declarations of a desire to make the union more inclusive, Duweik made clear that she was first and foremost a PSD activist. Whether as part of a desire to distance herself as much as possible from her discredited predecessor or as a result of her lack of ease in dealing with professional and intellectual women, Duweik allowed the *alliances* to atrophy, thus sacrificing one of the few dynamic structures that remained to the UNFT.[33]

EVALUATION

The fossilization of the UNFT must be understood in the context of the broader crisis in the Tunisian political system and as part of the more specific process of lack of turnover or renewal among PSD cadres. Fathia Mzali's personal ambition—her assumption of the ministership and failure/refusal to relinquish responsibility for the union—was both cause and effect of the union's problems. The union would wait another several years before a serious initiative aimed at revival was launched.

The 1981 change in the Code du Statut Personnel (CSP)

By the mid-1960s, the legislation underpinning Bourguiba's developmentalist program was in place. Central, of course, was the CSP. The 1970 attempt by the UNFT under Radhia Haddad to push forward amendments to the CSP was quickly quashed by Bourguiba, who made clear that *he* and he alone was responsible for this portfolio. In any case, no new changes were introduced into the CSP until February 1981. As noted in the previous chapter, the idea to revise the law came as a result of the president's concern that a widow or divorcée be able to maintain a decent standard of living after losing her husband. To change the law to that end, in November 1980 the minister of justice assembled a committee of fourteen, including five women. About one-third of the members were Islamists, who were not terribly inclined to change the law, about one-half were secularists, who wanted to further develop Tunisian law, and the rest wanted only narrow changes.[34]

Several months were spent in deliberations, although not long enough according to some who felt that such serious topics merited a longer period of reflection.[35] Because of the relative balance between contending strains of opinion, the committee went back to the president for consultations. The president had been convinced of the need to find a system of sharing the fruits (*makasib*) of marriage, something along the lines of the idea of community property. However, at the meeting with the president, some members of the committee advised against the idea of an equal sharing, arguing that this was a European idea with no basis in Islam, and would, therefore, not be accepted by Tunisian society. Some even expressed the fear that not only would the desired goal (protecting these women) not be achieved, but that a backlash could occur; for example, women might be killed rather than divorced so that the husband could avoid dividing up property. In the end, therefore, it was the third group, those who supported the idea of only very narrow reforms, who won the day.[36]

EVALUATION

While it is true that this initiative came as the Islamists were beginning to flex their muscles (see chapter 7), there is no evidence to suggest that the president made the decision that the code needed to be revised because he wanted to reaffirm the state's concern with women in order to be sure, for example, that he could count on their support to counter this domestic political challenge. In the first place, testimony, both written and oral, insists that the sufferings of some divorced women *happened* to reach the president's ears, and he decided to act.[37] And, while it is true that these changes were implemented during the period of liberalization, it seems that this was an example of the president's acting independently and because he chose to do so. The only role that the liberalization may have played at this time was that the realm for public and media discussion of the changes was greater than it would otherwise have been.[38]

The Appointment of Two Women Ministers and the Creation of a New Ministry

There had been, for some time a discussion of the possibility of a woman's being appointed minister. Several names had been bandied about, including that of Fathia Mzali. Then, during the discussions of the 1983 budget, a number of female deputies had called for the revival (*ba'th*) of a high-level women's structure to look after the concerns of women.[39] Given that women's concerns were addressed by a number of ministries—justice, education, social affairs, health—the idea of the new Ministry for the Family and Promotion of Women was not that it be one devoted to actual administration and running of women's affairs, but rather one concerned with conceptualizing problems and solutions, of studying and making proposals that would harmonize the work of the other ministries on "women's issues" such as family planning, employment, women's rights, family assistance, and better integrating women into the development process. It was not intended to take over from other ministries their existing projects dealing with women, but to help coordinate policies. To that end the minister or the ministry was to be represented in all other bodies and agencies whose tasks dealt directly with women and the family.[40] The other unusual aspect of the ministry's structure was that, like the Ministry of Defense, it was to have an organic link directly with the president.[41] It is worth noting that at the same time Mzali was appointed to head this new ministry, another woman, Souad Yaacoubi, was appointed minister of state for public health, a position that later became a full-fledged ministership under her direction. (Unlike Mzali, Yaacoubi outlasted the *changement*, remaining at her post until the ministerial changes following the April 1989 elections.)

Mzali succeeded in recruiting to work with her several high-powered women who had been active in her *rabitat*, especially the one for women from legal professions (including Faiza Kefi from the Ministry of Planning, who assumed the presidency of the UNFT in 1993). Beyond that, the available record indicates two major accomplishments. The first is the brief publication of a new journal entitled *al-Mar'ah al-'A'ilah w-al-Sukkan* (Women, Family, and Population). The second was the union's supervision of the national committee to evaluate Tunisia's performance during the Women's Decade 1975–84. This involved the preparation, distribution, compilation and analysis of questionnaires for a report for the 1985 UN meeting in Nairobi.[42] In evaluating the impact of this ministry, beyond these two projects, it is difficult to point to anything more than symbolic importance. Although Mzali was appointed on November 1, 1983, the specifications of the ministry were not published until February 1984, and the ministry was closed by presidential decree on June 23, 1986, shortly before Muhammad Mzali was dismissed as prime minister. The *Journal Officiel de la République Tunisienne (JORT)*, the equivalent of an official gazette, was still publishing appointments of people from other government positions to work in the new ministry, as well as notices of basic job openings, up until the time the ministry was closed.

EVALUATION

The establishment of this ministry fit well with the modernizing image of Bourguiba's Tunisia. The announcement of the appointment of Fathia Mzali and Souad Yaacoubi to ministerial positions and the creation of a new ministry, which Mzali was to head, came at the height of Muhammad Mzali's power, November 1983. The question that arises, why did this happen in 1983?

Given the jockeying for power between Mzali and "the palace," one might have expected that the explanation lay in an attempt by the prime minister to fill the cabinet with those who were loyal or beholden to him. His wife was quite ambitious, and she had been pushing since 1978 for the establishment of a ministry to deal with women.[43] She must have assumed she would be the logical choice to head such an institution.

Another explanation, which seems eminently plausible given the nature of the regime and given the story behind the 1981 CSP changes, was that it had more to do with presidential whim.[44] Observers of the political scene at the time argued that the catalyst was the presence in the delegation that had accompanied President Mitterrand, on a recent visit to Tunisia, of Georgina Dufoix, recently appointed minister of social affairs and national solidarity in charge of family, population, and immigrant workers. Bourguiba was already sensitive to the issue of appointing a woman minister, had reportedly been thinking about it for some time, thought that its time had come, and the presence in such a delegation of Dufoix led him to act. Thus, according to this explanation, it was a presidential, not a prime ministerial, decision. It was also Bourguiba who reportedly defined the extent of the ministry's purview.

Again, it is difficult to see in these developments contestation or negotiation of broader social forces at work as the result of political liberalization. The president decided the establishment of this ministry and the appointment of two women was the appropriate next step in his continuing championing of the cause of women. While Mzali's position as prime minister cannot have hurt his wife's appointment chances, she had a very long and strong record with the PSD in her own right, which made her the logical candidate for this job, quite apart from the identity of her spouse. In the end, the ministry's life and Mzali's tenure were too short to make a longlasting impact.

The MTI's Challenge to the CSP[45]

The growing strength of the MTI ultimately led in summer 1985 to an unprecedented move: an open call for a referendum on the CSP. In an interview in *Jeune Afrique*, MTI leader A. Mourou argued that it was not the rights of women, but the rights of the *family* that the CSP should defend. He contended that there were gaps in the code that needed to be addressed and that the MTI was therefore calling for the establishment of a national council composed of specialists to review the CSP and the reasons for the deterioration of the cohesion of the Tunisian family.[46]

The MTI's challenge cannot be separated from the broader economic and political context. It will be remembered that following the riots of 1984, Mzali abandoned his attempt to coopt labor as a power base. In the meantime, he had been dealing with Islamists in one way or another, and while still not formally licensed, they were able to take advantage of the liberalization (and Mzali's political predicament) to assert themselves more forcefully. At the same time, a number of economic factors rendered their calls more acceptable. The economic crisis of the 1980s led increasing numbers of people in the political parties and unions to blame women for the economic and social deterioration. Unemployment, delinquency, and increasing instability in the family structure were all laid at the feet of a purported excessive liberation of women. The prescribed solutions were familiar: returning women to the home (from the labor market); reinstating polygamy; and making obtaining a divorce more difficult.

Even with the increasing economic pressures, however, most Tunisians did not respond to the MTI's call. Hence, it abandoned the idea of a referendum on the CSP, and instead called for a law forbidding mixed (Muslim female/non-Muslim male) marriages. A circular to this effect had been issued by the Ministry of Justice in November 1973, but such marriages continued to take place in the country. By focusing on this issue, the MTI was able to advocate the virtues of returning to the *shari'a* without directly confronting the CSP. Such a position enabled them to rally the largest number of people around their demand while neutralizing those who defended women's rights.

The UNFT was silent on this issue, but other groups were not, and there were numerous exchanges in the press on the subject during this period. Further fueling the debate was the fact that the LTDH was engaged in drafting its charter, and the secularists took advantage of this opportunity to propose the inclusion in it of an article calling for complete freedom of spousal choice.[47] This then triggered an even wider controversy. In the end there was no new law on mixed marriages. Instead, on August 13, 1985, the anniversary of the promulgation of the CSP, the mufti of the republic published a juridical-religious opinion forbidding such unions. For its part, the LTDH backed down and simply omitted any reference to religion from the article in question.[48]

EVALUATION

The combination of Mzali's equivocation in dealing with the Islamists, which offered them the equivalent of a political opening, and the growing economic crisis in the country helped to create an atmosphere in which Mourou's call for a reexamination of the CSP could not only be voiced openly but also strike a responsive cord with a segment of Tunisian society. While the Islamists were not yet in a position to challenge the state, in part because secular sentiment was still so strong, they were viewed as sufficiently powerful to force the LTDH to back down from its position on mixed marriages and to lead the state to reaffirm its opposition to such unions.

THE CHANGEMENT: PLURALISM ASCENDANT . . . PLURALISM QUASHED

The story of the place of women in the maneuvering and bargaining that took place under Ben 'Ali began immediately after the *changement*. Just as women and the CSP were a central part of the legitimacy formula of the Bourguiba regime, so they became under the new president. As was the case in the first section of this chapter, several developments will be examined to explore the relationship between women and the state during the period of liberalization and its aftermath. A final section, which examines developments as the state abandoned its experiement with political liberalization, is included to provide a contrast, especially since the Tunisian state has engaged in a number of high-profile initiatives apparently in support of women since the liberalization ended.

Ben Ali, the Islamists[49] and the Women

One author divides the post-Bourguiba period into three phases, and they are useful for organizing this discussion.[50] The first is the period of anticipation and uncertainty, which began with the "constitutional coup." Although women were one of the most important sectors referred to in Ben 'Ali's November 7 declaration, immediately thereafter rumors began to circulate that the new president intended to reverse some of Bourguiba's policies. According to testimony, men began to taunt women, taking special pleasure in menacing them with the possibility that the CSP would soon be a relic of the past.

Even more threatening, early moves by Ben 'Ali to relax the secularism of his predecessor's regime led some to conclude that a competition had developed between the PSD and the MTI over who was more Islamist.[51] The state's initial silence in the face of the questioning of women's gains even by some *deputies* was interpreted as meaning that the CSP was in jeopardy. Moreover, the swift move to Islamize state discourse—the introduction of television broadcasting of the calls to prayer, Ben 'Ali's making the *hajj*, and his references to the need to be faithful to the country's Arabo-Islamic heritage—gave Islamists hope, just as they troubled many women.[52]

Growing concern with the power of the Islamists began to lead to the coalescing of a group of democratic, liberal, reformist, and leftist women and men. On International Women's Day 1988, many who were concerned with the new direction in regime policy organized a series of activities to celebrate the CSP, women's other gains, citizenship, and secularism more broadly. In a speech on this occasion, the head of the LTDH stated that the time was not appropriate for pressing for more rights for women. Instead, the focus needed to be on protecting and reinforcing existing rights. In this way, men again took charge of the women's struggle, and limited it to one of a rear-guard defensive action in which the battle lines would be clearly drawn, and the only enemy would be the fundamentalists.[53] Whether the Tunisian men's response was because they were truly afraid of an Islamist backlash that would trigger instability or whether they simply used this to cover their own sexism is an open question.

Perhaps as a result of this series of events, in a March 20, 1988 address, Ben 'Ali called the CSP "un acquis civilisationnel irreversible." He thereby closed the book on any discussion of overturning the CSP and presented the state as the guarantor of the code. However, the president's position, similar to that of the LTDH, was also intended not to upset conservative sensitivities. His phrase, "Tout le CSP, mais rien que le Code," captured the new approach to women's rights: what had been granted would be preserved, but no amendments were envisioned. This speech marks the beginning of the second period, characterized by bargaining with and attempted cooptation, not only of the Islamists[54] but also, increasingly, of women.

At the end of the summer, the president announced his intention to assemble working committees to draft a National Pact. Participants in the discussions were to include representatives from the political parties, including the Islamists, as well as a variety of other organizations: the UGTT, the LTDH, UNFT, and even the unlicensed FD (later ATFD), as well as the doctors and engineers associations. The work was to focus on defining and agreeing upon the bases and principles required to preserve an *état de droit* (a state based on the rule of law). During the course of the discussions, great differences emerged. For example, the government and others wanted the Islamists to renounce violence as well as their desire to turn the clock back on certain issues. The MTI's primary goal at the time was to secure legal political party status, and it was willing to make substantial compromises to achieve it. The bargain that was finally struck to include the Islamists as signatories to the pact involved the MTI's acceptance of the designation of the CSP as an "irreversible civilizational gain" in exchange for the inclusion in the text of a phrase insisting upon Tunisia's Arabo-Islamic identity. In the end, the president declared that women were in fact responsible for safeguarding this identity, a charge that made many non-Islamist women extremely uncomfortable. Once again, the women's struggle had been redefined by the state to serve its interests.[55]

Despite the MTI's formal acceptance of the CSP through its adherence to the National Pact, Islamist candidates during the campaign for the April 1989 elections regularly attacked the code, often attracting large, supportive crowds. The Islamists placed women center-stage in their program, campaigning on the theme of "women and morals," lambasting "the modern woman" and glorifying "the veiled woman."[56] In response, on March 31, 500 women participated in a demonstration led by the still unlicensed ATFD, although the president of the UNFT, Neziha Mezhoud, was also present. Slogans called for no retreat on women's rights and for equality.[57]

In the end, the PSD turned RCD (Rassemblement Constitutionnel Démocratique) received 77.7 percent of the female vote (39.8 percent of eligible women), and 70.5 percent of the male vote (47.3 percent of the eligible men). Six RCD women were elected; the previous parliament had had seven. The success of the Islamists, who ran as independents, was estimated officially at 13 percent of the vote; however, according to informed observers, the percentage was actually much higher, especially in the urban areas and in Tunis in particular.[58]

Ben 'Ali was apparently surprised by their strong showing and stage three in the drama began in the wake of the elections.[59] As the Islamist threat appeared to increase both from abroad (Algeria) and domestically, Ben 'Ali's policy gradually turned into full-scale assault against al-Nahdah, while adopting a policy of more actively supporting women, at least in terms of form. While a concern for religious conservatism had clearly insinuated itself into regime, the threat that the state would make concessions to the Islamists on women or any other issue had dissipated. Whatever the brutality of the measures, many women (and other non-Islamists) justified the assault as the only means of preventing religious elements from taking power.

EVALUATION

One of the most interesting characteristics of the early Ben 'Ali period is the degree to which the regime's policy toward the Islamists became increasingly inseparable from its policy toward women. The important place that women and the CSP had had under Bourguiba meant that they would certainly be a target of Islamists seeking to restore Islam and women to their "proper place." Beginning with an ambivalent attitude toward women's concerns as it Islamized state discourse, the state gradually came to view women as a natural first defense line against the Islamists. With nowhere else to go, the women had little choice but to seek the protection of the state. Once the state decided to crack down, it was able to use its concern for women as a justification for its policy and as proof, especially to the outside world, of its continuing commitment to modernity and human rights, regardless of the brutality to which it had resorted.

The UNFT: the Struggle for Redefinition

As noted in the previous chapter, the UNFT was the central institution used by the state to channel women's activities. Over the years, several attempts by the UNFT to assert a degree of autonomy, or generate from within its ranks ideas for improving women's status, had been met with resistance, as the president kept women's affairs as his personal portfolio. Interest aggregation from the bottom up was neither envisioned nor appreciated.

The *changement* opened the way for change in the UNFT. In December 1987, it held a meeting in which independents joined with some members of the executive committee to issue the first call for autonomy of the organization from the PSD. A more serious discussion of this issue, however, had to await other developments. In February 1988, the RCD congress failed to reelect Fatima Duweik to its central committee, thus in effect forcing her to resign from the presidency of the UNFT. Dr. Neziha Mezhoud, who had been a member of the executive committee of the UNFT holding the health, social affairs, and social services portfolio but who had remained aloof from the conflicts that had recently plagued the union, was unanimously elected by the executive on August 9 to take Duweik's place.[60] The celebration of her installation later that month marked the first time that women from outside the union—the opposition—were invited to attend such an event. Mezhoud stressed that she wanted to break monopolies in the women's field and encourage independent associational activity.[61]

On September 8–9, 1988, the UNFT central council met to confirm the election of Mezhoud and to begin to address three basic issues: setting new general directions and ways of working; restructuring the union and its by-laws; and participating in drafting the National Charter. The 1988 congress of the PSD turned RCD had declared its interest in preserving the independence of national organizations like the UNFT. Thus at the September meeting discussion began of the nature of the union's relationship with the RCD. The UNFT executive agreed upon the principle of union independence, but in the framework of preserving cooperation and some ties with the RCD. The union's growing financial problems, the need to seek funding from international agencies, and the importance of reinvigorating the *alliances* were also addressed.[62] In order to reinterest women in the UNFT and stem what she and others saw as growing marginalization, Mezhoud invited all women of good will to put their interest in women's issues above partisan concerns. From the UNFT's side she promised a change in modus operandi, including more varied and mobilizing programs of action.[63]

In keeping with her invitation of non-UNFT or RCD women to her installation, one of Mezhoud's first initiatives was to broaden the appeal of the UNFT by organizing the coordination of women of different political backgrounds, including the ATFD women, to solicit their opinion regarding the union. Many insisted upon an end to the union's dependence upon the party as a condition for their further involvement. Some expressed skepticism regarding the move toward greater autonomy when the UNFT was taking its budget directly from the RCD, its president continued to be a member of the party's central committee, and the majority of its members were recruited from RCD ranks.[64] A meeting was held on November 9, 1988, which did include a few women from outside the UNFT and the RCD, to discuss the future relationship between the woman's organization and the party, but little progress was made.[65]

On January 19–20, 1989, the union's national council, comprising 200 delegates, met. No political parties were invited, but some independent women received invitations. This was the first meeting of the national council since the *changement*. The central issue under discussion was the UNFT-RCD relationship, and two proposals were put forward. The first was to adjust the relevant paragraph in the bylaws to read that there would be relations of cooperation with the RCD and mutual assistance with other organizations working to emancipate women. The second was to remove the paragraph altogether so that there would be no reference to the nature of the relationship between the party and the UNFT. Not surprisingly, there were strong differences of opinion between the two camps. The larger, but less cohesive, of the two wanted the union to become independent. The other group wanted to maintain a special relationship with the party based on only partial independence, and although smaller, it enjoyed a certain historic legitimacy in the union.[66] While initially the council seemed to be moving toward autonomy, the old guard flexed its muscle to secure a reaffirmation of the traditional relationship between the UNFT and the party.[67] In the end, the bylaws were changed largely in line with the opinion of the more powerful minority, so that the UNFT became an organization with "privileged ties" with the RCD.[68]

While this was the most critical issue addressed by the conference, dissatisfaction in the ranks was manifested in discussions of other issues as well, including many that had been raised in 1986 at the previous congress: problems of finance, centralization of power, the place of women in political leadership positions, the undervalued role of UNFT representatives in rural areas, and so on.[69]

In the meantime, there did appear to be some positive changes in the UNFT. The very fact that its president was pushing the question of autonomy from the RCD was nothing short of revolutionary. The UNFT line had also begun to evolve, as was evident in Mezhoud's interviews on radio and television. The journal *Al-Mar'ah* had received a facelift and expanded publication (4,700 copies in June 1991, 18,500 in August 1991). Its more streamlined version was bilingual (the old version had been almost exclusively in Arabic), and had regular sections devoted to issues such as health, children, food, beauty, culture, and short stories. The UNFT structure also underwent a change: 60.9 percent of its women in leadership positions changed, and of the new totals, 83 percent were between twenty and forty years-of-age.[70] In addition, Mezhoud founded new *alliances* dealing with the sectors of education, health, social affairs, and office/government employees.[71] Perhaps more important were some of the public positions that the union took on political issues. For example, it denounced the negative attitudes expressed by a parliamentary deputy (RCD) regarding women's participation in political life mentioned in chapter 1. It expressed its support for Minister of Education Charfi, when the Islamists launched their campaign against him, and it joined the ATFD in a demonstration on the eve of the April 1989 parliamentary elections. The UNFT cast itself as appealing to women who wanted to work but thought of themselves as moderates, those who were looking for dialogue and evolutionary change, not those who wanted to, as they put it—no doubt referring to those women of an ATFD inclination—"shock public opinion."[72]

But change in such an organization does not come easily, and despite attempts by Mezhoud at renewal, there appeared to be little change in the tone or level of the discussions from the 1986 meeting.[73] Indeed, the UNFT Congress held December 7–9, 1989, at which Mezhoud was re-elected, reflected many of the more general problems from which the UNFT suffered. Although she stressed the importance of reasserting the value of the role of the UNFT at a juncture marked by the emergence of "retrograde, reactionary and extremist tendencies," in general, there was no spirit of struggle or volunteerism among the participants.[74]

EVALUATION

Several factors explain the UNFT attempts at revival. The first was a general revival in the party and government itself announced and pushed by Ben 'Ali. In this atmosphere of renewed enthusiasm about politics, many who had left the union or had never thought seriously of joining began to show interest. The focus on pluralism and the limited period of greater freedom of expression also opened the way for a discussion of union autonomy, a subject that could not have been broached before. Perhaps further triggering action was the presence of the ATFD and the feeling on the part of the UNFT that it needed to position itself in rela-tion to ATFD demands.

At the same time, the brief opening created threats to the union in terms of its relationship to the party. For example, at the time of the designation of the new central committee of the RCD as well as at the time of the 1989 legislative elections, it became clear that the UNFT no longer constituted the sole training ground for RCD women candidates. Similarly, the women of the RCD, even those of the central committee, have not felt obliged to join the UNFT. Some have even tried to create women's groups within the party, attempts against which the UNFT has protested, since it considers these unnecessary parallel structures.[75] It has also lost its monopoly posi-tion among state organizations as the regime has created a number of gov-ernmental NGOs dealing with women. Moreover, the state's adoption of the discourse of pluralism has led to the licensing of real NGOs that in ef-fect compete with the UNFT in a variety of areas that had long belonged solely to it. At the same time, however, the RCD continues to treat the UNFT as a part of the party's field of control. Hence, it has gained neither substantive autonomy nor maintained the power it once exerted within the party and state structures.

The Story of the ATFD

The eventual legalization of the Femmes Démocrates, the first indepen-dent women's organization with a clearly activist (as opposed to research) agenda, is one of the most important stories of this period. Following the *changement*, the ATFD published a declaration carrying eighty signatures and underlining the importance of the CSP, among other issues.[76] Although still unlicensed, the women were consulted on the National Pact in fall 1988, and five ATFD members were granted an audience with the president during which they were promised that their organization would be licensed.

They first asked for a *visa* (license) in late November 1988, but were denied the right to hold a press conference on that occasion. A formal request for licensing in February 1989 was also denied. ATFD members suggested that the UNFT had exerted pressures so that they not be legalized. (The UNFT president did state that it was very painful for them to see the emergence of another women's group, especially one that had such dislike for the UNFT.)[77] In any case, they then approached the minister of the interior for clarification. In late July 1989 they were asked to reformulate certain articles of their statutes. After doing so they presented a new request, which was approved and announced on August 11.[78] Despite the long-standing antagonism between the two, in the face of rising interest in Islam by the state, the ATFD and the UNFT moved closer together, first, just prior to the 1989 parliamentary elections and then again on December 27, 1990, against positions taken by certain deputies calling into question women's rights. They also organized a series of meetings in support of Algerian women.[79] In general, however, it was the ATFD that initiated such activities.

ATFD goals include the elimination of discrimination against women, defending existing rights, and developing Tunisian legislation so that there is greater real equality between the sexes. They also seek to change patriarchal and discriminatory attitudes, to encourage women to take charge of their struggle themselves (rather than continuing to rely on "gifts" from the state), and to encourage women to participate in civil and political life. They view women's rights as an inseparable part of human rights, and the struggle to achieve these rights as part of a larger battle against all forms of discrimination, and part of the struggle for true democracy.[80]

Despite quite limited resources, the ATFD has sponsored numerous conferences and workshops on women's rights and concerns. The newspapers of the period carried periodic statements from the ATFD in response to statements by members of al-Nahdah or the government which challenged women's rights. They also made clear their desire to participate in government discussions relative to women's status (such as the Women and Development commission intended to prepare suggestions for the eighth development plan) by suggesting and calling for the need to change or amend certain legislation.

While it continues to argue for changes in Tunisian legislation to improve women's status, the gradual closing of the "opening" has left the ATFD less and less room to militate on this front. Perhaps as a result, since 1991, one of the primary foci of their programs has been the campaign to sensitize men and women to the problem of violence against women. Although the UNFT and the Ministry of Women's Affairs also officially have structures to address this problem, the ATFD was the first to push for a more open discussion of it. They began with a poster campaign and then organized an international seminar on the topic. This was followed by a series of roundtables and workshops to train women to work at what became a violence counselling center at its headquarters supported by small contributions from Italian, German, and American institutions.[81]

EVALUATION

The ATFD is the one women's NGO in Tunisia with a clearly political message and program. The inheritors—indeed in many cases the original activists—of the independent women's study groups of the 1980s were finally able, in the ATFD, to agree upon an organizational structure and receive a license from the government. This was no mean achievement and cannot be explained except in the framework of the conditions surrounding the *changement*, including the Islamist challenge. As one analyst argued, "[u]ltimately the government granted the union a visa, not out of respect for free contestation but rather because it realized the UFD [*sic*] could mobilize a significant force of feminists behind the regime's campaign to battle the Islamists."[82] At the same time, the presence of a legalized ATFD served other regime interests as well, since, as one former activist described it, it was "a nice decoration when the question of civil society or democracy was raised."[83]

While its mere existence is extremely significant, for reasons related to broad political constraints as well as the feminist aspects of its program, membership remains small, and women come and go depending upon the political atmosphere. In 1989, when women were worried about the fundamentalists, many joined the ATFD ranks. Some were demobilized after the regime began its assault against the fundamentalists and the danger to the CSP appeared to fade.[84] However, the increasing coercion resorted to by the state against even non-Islamist opposition forces has led some ATFD activities to be canceled, and the narrowing of the realm of activity has hurt the appeal of an organization that continues to guard its autonomy and work on political issues. The women are faced continuously with the dilemma of maintaining relevance (through an acceptable level and variety of activities), which requires some form of working or cooperating with the state, and avoiding cooptation.[85] As the margin of freedom of activity has narrowed, it has become increasingly difficult for the women to remain both relevant to political developments and true to their principles.

BEN ALI, THE PROLIFERATION OF WOMEN'S ORGANIZATIONS, AND THE PROMOTION OF WOMEN

Starting with the discussions leading to the issuance of the National Pact, but especially since the beginning of the battle against the Islamists, government officials have stressed the importance of associational life or civil society. As al-Nahdah's fortunes declined and women's currency with the state began to increase in value, one of the most notable developments has been the state policy of institutionalizing a concern for women along with an (obviously selective) promotion of women to high profile positions. This period has also produced a variety of apolitical women's organizations.

In June 1991 Ben 'Ali announced the establishment of a National Consultative Commission on Women and Development, which was to prepare a report for consideration during discussions of the Eighth National Development Plan. While this was viewed as a positive development, it came after the initial working groups had already been assembled, and criticism was raised that there was no special working group on women. In the wake of the criticisms, such a group was convened, but it had only two months to prepare a report that the other sectoral commissions had had two years to write. A variety of individuals as well as institutional actors, including the ATFD, were involved in the commission's discussions, which focused on education and literacy, health and family planning, vocational training and development, and information, culture, and communication. The ATFD women felt that most of the content had largely been predetermined. However, they were able to argue that schooling should be made compulsory and in 1992 the education law was amended to make schooling a requirement, not just a right.[86]

The real move to reinforce the state's position vis-à-vis women was initiated on December 31, 1991 (following the first round of the ultimately aborted Algerian elections), when Ben 'Ali called for a commission to examine women's legal status—especially, but not exclusively, the CSP—to explore ways to reinforce and develop women's gains without contradicting the country's Arabo-Islamic identity. The commission began meeting in February 1992 to review all laws. It comprised fifteen members, including seven women: one, an adviser to the president; two law professors; three lawyers, and a theologian. Its recommendations were announced on Women's Day, August 13, 1992, and finally came into effect a year later. As the previous chapter detailed, the new CSP revisions included some very positive elements. However, in announcing these changes, the president concluded his speech by mentioning the coming "payback dates" (presumably elections) which would allow the state to evaluate how women were shouldering their responsibility.[87]

In the realm of high-level appointments, in January 1992 a woman was named vice-president of the parliament, and a municipal councilor from Gabes and member of the RCD, Chadlia Boukhchina, was named by Ben 'Ali as a political adviser, the first woman ever to serve the president in such a capacity. At about the same time, party faithful Naziha Zarrouk was appointed permanent secretary in charge of RCD women's affairs. The party then also appointed regional RCD women's coordinators. On August 17, 1992, the president announced the nomination of two women to the government: Nabiha Gueddana, state secretary attached to the prime ministry charged with women's and family affairs; and Neziha Mezhoud (who had been the head of the UNFT), state secretary attached to the Minister of Social Affairs. At the same time, six women were appointed *chargées de mission* at the ministries of foreign affairs, international cooperation and foreign investment, national economy, housing, transportation, and professional training and employment.[88] Following the RCD congress in early September 1993, Gueddana, who was not on the new RCD central committee, was replaced by Mezhoud, and the position was upgraded to full ministerial status. At the same congress, Neziha Zarrouk became only the second woman to win a place on the RCD Politburo.

If one moves to the realm of governmental NGOs, perhaps no institution has as high an external profile as CREDIF (Centre de Recherche, d'Etudes, de Documentation, et d'Information sur la Femme.) Created in August 1990 as an administrative service, it was made a public establishment by a subsequent change in the law. It continued to receive state money under the supervision of the Ministry of Women's and Family Affairs, but was thereby accorded greater autonomy. It is housed in a large three-story building in the upscale al-Manar district, where it has a small but impressive and growing library. CREDIF is responsible for monitoring the condition of Tunisian women in order to provide data to decisionmakers. It has developed a data bank on women and women's issues and has initiated and is the focal point of a network of information on women for Tunisia and North Africa. The center has also produced a number of studies on women's condition, Tunisian women's oral histories, women's legal status, and the like, in addition to publishing a regular magazine and bulletin. Not surprisingly. CREDIF has already become a prominent reference center in its area of expertise. It also organized and hosted a series of conferences, including some in preparation for Tunisia's participation in the 1995 UN conference on women in Beijing.[89]

There has also been a proliferation of real, as opposed to governmental, NGOs dealing with women, although they are either clearly humanitarian or developmentalist in thrust. Before concluding, it is worth discussing one last organization: Rihana, the network of NGOs that participated together in the Beijing conference. Initially, the NGOs had been approached by Minister of State for Women and Family Affairs, Nabiha Gueddana, for input into the Tunisian governmental report for Beijing. Her/the state's desire was that all activity be coordinated through the ministry, but the NGOs refused. Then came an initiative of the UNFT, to establish the network which they named Rihana. Nine women's NGOs, among them the UNFT and ATFD, agreed to work together for a number of goals while preparing for the international women's conference. This type of coordination was unprecedented and was especially notable since it involved working with the UNFT. In a way it was still the state's highly touted *partenariat* (partnership between civil society and the state) formula, but with an organization identified as not completely coincident with the state.[90] The discussions were not always easy, and the difficulty of working together was clear in interviews with UNFT and ATFD women.(None of the other organizations had the same history of nonrecognition or antagonism.) But for three years, women who had previously refused to set foot in each other's headquarters met on a weekly basis.[91] Not all were pleased with the outcome of the joint presentation at Beijing (a workshop and a video presentation), but both sides insisted that they had learned a great deal from the experience and that it had, at very least, de-demonized the other.[92]

EVALUATION

Given that women had lined up behind the state as it cracked down on the Islamists, as the assault was ending in late 1991 and in 1992, Ben 'Ali in effect "rewarded" the women with a series of gestures of support, both symbolic and concrete, but all in the framework of reinforcing domestic stability, Tunisia's image of progress and pluralism, and women's dependence upon the state. His 1988 speech closing the door to any revisions of the CSP had already reasserted the president's special prerogative in addressing the women's portfolio. However, the introduction of new amendments to the CSP in 1992 was the first clear demonstration of the president's intent publicly to promote women's issues. In so doing he was operating in the Bourguibist tradition. Yet, by simultaneously making a number of appointments of women to key party and governmental positions and promoting the development of associational life (if in a highly constrained or controlled form), Ben 'Ali also clearly distinguished himself from his predecessor's legacy of a one-party state.

CONCLUSIONS

Under both periods of liberalization and subsequent retrenchment examined above, women's issues became sources of contention between regime and opposition, but to different degrees. The opening under Mzali offered the first real opportunity since independence for women to come together outside the framework of the UNFT monopoly. While the women's efforts were limited by their lack of experience, their small numbers, and the continuing pressures from an authoritarian state, they nonetheless carved out a certain space that they continued to develop and eventually built into an independent women's organization. At the same time, however, the combination of regional factors and a growing domestic political crisis meant that the liberalization under Mzali also opened the door to other non-PSD Tunisians to operate more freely. While some of the minor opposition parties certainly took advantage of this opportunity, the group whose strength continued to grow through the period was the Islamists.

Just as questions related to women's status had been central to Bourguiba's modernization project so they were to the Islamists' program for putting Tunisian society back on the road to fuller implementation of *shari'a*, a program that, on the basis of MTI's own discourse, many women understood to portend major retreats from the rights they enjoyed. Although Mzali's flirtation with the Islamists as he searched for coalition partners to reinforce his position made many Tunisian women nervous, as long as Bourguiba was in power there seemed little chance of the prime minister's ceding ground on the CSP. The cases of women-state interaction examined above to a large extent reflect the president's continuing personal monopoly of decisions related to women, not a real response by the state to pressures from below, Islamist or feminist. The only exceptions are the development of the ATFD precursor groups (the most obvious example of women's ability to take advantage of a political opening) and the increasing assertiveness of the MTI.

Under Ben 'Ali, the stakes were raised. Despite the general relief that Bourguiba had been removed from the presidency without bloodshed or civil unrest, Ben 'Ali still needed to consolidate his position and distinguish himself from his predecessor. At the same time, he had to address the pressures for change in the political system, including the growing Islamist movement. The examples above have outlined how regime policy gradually shifted from one of compromise with or cooptation of the Islamists to one of treating women as the first line of defense against them. While Ben 'Ali "rewarded" his female reservists with a variety of legislative amendments and high-level promotions after the battle was won, the approach is fraught with dangers: it leaves women dependent upon the state to defend their rights and makes them the most likely target of backlash should the regime change.

The state under Ben 'Ali has certainly recognized women as a pressure group of importance, but it has also decided that any further evolution of law or status has to be within a more conservative framework.[93] Many Tunisian women are unwilling to criticize the regime's approach. They have been profoundly affected by developments in Algeria and believe that their choice is between the current Tunisian government and the Islamists. They also compare their status to women elsewhere and see that they have many advantages. The women of the ATFD, on the other hand, argue that there has been a real retreat in the women's situation in Tunisia, regardless of the changes introduced in 1993. They are most concerned with the continuing conservative nature of a state discourse pervaded by Islamic idiom. They are uncomfortable with the National Charter's reference to the country's Arabo-Islamic heritage, viewing it as a serious departure from the more secular orientation of the Bourguiba years. The state has refused to define what it means by this phrase, and thus there is always the possibility that it could be used to justify a retreat in the field of women's rights.[94]

The National Charter called for a *partenariat* (partnership) between the state and civil society. This means some form of cooperation, but it is not supposed to involve absorption. Yet, Ben 'Ali's successes in coopting opposition members have already been mentioned. What must be stressed in conclusion is that while the state discourse is one of pluralism, civil society, and tolerance (the code word for anti-fundamentalism), the practice is that of demobilization, depoliticization, and coercion—to the extent that all opposition, even secular and loyal, is treated as threatening. Even the concept of citizenship remains problematic. Despite the degree to which Bourguiba's reforms helped to liberate Tunisian women, as one analyst has pointed out, this "liberation in the framework of her private family space was accompanied by an infantilization of the individual Tunisian (man and woman) in the framework of public space"[95] through the institution of the single party and its affiliated structures and by the broader authoritarian nature of the regime. Under Ben 'Ali there is a window dressing of political pluralism, but the levels of coercion remain high. The regime plays on Tunisians' fears of a spillover from Algeria to justify its continuing repressive policies. It is not a situation which bodes well for the further development of any rights; indeed, the trend is clearly one of erosion. Yet, as long as the economy appears to perform well and the country is stable, many Tunisians, women and men, will be unwilling to risk the rise of Islamist influence and the losses they believe it would bring, by pushing for a greater opening of the system.

CONCLUSIONS

MENA Women and Political Liberalizations: Years of Living Dangerously?

Women establish new organizations with political programs and seek legalization, but operate in the absence of formal licensing. Of various political stripes, they run for parliamentary and municipal election, often against daunting odds. They collect signatures demanding changes in personal status laws against the backdrop of charges of apostasy. Some open violence hotlines or dare for the first time to report domestic abuse. Islamist women insist upon their right to veil; secular women argue against programs aimed at sex segregation. There are those who become engaged in literacy, health awareness, and child-rearing programs, while others demand the release of political detainees and greater respect for human rights. Women are lauded by some for efforts to eliminate discriminatory elements in labor and pension laws; they are attacked, sometimes physically, by others who deplore their insistence upon greater visibility and power in the so-called public realm.

These are but a few of the images of MENA women during the periods of liberalization examined in this study. Their efforts range from the modest to the heroic. In political climates in part characterized by increased possibilities, the authors of these stories—whether Islamist or secularist, young or old, rich or poor—have been engaged in efforts aimed at laying the bases for improvements in their lives, as well as those of their families and their societies more broadly. At the same time, as the images recalled above make clear, the atmosphere of increased opening has also often meant that women have had to confront threats, some of them quite serious, to existing rights. Political liberalizations, like other forms of regime change, can be characterized by increased perils. The fact that in each of the three cases examined here women at the time of this writing appeared to have been spared or overcome challenges to their rights that emerged with the beginning of the liberalizations does not change the fact that at various points during the transitions—according to their own testimonies, which I have accepted—they felt or knew themselves to be under siege.[1]

I undertook this study with the goals of determining and detailing the interaction of key factors that affected women's fates during these periods. The three MENA cases examined in detail have underlined the importance of a number of the same elements first suggested by the brief examination of several Latin American and Eastern European cases:

- the nature and source of the liberalization;
- the relationship between women and the state prior to liberalization;
- the role that organized women's groups played in triggering the transition;
- the relationship between conservative forces (religious or others) and the regime both prior and subsequent to the beginning of the liberalization;
- and the balance of forces on the political stage as the new (or reconstructed) regime seeks to consolidate itself.

In addition, for the MENA cases, I gave detailed consideration to the impact of external factors. The lessons or generalizations that emerge from these cases are presented below.

THE NATURE AND SOURCE OF THE LIBERALIZATION

One major distinction among liberalizations is whether they fall closer to the shock or the gradual end of the transition spectrum. Few liberalizations may be characterized as single shock, although several have been encountered in this study. Most are the result of more extended processes. Among the three cases considered in detail, Tunisia's opening of the early 1980s, Jordan's of the mid-1950s, and Morocco's more recent liberalization are examples of gradual openings. In the case of Tunisia, although the liberalization unfolded against the backdrop of economic crisis, it nonetheless apparently owed more to jockeying for power position among Bourguiba's potential successors. In Jordan, the country's first democratic experiment owed to a combination of regional political ferment and the youth and inexperience of the monarch. Morocco's liberalization since the second half of the 1980s has derived from Hassan's desire to overcome malaise in both the economic and political systems. It has also been an attempt to reach out to constituencies that were perceived to be of growing importance domestically (particularly the urban middle classes) and internationally, given his desire for fuller membership in the European Union.

In contrast, both Jordan (1967 and 1989) and Tunisia (1987) experienced openings triggered by a single, identifiable event. In the case of Tunisia, Ben 'Ali reportedly decided to retire the aging president on November 7, 1987 because of the imminent possibility of an Islamist move against the state. Whether the explanation is accurate or not is less important for our purposes than the fact of Bourguiba's swift replacement. Although Ben 'Ali had risen through the Bourguibist ranks and hence cannot be viewed as an outsider, once in charge he was forced to consolidate support for his rule against the backdrop of the formidable legacy of Tunisia's leader since independence. In Jordan, in 1967 the opening resulted from the defeat in the June war, which discredited the regime and its security forces. In April 1989, on the other hand, economic riots triggered the decision to liberalize, although political and economic crisis or malaise constituted the broader backdrop. The prime minister was ousted, but as in 1967, the king remained, thus ensuring a certain continuity. Nonetheless, the fact that the riots had broken out among a sector of the population long assumed to be the bedrock of regime support called into question the stability or solidity of the ruling coalition and raised the possibility of reconsolidation along modified lines.

The evidence presented in these cases, as well as those from Latin America and Eastern Europe, suggests that a transition closer to the shock end of the spectrum poses more possibilities as well as threats to women. It is the uncertainty regarding the possibility for domestic coalitional alliance shifts during this period of (re)consolidation, that is the basic source of opportunities and perils. Gradual transitions may be less dramatic, but they may also be much safer, since the leadership is either not overthrown, or is removed from power through a progressive unfolding of events that lessen the uncertainty involved in the search for new allies. I will explore this point again below.

WOMEN AND THE STATE PRIOR TO LIBERALIZATION

The Tunisian case underscores the importance of evaluating the legal and social status of women prior to the liberalization in order to understand the outcome. While improving social welfare indicators was certainly an important part of Jordanian domestic policy, Tunisia is the only one of the three cases in which the regime had made support for improvement in women's status (if within certain limits) a central part of its program. In Tunisia, the stress on education and the availability of contraceptives from the early 1960s meant that women were not only trained to participate in the labor force, they also had a certain degree of reproductive choice. While their participation in the political life of the country was not extensive, some did join the PSD, and several women reached positions of prominence. Although not initially conceived of in this way, Bourguiba's CSP became one of the defining features of his regime. Over the years he counted upon women—to whom *he* had granted the right to education, contraception, and freedom from the fear of polygamy—as a reliable base of regime support.

The situations in Jordan and Morocco were somewhat different. In the case of Jordan, while there have been notable efforts to expand social and educational infrastructure, the higher levels of literacy and education among Jordanian (both Palestinian and Transjordanian) women, did not translate into a noticeable increase in women's participation in either the formal sector workforce or in other aspects of public life. Education of women continued (and continues to this day, if to a decreasing extent) to be viewed as a means of preparing a woman to be a more attractive marriage partner to someone who would be able to ensure that she need not work outside the home. Moreover, the conservative nature of the society, the underindustrialized nature of the economy, and the suppression of civil society activity in general combined to lead to a limited presence of women in the so-called public sphere.

Unlike Jordan, in which the state has directly reached the most remote corners of the kingdom through, most notably, recruitment into the army, the state in Morocco has continued to rely on a much more indirect form of control, ruling through rural notables.[2] As a result of its less than benign neglect of rural areas combined with deteriorating economic conditions since the mid-1980s, literacy levels are relatively low, and some argue that they are dropping under the weight of various structural adjustment policies. The importance of women's labor in the agricultural sector as well as their role in the informal sector (as economic conditions have worsened) has meant that despite their inferior legal status and educational levels, women's labor force participation rate in Morocco is similar to that of Tunisia. Nonetheless, it is largely the women of the post-independence urban middle class, with their access to state schooling and fellowships, who have entered the higher profile public arena.

The strength of the women's movement or of women's organizations and their relationship to the state prior to the political transition are two additional factors of crucial importance under this general rubric. In the cases of Jordan and Morocco, while women's groups had long been active in a range of charitable and other efforts, the number of women involved in groups that sought serious change in women's status was small, and some groups were neither formally licensed nor recognized. They were, therefore, not in a position to be involved in the push for liberalization. In Jordan, women's organizations had suffered a fate similar to that of other civil society organizations: anything that smacked of politics or of a challenge to the system was generally swiftly shut down. The one clear attempt by the state to establish a women's union (the GFJW) was apparently undertaken with the aim of controlling women's organizational activity. In the case of Morocco, Hassan did establish the UNFM as a national women's organization, but its activities have been largely limited to charitable activities and sending congratulatory cables on the occasion of national holidays. While it has offices across the kingdom, they have never had a mobilizational function. In contrast, in Tunisia, Bourguiba's single-party state established the UNFT, which extended its branches and activities throughout the country. However, like the PSD of which it was an extension, it had grown sclerotic long before the 1987 coup and had never had a mandate to mobilize women to express grassroots demands.

THE ROLE OF WOMEN IN FORCING THE TRANSITION

While women in all three countries have played roles in opposition groups or parties, none of these groups can be credited with "forcing the opening." Instead, despite differences in numbers and previous experience, in all three cases, there were women who had been champing at the bit to exploit a greater organizational opening, as well as women who, once the opening appeared, eagerly took advantage of it. Indeed, one of the notable characteristics of the liberalizations in all three countries has been the attempts by a variety of organizations to seek formal recognition (the UAF and ADFM in Morocco, the ATFD in Tunisia), or to revive repressed or frozen organizations (the JWU in Jordan).

The MENA women's experiences contrast sharply with the Latin American cases, in which women actually put themselves on the front lines of the battle against the authoritarian regimes, even if in some cases it was in their roles as wives and mothers. While women's active involvement in political movements has not necessarily meant special consideration in the aftermath of the struggle, in the case of the women in Latin America, the fact that they were an important and visible part of the grassroots movement that helped topple the dictators seems to have been an important factor in investing them with power during the transition. The transitional regimes appear to have recognized not only the women's role, but also their continuing importance as a political constituency. Similarly, the *absence* of prominent women's organizations in the transitions in the Eastern European cases (and the association of the existing ones with the former communist regimes) seems to account in part for the treatment women's concerns received from the successor governments. The three MENA cases resemble the Eastern European experience on this point.

THE STATE AND CONSERVATIVE FORCES

The relationship between women and the state/regime prior to the liberalization is clearly connected with another, extremely important, factor: the relationship between the regime and conservative forces. In the MENA context of the 1980s and 1990s, the most important oppositional forces have been Islamist, of various stripes. It must be stressed, however, that there is nothing to suggest that across time and space this is the only possible expression of conservatism, nor that such groups should constitute the most important opposition. Indeed, if one looks at the 1950s, 1960s and 1970s, the relative weight of groups along the political spectrum in the MENA region was quite different than it is today.

In any case, the weight and composition of conservative forces is critical for this analysis. Unlike Bourguiba's republican regime, which preached a not-so-veiled secularism and which had fired its opening shot in its quest to consolidate power at the religious elite, the monarchies of both Jordan and Morocco are dependent to one degree or another for their legitimacy on their relationship to Islam and to the religious establishment. In the case of Morocco, Hassan claims descendance from the Prophet Muhammad, and the *ulama* have long been a key source of regime support. Given that issues related to women and the family are viewed by such forces as falling within the purview of Islamic law, any attempt at reinterpretation that appears to challenge Islamic teachings may be expected to be fought vigorously by the *ulama* and certainly be viewed warily by the king. Viewing the field of potential allies as the liberalization unfolded, Hassan, who is neither democrat nor liberal, would have found few incentives to risk alienating a long-standing source of support for the sake of a sector of the population (women) that had yet to demonstrate much power or coherence.

In the case of Jordan, Husayn also claims descendance from the Prophet, although, unlike Hassan, he has never asserted a right to rule on matters related to religion. The relationship between the regime and conservative religious elements is best exemplified by the generally cooperative ties the leadership had with the Muslim Brotherhood over the years. Husayn has long presented Jordan as a forward-looking country and has promoted education and interaction with the West, yet he has never challenged the complex of societal and religious structures and practices that underpin the second-class status of Jordanian women. He has no doubt been aided by the fact that most of the country's politically aware population has been preoccupied with the

Arab-Israeli conflict over the years. Since the liberalization, the king's sister, Princess Basma, has assumed the women's portfolio. In so doing, however, she has been careful to place any suggestions for change within the framework of the country's Islamic heritage and traditions.

To sum up, in the case of both Jordan and Morocco, the relationship between the regime and religious or socially conservative forces in the country has generally been quite good, while in Tunisia, despite an apparent courting by Mzali of the MTI in the early 1980s, relations have been tense. This was certainly the case at the time Ben 'Ali made his decision to retire Bourguiba. The question then arises as to the salience of the nature of such relations for women and the state in the framework of political liberalization. To address this issue, however, a presentation of the political landscape at the time of the initiation of the change is needed.

THE POLITICAL LANDSCAPE AT THE TIME OF LIBERALIZATION / RECONSOLIDATION

In the case of Morocco, in which there has been a very gradual transition, the regime has remained largely unchanged. Although Hassan has instituted political reforms intended ultimately to lead to an *alternance* (a rotation of power in parliament between the royalist and so-called opposition parties), the bases of the regime have remained their conservative selves. The role of Islamist groups continues to be of some concern to the regime, but they appear to be either coopted or largely in tow, and the secular or leftist "opposition" is fully implicated in the system. As a result, in the Moroccan case there has been no attempt by conservative forces as the liberalization unfolded to use the relatively greater freedom to push for a retreat in women's position or rights.

In the case of Jordan, the fact that it was the solidly Transjordanian south—areas and towns from which much of the Jordanian army is recruited—that rioted in 1989 clearly called into question one of the traditional bases of the regime's support. The story of the forces and coalitions at work in the 1989 and 1993 parliaments will not be repeated here. What is important to remember is that the Brotherhood and its allies clearly emerged as *the* force to be dealt with in the immediate aftermath of the 1989 elections: the regime's traditional opponents, the leftists and Arab nationalists, had not won enough seats to pose a threat. While the Brotherhood was hardly an unknown quantity, one thing had changed: it was now in a position to push for parts of its program through legislation. Given the Islamists' numbers in parliament and the clear support they enjoyed among the population, the regime was in effect forced to negotiate over Ikhwan demands. Like their counterparts elsewhere, the Jordanian Ikhwan had a program that included women and the family, but it was a program that non-Islamist women (as well as many men) saw as inimical to their (or society's) interests. As a result, prior to the appointment of Tahir al-Masri as prime minister in June 1991, the possibility of a rollback or restricting of rights in a number of areas of concern to women seemed quite real.

In the case of Tunisia, the shock transition combined with the previous regime's long-standing support for women's rights was the most threatening situation of all. Ben 'Ali needed to consolidate support; he also needed to reinvigorate a fossilized political and party system. Just as there were those who were relieved to see that the succession issue had finally been solved peacefully, there were those who were opposed to a change in PSD structure and style. The pluralism proposed by the new president simply did not sit well with many of the party faithful. Ben 'Ali had to confront and defeat these cadres at the same time that he had to address the existing crisis between the state and the Islamists.

From his assumption of power in November 1987 until his speech in March 1988 committing himself to the CSP, Ben 'Ali may have toyed with the idea of turning back parts of the Code. He certainly made numerous gestures to court the more conservative segments of the population, many of whom had been alienated by what they saw as Bourguiba's excessively secularist program. For a leader seeking to distinguish himself from a predecessor who was known as the Liberator of Tunisian Women, what better way in a time of religious resurgence than to overturn parts of the CSP? Indeed, for a number of months it appeared that the long years of support offered women by Bourguiba would end in a backlash against women's rights.

In both Tunisia and Jordan, other factors intervened to deprive the Islamists of the role they sought to play and to avoid the full realization of the threats that many women feared. In Jordan, one factor may have been the Ikhwan's legislative and ministerial behavior. More important, the imperative to enter peace talks with Israel following the debacle of the Gulf War meant that the king had to have a government that would accept such a move. This required the Ikhwan's departure from the cabinet. In the case of Tunisia, women responded to the regime's overtures to the Islamists and the Islamists' challenges to the CSP by vocally insisting upon its preservation. It is unclear to what extent their early mobilization against the Islamists may have influenced Ben 'Ali, but it seems likely that the percentage of votes the RCD received from women in the April 1989 elections made an impression on the president, particularly given how well the Islamists did. Al-Nahdah's unexpected electoral successes led the regime to decide that it was time to replace the carrot with the stick. The rise of the FIS in neighboring Algeria may have sealed the regime's decision that Islamists were not to be trusted, but it appears that the election results, not external forces, were the primary reason behind the initial crackdown. Overtures continued to be made to coopt religious elements, but the policy of treating with al-Nahdah in such a way as to allow it an independent and oppositional position was abandoned. Of course, the corollary to the repression of Islamists has been the gradual increase in repression against any even marginally independent civil society groups with a political agenda.

THE ROLE OF EXTERNAL ACTORS

Given the common complaints by Middle Easterners and North Africans that their domestic affairs are highly penetrated or influenced by outside actors, it seemed critical to consider this factor in the in-depth case studies. All of these liberalizations have unfolded in an environment in which a variety of multilateral institutions have been preaching the gospel of economic liberalization, human rights, and democratization (loosely defined). In the case of Morocco, there is no question that the European view of the kingdom's human rights record has become a major concern, primarily because of Hassan's ambitions to make his realm a fuller economic member in the European Union. For Jordan, the holding of free elections in 1989 was certainly a feather in the king's cap in the eyes of the West. After the Gulf War deprived Amman of its traditional donors, the imperative to find new aid sources from the industrialized states no doubt encouraged Husayn and his government to emphasize the democratization angle, along with the kingdom's adherence to a program of IMF-scripted domestic economic reforms.

Tunisia is interesting in this regard because external actors have seemed willing to overlook in Ben 'Ali's realm the very human rights abuses they decry in Morocco. Tunisia's record in this regard owes to two primary factors. First, the country has been dutiful in following prescriptions for economic reforms in a region where there are more recalcitrants than faithful implementers. Second, and probably more important for Tunisia's European audience, has been the fact that the human rights abuses have been largely committed in the quest to conquer "the forces of intolerance and obscurantism," i.e. the Islamists. No one in Europe is anxious to have another Algeria on the Mediterranean's southern littoral. At the same time, while perfecting his police state, Ben 'Ali has continued to speak the language of pluralism, and the proliferation of "civil society" organizations appears to bear witness to the state's commitment to letting a thousand flowers bloom.

Within this broader context, of course, there has been an international focus on promoting women's rights, which received even greater attention as preparations were undertaken for the Beijing conference. The availability of funds from foreign donors, both official and NGO, for projects related to improving women's status was a hallmark of this period. While it would be difficult to argue that foreign donors have forced the local governments to modify their policies to be more supportive of women, there are clear examples of these governments' taking steps in the prelude to Beijing which must have been directed at least in part at making a positive impression on the international conference and international donors.

However, with the exception of Morocco, these benefits were realized largely after the transitions had ended. It would be difficult to point to an example of an external organization that truly made a difference, swaying the regime on issues related to women. In Jordan, the major defeat of the Islamists' 1991 efforts came, it appears, thanks to the combination of an ad hoc lobby composed of vocal and relatively elite Ammanites and the approach of the peace process. In Tunisia, it was the regime itself that changed its tune regarding al-Nahdah, while in Morocco the issue never came to a head. In the Moroccan case, the majority of funds for activist (as opposed to research and publishing) activities has been contributed or put into projects since the impressive *mudawwanah* campaign, which was the effort of a single women's group, the UAF.

SUMMARY

To sum up the broad conclusions, most basically, shock transitions appear to offer the greatest opportunities and the most serious challenges to women. They are initiated either as the result of a trauma, such as massive rioting, or are the product of a coup d'état, or a related system breakdown. In such situations, the leadership as well perhaps as certain aspects of the political system may be challenged or overturned. In the period of (re)consolidation that follows, the source of the trauma must be addressed, and the (new) leadership may well be forced to seek new allies and strike new political bargains. Weakened central states have traditionally allowed for increased political possibilities; yet, as preexisting relationships and structures are called into question, those that may have traditionally protected some segments of the population may also be up for discussion.

We have seen that in the case of a shock transition that sets aside a leadership or a regime that was viewed as women-friendly and in which the most powerful opposition forces in the new system are conservative/religious, women are set up for a backlash of potentially dangerous proportions. This is the situation that best characterizes the Tunisian case. (It also has parallels with Eastern Europe even though in Poland and Russia the transitions were gradual.) A slight contrast is that of the case of Jordan, which witnessed a shock transition, and in which the most powerful opposition forces were conservative/religious ones but in which the previous regime, itself conservative, had had a good relationship of long standing with these forces.

In none of these cases was there a women's movement or a mobilizing women's organization that either participated in the transition or was in a position to impose its will on the new regime. This situation resembles that of a number of Eastern European countries, in which the preexisting women's organizations were discredited through their association with the communists. Only in the case of Tunisia do we see some role for women's groups after the November 7 coup, but their successes must be put in the context of the new leadership's failure to coopt Islamists to its satisfaction and its subsequent decision that women, even if not mobilized in politically powerful organizations, could, as they had under Bourguiba, serve as a bulwark of the regime.

Gradual transitions are another major category, the only example of which examined in detail in this study is the continuing liberalization in Morocco. Hassan has not had to operate in a crisis mode characterized by a search for new allies to shore up a faltering system. As a result, the opening has offered increasing organizational and expressional possibilities to a growing range of civil society actors, many of them women. In my opinion, the most remarkable of the critical junctures explored in this work was the *mudawwanah* campaign: a grassroots effort of unprecedented scope and nontraditional nature that forced itself into the king's considerations and calculations. While its results were disappointing to many, the victory it represented should not be underestimated. At the same time, while the women involved were harassed by non-Islamist politicians and charged with apostasy by Islamists, neither Islamist nor other groups made any attempt to promote more conservative policies and discourse as a result of the liberalization. Again, this owes largely to the preexisting conservative set of laws governing Moroccan women's status and to the close ties between the regime and religious and other conservative forces.

The Latin American cases, although in a number of respects quite different, help underline some of these points. The transitions were generally gradual, but the new regimes had markedly different programs from their authoritarian predecessors. In Latin America, it was rightist regimes that were brought down. Hence the primary opposition was not, as we found in the MENA region or Eastern Europe, from the religious/conservative right, but rather from the center or left of the spectrum. The discrediting of the previous regimes (whose programs promoted conservative notions of women's role and place) opened up the space to push for progressive changes in women's status. What also sets the Latin American cases apart is the fact that women's organizations had played a role in pushing for regime change. Their past and potential mobilizational role was clearly understood by the leaders of the successor regimes. Women had made themselves political players of consequence in a way that MENA and Eastern European women's groups have yet to match.

TAKING ADVANTAGE OF THE OPENING

This study would not be complete without an examination of what women have been able to accomplish during or as a result of political liberalization. As we saw in the introduction, the Latin American experiences were very rich in producing new organizations, promoting elements of a women's agenda, and increasing the state's attention to women's concerns, even if not to the extent that was initially hoped.

A variety of factors shape women's ability to take advantage of an open-ing. The first is its length and fate. The MENA cases are perhaps the most limited in accomplishments in part because the political transformations in the region have stalled or been reversed. For example, in the case of Tunisia, the opening of the early 1980s was of sufficient duration that the first non-state affiliated women's group was allowed to emerge, if not be li-censed. During the short opening following Ben 'Ali's assumption of power, a group of women was able to obtain a license, but has had great dif-ficulty expanding activities or even maintaining its independence as the lib-eralization has been reversed. On the other hand, in Morocco, the contin-uing margin of freedom of organizing and expression has opened up many possibilities for women's organizations.

A second element concerns the degree of women's mobilization before the opening. While in the Eastern European cases, as well as those of Chile and Tunisia, state-sponsored women's organizations were in place prior to the transformation, the discrediting of the previous regime or the malaise in the organizations themselves deprived them of the legitimacy to play a mobilizational role in the new period. Hence, new or previously illegal or-ganizations have had to emerge to constitute a legitimate voice for women. In the MENA region, these organizations have been relatively weak, with members recruited from an educated, urban elite, although generally not from the wealthiest sectors of society.

Women's and society's own view of such organizations must also be con-sidered. If they are associated in any way with the previous, discredited regime, there is likely to be little interest. Even if they are new, a great deal of skepticism remains about possible ties to the state, influence from out-side (if there is any hint of feminism to them), or effectiveness. One hears frequently in Jordan and Morocco that there are too many women's orga-nizations, that the movement is too fractured and plagued by rivalries and infighting. It is interesting that while such a characterization is also quite appropriate for the broader political scene, that is, the male-dominated parliaments and political parties, the criticism is most often directed against women. One can certainly make the case that for women, as an underempowered group, the inability to work together is particularly harmful. However, part of the problem is the image that society (including women) constructs and perpetuates regarding women: that their primary responsibilities continue to be in the home and that they are not as capable as men in the political arena.

Indeed, a number of factors that helped to discourage women's activism under the (more) authoritarian predecessor regimes continue to play a role. Primary among these is the issue of time. To combine a job with family is no small undertaking. To add to that a commitment to another organization is something that many women simply cannot manage. In addition, however, are societal pressures regarding a woman's activity in the public sphere beyond her job. For many MENA women, mobility outside the home continues to be restricted, especially when the movement is for meetings in the evening or when the issue is politics, since the long experiences with authoritarianism have led people to associate political activity with jail, and jail with loss of a woman's honor. There is an economic angle as well: not only the opportunity cost of the time spent at or going to and from the meetings, but also the cost of transportation. For many women, spending on such "luxuries" is out of the question.

Also of critical importance are the goals that women seek to achieve. While the right to an education and to enter the workforce are demands of many women, they are by no means the demands of all. As was discussed in the introduction, while "it is true that at a certain level of abstraction women can be said to have some interests in common, there is no consensus over what these interests are or how they are to be formulated."[3] This study has concentrated on issues dealt with at the national level, and even here one finds divergent opinions among women regarding focus and priorities. The picture becomes even more complex when one tries to factor in more carefully elements such as region, class, ethnicity, and so on. Kandiyoti's point on women's conservatism regarding policies or developments that might challenge the family structure is also relevant here: "Women often resist the process of transition because they see the old order slipping away from them without any empowering alternatives."[4] Having played within the patriarchal rules for so long, they are loathe to challenge the system in ways that might deprive them of the benefits they have earned, particularly as they age and their authority in the family increases. Women in effect become active collaborators in their own oppression and in reproducing the oppressive system. All these points need to be borne in mind as we seek to evaluate the changes since the beginnings of the liberalizations.

If we examine the actual achievements during the liberalizations in the three countries examined here, the greatest amount of activity of a non-top-down nature—it is difficult to call it purely grassroots, since it still generally involves an urban, middle to upper-middle class elite—has been in Morocco, the only case in which a gradual liberalization continues. Here a number of women's organizations have become involved, largely since the *mudawwanah* campaign of 1992, in raising awareness regarding the continuing discrimination against women in Moroccan law. They have also taken the initiative in addressing the issue of violence and sexual harassment against women at home, in the street, and in the workplace. They have emphasized the need for women to become involved more actively in the political process whether as informed voters or as candidates on the municipal or national level. Their activity remains limited largely to Rabat and Casablanca, but the liberalization has provided small groups of activist women opportunities to begin to work for a reduction in the glaring difference between Moroccan women's social reality and their legal status.

In Jordan, the attempts to revitalize the GFJW and the JWU were both products of the new possibilities offered by the liberalization. While the GFJW languished, mired in a power struggle between Islamist and non-Islamist women, the JWU took advantage of the opening to address many of the same kinds of issues being worked on in Morocco: changing laws that discriminate against women, making women aware of their rights, providing counseling and legal services, and breaking the taboo against discussing the issue of violence against women. However, one of the most important parts of the story in Jordan concerns the reassertion of the state's role in women's activity through Princess Basma. While the profile she brings to her efforts is unmatched by any other woman in the kingdom, her association with the regime draws boundaries around the kinds of activities her National Forum is likely to undertake, just as it can potentially be used as a means of harnessing women's support for the regime. There is no denying that her efforts, in combination with some high-level appointments of women made by the king, have helped to eliminate the novelty of seeing a Jordanian woman involved in politics. It remains to be seen whether such efforts can ultimately help other women, not affiliated with the princess' efforts, play a more effective role.

Finally, in Tunisia, despite the liberalization's initial component of energizing the RCD and promoting pluralism, an expansion of women's groups (or any group for that matter) involved in politics and espousing other than a 100 percent RCD line is clearly not something in which the regime is interested. Indeed, the majority of women's organizations are involved in activities related to reinforcing the role of motherhood and the family, developmentalist work in rural areas, or encouraging women entrepreneurs. One cannot meaningfully talk about women's having taken advantage of the liberalization, because it was of too short a duration, and has been followed by a serious retreat into authoritarianism. Instead, frightened by the prospects of an Islamist surge that might have deprived them of their rights and lacking meaningful alternative allies, the women, whether RCD or not, were in effect forced into an alliance with the regime.

In this context it is also important to note that while the liberalization in Jordan has stalled, and that in Tunisia has been turned back with a vengeance, this has not meant that on the surface, women's rights or status as defined by the regime has suffered the same fate. In Tunisia, Ben 'Ali further amended the CSP, has made additional high-level appointments of women, and put state money into developing women's institutes such as CREDIF. In Jordan, getting women involved in the political process and working to end discrimination against women in certain laws continues to attract high-level attention and efforts, most notably those of the princess. Yet it would be difficult to classify these developments as constituting meaningful empowerment, at least in the near to medium term. The degree of progress is more apparent than real, and the benefits are likely to redound most immediately to the leadership rather than to women. If anything, such high-profile efforts resemble those of earlier periods of state feminism, and once again place women in a position of being beholden to the state for their position. This raises anew the specter of backlash in the event of a future regime change.

Finally, all of these cases raise serious questions about the suggestion in the civil society literature, noted in the introduction that women's organizations may play a vanguard role in pushing for greater democratization. The lessons from the MENA and the other regional cases appear to be that until women's organizations impose themselves on the political scene as capable of mobilizing to achieve what may be oppositional demands (and not just as capable of channeling women's energies into activities blessed by the state), the state and other political actors will not feel *obliged* to respond to their demands (although they may choose to do so as part of a larger political bargain with other actors). Also crucial is the fact that despite the discourse, with only a few exceptions, MENA women's organizations do not seem to have overcome the problems of internal authoritarianism or what one might call the *za'im* (political boss) syndrome. Women's groups appear to be no more democratic in internal practices and structures than many other "civil" society organizations. The most frank admission and open attempts to deal with these problems came in Tunisia, from women in the various precursors to the ATFD, who were brave and honest enough to engage in a serious autocritique. Such efforts remain the exception rather than the rule.

BENEFITS ACCRUING TO THE REGIME OR STATE

The most obvious benefit to the state in the cases of managed liberalizations has been the revival or salvation of the existing regimes, with only minor changes. However, beyond this factor, there are several less obvious developments of which one should take note. The first concerns the benefits that accrue from the expansion of so-called civil society. Here, we have focused specifically on the women's sector, although examples affecting other sectors abound. The expansion of interest on the part of international aid agencies and other funders has meant that a variety of projects that would otherwise not have been undertaken have been embarked upon. While not all such projects can be described as in line with state priorities, they are also not projects that contradict state interests, and the outside funding enables the civil society organizations to provide a variety of services that they could not have otherwise. As a result, some have charged that the international focus on encouraging NGO development has in fact facilitated the state's abdicating responsibility for providing critical services.

What appeared more salient in the course of this research was the degree to which the state had succeeded in reconstructing parts of itself as NGOs so as to please international patrons and benefit from the available funding, and yet at the same time maintain control over certain sectors or activities.[5] This problem was obvious in the case of the JNWF, the Noor al-Hussein Foundation, and the Queen Alia Fund for Social Development in Jordan. More problematic was donor support for Tunisia's UNFT following the *changement*, after a bitter debate left the union—organizationally and in terms of personnel—still firmly within the control of the RCD. These organizations may well have a greater absorptive capacity and broader reach, but they also threaten to strangle or severely limit the development of genuine civil society activity.

This last point underscores a theme that has run throughout this study, the complex nature of the state. Depending upon time and context, one may find the state promoting women's rights (e.g. the CSP in Tunisia) or thwarting attempts at reform (e.g., the Jordanian experience regarding the Personal Status Code). There are also examples of apparently contradictory policies at work at the same time in the same country. The explanation is rather simple. States are sets of relations and institutions upon which competing demands are made and through which conflicting interests are contested. Only in the most rudimentary and simple of states might one expect all policies on a given issue—women or otherwise—to be internally coherent and consistent. The state can be a primary instrument in improving women's status—as the policies of state feminism of a variety of regimes have shown—within certain boundaries. At the same time, it may also be the most formidable obstacle to women's achieving rights of which the leadership or society is skeptical. Classifying states or regimes as women-friendly (or not) oversimplifies the issues involved just as it obscures what is a continuing political process of defining and redefining state/regime policy and interests on these and other issues.

THE ROLE OF CULTURE

This study has shown that a range of shared political factors has served to form the broad outlines of the possibilities and perils women may encounter during periods of political liberalization: the nature of the transition and the reasons behind it, women's place in the political system and the public sphere, the role of religious or other conservative groups, and so on. The similarities across regions are striking. During such periods, political and social conservatives of various stripes—and in some cases even so-called progressives—whether of Hispanic, Slavic, or Arab background, and whether Catholic, Orthodox, or Muslim, construct similar programs for women when given free rein and voice: glorification of motherhood, promotion of women as repositories of family honor and societal values, the retreat of women from the work place, restriction of access to various forms of public space, and the like.

Having said that, there is no question that emphases differ. In the Latin American cases, women had to fight for respect for human rights as well as more meaningful state consideration of labor and child care concerns. In Eastern Europe, the record was mixed, and the greatest concern was with economic issues, but the question of abortion seemed to be a unifying theme. In the MENA region, it is the personal status laws, especially those elements relating to marriage, divorce and inheritance, which are the most oppressive and which are the most intractable in the current period because of the prevailing literalist interpretations of the Quran.

One important difference in the role of organized religion relates to the emergence within the Catholic Church of liberation theology. Although clergy and nuns generally did not support a more liberal approach to the questions of birth control and abortion, in some countries they did break with the stance of the church to advocate forms of empowerment that involved both sexes and a right to resist repressive regimes. Indeed, they became a critical part of the support structure for those who opposed authoritarianism as well as, in some countries, a moral conscience, calling for respect for human rights. In the case of Islam, despite the existence of an official religious establishment in most countries, Islamist groups either in legal opposition or completely outside the state have for some time constituted the only significant and broadly recognized oppositional voice in MENA countries. A number of these groups claim to subscribe to pluralistic principles, and given the fact that they have never been put to the test, it would be unfair to dismiss them. The experiences of the Sudan and Algeria (prior to the 1992 coup) certainly give reason for pause, although MENA's secular "republican" regimes over the years have hardly been paragons of pluralism. Moreover, the surprise outcome of the 1997 presidential elections in Iran shows clearly that Islamic regimes or governance defy simplistic categorizations. The absence of a reformist Islam with a program of public-sphere empowerment of the average citizen (or subject), male or female, is a major difference between the Latin American and MENA cases. Some would argue that Islam is inherently inimical to such a variation. In its current forms, that may appear to be the case, but Catholicism and various forms of Protestantism could easily have been similarly charged in the past. The essentializing of Islam and Islamist societies is as misleading in the MENA region as would be the case for other religions in their home societies.

One could continue to elaborate the particular influence that different cultures have had in further refining the boundaries of the outcomes of the liberalization processes. Suffice it here to end with two points. The first is that while culture clearly does matter, the empirical material does not indicate that it is a variable with exceptional explanatory power, and we delude ourselves if we continue to use it to proclaim broad bases of MENA regional particularism. Second, and more basic, despite the variations in history, culture, religion, and experience, all these cases make quite clear that until women constitute a political force capable of imposing themselves and their program(s) on the national or local stage, they will continue to be in the unenviable position of being bargained above and over by those actors who can and do impose themselves. For women to be full beneficiaries of liberalization, they must be full players in the game. Conversely, for true political liberalization to be achieved, it must meaningfully include women's movement toward the citizen end of the subject-citizen spectrum. Otherwise, the transitions will remain incomplete, deficient, and unjust. That said, the cases examined here suggest that for many women—in the MENA region and beyond—future periods of political transition will continue to constitute years of living dangerously.

NOTES

INTRODUCTION

1. From Samuel J. Huntington's title, *The Third Wave: Democracy in the Late 20th Century* (Norman: University of Oklahoma Press, 1991).

2. This is huge literature. See, for example, Guillermo O' Donnell and Philippe C. Schmitter, *Transitions from Authoritarian Rule: Tentative Conclusions about Uncertain Democracies* (Baltimore: Johns Hopkins University Press, 1986); John Higley and Richard Gunther (eds.), *Elites and Democratic Consolidation in Latin America and Southern Europe* (New York: Cambridge University Press, 1992); George A. Lopez and Michael Stohl (eds.), *Liberalization and Redemocratization in Latin America* (New York: Greenwood Press, 1987); Richard Gunther, P. Nikiforos Diamandouros, and Hans Jurgen Puhie, *The Politics of Democratic Consolidation: Southern Europe in Comparative Perspective* (Baltimore: Johns Hopkins University Press, 1995); Jorge I. Dominguez and Abraham F. Lowenthal (eds.), *Constructing Democratic Governance: Latin America and the Caribbean in the 1990s—Themes and Issues* (Baltimore: Johns Hopkins University Press, 1996); Scott Mainwaring, Guillero O'Donnell, and J. Samuel Valenzuela (eds.), *Issues in Democratic Consolidation: The New South American Democracies in Comparative Perspective* (Notre Dame: University of Notre Dame Press, 1992).

3. The emphasis must be placed on *dramatic*, for as the case studies will show, each of the MENA countries under examination, as well as others not examined in detail—notably Egypt—witnessed periods of slight loosening of political control or of opening well before the wave of the late 1980s.

4. This is also a huge literature. See, for example, Luiz Carlos Bresser Pereira, Jose Maria Maravall, and Adam Przeworski, *Economic Reforms in New Democracies: A Social Democratic Approach* (New York: Cambridge University Press, 1993); Adam Przeworski, *Democracy and the Market: Political and Economic Reforms in Eastern Europe and Latin America* (New York: Cambridge University Press, 1991); Edward Friedman, *The Politics of Democratization: Generalizing the East Asian Experiences* (Boulder: Westview, 1994); Arendt Lijphart and Carlos H. Waisman (eds.), *Institutional Design in New Democracies: Eastern Europe and Latin America* (Boulder: Westview, 1996); Constantine Menges (ed.), *Transitions from Communism in Russia and Eastern Europe: Analysis and Perspectives* (Landham, MD: University Press of America, 1994); Daniel N. Nelson *After Authoritarianism: Democracy or Disorder* (Westport, Conn.: Greenwood Press, 1995); Joan Nelson (ed.), *A Precarious Balance* (San Francisco: ICS Press, 1994); George Pridham, Eric Herring, and George Sanford (eds.), *Building Democracy: The International Dimension of Democratization in Eastern Europe* (New York: St. Martin's, 1994).

5. Christine Fauré, *Democracy Without Women: Feminism and the Rise of Liberal Individualism in France* (Bloomington: Indiana University Press, 1991), p. 120.

6. See for example, Valentine Moghadam (ed.), *Modernizing Women: Gender and Social Change in the Middle East* (Boulder: Lynne Rienner, 1993), chapter 6.

7. Algeria is one of the most notorious cases. See, for example, Boutheina Cheriet, "Gender, Civil Society and Citizenship in Algeria," *Middle East Report*, no. 198 (Jan.–March 1996): 22–26; Marnia Lazreg, *The Eloquence of Silence: Algerian Women in Question* (New York: Routledge, 1994); and Djamiila Amrane, *Les Femmes Algériennes dans la Guerre* (Paris: Plon, 1991). For a discussion of Palestinian women's concerns with this issue see Rita Giacaman, Islah Jad, and Penny Johnson, "For the Common Good? Gender and Social Citizenship in Palestine," *Middle East Report*, no. 198 (Jan.–March 1996): 11–16.

8. O'Donnell and Schmitter, *Transitions*, p. 7.

9. This process has generally been discussed in the framework of "pacts," Ibid., pp. 37–47. See also Michael G. Burton and John Higley, "Elite Settlements," *American Sociological Review* 52 (3): 299–301.

10. There is a problem, of course, in talking about "outcomes" in such situations, since in the case of liberalization we are clearly talking about a process, a moving train. The interest in this study, has been in the earliest stage in the liberalization, in which the most serious problems of regime consolidation and legitimation arise. Admittedly, such phases are not always easy to delineate.

11. For a discussion of the convergence of Islamist and secular programs for women in Egypt see Mervet Hatem, "Egyptian Discourses on Gender and Political Liberalization: Do Secularist and Islamist Views Really Differ?" *Middle East Journal* 48 (4) (Autumn 1994): 661–676.

12. Maxine Molyneux discusses the difficulties involved in defining and generalizing about what constitutes "women's interests, in "Mobilization without

Emancipation? Women's Interests, the State and Revolution in Nicaragua," *Feminist Studies* 11 (2) (Summer 1995): 231–232.

13. Ibid., p. 232–233.

14. Su'ad Joseph, "Gender and Citizenship in Middle Eastern States," *Middle East Report*, no. 198 (January–March 1996), p. 4.

15. The contrasting views of the role of the state can clearly be seen in the different schools addressing questions of economic development. Traditionally, structuralist schools saw a clear and necessary positive role for state intervention to achieve both industrial development and social welfare goals. On the other end of the spectrum, neo-liberals regard state involvement as a source of inefficiencies and rent-seeking behavior. See, for example, John Brohman, "Economism and Critical Silences in Development Studies: A Theoretical Critique of Neoliberalism," *Third World Quarterly* 16 (2) (June 1995): 297–318.

16. I am grateful to Greg White for encouraging me to clarify this point.

17. See Hicham Ben Abdallah al-Alaoui, "Etre Citoyen dans le Monde Arabe," *Le Monde Diplomatique*, July 1995, p. 11.

18. See Carol Pateman, *The Sexual Contract* (Stanford: Stanford University Press, 1988). I have applied Pateman's analysis to Jordan in "Women and the State in Jordan: Inclusion or Exclusion" in John Esposito and Yvonne Haddad (eds.), *Islam, Gender and Social Change* (New York: Oxford University Press, 1998), pp. 100–123.

19. See Pateman, *The Sexual Contract* and Joseph, "Gender and Citizenship," pp. 7–9.

20. See Floya Anthias and Nira Yuval-Davis, "Introduction," in Anthias and Yuval-Davis (eds.), *Woman—Nation—State* (London: Macmillan, 1989), pp. 6–7.

21. O' Donnell and Schmitter, *Transitions*. In O'Donnell's p. 57 listing of sectors or groups that played a role in the transitions, he does not mention women at all.

22. Most notable are: Valentine M. Moghadam (ed.), *Democratic Reform and the Position of Women in Transitional Economies* (Oxford: Clarendon Press, 1993); Nanette Funk and Magda Mueller (eds.), *Gender Politics and Post-Communism* (New York: Routledge, 1993); and Shirin Rai, Hilary Pilkington, and Annie Phizacklea (eds.), *Women in the Face of Change: The Soviet Union, Eastern Europe and China* (New York: Routledge, 1992). The latter two books do provide some coverage of the political aspects of the transition.

23. See Jane S. Jaquette (ed.), *The Women's Movement in Latin America: Participation and Democracy*, 2nd ed.(Boulder: Westview, 1994); Sarah A. Radcliff and Sallie Westwood (eds.), *Viva: Women and Popular Protest in Latin America* (New York: Routledge, 1993). See also Georgina Waylen, 'Women and Democratization: Conceptualizing Gender Relations in Transition Politics," *World Politics* 46, (3) (April 1994): 327–354.

24. Afaf Marsot, *Women and Men in Late Eighteenth-Century Egypt* (Austin: University of Texas Press, 1995).

25. Margot Badran, *Feminists, Islam and Nation: Gender and the Making of Modern Egypt* (Princeton: Princeton University Press, 1995).

26. Julie M. Peteet, *Gender in Crisis: Women and the Palestinian Resistance Movement* (New York: Columbia University Press, 1991).

27. See the contributions in Deniz Kandiyoti (ed.), *Women, Islam and the State* (Philadelphia: Temple University Press, 1991).

28. Mervet Hatem has defined state feminism (under the regime of Gamal 'Abd al-Nasir in Egypt) as "ambitious state programs that introduce important changes in the reproductive and productive roles of women," as quoted in As'ad AbuKhalil, "Toward the Study of Women and Politics in the Arab World: The Debate and the Reality," *Feminist Issues* 13 (1) (spring 1993): 17.

29. As Deniz Kandiyoti has argued "Of all the concepts generated by contemporary feminist theory patriarchy is probably the most overused and, in some respects, the most undertheorized" (p. 274). She notes that radical feminists have applied it to virtually any form or instance of male domination, while socialist feminists have focused on the relationships between patriarchy and class under capitalism. Kandiyoti offers a more nuanced approach, arguing that women "strategize within a set of concrete constraints that reveal and define the blueprint of" what she terms "patriarchal bargains" in a given society. These "bargains" will vary according to class, caste, and ethnicity. "They influence both the potential for and specific forms of women's active or passive resistance in the face of their oppression" (p. 275). See, D. Kandiyoti, "Bargaining with Patriarchy," *Gender & Society* 2 (3) (September 1988): 274–290.

30. Mervet Hatem, "Egyptian Discourses on Gender and Political Liberalization: Do Secularist and Islamist Views Really Differ?" *Middle East Journal* 48 (4) (Autumn 1994): 661.

31. Mervet Hatem, "Political Liberalization, Gender, and the State," in Rex Brynen, Bahgat Korany, and Paul Noble (eds.), *Political Liberalization and Democratization in the Arab World* 1 (Boulder: Lynne Rienner, 1995), p. 187.

32. See for example, Moghadam (ed.), *Democratic Reform*; Funk and Mueller (eds.), *Gender Politics*; Rai, Pilkington and Phizacklea (eds.), *Women in the Face of Change*; Nahid Aslanbeigui, Steven Pressman, and Gale Summerfield, *Women in the Age of Economic Transformation: Gender Impact of Reforms in Post-Socialist and Developing Countries* (New York: Routledge, 1994); Chris Corrin (ed.), *Superwoman and the Double Burden: Women's Experience of Change in Central and Eastern Europe and the Former Soviet Union* (Toronto: Second Story Press, 1992).

33. See Funk and Mueller (eds.), *Gender Politics*; Jane Jaquette, *The Women's Movement*; Barbara Einhorn, *Cinderella Goes to Market: Citizenship,. Gender and Women's Movements in East Central Europe* (London: Verso, 1993); Marilyn Rueschmeyer (ed.), *Women in the Politics of Postcommunist Eastern Europe* (London: M. E. Sharpe, 1994); "Women and Political Transitions in South America and Eastern and Central Europe: The Prospects for Democracy," (Los Angeles: The International and Public Affairs Center, Occidental College, working paper, 1992).

34. Renata Siemienska, "Women and Social Movements in Poland," *Women & Politics* 6 (4) (winter 1986): 24.

35. Ibid., p. 16.

36. Barbara Einhorn, "Democratization and Women's Movements in Central and Eastern Europe: Concepts of Women's Rights," in Moghadam (ed.), *Democratic Reform*, p. 48.

37. Doina Pasca Harsanyi, "Women in Romania," in Funk and Mueller (eds.), *Gender Politics*, pp. 48.

38. Ibid., p. 49

39. Siemienska, "Women and Social Movements in Poland," pp. 29, 30 and 32.

40. Ewa Hause, Barbara Heyns, and Jane Mansbridge, "Feminism in the Interstices of Politics and Culture: Poland in Transition," in Funk and Mueller (eds.), pp. 262–63.

41. Małorzata Fuszara, "Abortion and the Formation of the Public Sphere in Poland," in Funk and Mueller (eds.), p. 243.

42. Ibid., pp. 249, 251.

43. The law was finally liberalized again in August 1996. *LA Times*, August 31, 1996. For the background to the shift see Daniel Singer, "Of Lobsters and Poles," *The Nation*, December 20, 1993, p. 765.

44. Anastasia Posadskaya, Changes in Gender Discourses and Policies in the Former Soviet Union," in Moghadem (ed.), *Democratic Reform*, p. 164.

45. Katrina vanden Heuvel, "Right-to-Lifers Hit Russia," *The Nation*, November 1, 1993, pp. 489–492.

46. Gail Warshofsky Lapidus, "Gender and Restructuring: The Impact of Perestroika and its Aftermath on Soviet Women," in Moghadam (ed.), *Democratic Reform*, pp. 154–55.

47. Elizabeth Waters, "Finding a Voice: The Emergence of a Women's Movement," in Funk and Mueller (eds.), p. 300.

48. See "Russia's Church: A Material Calling," *LA Times*, September 4, 1997.

49. Sonia Alvarez, "The (Trans)formation of Feminism(s) and Gender Politics in Democratizing Brazil, in Jaquette (ed.), *The Women's Movement*, pp. 15–16.

50. Patricia M. Churchryk, "From Dictatorship to Democracy: The Women's Movement in Chile,"" in Jaquette (ed.), *The Women's Movement*, p. 77.

51. O'Donnell and Schmitter, *Transitions*, p. 52.

52. Maria del Carmen Feijoo with Marcela Maria Alejandra Nari, "Women and Democracy in Argentina," in Jaquette (ed.), *The Women's Movement*, p. 117.

53. Alvarez, "Democratizing Brazil," pp. 41–43.

54. Churchryk, "The Women's Movement in Chile," pp. 79, 86, 88–89.

55. Feijoo with Nari, "Women and Democracy in Argentina," pp. 117, 121–122, and 126.

56. For a discussion of the question of Middle Eastern or Arab exceptionalism see Ghassan Salameh, 'Introduction: Where are the Democrats?," and John Waterbury, 'Democracy Without Democrats," in Ghassan Salame (ed.), *Democracy Without Democrats: The Renewal of Politics in the Muslim World* (New York: I. B.

Tauris, 1994). See also Fred Halliday, *Islam and the Myth of Confrontation: Religion and Politics in the Middle East* (New York: I. B. Tauris, 1996) and Olivier Roy, *The Failure of Political Islam* (Cambridge: Harvard University Press, 1994).

I. IN THE REALM OF THE COMMANDER OF THE FAITHFUL

1. Mark Tessler, "The Uses and Limits of Populism: The Political Strategy of King Hassan II of Morocco," *Middle East Review* (Spring 1985): 47.
2. Henry Munson, *Religion and Power in Morocco* (New Haven: Yale University Press, 1993), especially chapters 5–7. See also the annual reports of Amnesty International.
3. Interview with Khalid Jamai, editor of the PI's French-language daily, *L'Opinion*, in Rabat, June 30, 1995.
4. *Annuaire de l'Afrique du Nord* (hereafter, *AAN*), 1986 (Paris: CNRS, 1986).
5. *Middle East International* (hereafter, *MEI*), August 28, 1993.
6. *AAN* 1986, p. 743.
7. *MEI*, January 7, 1994.
8. See "Political Economy Review of Morocco," unpublished draft submitted to Chemonics, International, June 1992, pp. 8–9. It states that in 1979, 45% of the rural population alone (11.8 million at the time) was living in absolute poverty.
9. Interview with Lahcen Oulhadj, editor of the Berber journal *Tifawt*, in Rabat, August 4, 1995.
10. Tessler, "Uses and Limits of Populism," p. 44.
11. Ibid., p. 45.
12. *AAN* 1985, p. 650.
13. *AAN* 1986, pp. 754–55.
14. *MEI*, July 25, 1987.
15. *EIU*, no. 2, 1988, p. 7.
16. *EIU*, no.1, 1989, p. 11.
17. Interview with 'Abd al-'Aziz Bennani, head of the OMDH, in Rabat, July 5, 1995.
18. *MEI*, March 2, 1990.
19. *AAN* 1990, pp. 717–18.
20. Gilles Perault, *Notre Ami le Roi* (Paris: Gallimard, 1990).
21. Amnesty International, *Morocco: Breaking the Wall of Silence: The Disappeared in Morocco* (New York: Amnesty, 1993).
22. *AAN* 1986, p. 764. Headed by personalities close to the king or ministers, by 1988 these associations could be found in almost all large Moroccan cities.
23. *AAN* 1988, pp. 685–86.
24. *AAN* 1989, pp. 618–19.
25. The next two chapters carry full details on these changes.
26. Guilain Denoeux and Laurent Gateau, "L'Essor des Associations au Maroc: à

la Recherche de la Citoyenneté?" *Maghreb-Machrek*, no. 150 (Oct.–Dec. 1995): 19–39.

27. *AAN* 1990, p. 721.
28. *AAN* 1989, p. 620.
29. *MEI*, December 21, 1990.
30. *MEI*, February 8, 1991.
31. *AAN* 1991, p. 786.
32. *AAN* 1990, pp. 722–23.
33. *AAN* 1991, p. 789.
34. *AAN* 1992, p. 837.
35. Ibid., p. 838.
36. See *Jeune Afrique*, April 23, 1992.
37. *AAN* 1992, p. 837.
38. *EIU*, no. 4, 1992, p. 8.
39. *EIU*, no. 1, 1993, p. 8.
40. *AAN* 1992, pp. 843–44.
40. *AAN* 1992, p. 846.
42. *EIU*, no. 4, 1993, pp. 9–10.
43. *MEI*, March 31, 1995.

2. IN THE SHADOW OF THE *MUDAWWANAH*

1. Zakya Daoud, *Féminisme et Politique au Maghreb* (Casablanca: Editions Eddif, 1993), pp. 243–245, 250. (Hereafter Daoud.) The reader will note a fairly heavy reliance on this work. That is a result of the paucity of other materials on particularly the early part of the period under discussion.
2. Ibid., pp. 243 and 253.
3. Aicha Belarbi, "Al-Harakah al-Nisa'iyyah w-al-Intiqal nahwa al-Dimuqratiyyah," in Friedrich Ebert Stiftung, *Femmes & Société Civile au Maghreb* (Marrakech: Publications Universitaires du Maghreb, n.d.), p. 11.
4. Daoud, pp. 262–63.
5. Leila Chafai, "Le Mouvement des Femmes au Maroc," draft paper, p. 12 (hereafter Chafai); and Daoud, pp. 269–271.
6. Daoud, p. 276.
7. Sophie Bessis and Souhayr Belhassan, *Femmes du Maghreb: l'Enjeu* (Casablanca: Editions Eddif, 1992), p. 74.
8. Interview with Amina Lamrini, president of the Association Marocaines des Femmes Démocrates (AMDF), in Rabat, 18 July 1995.
9. Daoud, p. 290.
10. Chafai, pp. 9–10.
11. Daoud, p. 288.
12. Chafai, pp. 10–11.
13. Daoud, p. 287.
14. Chafai, p. 10.

15. Daoud, p. 286.

16. Ibid., pp. 289, 298–290, 307.

17. Patrick Haenni, "Le Théâtre d'Ombres de L'Action Féminine: Femme, Etat, et Société Civile au Maroc" (hereafter cited as Haenni) thesis for the D.E.A. d'études politiques (AMAC), I.E.P. de Paris, 1993, p. 20.

18. Chafai, p. 26.

19. Haenni, p. 37.

20. Chafai, pp. 20–21.

21. Ibid., p. 456.

22. Interview with journalist and former student activist Leila Chafai, in Rabat, July 4, 1995.

23. Haenni, p. 41.

24. Chafai interview.

25. Daoud, pp. 413–14.

26. Ibid., pp. 316–17.

27. Interview with Aicha Loukhmas, an editor of *8 Mars* and a member of the UAF, in Casablanca, July 21, 1995.

28. Interview with Aicha Chenna, head of Association of Women's Solidarity, in Casablanca, July 11, 1995.

29. Aicha Belarbi, "Mouvement des Femmes au Maroc," *Annuaire de l'Afrique du Nord* 28 (1989): 463–64.

30. Lamalif is a word that combines the names for two Arabic letters (lam and alif) which spell the word meaning "no."

31. For full details of Mernissi's programs see *Femmes Maghreb Deux Mille Deux: cinq ans après* (Rabat: AFJEM, n.d.)

32. Interview with Najat Razi, former student activist and member of the Association Marocaine des Droits des Femmes, in Casablanca, July 11, 1995.

33. Interview with Nadia Yacine, in Sale, August 10, 1995. For a more detailed presentation on 'Abd-Salam Yacine and the Justice and Charity party see Henry Munson, *Religion and Power in Morocco* (New Haven: Yale University Press, 1993), pp. 162–179.

34. Al-Rayah, April 16, 1996.

35. Interview with Khadijah Ahmad, member of Tajdid al-Wa'i al-Nisa'i, in Rabat, April 23, 1996.

36. Haenni, p. 52.

37. Centre d'Etudes et de Recherches Demographiques (CERD), *Statut Economique et Social de la Femme au Maroc: Recueil Analytique des Textes* (Rabat: Ministère du Plan, Direction de la Statistique, 1990), pp. 246–51.

38. Ibid., pp. 252–59.

39. Moulay Rachid Abderazak, *La Femme et La Loi au Maroc* (Casablanca: Editions Le Fennec, 1992), p. 116.

40. Daoud, pp. 255, 258, and 260. "We were the pioneers. Our dignity, our emancipation was in literacy, education. Everything was the result of ignorance. For us, the *mudawwanah* was a secondary concern."

41. Abderazak, pp. 54–64; 62–63.

42. Ibid., pp. 64–73.

43. Leila Abuzayd, "Ta'dil Mudawwanat al-Ahwal al-Shakhsiyyah," *Al-Minbar al-Libirali*, April 19, 1995, p. 25.

44. Daoud, p. 300.

45. Ibid., p. 301.

46. *8 Mars*, no. 57, p. 2.

47. Interview with MP Badi'a Sqalli, in Rabat, July 19, 1995.

48. *Al-'Alam*, 8 March 1994.

49. Sqalli interview.

50. Daoud, p. 337.

51. Interview with Professor of Sociology and USFP member Aicha Belarbi, in Rabat, June 29, 1995.

52. Interview with Konrad Adenauer Representative in Morocco, Dr. Bernd Weischer, in Rabat, June 27, 1995.

53. Interview with Friedrich Ebert Representative in Morocco, Dr. Peter Hunseler, and his assistant, Najat Saher, in Rabat, June 23, 1995.

54. Interview with Amideast Director for Morocco, Sue Buret, in Rabat, July 26, 1995.

55. Discussion with USIS Information Officer Nabil Khoury, in Rabat, July 21, 1995.

56. Interview with Wafa Ouichou, WID Officer, AID Morocco, in Rabat, July 28, 1995.

57. Ouichou interview.

58. Discussion with USIS Cultural Affairs Assistant Laura Berg, in Rabat, July 18, 1995.

59. Belarbi, "Mouvements," p. 464.

3. CONFRONTING THE MAKHZEN

1. *Jeune Afrique*, April 23, 1992.

2. Interview with Fatima Meghnawi, officer in the UAF, in Rabat, July 25, 1995.

3. *8 Mars*, no. 58, p. 11.

4. The citation is taken from Patrick Haenni, "Le Théâtre d'Ombres de L'Action Féminine: Femmes, Etat, et Société Civile au Maroc," (hereafter cited as Haenni) thesis for the D.E.A. d'études politiques (AMAC), I.E.P. de Paris, 1993, p. 69.

5. Meghnawi interview.

6. Interview with journalist and former student activist Leila Chafai, Rabat, July 4, 1995.

7. Zakya Daoud, *Féminisme et Politique au Maghreb* (hereafter cited as Daoud) (Casablanca: Editions Eddif, 1993), p. 335.

8. Khadija 'Amti, "Al-Nisa'i bayna Sultat al-Taqlid w-al-Hadathah: Mudawwanat al-Ahwal al-Shakhsiyyah ka-Halah," in *Femmes et Société Civile au Maghreb* (Marrakech: Publications Universitaires du Maghreb, n.d.), p. 58.

9. Daoud, p. 338; 'Amti, "Al-Nisa'i," pp. 58–68; and M. Ahnaf, "Maroc: Le Code

du Statut Personnel,"(hereafter cited as Ahnaf) *Maghreb-Machrek*, no. 145 (Juillet–Septembre 1994), pp. 12–13.

10. *Al-Rayah*, July 20, 1992.

11. *Al-Rayah*, June 1, 1992.

12. Interview with 'Abdalillah Benkirane, head of *Islah w-al-Tajdid*, Rabat, April 18, 1996.

13. *Al-Bayan*, April 21, 1992.

14. *Al-Rayah*, July 20, 1992.

15. 'Amti,"Al-Nisa'i," p. 57.

16. Al-Islah w-al-Tajdid, "Bayan Hawla al-Intikhabat al-Jama'iyyah," 15 October 1992.

17. Ahnaf, p. 17.

18. *8 Mars*, no. 58, p. 13.

19. Haenni, pp. 70–71.

20. "A Propos du Code de Statut Personnel," in *L'Organisation Marocaine des Droits de L'Homme à Travers ses Communiqués et Déclarations: Mai 1991–Décembre 1992* (n.p.: OMDH, 1993), pp. 92–93.

21. See chapter 1 for more on the political context.

22. Daoud, pp. 342–43.

23. Ahnaf, pp. 17–18.

24. Interview with author Leila Abouzeid, Rabat, June 22, 1995.

25. Haenni, p. 72.

26. OMDH, p. 102.

27. Daoud, p. 344.

28. Leila Abouzeid, "Ta'dil Mudawwanat al-Ahwal al-Shakhsiyyah," *Al-Minbar al-Libirali*, April 19, 1995, p. 25.

29. *Al-'Alam*, March 8, 1994.

30. Ahnaf, p. 17.

31. *Jeune Afrique*, March 25, 1993.

32. Ibid.

33. Haenni, p. 75.

34. *Al-'Alam*, April 3, 1993.

35. Haenni, p. 77.

36. *Anoual*, April 1, 1993.

37. Interview with Professor of Sociology and USFP activist Aicha Belarbi, June 29, 1995.

38. *Al-Bayane*, February 28, 1993.

39. *Liberation*, March 13, 1993.

40. *Anoual*, April 8, 1993.

41. *Al-Rayah*, March 9, 1993.

42. "Observations générales sur le procès 'Tabit,' " in *O.M.D.H. à Travers ses Communiqués et Déclarations, Decembre 1992 - Mai 1994* (Casablanca: Les Editions Maghrebines, n.d.), pp. 37–9.

43. Haenni, p. 78.
44. Interview with 'Abdallah Saaf, Chair of the Department of Public Law, Muhammad V University, Rabat, July 1, 1995.
45. *Anoual*, April 1, 1993.
46. *Al-Bayane*, March 11, 1993.
47. *Anoual*, April 2, 1993.
48. Interview with 'Aicha Loukmas, lawyer, editor of *8 Mars*, in Casablanca, July 21, 1995.
49. This section is taken in its entirety from my interview with Amina Lamrini, Rabat, July 18, 1995.
50. Although the original four-party (PI, USFP, PPS, and OADP) *kutlah* broke down well before the parliamentary elections, the PI and USFP did construct and electoral alliance, which people continued to refer to as the *kutlah*, which involved running joint candidates.
51. This section is taken in its entirety from my interview with MP Sqalli, Rabat, July 19, 1995.
52. The translation of *populaire* (Fr.) or *sha'bi* (Ar.) into English poses a bit of a problem. The word implies a lower-middle class area, has a working-class connotation, but also implies a certain traditionalism and sense of community.
53. Interviews with UAF activists Meghnawi and Loukhmas.
54. This was off-the-record, April 1966. My interviewee reported that a member of the OFI who was appointed to a position in the Ministry of Foreign Affairs responsible for liasing with international organizations apparently lobbied against the report because of the UAF's role in it. She referred to UAF women as atheists who were outside the framework of Islam.
55. It is probably instructive that the *8 Mars*, no. 59, p. 5 article which details the history of this period does not mention the UNFM by name. I learned it by chance in an unrelated interview, and another activist subsequently confirmed it.
56. Off-the record comments by a woman activist, July 1995.
57. *8 Mars*, no. 59, p. 5.
58. Ibid.
59. Meghnawi interview.
60. *8 Mars*, 60/61, pp. 7–16.

4. GOD, HOMELAND, KING

1. For a discussion of the political role of these unions, see Laurie A. Brand, *Palestinians in the Arab World: Institution Building and the Search for State* (New York: Columbia University Press, 1988), pp. 177–79.
2. Circassians are a minority group from the Caucasus that was offered refuge in what is now Jordan and other parts of the Ottoman empire in the late 1880's. Christians are an indigenous minority that make up about 5–6% of the Jordanian population.

3. See Laurie A. Brand, *Jordan's Inter-Arab Relations: The Political Economy of Alliance Making* (New York: Columbia University, Press, 1994).

4. See Robert Satloff, *From Abdallah to Hussein* (New York: Oxford, 1995).

5. The breakdown of population between Transjordanians and Jordanians of Palestinian origin is a subject of great sensitivity as well as speculation. The results of the 1995 national census, which would have provided answers to this question, have not been released, for political reasons. Palestinians tend to overestimate their numbers, while Transjordanians have a tendency to underestimate the numbers of Jordanians of Palestinian origin. On the basis of my own calculations and observations, and the results of sampling that was part of public opinion surveys conducted by the Center for Strategic Studies of Jordan University, I am convinced that the breakdown is within a couple of percentage points of 50–50, with the balance tipping slightly to the Palestinian side.

6. "Jordan," *Amnesty International 1990 Report* (New York: Amnesty International Publishing, 1990), p. 137.

7. Malik Mufti, "Elite Bargains and Political Liberalization in Jordan," draft article accepted for publication by *Comparative Political Studies*, pp. 7–9. From interviews with the small circle of advisors to the king at this time, Mufti argues that the opening was viewed as tactical. He also shows just how fragile the initial decision to liberalize was.

8. *Middle East International* (hereafter, *MEI*) September 22, 1989.

9. Pascaline Eury, *Jordanie: Les Elections Législatives du 8 Novembre 1989* (Beirut: Centre d'Etudes et Recherches sur le Moyen Orient Contemporain,CERMOC, 1991), p. 43. Toujan Faisal, who directly addressed their insults and criticisms, was targeted with an unprecedented campaign of harassment, including charges that she was an apostate and could therefore be killed. The Faisal affair, which became famous well beyond Jordan, is examined in detail in chapter 6.

10. Eury, *Jordanie*, pp. 55–57.

11. Mufti, "Elite Bargains," p. 11. He cites high-level interviewees who told him that although government-commissioned polls had "accurately predicted the election results, the intelligence services remained convinced that the Islamists would win only 8–15 seats . . ."

12. The numbers of Islamists vary, depending upon which source one consults. The problem derives from defining who is an independent Islamist. I found the number of Islamist MPs given to be as many as 34, and as few as 28. Most often 28 or 30 is cited. What seems most important is that even if one takes the lowest figure, Islamists controlled more than one-third of the 80-seat house.

13. The Muslim Brotherhood in Jordan is an offshoot of the movement of the same name founded in Egypt in the 1930s. While it accounts for the majority of Islamists in Jordan, struggles internal to the movement as well as approaches outside the Ikhwan have meant that there are a significant number of independent Islamists as well.

14. *MEI*, 25 May 1990.

15. Mufti argues that Husayn was not inclined to reject the election results so soon after the opening and accepted the arguments of the pro-liberalization group among his advisers that oppositional voices could be contained—through various forms of cooptation and implication in the system. Mufti, "Elite Bargains," p. 13.
16. Eury, *Jordanie*, p. 67.
17. Louis-Jean Duclos, "Les Elections Législatives en Jordanie," *Maghreb-Machrek* 129 (Juillet–Septembre 1990): 66. Mufti argues that the Ikhwan was not interested in cabinet participation at this point. Mufti, "Elite Bargains," p. 15.
18. *Jordan Times* (hereafter, *JT*), January 3, 1990.
19. The Islamists' candidate, Yusuf Mubayyidin, lost to a Transjordanian political conservative, Sulayman 'Arar, 44–36.
20. *JT*, February 6, 1990. *Zakat* is a form of tithing in Islam.
21. Eury, *Jordanie*, p. 68.
22. *JT*, 15 May 1990.
23. While the category "Islamists" is broader than the Ikhwan, the word "Ikhwan" is often used by Jordanians to refer to all Islamists.
24. *JT*, May 8, 1990.
25. Sultan Hattab, "The Muslim Brotherhood: The Road to Government," *JT*, November 19, 1990.
26. The details of a number of such laws and deals are provided in one of the cases in chapter 4.
27. *MEI*, January 11, 1991.
28. *MEI*, June 28, 1991.
29. Ibid.
30. *JT*, June 22, 1991.
31. In the Jordanian political system, members of the lower house may also serve simultaneously as cabinet ministers.
32. *JT*, December 19–20, 1991.
33. See the series of *JT* articles written by Lamis Andoni analyzing the failure of the Masri government, November 23, 24, and 27, 1991.
34. *MEI*, January 24, 1992.
35. Interview with Tahir al-Masri, May 11, 1993.
36. *JT*, December 19–20, 1991.
37. *JT*, December 1, 1991.
38. *JT*, March 23, 1993.
39. "Chronology: Jordan," *Middle East Journal* 47 (2) (Spring 1993): 327.
40. *JT*, March 11–12, 1993.
41. Ibid.
42. Interview with Senator Layla Sharaf, July 1, 1993; interview with Professor of Psychology at Jordan University and women's activist Arwa al-'Amiri, May 10, 1993.
43. Commentary by Walid Sa'adi, *JT*, March 1, 1993.
44. *JT*, August 28, 1993.

45. It should be noted here that, owing to the existing electoral district boundaries, which do not capture comparable numbers of voters in each district, the urban areas—especially Amman and Zarqa—are grossly underrepresented. Given that Palestinians live in greatest concentration in just these urban areas, this means that the kingdom's citizens of Palestinian origin are underrepresented in parliament.

46. As noted earlier, this story will be dealt with in depth in chapter 6.

47. *JT*, May 30, 1994.

48. *JT*, May 31, 1994.

49. *JT*, June 4, 1994.

50. See editorial by Musa Keilani, *JT*, August 6, 1994. My recollection of the broadcast differs markedly from that of Keilani.

51. *JT*, December 6, 1994.

52. *MEI*, January 20, 1995.

53. A survey conducted by Jordan University's Center for Strategic Studies, "Formation of the New Government, February 1996," indicated that among the public at large, 51.7% were optimistic about Kabariti himself, but only 32.2% were optimistic about his cabinet selections.

54. Masri interview.

55. It has been argued that the king was in fact in control from the beginning and that the legalization of political parties (particularly the leftists) was undertaken to counterbalance the power of the Islamists, since it was believed that these two groups would not support the same position on any issues. See Eury, *Jordanie*, p. 68. However, this seems to assume more control and knowledge of the balance of forces than, at very least, the regime's expectations of the 1989 election results would have suggested. Moreover, if correct, it would represent another mistaken assumption, since the leftists and the Islamists were in accord on the issue of expanding public freedoms, and some of their members continued to vote together in opposition to the various government-proposed budgets as well as the peace treaty.

56. *MEI*, January 24, 1992.

5. THE STRUGGLE FOR VOICE

1. Emily Bisharat, "Muhattat Mudi'ah fi Tarikh Masirat al-Mar'ah al-Urdunniyyah ," *Al-Dustur*, June 29, 1993. (Hereafter cited as Bisharat.)

2. Haifa Jamal, "Juhud Ittihad al-Mar'ah al-Urdunniyyah fi Sabil Tatwir al-Tashri'at al-Khassah b-il-Mar'ah," unpublished paper presented at the First Conference of the JWU, 13–15 June 1995, p. 3. (Hereafter cited as Jamal.)

3. Bisharat. It should be noted that Bisharat and Suhayr al-Tall, *Muqaddimat Hawla Qadiyat al-Mar'ah w-al-Harakah al-Nisa'iyyah f-il-Urdunn* (Beirut: al-Mu'assasah al-'Arabiyyah l-il-Dirasat w-al-Nashr, 1985; hereafter cited as al-Tall), are the only two accounts that cover this entire period and, unfortunately, they do not always agree. In cases of lack of complementarity I have relied

on al-Tall, who is a researcher and whose account is much more detailed and critical. Bisharat, whose piece is, admittedly, much shorter, has clearly omitted a number of important events, presumably for political reasons.

4. Al-Tall, p. 111.
5. Ibid., pp. 122 and 124.
6. Ibid., p. 126.
7. Jamal, p. 3.
8. Ibid., p. 6.
9. Bisharat.
10. Ibid.
11. Al-Tall, p. 129.
12. Bisharat.
13. Ibid.
14. Al-Tall, p. 115.
15. Laurie A. Brand, *Palestinians in the Arab World: Institution Building and the Search for State* (New York: Columbia University Press, 1988), pp. 199–200.
16. Al-Tall, p. 58.
17. The name is significant: The Women's Federation in Jordan rather than the Jordanian Women's Federation, or some similar formulation. It allowed for both Transjordanian and Palestinian women to participate without feeling they were compromising their communal identities. There was a conscious effort at this point—when the memories of 1970 were still quite strong—to bring together women from both communities to work together in a common framework.
18. Da'd Mu'adh, "Tajribat al-Ittihad al-Nisa'i (1974–1981)," *Al-Urdunn al-Jadid*, no. 7 (spring 1986), p. 60 (hereafter cited as Mu'adh); al-Tall, pp. 117 and 130.
19. Al-Tall, pp. 131–32.
20. Ibid., p. 134; Mu'adh, p. 61. While Mu'adh cites the same total numbers, she attributes only 800 members to the capital. In most respects, however, her presentation follows that of al-Tall extremely closely.
21. Al-Tall, pp. 141–42.
22. Ibid., p. 161; Mu'adh, p. 63.
23. Al-Tall, pp. 162–63.
24. Ibid., p. 164.
25. Mu'adh, p. 64.
26. Al-Tall, p. 157.
27. Ibid., pp. 155–56.
28. It is interesting that in her long newspaper article on the history of the women's movement, Bisharat simply notes that the union was closed. No comment or explanation is offered.
29. Brand, p. 202. I am grateful to Amal Sabbagh, who pointed out to me that the GFAW was not united in its rejection of the GFJW.
30. Majidah al-Masri, "Al-Azmah al-Rahinah l-il-Harakah al-Nisa'iyyah f-il-Urdunn," *Al-Urdunn al-Jadid*, no. 7 (Spring 1986), pp. 67 and 69.

31. Business and Professional Women's Club, "Grassroots Democracy Project," unpublished report. Amman, March 1994.

32. A number of very dismaying stories were recounted to me spontaneously by women whom I was not interviewing for the project when they heard that I was conducting research on women's organizations.

33. Interview with Suhayr al-Tall, author and researcher on social issues, June 3, 1996.

34. Al-Tall, p. 65; Husayn Shikhatra, *Al-Mar'ah al-Urdunniyyah: Haqa'iq wa Arqam* (hereafter cited as Shikhatra) (Amman: BPWC, 1992), pp. 19, 23–30.

35. Nasrin Mahasanah, "Wad' al-Mar'ah al-Urdunniyyah fi Tashri'at al-Qanuniyyah" (hereafter cited as Mahasanah), unpublished study sponsored by the General Secretariat, National Assembly, Hashemite Kingdom of Jordan, 1994, p. 19.

36. Ibid., p. 22; al-Tall, p. 105.

37. Nadia Takriti Kamal and Mary Qa'war, "The Status and Role of Women in Development in Jordan," Manpower Division, Ministry of Planning, Hashemite Kingdom of Jordan. Unpublished paper presented at the ILO meeting on "Women in the Jordanian Labor Force" held at the Royal Scientific Society, Amman, December 1990, Table 4.

38. Mahasanah, p. 8.

39. Shikhatra, p. 36; Kamal and Qa'war, "The Status and Role of Women in Development in Jordan,"p. 16.

40. Mahasaneh, p. 5; al-Tall, p. 98.

41. Mahasanah, p. 20. Interview with Amal Sabbagh, the Ministry of Social Development, July 19, 1993. In late 1996, apparently thanks to the efforts of Princess Basma, a number of key issues related to such difficulties were put at the discretion of the head of the Civil Status and Passports Department. This change was intended to facilitate the access of widows, divorced women, and Jordanian wives of foreign nationals to separate family books. *Jordan Times* (hereafter, *JT*), December 17, 1996.

42. *JT*, October 6–7, 1994.

43. In a tragic twist on the concept of an honor crime, the *JT* December 25, 1995 reported the story of parents who killed their newborn son because he was conceived out of wedlock, and then received reduced sentences because it was *their* child. This further problematizes the notion of citizenship (in terms of meaning protection under the law).

44. *JT*, October 6–7, 1994.

45. Interview with Suhayr al-Tall, 20 July 1994; *JT* December 31, 1994.

46. Interview with Senator Layla Sharaf, July 1, 1993.

47. *JT*, July 11, 1993.

48. *The Star*, May 12, 1994.

49. Interviews with Senator Na'ila Rashdan, August 6, 1994 and May 22, 1996.

50. *Al-Dustur*, May 19, 1996.

51. *Al-Ra'y*, June 7, 1995.

52. *JT*, August 28, 1995.

53. Jordanian National Women's Committee, "National Strategy for Women in Jordan," (a booklet) September 1993, p. 11; "The National Report on the Jordanian Woman for the International Conference, Beijing 1995," (in Arabic), pp. 44–48.

54. *JT*, September 10, 1994.

55. *JT*, February 1, 1995.

56. The crown prince raised the issue again at a symposium organized by the Public Security Department in August 1997. See *JT*, August 27, 1997.

57. *JT*, November 30, 1997.

58. *JT*, September 14–15, 1995.

59. Women in Development Team, USAID/Amman, "Proposed National Strategy and Action Plan for the National Women's Committee," draft, June 30, 1992, from the executive summary.

60. Much of the material in this section is taken from an interview with Janine al-Tall, Director of AMIDEAST, Amman, March 12, 1996.

61. The experience of Toujan Faisal during the fall 1989 parliamentary campaign will be examined in detail in chapter 6.

62. The Asia Foundation, "Women in Politics Program," an information page.

63. National Endowment for Democracy, *1994 Annual Report*, p. 5.

64. National Democratic Institute, *Democracy and Local Government in Jordan: 1995 Municipal Elections* (Washington. D.C.: NDI, September 1995).

65. National Endowment for Democracy, *1994 Annual Report*, p. 55.

66. See section on GFJW in next chapter.

6. THE STATE RETREATS, THE STATE RETURNS

1. Nancy Gallagher, "Gender, Islamism and Democratization in Jordan: The Case of Tujan al-Faysal), draft paper, 1993, pp. 7–8.

2. Ibid., pp. 10–15.

3. *Jordan Times* (hereafter, *JT*), 4 November 1989.

4. Ibid.

5. Ibid.

6. Gallagher, "Gender, Islamism and Democratization," p. 17.

7. Ibid., pp. 26–28.

8. *JT*, 22–23 February 1990.

9. Ibid.

10. Gallagher, "Gender, Islamism and Democratization," pp. 21–22.

11. Interview with Professor of Psychology at Jordan University and women's activist Arwa al-'Amiri, May 10, 1993.

12. Inas al-Khalidi, "Al-Himayah al-Qanuniyyah l-il-Mar'ah al-Urdunniyyah," unpublished paper presented at the First Conference of the JWU, June 13–15, 1995, p. 9.

13. In my May 11, 1993 interview with MP and former PM Tahir al-Masri, he denied that such charges were true and contended that only in the case of the Miri land law had women's rights been compromised.
14. *JT*, July 10, 1990.
15. Interview with Majida al-Masri, member of the JWU executive committee and Rand, June 9, 1996. The cynicism in the evaluation is mine; she saw the GFJW attempts at revitalization as part of strategy to prevent the union from descending into irrelevance.
16. *JT*, June 20, 1990.
17. *JT*, July 10, 1990.
18. *JT*, July 31, 1990.
19. Commentary by Na'ila Rashdan in *al-Ra'y*, February 20, 1993.
20. *JT*, July 10, 1990.
21. This was the evaluation of Majida al-Masri in my interview with her.
22. This was the evaluation of Senator Na'ila Rashdan, who was close to the Islamist camp. Interview with Senator Rashdan, who was active with the GFJW during the period, August 6, 1994.
23. *JT*, July 21, 1990.
24. *JT*, July 20, 1990.
25. *JT*, August 31, 1990.
26. *JT*, July 29, 1990.
27. Mu'nis al-Razzaz in *al-Dustur*, July 31, 1990; Ahmad Dabbas in *Sawt al-Sha'b*, July 30, 1990.
28. Muna Banduqji Abu Ghunayma in *al-Dustur*, August 1, 1990.
29. *JT*, August 4, 1990.
30. Haifa Malhas in *al-Ra'y*, August 4, 1990.
31. *Al-Ra'y*, August 4, 1990.
32. *JT*, January 28, 1991.
33. Na'ila Rashdan in *al-Ra'y*, February 20, 1993.
34. *JT*, July 25–26, 1991.
35. Interview with Dr. 'Abla 'Amawi, UNDP, formerly with the Noor al-Hussein Foundation, March 18, 1996.
36. "Jordanian Women Federation Elections," an unsigned (although clearly from Islamists) statement dated September 15, 1991 and found in the archives of the *Jordan Times*.
37. *JT*, October 20, 1991.
38. Rashdan interview, May 22, 1996.
39. *The Star*, August 27, 1992.
40. Rashdan interview, May 22, 1996.
41. *JT*, May 23–24, 1991.
42. Off-the-record interview.
43. *JT*, June 13–14, 1991.
44. Off-the-record interview.
45. Off-the-record interview.

46. See "Draft Project Proposal: Support to JNCW for Implementation of the Political Domain of the National Strategy for Women in Jordan," submitted to NDI, January 1996, and USAID, "Proposed National Strategy and Action Plan for the National Women's Committee," June 30, 1992. I am skeptical of many details about the source of initiatives. (One source indicated that a women's committee had in fact been in existence since the prime ministership of Tahir al-Masri (June–November 1991), although it did not meet until bin Shakir's second premiership, in spring 1992.) Having observed their emergence and development, the logic or coherence of the projects appears only in hindsight.

47. I attended this meeting as an observer.

48. Off-the-record interview with one of the women who was in attendance at the session.

49. Off-the-record interview.

50. QAF, "QAF facts: Women on the Move," n.d., p. 1.

51. *JT*, July 16, 1995.

52. *Al-Aswaq*, March 11, 1996.

53. *Al-Aswaq*, November 20, 1995.

54. *Al-Dustur*, March 1, 1996.

55. *Al-Dustur*, December 30, 1995.

56. *Al-Dustur*, April 1, 1996.

57. PBWRC, brochure and press release, no date.

58. *The Star*, April 1, 1996.

59. *Al-Aswaq*, March 11, 1996.

60. Interview with Maha al-Khatib, director of UNIFEM office, Amman, February 27, 1996.

61. Interview with IAF member Hayat al-Musaymi, June 16, 1996. She said that the extent of their involvement was having obtained a copy of the report and submitting input on an informal basis.

62. *Al-Ra'y*, February 10, 1996.

63. *JT*, 14–March 15, 1996.

64. Rashdan interview.

65. Interview with Asma Khadr in *The Star*, March 24, 1994.

66. *JT*, January 8, 1994.

67. *JT*, September 25, 1995.

68. *The Star*, April 14, 1994.

69. Comments by Asma Khadr at a panel on women at a conference co-sponsored by the New Jordan Research Center and Friedrich Ebert Stiftung, "Jordan's Democratic Path," May 31, 1994.

70. *The Star*, June 29, 1995.

71. Musaymi interview.

72. *JT*, April 27, 1993.

73. *JT*, July 17, 1993. I attended this session as an observer.

74. *Al-Aswaq*, March 11, 1996.

75. Off-the-record interview.
76. 'Amawi interview. 'Amawi did not coin or use the term RONGOs.
77. Off-the-record conversations.

7. BOURGUIBA AND HIS LEGACY

1. Eva Bellin, "Civil Society in Formation: Tunisia," in R. Augustus Norton (ed.), *Civil Society in the Middle East* (Leiden: Brill, 1994), p. 128.
2. Zakya Daoud, *Féminisme et Politique au Maghreb* (Casablanca: Editions Eddif, 1993), p. 51.
3. Interview with activist and member of the Association Tunisienne des Femmes Démocrates (ATFD) Raouda Gharbi, in Tunis, October 24, 1995.
4. M. Ahnaf, "Tunisie: un débat sur les rapports Etat/religion," *Maghreb-Machrek*, no. 126 (October–December 1989), p. 94.
5. Souad Chater, *La Femme Tunisienne: citoyenne ou sujet?* (Tunis: Maison Tunisienne de L'Edition, n.d.), pp. 91–92.
6. Sophie Bessis and Souhayr Belhassan, *Femmes du Maghreb: l'enjeu* (Casablanca: Editions Eddif, 1992), p. 130.
7. Ibid., pp. 143, 148–149.
8. Bellin, "Civil Society in Formation," p. 130.
9. Sophie Bessis and Souhayr Belhassan, *Bourguiba, vol. 2: Un si long règne* (Paris: Jeune Afrique Livres, 1989), p. 13.
10. Interview with Hedia Jrad, president of the ATFD, in Tunis, October 23, 1995.
11. Bessis and Belhassan, *Femmes*, p. 141.
12. Mark Tessler, John Entelis and Gregory White, "The Republic of Tunisia," in David E. Long and Bernard Reich (eds.), *The Governments and Politics of the Middle East and North Africa* (Boulder: Westview, 1996), pp. 440–441.
13. Remy Leveau, "La Tunisie du Président Ben Ali: équilibre interne et environnement arabe," *Maghreb-Machrek*, no. 124 (Avril–Juin 1989), pp. 14–15.
14. *Annuaire de l'Afrique du Nord* (hereafter *AAN*), 1990 (Paris: Editions de CNRS, 1990), p. 788.
15. See, for example, press reports of the visit of French President Jacques Chirac to Tunisia, October 5–6, 1985 in *al-Sabah* and *La Presse*.
16. Bessis and Belhassan, *Bourguiba*, p. 97.
17. Ibid., p. 106.
18. Bellin, "Civil Society in Formation," p. 129.
19. Tessler et al., "Republic of Tunisia," p. 429.
20. Bellin, "Civil Society in Formation," p. 130, footnote, 20.
21. Eva Rana Bellin, "Civil Society Emergent?: State and Social Classes in Tunisia," doctoral dissertation, Princeton University, 1992, pp. 278–279.
22. Souad Chater, *Les Emancipées du Harem: regard sur la femme tunisienne* (Tunis: Editions La Presse, 1992), pp. 31–32.
23. Bessis and Belhassan, *Bourguiba*, pp. 149–150.
24. Bellin, "Civil Society in Formation," p. 130.

25. *AAN* 1979, p. 560.
26. *AAN* 1980, p. 595.
27. Bessis and Belhassan, *Bourguiba*, p. 186.
28. Tessler et al., "Republic of Tunisia," p. 431.
29. Bellin, "Civil Society in Formation," p. 131.
30. *Ibid.*, pp. 614–15.
31. Bessis and Belhassan, *Bourguiba*, p. 196.
32. *AAN* 1981, p. 623.
33. L.B. Ware, "Ben Ali's Constitutional Coup in Tunisia," *Middle East Journal*, vol. 42, no. 4 (autumn 1988), p. 591.
34. *Jeune Afrique*, 30 November 1983.
35. *Jeune Afrique*, 23 July 1986.
36. *AAN* 1983, p. 899.
37. *AAN* 1984, pp. 979–980.
38. *AAN* 1985, p. 698.
39. *Jeune Afrique*, 19 June 1985.
40. *AAN* 1987, 708.
41. Aziza Dargouth Medimegh, *Droits et Vécu de la Femme en Tunisie* (Paris: L'Hermès Edilis, 1992), p. 132.
42. *AAN* 1985, p. 708.
43. *AAN* 1987, p. 650.
44. Kevin Dwyer, *Arab Voices: The Human Rights Debate in the Middle East* (Berkeley: University of California Press, 1991), p. 149.
45. *AAN* 1987, p. 746.
46. *AAN* 1988, p. 745.
47. Ahnaf, pp. 98–105.
48. Bellin, "Civil Society in Formation," pp. 133–34.
59. Economic Intelligence Unit, Quarterly Report, (hereafter, EIU), *Tunisia*, no. 4, 1988, p. 7.
50. *AAN* 1989, pp. 682–3.
51. *Middle East Journal*, "Chronology," for January 29, 1989.
52. See Amnesty International Reports: "Tunisia: Heavy Sentences after Unfair Trials," (October 1992); and "Tunisia: Prolonged Incommunicado Detention and Torture," (March 1992).
53. Leveau, "La Tunisie du Président Ben Ali, p. 6.
54. Ibid., p. 15.
55. *EIU*, no. 2, 1989, p. 7.
56. *Al-Sabah* (Tunis), 28 December 1989.
57. *AAN* 1989, pp. 685–6.
58. *AAN* 1989, p. 688.
59. *AAN* 1989, 689–90; and *Middle East International*, (hereafter, *MEI*), October 20, 1989.
60. *MEI*, 2 March 1990.

61. *EIU*, no.2, 1990, p. 9.
62. Ibid., p. 17.
63. *AAN* 1990, p. 784.
64. *EIU*, no. 4, 1990, p. 10.
65. *AAN* 1990, p. 793.
66. Ibid., p. 795.
67. *EIU*, no.1, 1991, p. 11.
68. *EIU*, no. 2, 1991, p. 15.
69. For a personal story of that period by a man who was merely suspected of having Islamist sympathies see Ahmed Manai, *Supplice Tunisien: Le jardin secret du général Ben Ali* (Paris: Editions la Decouverte, 1995).
70. *AAN* 1991, pp. 949–950. See also the annual reports of Amnesty International for that period.
71. Bellin, "Civil Society in Formation," p. 136.
72. Ibid., pp. 140–41.
73. *EIU*, no. 4, 1992, p. 10.
74. Off-the-record discussion with an official at the U.S. Embassy, Tunis, October 6, 1995.

8. CITOYENNES À PART ENTIÈRE?

1. Ilhem Marzouki, *Le Mouvement des Femmes en Tunisie au XXème siècle* (Paris: Maisonneuve et Larose, 1993), pp. 89, 96–97 (hereafter cited as Marzouki), and 108. This section relies heavily on Marzouki's work because it is the most comprehensive. The only other full treatment of which I am aware, and which I cite on several occasions below (as Daoud), is that of Zakya Daoud, *Féminisme et Politique au Maghreb* (Casablanca: Editions Eddif, 1993). Unfortunately, I have discovered a number of errors in this work of Daoud's, leading me to a more cautious use of it.
2. Marzouki, p. 139.
3. Ibid. p. 76.
4. Ibid. p. 77.
5. Ibid. p. 141.
6. Ibid. p. 139–140.
7. Ibid. p. 158.
8. Samya El-Mechal, "Femmes et Pouvoir en Tunisie," *Les Temps Modernes*, no. 436 (November 1982), p. 983.
9. Ibid., p. 984.
10. Marzouki, p. 189.
11. Daoud, p. 56.
12. Marzouki, p. 187.
13. Ibid. p. 160.
14. Daoud, p. 65.
15. Susan E. Waltz, "Another View of Feminine Networks: Tunisian Women and

the Development of Political Efficacy," *International Journal of Middle Eastern Studies* 22 (1990), pp. 30–31.

16. Marzouki, p. 205.

17. Souad Chater, *Les Emancipées du Harem: regard sur la femme tunisienne* (Tunis: Editions La Presse, 1992), pp. 173–78.

18. Marzouki, p. 170.

19. Ibid. pp. 201–2.

20. Daoud, p. 68.

21. This was clear in my interviews, a full decade after Fathia Mzali's political demise.

22. Daoud, p. 69; Marzouki, p. 183.

23. Marzouki, p. 186. My translation.

24. Ibid., pp. 184 and 192.

25. Ibid., p. 185.

26. Mounira Charrad, "Repudiation versus Divorce: Responses to State Policy in Tunisia," (hereafter cited as Charrard) in Esther N. Chow and Catherine W. Berheide (eds.), *Women, The Family and Policy: A Global Perspective* (Albany: SUNY Press, 1994), pp. 56, 59, 65–66.

27. Alia Cherif Chamari, *La Femme et La Loi en Tunisie* (Casablanca: Editions Le Fennec, 1991), (hereafter cited as Chamari) pp. 45, 47, 52–53.

28. CREDIF, *Femmes de Tunisie: Situation et perspectives* (Tunis: SIMPACT, 1994), p. 15

29. Ibid. pp. 64, 74, 77.

30. Marzouki, p. 249.

31. CREDIF, pp. 134, 137, 144–148.

32. Chamari, p.90.

33. Chamari, p. 117.

34. Ibid., pp. 47, 120–21.

35. CREDIF, pp. 103–104.

36. Sophie Bessis and Souhayr Belhassan, *Femmes du Maghreb: l'enjeu* (Casablanca: Editions Eddif, 1992), p. 101.

37. Chamari, 82.

38. For a full discussion of the issues involved in the 1981 CSP changes, see the next chapter.

39. Chamari, pp. 67–68.

40. See the interventions of lawyer Fathia Bahri in "Amendement du code du statut personnel," *Le Maghreb*, April 11, 1981, p. 37.

41. Charrad, p. 60.

42. Chamari, p. 70.

43. This section is taken largely from the pamphlet by CREDIF for the Ministry for Women and the Family entitled, "The Legal Status of Women: 1993 Reforms."

44. *Jeune Afrique*, July 13, 1995.

45. Interview with David Painter, AID, Bureau of Urban Development, in Tunis, October 12, 1995.

46. Interview with Radhia Riza, former vice-president of the UNFT, in Tunis, November 9, 1995.

47. UNFT, "Rapport Général sur les Projets Financés dans le cadre du programme de coopération avec USAID, 1995."

48. Ibid. It is interesting, and probably instructive, that in the UNFT's journal's article on these activities, no mention was made of USAID funding. See *Femme*, March–April 1995.

49. "Rapport sur les activités du Reseau Rihana, 95," September 27, 1995.

50. This section is based on my interview with Jim Coffman, Director, Amideast, Tunis, in Tunis, November 8, 1995.

51. This section is based on my interview with Gabriele Noack-Spaeth, permanent representative of the Friedrich Naumann Foundation, in Tunis, November 10, 1995.

52. This section is based on my interview with Rym Ben Halima, coordinator, ACDI, in Tunis, November 10, 1995.

53. Noack-Spaeth interview.

54. Coffman interview.

9. THE CHANGING GUISE OF STATE FEMINISM

1. CREDIF, *Femmes de Tunisie* (Tunis: SIMPACT, 1994), p.74.

2. Ibid., p. 134.

3. Neila Zoughlami, "Quel Féminisme dans les groupes-femmes des années 80 en Tunisie?" (hereafter Zoughlami) *Annuaire de l'Afrique du Nord* (hereafter *AAN*), 1989 (Paris: CRNS, 1989), p. 445.

4. Azza Ghanmi, *Le Mouvement Féministe Tunisien: terminologie sur l'autonomie et la pluralité des femmes, 1979–1989* (hereafter cited as Ghanmi) (Tunis: Editions Chama, 1993), pp. 28–29; and Amel Ben Aba, "Clore pour éclore à l'aube du féminisme tunisien," in AFTURD, vol. 2.

5. Ghanmi, pp. 43–44.

6. Ibid., pp. 27–28.

7. Kevin Dwyer, *Arab Voices: The Human Rights Debate in the Middle East* (Berkeley: University of California Press, 1991—hereafter cited as Dwyer), p. 195.

8. Ghanmi, pp. 50–54.

9. Dwyer, pp. 196, 199–200.

10. Ilhem Marzouki, *Le Mouvement de Femmes en Tunisie au XXème siecle* (Paris: Maisonneuve et Larose, 1993—hereafter cited as Marzouki), pp. 261, 265.

11. Ghanmi, p. 58.

12. Ibid., p. 59.

13. Zoughlami, p. 446.

14. Ghanmi, pp. 60–61.

15. *Le Maghreb*, June 30, 1989.

16. Zoughlami, p. 446.

17. Ghanmi, pp. 59–60. See discussion of this period in chapter 7.
18. Marzouki, p. 266.
19. Ghanmi, pp. 67 and 70.
20. Marzouki, p. 267.
21. Dwyer, p. 202.
22. Ghanmi, p. 77. At the time, 50 TD was worth about US$42.
23. Dwyer, p. 206.
24. Marzouki, p. 295.
25. Zoughlami, p. 447.
26. Dwyer, p. 207.
27. Zoughlami, p. 448.
28. *Dialogue*, April 6, 1981.
29. The press dossiers at the Centre National de Documentation had very little on the UNFT from 1983 to 1988.
30. *Haqa'iq*, July 13–19, 1990.
31. *Al-Sabah*, April 4, 1987.
32. *Al-Sabah*, April 7, 1987.
33. Interview with Radhia Riza, former vice-president of the UNFT, Tunis, November 9, 1995.
34. Al-Tayyib al-Lumi, "Al-Jadid fi Majallat al-Ahwal al-Shakhsiyyah," (hereafter cited as al-Lumi), in 'Ayyad Ibn 'Achour (ed.), *Thulathiyyat al-Majallah al-Qanuniyyah al-Tunisiyyah, 1953–1983, 'Adad Khass* (Tunis: Kulliyyat al-Huquq w-al-'Ulum al-Siyasiyyah w-al-Iqtisadiyyah bi Tunis, 1985), p. 66.
35. See the interventions of law professor Sassi Ben Halima in "Amendement du code du statut personnel, *Le Maghreb*, April 11, 1981.
36. Al-Lumi, pp. 67–68.
37. Interview with Hedia Jrad, president of the ATFD, in Tunis, October 23, 1995. Al-Lumi confirms this point as well.
38. See the interventions of lawyer Fathia Bahri in "Amendement," *Le Maghreb*, April 11, 1981.
39. *Al-Sabah*, April 11, 1984.
40. See Order 107 of 1984, published in *al-Mar'ah al-'A'ilah w-al-Sukkan*, February 1985.
41. *Le Maghreb*, November 5, 1983.
42. *L'Action*, April 7, 1984.
43. Riza interview.
44. Jrad interview. Interview with author and consultant Souad Chater, in Tunis, October 31, 1995.
45. This section is taken largely from Rachida Ennaifer, "Des Acquis en Péril," *Kalima*, no. 1, February 1986.
46. *Jeune Afrique*, August 7, 1985.
47. *AAN*, 1985, p. 704.
48. Souad Chater, *Les Emancipées du Harem* (Tunis: Editions La Presse, 1992) p. 38.

49. For a discussion of the diversity among Islamists in Tunisia see Douglas K. Magnuson, "Islamic Reform in Contemporary Tunisia: Unity and Diversity," in I. William Zartman (ed.), *Tunisia: The Political Economy of Reform* (Boulder: Lynne Reinner, 1991), pp. 169–192.

50. Aziza Dargouth-Medimegh, *Droits et Vécu de la Femme en Tunisie* (Paris: L'Hermès Edilis, 1992—hereafter cited as Dargouth-Medimegh), p. 144.

51. Ghanmi, p. 120.

52. Dargouth-Medimegh, p. 144.

53. Ghanmi, pp. 120–21.

54. Dargouth-Medimegh, p. 144.

55. Ghanmi, 122–23.

56. Dargouth-Medimegh, p. 145.

57. *Al-Sabah*, April 1, 1989.

58. Dargouth-Medimegh, pp. 154, 158, and 181.

59. Dargouth-Medimegh says this period starts with the president's speech closing the campaign, p. 144.

60. *Le Maghreb*, September 30, 1988.

61. *Al-Musawwar*, August 19, 1988.

62. *Al-Mar'ah*, special issue, November 1988.

63. *Le Maghreb*, September 30, 1988.

64. Ibid., short interviews, pp. 11–13.

65. *Le Maghreb*, November 11, 1988.

66. *Al-Akhbar*, December 12, 1988.

67. *Le Maghreb*, January 27, 1989.

68. Ghanmi, p. 129.

69. *Al-Hurriyyah*, January 22, 1989.

70. *Le Maghreb*, December 8, 1988.

71. *Le Renouveau*, November 27, 1988.

72. Interview with Faiza Kefi, president of the UNFT, in Tunis, October 25, 1995.

73. *Al-Hurriyyah*, January 22, 1989.

74. *Al-Akhbar*, December 16, 1989.

75. *Le Maghreb*, December 8, 1989.

76. Reproduced in Ghanmi, pp. 93–95.

77. Kefi interview.

78. *Le Temps*, August 12, 1989.

79. Zakya Daoud, *Féminisme et Politique au Maghreb* (Casablanca: Editions Eddif, 1993), p. 107.

80. *Al-Sha'b*, August 11, 1992.

81. Interview with Sana Jelassi, member of ATFD and administrator of the violence counseling center, in Tunis, October 10, 1995.

82. Eva Bellin, "Civil Society in Formation: Tunisia," in Augustus Richard Norton (ed.), *Civil Society in the Middle East* (Leiden: Brill, 1995), in note, p. 146.

83. Discussion with former ATFD activist and professor of history Dalenda Larguech, in Tunis, October 12, 1995.

84. Ghanmi, pp. 99–100.

85. Interview with Nadia Hakimi, secretary-general of the ATFD, in Tunis, 10 October 1995.

86. Jrad interview.

87. Daoud, pp. 121–123.

88. Ibid., pp. 117–118.

89. *InfoCredif*, November 6, 1994. Also, interview with Dr. Soukaina Bouraoui, director of CREDIF, in Tunis, October 21, 1995.

90. Jrad interview.

91. Kefi interview.

92. Kefi and Hakimi interviews; interview with Fathia Harzallah, member of AF-TURD, in Tunis, October 18, 1995.

93. Dargouth-Medimegh, pp. 183–184.

94. Jrad interview.

95. Abdelkader Zghal, "La circulation des femmes dans le commerce politique, "*Revue Tunisienne des Sciences Sociales*, no. 88/91, 1987, p. 28.

CONCLUSION

1. Determining what constitutes a threat and who defines it is not a simple matter. It is certainly the case that states can construct a threat where none exists, or exaggerate the dangers involved in a situation in order to justify state policy or distract public attention from other, possibly more substantial, problems. One could argue, quite plausibly, that since its crackdown on the Islamists in 1991–1992, that is exactly what the Tunisian state has done. However, I have also felt obliged to report the feelings and perceptions of the many women whose works I read or whom I interviewed in Jordan, Tunisia, and Morocco during the course of my research. (See list in bibliography.) If they expressed the sentiment that at a particular point they felt threatened or under siege, I certainly did not feel in a position to dispute the veracity or authenticity of their testimony: they lived through these periods, not I. Again, the fact that some women's worst fears were not realized does not mean there was no threat. It means that certain factors or elements have intervened to remove the threat.

2. For a thorough discussion of the relationship between the state and rural notables in Morocco see Remy Leveau, *Le Fellah Marocain: Défenseur du Trône* (Paris: Presses de la Fondation Nationale des Sciences Politiques, 1985).

3. Maxine Molyneux, "Mobilization without Emancipation? Women's Interests, the State and Revolution in Nicaragua," *Feminist Studies* 11 (2) (Summer 1995): 231.

4. Deniz Kandiyoti, "Bargaining with Patriarchy," *Gender and Society* 2 (3) (September 1988): 279 and 282.

5. I am grateful to Roula Majdalani, ESCWA Amman, for a series of discussions in July 1996 regarding NGOs and the state which helped to shape my thinking.

INTERVIEWS

MOROCCO

Abouzeid, Leila. Author. Rabat. June 22, 1995.

Ahmed, Khadija. Member of the Tajdid al-Wa'i al-Nisa'i organization. Rabat. April 23, 1996.

Belarbi, Aicha. Professor, Faculty of Educational Sciences, Muhammad V University, and member of the USFP. Rabat. June 29, 1995.

Benkirane, 'Abdalilah. Leader of the Islah w-al-Tajdid movement. Rabat. April 18, 1996.

Bennani, 'Abd al-'Aziz. President of the OMDH. Rabat. July 5, 1995.

Benzekri, Driss. OMDH activist. Rabat. July 31, 1995.

Berg, Laura. Cultural Affairs Assistant, USIS. Rabat. July 18, 1995.

Bourquiah, Rahma. Professor, Department of Sociology, Mohammad V University. Rabat. July 5, 1995.

Buret, Sue. Director, AMIDEAST, Morocco. Rabat. July 26, 1995.

Chafai, Leila. Journalist and fromer student activist. Rabat, July 4, 1995.

Chenna, Aicha. Founder of the Association of Women's Solidarity. Casablanca. July 11, 1995.

Ghassasi, Dr. Fawzia. Professor, Department of English, Mohammad V University. Rabat. July 6, 1995.

Hunseler, Dr. Peter. Resident Representative of the Friedrich Ebert Foundation, Morocco. Rabat. June 23, 1995.

Lamrini, Amina. President of the ADFM and member of the PPS executive. July 18, 1995.

Loukili, Fatima. Journalist. Office of Press Affairs, Mohammad V Airport. Casablanca. July 11, 1995.

Loukmas, Aicha. Lawyer, editor of *8 Mars*, and member of the UAF. Casablanca. July 21, 1995.

Jamai, Khalid. Editor, *L'Opinion*. Rabat. July 30, 1995.

Khoury, Nabil. Information Officer, USIS. Rabat. July 21, 1995.

Meghnawi, Fatima. Member of the UAF. Rabat. July 25, 1995 and April 12, 1996.

M'jid, Dr. Najat. President of L'Heure Joyeuse, private women's and child welfare association. Casablanca. July 12, 1995.

Miadi, Zineb. Lawyer, member of OMDH and director of Center for Battered Women. Casablanca. July 10, 1995.

Naciri, Rabea. Member of the ADFM and head of the Collectif 95. Rabat. June 26 and July 27, 1995.

Ouichou, Wafa. USAID WID officer, Morocco. Rabat. July 28, 1995.

Oulhadj, Lahcen. Editor of Berber journal *Tifawt*. Rabat, August 4, 1995.

Razi, Najat. Former student activist and president of the AMDF. Casablanca. July 11, 1995.

Riyadh, Khadija. Activist with the UMT. Rabat. August 1, 1995 and April 12, 1996.

Saaf, Dr. 'Abdallah. Chair of the Department of Public Law, Mohammad V University. Rabat. July 1, 1995.

Sbai, Noufissa. President of AFJEM. Rabat. June 30, 1995.

Sqalli, Badia. USFP MP. Rabat. July 19, 1995.

Weischer, Dr. Bernd. Representative of the Konrad Adenauer Foundation, Morocco. Rabat. June 27, 1995.

Yacine, Nadia. Unofficial spokesperson for the 'Adl w-al-Ihsan Society. Sale. August 10, 1995.

JORDAN

'Alami, Nisreen al-. UNIFEM, Amman. Amman. February 27, 1996.

'Amawi, Dr. 'Abla. UNDP; formerly with the NHF. Ammam. March 18, 1996.

'Amiri, Dr. Arwa al-. Professor of Psychology, Jordan University and member of the Women's Research Center. Amman. May 10, 1993 and July 31, 1994.

'Assaf, Rana. Civil engineer, formerly active with the Muslim Brotherhood's student organization. Amman. June 28, 1993.

Balakrishnan, Mr. USAID, Amman, responsible for the WID program. Amman, May 17, 1993.

Daghestani, Dr. Amal. Professor of Nursing, Jordan University. Amman. July 6, 1993.

Kamal, Nadiya Takriti. Long-time employee at the Ministry of Planning, July 11, 1993.

Khadr, Asma. Lawyer, human rights activist, and (subsequent to interview) president of the JWU. Amman. May 10, 1993.

Khalidi, Inas al-. Researcher at the Jordanian parliament. Amman, July 24, 1994.

Khawaldah, Dr. Samira al-. Educator, Princess Alia College and associated with the Muslim Brotherhood. Amman. May 27, 1993.

Khatib. Maha al-. Director UNIFEM office, Amman. Amman. May 18, 1993 and February 27, 1996.

Masri, Majida al-. Member of the JWU executive committee and of Rand (Hashd). Amman. June 9, 1996.

Masri, Tahir al-. MP; former foreign minister, prime minister, and MP. Amman. May 11, 1993.

Musaymi, Hayat al-. Member of the IAF. Amman. June 16, 1996.

Rashdan, Na'ila al-. Senator and member of the GFJW. Amman. August 6, 1994 and May 22, 1996.

Sabbagh, Amal. Director of CARDNE (Regional Center on Agrarian Reform and Development for the Near East). Amman. July 19, 1993 and May 30, 1996.

Salih, Firyial. Assistant Director, Community Development Association, Hayy Nazzal. Amman, July 21, 1994.

Saqqa, Su'ad al-. Pharmacist and member of Islamic charitable society Jam'iyyat al-Rubay'ah. Amman. July 18, 1993.

Sharaf, Layla. Senator, and former minister of information. Amman. July 1, 1993.

Tall, Suhayr al-. Writer and independent researcher on social issues. Amman. July 20, 1994, August 5, 1994, and June 3, 1996.

Tall, Janine al-. Director, AMIDEAST, Amman. Amman. May 18, 1993 and March 12, 1996.

Zu'bi. Salim al-. Former MP. Amman. May 15, 1993.

Zumaylah, Lutfiyyah al-. Islamist candidate for the GFJW presidency in 1990. Amman. July 18, 1993.

TUNISIA

Ben Halima, Rym. Agence Canadienne du Développement International. Tunis. November 10, 1995.

Blake, Robert. Political Officer, US Embassy, Tunisia. Tunis. October 6, 1995.

Bouraoui, Dr. Soukaina. Director of CREDIF. Tunis. October 21, 1995.

Chater, Souad. Author and consultant on women and family planning issues. Tunis. October 31, 1995.

Coffman, James. Director, AMIDEAST, Tunisia. Tunis. November 8, 1995.

Gharbi, Raoudeh. ATFD activist. Tunis. October 24, 1995.

Hakimi, Nadia. Secretary-General of the ATFD. Tunis. October 10, 1995.

Harzallah, Fathia. Member of AFTURD. Tunis. October 18, 1995.

Hassairi, Mohammad Ali. Formerly with USAID, WID. Tunis. October 20, 1995.

Jelassi, Sana. Administrator of the ATFD's Battered Women's Center. Tunis. October 10, 1995.

Johnson, Seneca. Economics Officer, US Embassy, Tunisia. Tunis. October 6, 1995.

Jrad, Hedia. President of the ATFD. Tunis. October 23, 1995.

Kefi, Faiza. President of the UNFT. Tunis. October 25, 1995.

Larguech, Dr. Dalenda. Professor of History, University of Tunis, and former activist with the ATFD. Tunis. October 12, 1995.

Noack-Spaeth, Gabriele. Permanent representative of the Friedrich Naumann Foundation, Tunisia. Tunis. November 10, 1995.

Painter, David. USAID, Regional Office, Bureau of Urban Development, Tunis. Tunis. October 12, 1995.

Riza, Radhia. Former vice-president of the UNFT. Tunis. November 9, 1995.

Walker, Vivian. Cultural Affairs Officer, USIS. Tunis. October 10, 1995.

Zghal, Dr. Abdelkadir. Director of CERES. Tunis. October 23 1995.

BIBLIOGRAPHY

BOOKS IN ENGLISH AND FRENCH

Association des Femmes Tunisiennes pour la Recherche sur le Développement (AFTURD). *Tunisiennes en devenir: Tome 1, Comment les femmes vivent; Tome 2, La moitié entière.* Tunis: CERES productions, 1992.

Abderrazak, Moulay Rachid. *La Femme et La Loi au Maroc.* Casablanca: Editions Le Fennec, 1991.

Akharbach, Latifa and Narjis Rerhaye, *Femmes et Politique.* Casablanca: Editions Le Fennec, 1992.

———. *Femmes et Média.* Casablanca: Editions Le Fennec, 1992.

Alahyane, Mohamed et al. *Portraits de Femmes.* Casablanca: Editions Le Fennec, 1987.

Alaoui, Cherifa et al. *Femmes et Education: Etat des Lieux.* Casablanca: Editions Le Fennec, 1994.

Amnesty International. *Morocco: Breaking the Wall of Silence: The Disappeared in Morocco.* New York: Amnesty International, 1993.

———. *Tunisia: Heavy Sentences after Unfair Trials.* New York: Amnesty International, 1992.

———. *Tunisia: Prolonged Incommunicado Detention and Torture.* New York: Amnesty International, 1992.

———. *Women in the Front Line.* New York: Amnesty International, 1990.

Association Marocaine de Soutien à l'UNICEF. *La Situation de l'Enfant dans les Communes.* n.p.: 1994.

Badran, Margot. *Feminists, Islam, and Nation: Gender and the Making of Modern Egypt.* Princeton: Princeton University Press, 1995.

Basri, Driss, et al., *Révision de la Constitution Marocaine. 1992: Analyses et Commentaire.* Imprimerie Royale, 1992.

———. *Le Maroc et les Droits de l'Homme: Positions, Réalisations et Perspectives.* Paris: L'Harmattan, 1994.

Bayer, Thomas C. *Morocco: Direct Legislative Elections June 23, 1993: Report of the IFES Monitoring and Observation Delegations.* Washington. D.C.: IFES. International Foundation for Electoral Systems), n.d..

Beck, Lois and Nikki Keddie, eds. *Women in the Muslim World.* Cambridge: Harvard University Press, 1978.

Ben Ammar, Zeineb. *Responsabilités des Entreprises Publiques dans l'Amélioration de la Condition de la Femme—Cas de la Tunisie.* Ljubljana: Centre international des entreprises publiques dans les pays en développement, 1983.

Bessis, Sophie and Souhayr Belhassen. *Femmes du Maghreb: l'Enjeu.* Casablanca: Editions Eddif, 1992.

— *Bourguiba, vol 2: Un si long regne.* Paris: Jeune Afrique Livres, 1989.

Boutarkha, Fatima. *Marocaines & Medias.* Casablanca: Editions Le Fennec, 1995.

Brand, Laurie A. *Jordan's Inter-Arab Relations: The Political Economy of Alliance-Making.* New York: Columbia University Press, 1984.

———. *Palestinians in the Arab World: Institution Building and the Search for State.* New York: Columbia University Press, 1988.

Brynen, Rex. Bahgat Korany, and Paul Noble. *Political Liberalization and Democratization in the Arab World,* vol. 1. Boulder: Lynne Rienner, 1995.

Camau, Michel. *Tunisie au Présent.* Paris: CNRS, 1987.

Centre d'Etudes et de Documentation Economique, Juridique et Sociale. CEDEJ). *Démocratie et Démocratisations dans le Monde Arabe.* Cairo: CEDEJ, 1992.

Centre d'Etudes et de Recherches Démographiques. *Femmes et Condition Féminine au Maroc: Documentation Statistique.* Rabat: Ministere du Plan, Direction de la Statistique, 1989.

Centre d'Etudes et de Recherches Démographiques. *Statut Economique et Social de la Femme au Maroc: Recueil Analytique des Textes.* Rabat: Ministere du Plan, Direction de la Statistique, 1990.

Centre de Recherche, de Documentation et d'Information sur la Femme. *Femmes de Tunisie.* Tunis: CREDIF, 1994.

Chamari, Alya Cherif. *La Femme et la Loi en Tunisie.* Casablanca: Editions Le Fennec, 1991.

Chater, Souad. *La Femme Tunisienne: Citoyenne ou Sujet.* Tunis: Maison Tunisienne de L'Edition, n.d.)

———. *Les Emancipées du Harem: regard sur la femme tunisienne.* Tunis: Editions La Presse, 1992)

Dargouth-Medimegh, Aziza. *Droits et Vécu de la Femme en Tunisie.* Paris: L'Hermès Edilis, 1992.

Daoud, Zakya. *Féminisme et Politique au Maghreb.* Casablanca: Editions Eddif, 1993.

Dawisha, Adeed and I. William Zartman. *Beyond Coercion: The Durability of the Arab State*. New York: Croom Helm, 1988.

Dwyer, Kevin. *Arab Voices: The Human Rights Debate in the Middle East*. Berkeley: University of California Press, 1991.

El-Khayat, Ghita. *Les Femmes dans l'Union du Maghreb Arabe*. Casablanca: Editions Eddif, 1992.

Eury, Pascaline. *Jordanie: Les Elections Législatives du 8 Novembre 1989*, Les Cahiers du CERMOC no. 2. Amman: CERMOC, 1991.

Faure, Christine. *Democracy Without Women: Feminism and the Rise of Liberal Individualism in France*. Bloomington: Indiana University Press, 1991.

Femmes & Violences. Marrakech: Editions Pumag, 1993.

Femmes Maghreb Deux Mille Deux: cinq ans après. 1989–1994. Rabat: AFJEM, 1994.

Ferber, Marianne E. and Julie A. Nelson. *Beyond Economic Man: Feminist Theory and Economics*. Chicago: University of Chicago, 1993.

Fontaine, Jean. *Ecrivaines Tunisiennes*. Tunis: Le Gai Savoir, second edition, 1994.

Friedrich Ebert Stiftung. *Femmes et Société Civile au Maghreb*. Marrakech: Publications Universitaires du Maghreb, 1996.

Friedman, Edward, ed. *Politics of Democratization: Generalizing East Asian Experiences*. Boulder: Westview, 1994.

Ghanmi, Azza. *Le Mouvement Féministe Tunisien: terminologie sur l'autonomie et la pluralité du mouvement des femmes, 1979–1989*. Tunis: Editions Chama, 1993.

Grant, Rebecca and Kathleen Newland, eds. *Gender and International Relations*. Bloomington: Indiana University Press, 1991.

Haddad, Radhia. *Parole de Femme*. Tunis: Editions Elyssa, 1995.

Hibri, Azizah al-, ed. *Women and Islam*. New York: Pergamon Press, 1982.

Hijab, Nadia. *Womanpower: The Arab Debate on Women at Work*. Cambridge: New York, 1988.

Jaquette, Jane, ed. *The Women's Movement in Latin America: Participation and Democracy*. Boulder: Westview Press, 1994.

Joekes, Susan P. *Female-Led Industrialization: Women's Jobs in Third World Export Manufacturing: the Case of the Moroccan Clothing Industry*. Sussex: Institute for Development Studies, 1982.

Jordanian National Committee for Women. *The National Strategy for Women in Jordan*. n.p.: September 1993.

Kahne, Hilda and Janet Z. Giele, eds. *Women's Work and Women's Lives: The Continuing Sturggle Worldwide*. Boulder: Westview, 1992.

Kandiyoti, Deniz, ed. *Women, Islam & the State*. Philadelphia: Temple University Press, 1991.

Leveau, Remy. *Le Fellah Marocain: Défenseur du Trône*. Paris: Presses de la Foundation Nationale des Sciences Politiques, 1985.

Manai, Ahmed. *Supplice Tunisien: Le jardin secret du général Ben Ali*. Paris: La Découverte, 1995.

Marsot, Afaf Lutfi al-Sayyid. *Women and Men in Late Eighteenth-Century Egypt*. Austin: University of Texas Press, 1995.

Marzouki, Ilhem. *Le Mouvement des Femmes en Tunisie au XXème siècle*. Paris: Maisonneuve et Larose, 1993.

Meknassi, Rachid Filali. *Femmes & Travail*. Casablanca: Editions Le Fennec, 1994.

Mernissi, Fatima. *Doing Daily Battle: Interviews with Moroccan Women*, translated by Mary Jo Lakeland. New Brunswick: Rutgers University Press, 1989.

———. *Beyond the Veil: Male-Female Dynamics in Modern Muslim Society*. Bloomington: Indiana University Press, 1987)

Mir-Hosseini, Ziba. *Marriage on Trial: A Study of Islamic Family Law — Iran and Morocco Compared*. New York: I.B. Tauris & Co., Ltd. 1993.

Moghadam, Valentine M., ed. *Democratic Reform and the Position of Women in Transitional Economies*. Oxford: Clarendon Press,1993.

———, ed. *Modernizing Women: Gender and Social Change in the Middle East*. Boulder: Lynne Rienner, 1993.

———, ed. *Identity Politics and Women: Cultural Reassertions and Feminisms in International Perspective*. Boulder: Westview Press, 1994.

Munson, Henry Jr. *Religion and Power in Morocco*. New Haven: Yale University Press, 1993.

National Endowment for Democracy. *Annual Report*, 1994.

Organisation Marocaine des Droits de l'Homme. *Organisation Marocaine des Droits de l'Homme à travers ses communiqués et déclarations, Mai 1988 - Mars 1991*. Casablanca: Editions Imprimerie, 1991.

———. *Organisation Marocaine des Droits de l'Homme à travers ses communiqués et déclarations, Mai 1991–Decembre 1992*. n.p., 1993.

———. *Organisation Marocaine des Droits de l'Homme à travers ses communiqués et déclarations, Decembre 1992–Mai 1994*. Casablanca: Les Editions Maghrebines, n.d..

———. *Organisations Marocaine des Droits de l'Homme au sujet du 3ème Rapport Gouvernemental au Comité des Droits de l'Homme des Nations-Unies*. Casablanca: Les Editions Maghrebines, 1994.

Pateman, Carole. *The Sexual Contract*. Stanford: Stanford University Press, 1988)

Peteet, Julie. *Gender in Crisis: Women and the Palestinian Resistance Movement*. New York: Columbia, 1991.

Peterson, V. Spike, ed. *Gendered States: Feminist Revisions of International Relations Theory*. Boulder: Lynne Reinner, 1992.

Peters, Julie and Andrea Wolper, eds. *Women's Rights, Human Rights: International Feminist Perspectives*. New York: Routledge, 1995)

Radcliffe, Sarah A. and Sallie Westwood, eds. *Viva: Women and Popular Protest in Latin America*. New York: Routledge, 1993.

Salameh, Ghassari (ed.), *Democracy Without Democrats: The Renewal of Politics in the Muslim World*. New York: I. B. Tauris, 1994.

Satloff, Robert. *From Abdallah to Hussein*. New York: Oxford University Press, 1994.

Sharabi, Hisham. *Neopatriarchy: A Theory of Distorted Change in Arab Society*. New York: Oxford, 1988.

Staudt, Kathleen, ed. *Women, International Development and Politics*. Philadelphia, Temple University Press, 1990.

———. *Administration, Women, Foreign Assistance and Advocacy* .New York: Praeger, 1985.

Tucker, Judith, ed. *Arab Women: Old Boundaries, New Frontiers.* Bloomington: Indiana University Press, 1993.

Tunisie. Ministère du Plan. Institute National de la Statistique. *L'Economie de la Tunisie en Chiffres.* Selected years.

Waterbury, John. *The Commander of the Faithful: The Moroccoan Political Elite—A Study in Segmented Politics.* New York, Columbia University Press, 1970.

I. William Zartman, ed. *The Political Economy of Morocco.* New York: Praeger, 1987.

———, ed. *Tunisia: The Political Economy of Reform.* Boulder: Lynne Reinner, 1991.

Union Nationale des Femmes Tunisiennes. *Les Femmes Européennes et Maghrebines se solidarisent contre l'intégrisme: colloque des femmes euro-maghrebines.* Tunis: Maison Tunisienne de l'Edition, 1992.

——— *L'Image de la Femme dans la Société Tunisienne.* Tunis: Orbis Impression, 1995.

Yuval-Davis, Nira and Floya Anthias, eds. *Woman—Nation—State.* London: Macmillan, 1989.

ARTICLES, CHAPTERS, AND MONOGRAPHS IN ENGLISH AND FRENCH

Ahnaf, M. "Tunisie: un débat sur les rapports Etat/Religion." *Maghreb-Machrek*, no. 126. Octobre-Decembre 1989): 93–108.

———, "Maroc: Le Code du Statut Personnel" *Maghreb-Machrek*, no. 145. Juillet-Septembre 1994): 3–26.

Belarbi, Aicha. "Mouvements de Femmes au Maroc." *Annuaire de l'Afrique du Nord* 28 (1989): 455–465.

Bellin, Eva. "Civil Society in Formation: Tunisia." In R. Augustus Norton. ed. *Civil Society in the Middle East.* Leiden: Brill, 1994, pp. 120–47.

Brand, Laurie A "Economic and Political Liberalization in a Rentier State: The Case of the Hashemite Kingdom of Jordan." In Iliya Harik and Denis Sullivan, eds. *Privatization and Liberalization in the Middle East.* Bloomington: Indiana University Press, 1992.

——— " 'In the Beginning Was the State. . .': The Quest for Civil Society in Jordan." In R. Augustus Norton, ed. *Civil Society in the Middle East.* Leiden: Brill, 1995, pp. 148–185.

——— "Women and the State in Jordan: Inclusion or Exclusion?" Yvonne Yazbeck Haddad and John L. Esposito, eds. *Islam, Gender and Social Change.* New York: Oxford University Press, 1998, pp. 100–123.

Charillon, Frédéric et Alain Mouftard. "Jordanie: les élections du 8 Novembre 1993 et le processus de paix." *Maghreb-Machrek* 144 (Avril–Juin 1994): 40–54.

Charrad, Mounira. "Les Cadres politiques au niveau en tunisie." In *Social Stratification and Development in the Mediterranean.* Mouton: Publications of the Institute of Social Studies, 1973.

———. "State and Gender in the Maghrib." *Middle East Report* (March-April 1990): 19–23.

————. "Repudiation versus Divorce: Responses to State Policy in Tunisia." In Esther N. Chow and Catherine W. Berheide, eds. *Women, The Family and Policy: A Global Perspective.* Albany: SUNY Press, 1994.

Curtiss, Richard. "Women's Rights: An Affair of State in Tunisia." *Washington Report on Middle East Affairs* (September/October 1993): 50–51.

Dammak, O.K. "Travail Feminin et Niveau de Vie en Milieu Ouvrier à Tunis." *Revue Tunisienne de Sciences Sociales* 17 (60) (1980): 57–89.

Daoud, Zakya. "Femmes tunisiennes. Gains juridiques et statut économique et social." *Maghreb-Machrek* 145 (Juillet–Septembre 1994): 27–48.

Denoeux, Guilain et Laurent Gateau. "L'essor des associations au Maroc: à la recherche de la citoyenneté?" *Maghreb-Machrek*, no. 150 (Octobre–Decembre 1995): 19–39.

Duclos, Louis-Jean. "Les éléctions législatives en Jordanie." *Maghreb-Machrek*, 129. Juillet–Septembre 1990): 47–75.

Ferchiou, Sophie. "Pouvoir/contre-pouvoir et société en mutation: L'example tunisien." *Peuples Mediterranéens* 48/49: 81–92.

Goetz, Anne Marie. "The Politics of Integrating Gender into State Development Processes: Trends, Oppotunities and Constraints in Bangladesh, Chile, Jamaica, Mail, Morocco and Uganda." Geneva: United Nations Research Institute for Social Development, May 1995. 62 pp.

Hatem, Mervet. "Egyptian Gender Discourses and Political Liberalization: Do Secularist and Islamist Views Really Differ?" *Middle East Journal* 48 (4) (Autumn 1994): 661–676.

Hermassi, Elbaki. "L'Etat Tunisien et le Mouvement Islamiste." *Annuaire de l'Afrique du Nord* 28 (1989): 297–308.

Joseph, Suad. "Women and Politics in the Middle East." *Middle East Report* (January-February 1986): 3–7.

Kandiyoti, Deniz. "Bargaining with Patriarchy." *Gender & Society* 2 (3) (September 1988): 274–290.

Karoui, Naiema. "La Notion d'Emancipation de la Femme à Travers la Presse." *Revue Tunisienne de Sciences Sociales* (44–51) (47) (1976): 93–124.

Kamal, Nadia Takriti and Mary Qa'war. "The Status and Role of Women in Development in Jordan." Manpower Division, Ministry of Planning, Hashemite Kingdom of Jordan, 1990. Unpublished paper presented at the ILO meeting on "Women and the Jordanian Labor Force." held in Amman, December 1990.

Larif-Beatrix, Asma. "L'évolution de l'Etat tunisien." *Maghreb-Machrek* no. 116 (Avril—Juin 1987): 35–44.

Lazreg, Marnia. "Feminism and Difference: The Perils of Writing as a Woman on Women in Algeria." *Feminist Studies* 14 (1) (Spring 1988): 81–107.

Leveau, Remy. "La Tunisie de Président Ben Ali." *Maghreb-Machrek*, no. 124 (Avril–Juin 1989): 4–17.

————. "Stabilité du pouvoir monarchique et financement de la dette." *Maghreb-Machrek*, no. 118 (Octobre–Decembre 1987): 5–19.

Marshall, Susan. "Paradoxes of Changes: Culture Crisis, Islamic Revival and the

Reactivation of Patriarchy." *Journal of Asian and African Studies* 19 (1–2) (1984): 1–17.

———. "Politics and Female Status in North Africa: A Reconsideration of Development Theory." *Economic Development and Cultural Change.* 1984): 499–524.

———. "Islamic Revival in the Maghreb: The Utility of Tradition for Modernizing Elites." *Studies in Comparative International Development* (Summer 1979): 95–108.

Mataillet, Dominique. "Tunisie: Les Femmes Contre les 'Frères.'" *Jeune Afrique* 32 (Septembre 1992): 24–30.

Mechal, Samya. "Femmes et Pouvoir en Tunisie." *Les Temps Modernes*, no. 436 (Novembre 1982): 975–1010.

Meziou, Kalthoum. "Féminisme et Islam dans la Réforme du Code du Statut Personnel du 18 Février 1981." *Revue Tunisienne de Droit* (1984): 252–282.

Munson, Henry Jr. "The Social Base of Islamic Militancy in Morocco." *Middle East Journal* 40 (2) (Spring 1986): 267–284.

Naciri, Rabea et Nadira Barkallil. "Société: Les femmes au Maroc ou les contradictions d'une évolution récente." *Corps Ecrit* 31 (L'Arabie Heureuse) 1989: 153–162.

Paul, Jim. "States of Emergency: The Riots in Tunisia and Morocco." *MERIP Reports* (October 1984): 3–6.

Seddon, David. "Winter of Discontent in Tunisia and Morocco." *MERIP Reports* (October 1984): 7–16.

Siemienska, Renata. "Women and Social Movements in Poland." *Women & Politics* 6 (4) (Winter 1986): 5–36.

Staudt, Kathleen. "Women, Development and the State: On the Theoretical Impasse." *Development and Change* 17 (1986): 324–33.

———, and Jane Jaquette. "Women's Programs, Bureaucratic Resistance and Feminist Organizations." In Ellen Boneparth and Emily Stoper, eds. *Women, Power and Politics: Toward the Year 2000.* 2nd ed. New York: Pergamon Press, 1988.

Tessler, Mark. "The Uses and Limits of Populism: The Political Strategy of King Hassan II of Morocco." *Middle East Review* (Spring 1985): 45–51.

———, John Entelis, and Gregory White, "The Republic of Tunisia." In David E. Long and Bernard Reich, eds., *The Governments and Politics of the Middle East and North Africa.* Boulder: Westview, 1996, pp. 423–445.

Vandewalle, Dirk. "From the New State to the New Era: Toward a Second Republic in Tunisia." *Middle East Journal* 42 (4) (Autumn 1988): 602–620.

Ware, L. B. "Ben Ali's Constitutional Coup in Tunisia." *Middle East Journal* 42 (4) (Autumn 1988): 587–601.

Waterbury, John. "Endemic and Planned Corruption in a Monarchical Regime." *World Politics* 25 (4) (July 1973): 533–55.

Waylen, Georgina. "Women and Democratization: Conceptualizing Gender Relations in Transition Politics." *World Politics* 46 (3) (April 1994): 327–354.

Zghal, Abdelkader. "La circulation des femmes dans le commerce politique." *Revue Tunisienne de Sciences Sociales* 88/89 (1987): 11–29.

Zoughlami, Neila. "Quel Feminisme dans les groupes-femmes des années 80 en Tunisie? " *Annuaire de l'Afrique du Nord* 28 (1989).

al-'Awd, Karim . "Wad' al-Mar'ah w-al-'Amal al-Siyasi b-il-Maghrib." For the Diplome at the Royal Institute li-Takwin al-Utur." Rabat, 1991.

Bisharat, Emily. "Muhattat Mudi'ah fi Tarikh Masirat al-Mar'ah al-Urdunniyyah." *Al-Dustur*, June 29, 1993.

al-Khudayri Salma . *Tanmiyat al-Mar'ah al-Rifiyyah fi-l-Urdunn*. Amman: Center for Women's Studies, 1993.

Lumi, Al-Tayyib al-. "Al-Jadid fi Majallat al-Ahwal-Shakhsiyyah." In 'Ayyad Ibn 'Ashour. ed., *Thulathiyyat al-Majallah al-Qanuniyyah al-Tunisiyyah, 1953–1983, 'Adad Khass*. Tunis: Kulliyat al-Huquq w-al-'Ulum al-Siyasiyyah w-al-Iqtisadiyyah bi Tunis, 1985, pp. 63–82.

Mahasanah, Nasrin. "Wad' al-Mar'ah al-Urdunniyyah f-il-Tashri'at al-Qanuniyyah." Unpublished study sponsored by the General Secretariat, National Assembly Hashemite Kingdom of Jordan, 1994.

Al-Mar'ah al-Urdunniyah w-al-'Amal al-Siyasi. Amman: New Jordan Research Center, 1993.

Masri, Majidah al-, Al-Azmah al-Rahinah l-il-Harakah al-Nisa'iyyah f-il-Urdunn." *Al-Urdunn al-Jadid* 7 (Spring 1986): 65–69.

Mi'adi, Zineb . *Al-Usra al-Maghribiyyah bayna al-Shar'i w-al-Khitab al-Sha'bi*. n.p.: Al-Markaz al-Watani li-Tansiq wa-Takhtit al-Bahth al-'Ilmi w-al-Taqni, 1988.

Mu'adh, Da'd. "Tajribat al-Ittihad al-Nisa'i. 1974–1981)" *Al-Urdunn al-Jadid*, no. 7. (Spring 1986): 59- 64.

al-Musaddiq, Ruqiyyah. *Al-Mar'ah w-al-Siyasah: Al-Tamthil al-Siyasi f-il-Maghrib*. Casablanca: Dar Tubqal, 1990.

Salamah, Hind. "Ayy Mawqi' Balaghithu Harakat al-Nisa' al-Tunisiyyat?" *Utruhat* 11/12 (1987): 49-51.

Shikhtra, Husayn. *Al-Mar'ah al-Urdunniyyah: Haqa'iq wa-Arqam*. Amman: Nadi Sahbat al-A'mal w-al-Mihn, 1992.

Tall, Suhayr al-. *Muqaddamat Hawla Qadiyyat al-Mar'ah w-al-Harakah al-Nisa'iyyah f-il-Urdunn*. Beirut: al-Mu'assasah al-'Arabiyyah l-il-Dirasat w-al-Nashr, 1985.

———. "Qa' al-Madina." *Jadal*, no. 4, 1993.

Wazarat al-Shu'un al-Ijtima'iyyah, al-Jumhuriyyah al-Tunisiyyah. *Taqrir Lajnat "Dawr al-Mar'ah f-il-Tanmiyah Khilal Al-Mukhattat al-Thamin, 1992–1996."* March 1992.

JOURNALS AND PERIODICALS

Africa Confidential
Annuaire de l'Afrique du Nord
Al-Dustur (Amman)
Quarterly Reports, Economist Intelligence Unit
Foreign Broadcast Information Service (FBIS)
Info CREDIF (Tunis)
Jeune Afrique

Jordan Times
Kalima (Morocco)
Lamalif (Morocco)
Le Maghreb (Tunis)
Al-Mar'ah (Tunis)
Al-Mar'ah, al-'A'ilah, w-al-Sukkan (Tunis)
Maghreb-Machrek
Middle East International
Al-Ra'y (Amman)
The Star (Amman)

UNPUBLISHED MATERIALS

Alami, Nisreen Z. "State, Bureaucracy, and the Institutionalization of Gender Policy: The Case of Jordan." Master's thesis submitted to the Faculty of Economics, London School of Economics and Political Science, 1994.

Bellin, Eva Rana. "Civil Society Emergent?: State and Social Classes in Tunisia." Doctoral dissertation, Princeton University, 1992.

Centre d'Etudes Maghrebines à Tunis. (CEMAT). "Femmes, Etat, et Développement au Maghreb." colloque, Octobre 10–14, 1991. Compilation of unpublished conference papers, including: "Féminisme d'Etat en Tunisie: Ideologie Dominante et Résistance Féminine" by Sophie Ferchiou.

Chafai, Laila. "Le Mouvement des Femmes au Maroc." Draft paper, no date.

Chemonics, Political Economy Review of Morocco, submitted June 1992.

Gallagher, Nancy. "Gender, Islamism, and Democratization in Jordan: The Case of Tujan al-Faysal," draft paper, 1993.

Haenni, Patrick. "Le Théâtre d'Ombres de l'Action Féminine: Femmes, Etat, et Société Civile au Maroc." D.E.A. d'études politiques. AMAC, I.E.P. de Paris, Septembre 1993.

Jamal, Haifa. "Juhud Ittihad al-Mar'ah al-Urdunniyyah fi Sabil Tatwir al-Tashri'at al-Khassah b-il-Mar'ah." Unpublished paper presented at the First Conference of the JWU, June 1995.

al-Khalidi, Inas. "Al-Himayah al-Qanuniyyah l-il-Mar'ah al-Urdunniyyah." Unpublished paper presented at the First Conference of the JWU, June 13–15, 1995.

Layachi, Azzedine. "Civil Society and Democratization in Morocco: Some Theoretical and Empirical Difficulties." Paper presented at the 29th annual meeting of the Middle East Studies Association, Washington, D.C., December 6–10, 1995.

"Al-Taqrir al-Watani hawla al-Mar'ah al-Urdunniyyah l-il-Mu'tamar al-Dawli/ Beijing 1995."

Union National de La Femme Tunisienne. "Rapport Général sur les Projets Financés dans le cadre du programme de coopération avec USAID. Projets no. 298–8249.93 et 298–8377.95." 1995.

Women in Development Team, USAID/Amman. "Proposed National Strategy and Action Plan for the National Women's Committee." Unpublished draft, June 1992.

INDEX

'Abdallah, King, 98

Abortion: Chile, 20; Jordan, 166; Morocco, 57; Poland, 14–16; Romania, 14; Russia, 16–17; Tunisia, 209

Abu Ghazalah, Dr. Haifa, 155, 166

Abu Risha, Zulaykha, 149

ACDI (Agence Canadienne du Développement Internationale), 217–19

Activism, women's, 13, 15, 18, 50, 259

ADFM (Association Démocratique des Femmes Marocaines), Morocco, 49, 51, 63, 82, 88

Adoption, 195

AFTURD (Association des Femmes Tunisiennes pour la Recherche sur le Développement), 216, 225

Al-Ahali, (publication), 114

Aicha, Lalla (Princess), 46, 47

Aicha (publication), 47

AID, see USAID

'Akaylah, 'Abdallah, 106, 113, 156–57

Akhwat al-Safa (Sisters of Purity), Morocco, 46

Alcohol, 103, 109, 110

Alfonsín, Raul, 20

Alfonsín administration, 17, 20

Algeria, 2, 7, 45, 182, 198, 200, 234, 245, 254

'Ali al-Kurdi, Shaykh 'Abd al-Rahman, 146

Alimony, 61, 149, 212; see also Divorce

Alliances (rabitat), 226, 227, 229, 236, 237

Alternance, 41, 44, 45, 77, 82

Amaoui, Noubir, 41

AMDF (Association Marocaine des Droits des Femmes), 37, 54, 80

AMDH (Association Marocaine des Droits de l'Homme), 37, 50–51, 54, 73, 80

Amideast, 64, 65, 141–42, 216–18

Amin, Qasim, 178

Amir al-mu'minin, "Commander of the Faithful," 32, 35

Amman, 102
Amnesty International, 37, 38, 100, 165, 183, 198
Anoual (publication), 75, 82
Approaches, 52, 63
Arab-Israeli wars, 96, 98, 253
'Arabiyyat, 'Abd al-Latif, 105
Arab League Rabat summit (1972), 100
Arab Organization for Human Rights, 165, 198
Arab Women's Federation, see AWF
'Arafat, Yasir, 101, 114
'Arar, Sulayman, 105
Argentina, 17, 19
Association Africaine pour la Recherche sur le Développement, 225
Association des Jeunes Musulmans, Tunisia, 202
Association al-Jusur, Morocco, 54
L'Association Marocaine des Femmes Progressistes, Morocco, 54
Association of Women's Solidarity, Morocco, 52
ATFD (Association Tunisienne des Femmes Démocrates), 219, 236, 238–40, 241, 251, 262
Al-'Athm, Yusuf, 106, 154, 157
Authoritarianism, 1, 261
AWF (Arab Women's Federation), Ittihad al-Mar'ah al-'Arabiyyah, Jordan, 121–23, 129
Awqaf Ministry, 157
Aylwin, Patricio, 20

Baccouche, Taieb, 223
Badran, Mudar, 9, 102–4, 106, 109, 117, 118, 154, 157
Baghdad Pact, 99, 122
Baghdad Summit (1977), 97
Bakr, Ibrahim, 127
Bar Association, Morocco, 37
Bashir, 'Awni, 154
Bashir, Haifa, 154

Basma, Princess, 136, 140, 155, 158, 159, 160, 161, 163, 170, 172, 260
Basri, Driss, 38, 44
Battered women, see Violence, against women
Beijing Women's Conference, 61, 63, 65, 255–56; "Beijing in Amman," 167; Jordan, 138, 143, 144, 155, 161, 163–64, 167, 169, 171, 172; Moroccan preparations for, 86–89, 90; Platform of Action, 162; Tunisia, 215–16, 218, 243
Belkhodja, Tahar, 185–86
Ben 'Ali, Zayn al-'Abdine, 181, 182, 183, 190–97, 199, 213, 232–35, 241–43, 249, 253, 255
Benani-Smires, Latifa, 61, 65, 76
Ben Mrad, Bechira, 203
Ben Salah, Ahmed, 181, 185
Ben Youssef, Salah, 178
Berbers, 35
Al-Bilad (publication), 114
Bin Shakir, Zayd, 101, 108–09, 115–16, 147, 159
Birth control, see Contraception
Bisharat, Emily, 121, 125
Boukhchina, Chadlia, 242
Bourguiba, Habib, xiii, 177, 178, 186, 188, 191, 199, 203, 257; health problems, 184, 189; Liberator of Tunisian Women, 204, 226; modernization program, 180, 209, 220, 244; ouster of, 1, 190, 244, 249; President for Life, 184, 191; secularism, 178–79, 254; women, program for, 180, 181, 205, 210–11, 212, 213, 235
Bourguiba, Wasila (Ben Ammar), 184, 185, 187, 188, 191
Boutros-Ghali, former UN Secretary General, 163
BPWC (Business and Professional Women's Club), Jordan, 128, 129, 134, 141

Brazil, 18, 19; National Council on
  Women's Rights, 19–20
Brazilian transformation, 7
British Mandate in Palestine, 121
Buret, Sue, 64

Camdessus, Michel, 183
Casablanca, 33; riots, 35
Catholic Church, see Religion
Catholic Relief Services, 65
CDT (Confédération Democratique
  de Travail), Morocco, 41
Ceausescu, Nicolae,14
CECF (Club d'Etudes de la Condition
  des Femmes), Tunisia, 221
Chaouche, Chehrezade, 227
Chaouni, Laila, 53, 63
Charfi, Muhammad, 196, 237
Chamari, A.C., 210
Chater, S., 205
Chenna, Aicha, 52
Children, custody of, 61–62
Chile, 18, 19, 20; Academy of
  Christian Humanism, 18; women's
  organizations, role of, 18–19;
  National Coalition of Women for
  Democracy, 20
Christians, see Religion
Circassians, 96, 275n2
Citizenship, 7, 8, 130–31, 139 210,
  213, 218
Civil rights, 36
Club de la Jeune Fille Tunisienne,
  202
Cold War, 182
Collectif 93-Maghreb Egalité, 63, 89,
  90
Comité de la Femme Ouvrière,
  Morocco, 71
Comité National pour la Promotion
  des Droits Politques de la Femme,
  Morocco, 83
Committee on Women's Labor,
  Tunisia, 226

Communes, 38
Communism, xiv; women and work,
  12–13
Community property, see Divorce;
  Inheritance laws
Conservatism, 234, 252, 259; defined, 6
Contraception, 180, 209, 211, 221,
  249, 263
Contracts, 61, 208
Convention Against the Exploitation
  of Children, 60
Convention Against Torture, 60
Convention on the Elimination of All
  Forms of Discrimination Against
  Women, 60
Convention Regarding the Minimum
  Marriage Age and Registering
  Marriage Contracts (1962), 135
Convention Regarding the Nationality
  of Married Women (1955), 135
Convention Regarding Political Rights
  of Women (1955), 135
CREDIF (Centre de Recherche,
  Etudes, Documentation, et
  Information sur la Femme),
  Tunisia, 216, 218, 219, 242, 261
Criminal code, 210, 213, 224
CSE (Commission Syndicale d'Etudes
  de la Condition de la Femme
  Travailleur), Tunisia, 223, 224
CSP (Code du Statut Personnel); see
  Tunisia
Culture, xv, 21, 263

Dabbas, Ahmad, 153
Daftar al-'a'ilah ("family book"), 132
Daghestani, Farah, 162
Dahhan, Umayma, 136, 169, 172
Damascus, 102
Damen-Masri, Salwa, 116
Daoud, Z., 47, 59
Dar Amerika, 65
Death penalty, 37, 224
Democracy, 7, 110

Democratic Institutions Initiative
(DII), see DII
Democratic transitions, 8, 12
Democratic Women's League, Jordan,
151, 162
Dhunaybat, 'Abd al-Majid, 115
DII (Democratic Institutions
Initiative), 64–65, 140, 142, 215,
216
Discrimination, 8, 58, 135, 210
Divorce: Chile, 20; Jordan, 122, 132,
149, 166; Morocco, 59–60, 62, 70;
Tunisia, 178, 194, 205, 208, 211,
212, 213, 231
Dowry, 208
Dufoix, Georgina, 230
Al-Dustur (publication), 154
Duweik, Fatima, 227, 235

East Bankers, see Jordan,
Transjordanians
Eastern Europe, 12, 251
Economic transitions, 8, 12
Editions Le Fennec, 53
Education, 122, 130, 156–57, 250, 180,
195, 205, 209, 211, 213, 218, 241,
249
Egypt, 9, 98, 200; controlled liberali-
zation in, 10; feminist movement, 9
8 Mars (publication), 52, 70, 73
Entitlements, 61, 131, 135, 210
EU (European Union), 32, 33, 35, 36,
181, 249

Faisal, Toujan, 113, 135, 145–48, 159,
169, 172, 276n9
Falklands-Malvinas war, 17
Fallaghas, 178
Family, 3, 52, 173, 180, 205; see also,
Personal status laws
Faris, Mu'tasim, 146
Fariz, Ziyad, 158
Al-Farqan (publication), 72
Al-Fassi, 'Allal, 46, 59

Al-Fassi, Malika, 46
Fatima, Zohra Lalla, 47
Fa'uri, Nawal, 162, 163
FD (Femmes Démocrates), Tunisia,
223, 226, 233, 238
Feminism, 18, 49; see also State
feminism
Femme et al Loi au Maroc, La
(publication), 53
Femmes et Media (publication), 53
Femmes Partagées: Famille-Travail
(publication), 53
Femmes et Politiqueu (publication), 53
Femmes et Pouvoir (publication), 53
Femmes 1980 (publication), 53
FEMNET, 87
FES (Friedrich Ebert Stiftung), 53, 54,
63, 143
Fez, riots in, 40
FIS (Front Islamique de Salut) , 35,
41, 45, 182, 194, 198, 254
FLN (Front de Libération Nationale),
Algeria, 182, 194
FNS (Friedrich Naumann Stiftung),
143–44, 217
France, 32, 183
French Revolution, 2; "Declaration of
the Rights of Man and the
Citizen," 2
Friedrich Ebert Stiftung (FES), see
FES
Friedrich Naumann (FN), see FN
Front Islamique de Salut (FIS), see FIS
Fundamentalism, see Religion

Gafsa, 182, 186
Gallagher, N., 147
Gender, 8; division of labor, 5, 170;
inequalities, 13; interests, 5, 6;
relations, 9
General Union of Palestinian Women,
Jordan, 123, 224
German Christian Democratic Party,
62

GFJW (General Federation of
Jordanian Women), 126–27, 129–
30, 134, 136, 150–55, 156, 158,
159, 165, 168, 260
Ghannouchi, 190
Ghassasi, Fawzia, 54
Global Women in Politics Program,
142
Great Britain, 96, 97, 99
Green March, 35
Gueddana, Nabiha, 242
Guide Juridique (publication), 215
Gulf War, 40, 53–55, 62, 67, 96, 157,
182, 197, 254

Haddad, Radhia, 206, 227
Haddad, Tahar, 178, 202
Haddaoui, Rafiq, 87
Hashemite Jordanian Women's
Society, 121
Hashemites, 98, state feminisim, 170
Hassan, Crown Prince, 115, 138, 147,
149
Hassan, King, 31, 32, 35, 36, 37, 38,
40, 41–42, 43–44, 69, 248, 252,
255; "commander of the faithful,"
32, 73; Green March, 35
Hassar, Fatima, 64
Hatem, M., 8, 10, 11
Higher Council on Human Rights,
Tunisia, 197
Hijab, 196
Hikmat, Tahir, 135
Hindawi, Dhuqan, 105, 111
Hizb al-Tali'a, Morocco, 54
Honor crimes, 133–34, 137, 139,
280n41
Al-Huda (publication), 72
Human rights: Jordan, 141; Morocco,
32, 35, 36–38, 40–41, 42; organiza-
tions, 37, 38; U.S. State Department
Human Right report, 38; Tunisia,
197, 199, 200, 216, 218, 239, 255;
see also Amnesty International

Human Rights Consultative Council,
Morocco, 38
Husayn, King, 95, 98, 99, 101, 104,
112, 252
Hussein, Saddam, 197

IAF (Islamic Action Front), Jordan,
109, 112, 113, 115, 117, 163, 168;
shura council, 162
Ibrahim, 'Abdallah, 49
Ijtihad, 57, 72, 178
*L'Image de la Femme dans la Société
Tunisienne* (publication), 215
IMF (International Monetary Fund),
97, 98, 100, 118, 181, 183
Infitah, 181
Inheritance laws, 105–6, 210–11,
228
Institut National de la Justice,
Morocco, 64
International Advisory Group, 163
International Federation of Business
and Professional Women, 128
International Monetary Fund (IMF),
see IMF
International Visitor (IV) program, 65,
217
International Women's Conference,
Mexico City (1973), 49
International Women's Day, 69, 162,
225, 233
Iranian revolution, 185
Iran-Iraq war, 96, 100
Iraq, 40, 97, 98, 106, 196
Islam (Islamists), xiv, 47, 57; "funda-
mentalist," xiv, 183; ijtihad, 57, 72,
178; in Jordan, 102, 103, 106, 108,
110, 111, 139, 156–57; in Morocco,
35, 91; in Tunisia, 178, 185, 188,
189, 190, 191–92, 193–94, 195,
200, 213, 228, 232, 241, 244; see
also Religion
Islamic Action committees, 154
Islamic Action Front (IAF), see IAF

Islamic Conference Organization, 49–50

Islamic family law, 180

Islamic inheritance law, 179; see also Inheritance laws

Islamic Tendency Movement, see MTI

Islamic Voluntary Societies, 154

Islamist organizations, 54, 55, 71, 179–80, 182, 185, 188, 191, 193, 194, 195, 197, 231–32, 234, 241, 244, 253, 254, 255

Islamists, see Islam 252; Ulama

Israel, 98, 116; occupation of West Bank, 100

Jaljuli, 'Adnan, 106

Jallaba, 50

Jamai, Khalid, 32, 80

JANDA (Jordanian Arab National Democratic Assembly), 107

Japan, 98

Jbabdi, Latifa, 52, 70, 87

Jeune Afrique (publication), 44, 186, 189

Jihad, 179

JNCW (Jordanian National Committee for Women), 134, 140, 141, 144, 158–63

JNWF (Jordanian National Women's Forum) (Tajammu' Lijan al-Mar'ah al-Watani al-Urdunni), 161, 164, 262

Jordan, 7, 96, 99, 100, 110; "family book" (*daftar al-'a'ilah*) 132; Baghdad Pact, 99; Charitable Societies Law, 121, 126; citizenship, 130–31, 139; Civil Defense Martyrs fund, 110; Civil Service Law, 136; Civil Status Law, 132, 166; Constitution, 104, 130; Constitutional Bloc, 107–8, 109; dairy project, 126–27; Democratic Bloc, 105; divorce and alimony, 122, 132, 149, 166; economy, 97–98, 105; educa-

tion, 122, 130, 156–57, 250; education portfolio, 102; Egypt, relationship with, 98; elections, 100, 101, 102, 103, 105, 110, 112, 122, 123, 124, 145, 146, 150, 153, 253, 255; Elections Law, 124; external agencies, role of, 140–44, 171; family, clan, and tribal ties, role of, 96; Great Britain, relationship with, 96, 97, 98, 99; Gulf crisis, 97, 105, 157, 165; hairdresser ban, 105, 118; health insurance, 135; IAF shura council, 162; Ikhwan, 102, 103, 104, 106, 107, 109, 117, 148, 154, 253; inheritance laws, 105–6; Iraq, relationship with, 98, 116; Islamic women, 152–53, 157, 168; Islamists, 102, 103, 106, 108, 110, 111, 139, 156–57; Israel, relationship with, 116; Jordanians of Palestinian origin, 99–100, 101, 106, 112; Labor Law, 131–32, 136, 166; Landlords and Tenants Law, 135, 139; liberalization, 101–14, 248; martial law, 96, 99, 101, 103, 104, 107, 149; Ministry of Social Affairs, 121; Ministry of Social Development, 125, 127, 150, 154, 157; Miri (state) land, 105, 134; MPs, 103, 109, 110; *mukhabarat*, 104; municipal councils law, 114 ; National Bloc, 152; National Charter, 104, 135; National Consultative Council, 100; National Forum, 260; National Women's Grouping, 124; Nationality Law, 137; Palestinian resistance, expulsion of, 99–100; Palestinians in, 96, 97; passport law, 137, 165; personal status laws, 122, 132, 137, 140, 142, 148, 149, 150; pluralism, 110; political history, early liberalizations, 98–101; political system and parties, 96–97, 101, 102; Press and

Publications Law, 114; refugees, influx of, 96, 97, 98, 166; Retirement Law, 131; riots, 100, 101, 118, 249; secretaries union, 165; sex segregation, 106, 110, 111, 114, 156, 157, 173; Soviet Union, relationship with, 99; Syria, relationship with, 98, 100; Transjordanians (East Bankers), 96, 97, 99, 106, 112, 113, 124, 164, 253, 276n5; United States, relationship with, 97, 98, 99; violence against women, 137, 138, 166; Violence Free Society, 138; West Bank, 98, 100; White Revolution, 116; women's movement in, 120–29, 168, 171, 250–251; Women's Week, 122; see also PLO

Jordanian Arab National Democratic Assembly (JANDA), see JANDA

Jordanian National Front, 113

Jordanian National Society for the Enhancement of Freedom and Democracy, 143

Jordanian National Women's Forum, 155

Jordan-Israel peace treaty, 118

Jordan Times (publication), 114, 137

Jordan Valley, 97

JORT (Journal Officiel de la République Tunisienne), (publication), 230

Joseph, Su'ad, 6, 8

Justice and Charity (al-'Adl w-al-Ihsan), Morocco, 54, 55

JWU (Jordanian Women's Union), 134, 137, 138, 140, 164–67, 172, 251

Kabariti, 'Abd al-Karim, 116–17, 149, 169

Kalima (publication), 53

Kandiyoti, D., 259

KAS (Konrad Adenauer Stiftung), 52, 62–63, 143

Kefi, Faiza, 215, 229

Khadr, Asma, 104, 165, 166, 172

Khalaf, Rima, 116, 169

Khalif, 'Abd al-Rahman, 196

Khalifeh, Majid, 106, 114

Khomeini, Ayatollah, 2

Al-Kilani, Ibrahim Zayd, 106

Konrad Adenauer Stiftung, see KAS

Kuwait, 96, 97, 154

Labor laws, and women's participation in, Chile, 20; Jordan, 131–32, 136, 166; Morocco, 57–58, 63, 250; Tunisia, 197, 209–10, 211, 213, 223

Lamalif (publication), 53

Lamrini, Amina, 65, 83–84, 86

Latin America: democratic transitions, 17; Catholic Church, role of, 18, 19; traditional image of women, 19; women's organizations, 19, 251, 257–58

Laws of Charitable and Voluntary Societies, 171

Al-Lawzi, Ahmad, 136

LDDF (Ligue Démocratique des Droits de la Femme), Morocco, 63

Leadership/regime, 3

Lebanon, 9, 224

Liberalization, "citizenness," 7, 8; decentralization in, 38; "decompression," 7; defined, 4; factors in, 22–23; Jordan, 101–14, 248; managed, 7; Morocco, 35–40, 248; nature of, 7–8; "subjectness," 7, 8; Tunisia, 183–88, 199–200, 228, 230, 248, 249, 261; women and, 8–12, 247

Libya, 36

Ligue Démocratique des Droits de la Femme, Morocco, 54

LMDH (Ligue Marocaine des Droits de L'Homme), 37

Loukhmas, Aicha, 79

LTDH, (Ligue Tunisienne des Droits

de l'Homme), 185, 190, 194, 200, 216, 231–32

Ma'aini, Subeiha, 169
Ma'arifah (publication), 185
Madres de la Plaza, Argentina, 18
Madrid conference (1989), 106–7, 108, 114, 158
Le Maghreb (publication), 189
Al-Majali, 'Abd al-Salam, 111, 112, 115, 169
Makhzen, 32, 38, 48, 54, 57, 58
Malekite tradition, 59
Manifeste de l'Independence, 46
Al-Mar'ah (publication), 226, 227, 237
Al-Mar'ah al -'A'ilah w-al-Sukkan
(Women, Family, and Population, publication), 229
Marrakesh, 36
Marriage: Jordan, 135; Morroco, 57, 60, 76; Tunisia, 208, 210, 231–32; see also Personal status laws
Marsot, A., 9
Marzouki, Moncef, 200
Al-Masri, Salwa Damen, 169
Al-Masri, Tahir, 106, 107, 108, 113, 118, 154, 254
Le Matin du Sahara (publication), 81
MCP (Moroccan Communist Party), 36, 46
MDS (Mouvement des Démocrates Socialistes), Tunisia, 187, 188, 189
Media, 81, 99, 114, 196, 197, 198, 200, 228, 239; see also Press
Meghnawi, Fatima, 87
Mères célibataires, 52
Mernissi, Fatima, 53, 63, 66
Methodology, 22–24
Mezhoud, Neziha, 235–36, 237–38
Mi'adi, Zineb, 83
Middle East peace conference, 107
Misbah, Princess, 120
Mitterrand, François, 230
Molyneux, M., 5

Moroccan Red Crescent Society (MRCS), 64
Moroccan Students Federation, 48
Morocco, 38, 40, 47; *alternance*, 41, 44, 45, 77, 82; Constitution, 41, 42–43, 57; Council on Human Rights, 35; divorce and alimony, 59–60, 61, 62, 70; economy, 32–35; elections, 35, 36, 39, 41, 42, 43, 49–50, 73–74, 80, 83–85; European relationship with, 32, 33, 35, 36; external factors, role of, 34–35; Finance Law of 1990, 60–61; human rights, 32, 35, 36–38, 40–41, 42; Islamic influence, 35; Istiqlal, 48, 49; *kutlah*, 43, 44, 45, 70, 74, 77; labor, women's participation in, 57–58, 250; Law of Engagements and Contracts, 61; legal status of women, 54, 57–62; liberalization, 35–40, 248; Ministry of Human Rights, 35, 64; Ministry of Youth, 51; "National Committee of Coordination to Change the *Mudawwanah* and to Defend the Rights of Women," 71; opposition parties, 36, 41, 43; penal code, 57, 61; Personal Status Code (*mudawwanah*), 49, 51, 52, 54, 57, 58–59, 60, 61, 63, 67, 76, 89, 260; Personal Status Code (*mudawwanah*), petition against, 69–77, 77, 256, 257; personal status laws, 43; political parties, women in, 48–50; political system in, 31–32; retirement, 61; riots, 35, 36, 40; SAP (sans appartenance politique) candidates, 43; Thabit Affair, 78–81, 82; tutor (*wali*), 57, 59, 70, 76; United States relationship with, 35; violence against women, 54, 63, 82, 83, 260; women's movement, 46–59, 250; women's organizations, role of external funders, 62–65

Mourou, A., 190, 232
Mouvement Populaire Démocratique et Constitutionnel, Morocco, 55
MRCS (Moroccan Red Crescent Society), 64
MTI (Mouvance de la tendance islamique), Islamic Tendency Movement, Tunisia, 179–80, 182, 185, 188, 191, 193, 231–32, 234, 244, 253
Mudawwanah, see Morocco
Al-Mufti, In'am, 125–26
Muhammad, Prophet, 111, 252
Muhammad V, 59
Muhammad V University, 62; Faculty of Letters, 52; Women's Study Group, 54
Muhaylan, Shaykh, 149
Munaththamat Tajdid al-Wa'i al-Nisa'i, The Organization for Renewing Women's Awareness, Morocco, 55
MUP (Mouvement de l'Unité Populaire), Tunisia, 188
Murad, Mansour, 108
Muslim Brotherhood, Egypt, 179
Muslim Brotherhood, Jordan, 102, 104, 106, 111, 113, 148, 154, 156, 252, 253, 276n13
Al-Mustaqbal (publication), 189
Mutlaq, 'Eida, 104, 149
Mzali, Fathia, 189, 190, 206, 226–27, 229, 230
Mzali, Muhammad, 180, 182, 186, 187–88, 189–90, 199, 206, 207, 223, 225, 230, 232, 244, 253

Al-Nabulsi, Faris, 111, 127
Nabulsi, Sulayman, 99
Naciri, Rabea, 82
Al-Nahdah, Tunisia, 193, 194, 195, 197, 234, 239, 241, 254, 255
Nairobi conference (1983), 89, 229
Napoleonic Civil Code, 2, 61

Al-Nasir, Gamal 'Abd, 99
National Action Front, Jordan, 113
National Charter on Human Rights, Morocco, 37
National Coalition of Women for Democracy, Chile, 20
National Democratic Institute (NDI), see NDI
National Endowment for Democracy (NED), see NED
National Islamic Front, Jordan, 115
Nationality, see Citizenship
National Office of Family Planning, Tunisia, 209
National Salvation Front, Romania, 14
National Solidarity Fund, 2606, Tunisia, 200
National Strategy for Women, Jordan, 140, 141, 158, 159, 160, 163, 164, 169
National Women's Forum, Jordan, 140
NDI (National Democratic Institute), 142–43
NED (National Endowment for Democracy), 142
Neo-Destour party, Tunisia, 203
New Jordan Research Center (NJRC), see NJRC
NGOs (non-governmental organizations): Jordan, 142, 159, 160, 168, 171; Morocco, 54, 62, 64, 66, 87–88; Tunisia, 198, 215–16, 217, 218, 219, 238, 240, 243; see also RONGOS
NHF (Noor al-Hussein Foundation), 143, 144, 171, 262
Nisa' al-Maghrib (Women of the Maghrib), publication, 51
Nissa (publication), 224, 225
NJRC (New Jordan Research Center), 142–43
Nongovernmental organizations (NGOs), see NGOs
Noor, Queen, 128, 158, 162

Noor al-Hussein Foundation (NHF), see NHF

Notre Ami Le Roi, (publication), 38

Notre Femme dans la Loi et dans la Société (publication), 202

Nouira, Hedi, 184, 185, 186

Nsour, 'Abdallah, 106

Al-Nur (publication), 71, 72

OADP (Organisation de l'Action Démocratique Populaire), Morocco, 43, 44, 52, 75

Obeidat, Ahmed, 104

OFI (Organisation de la Femme Istiqlalienne), Morocco, 51–52, 56, 71, 76, 88

Oil, 100

OMDH (Organisation Marocaine des Droits de l'Homme), 35, 37, 39, 54, 64, 73, 81, 83, 88

L'Opinion (publication), 32, 80

Organization for Renewing Womens' Awareness, Morocco, 55

Organisation Marocaine des Droits de l'Homme (OMDH), see OMDH

Organizations; civil society, 179, 198, 255, 262; licensing, 48, 187, 193, 197, 203, 238, 239, 258; see also *Utilité publique*; Women's organizations

Palestine Liberation Organization (PLO), see PLO

Palestinian intifada, 96, 101, 103

Palestinians, 9, 96, 97; guerrilla organizations, 123; resistance organizations, 99, 123

Pan-Arabism, 98, 119

Parti de la Renaissance et du Socialisme, Morocco, 71

Passports, 61, 103, 137, 165, 203

Patriarchy, 268n29

PCT (Tunisian Communist Party), 203

Penal code, 57, 61; see also Criminal code

Personal status laws, 43; Jordan, 122, 132, 137, 140, 142, 148, 149, 150; Morocco, mudawwanah, 49, 51, 52, 54, 57, 58–59, 60, 61, 63, 67, 76, 89, 260; Tunisia, CSP, 178, 180, 189, 192, 194, 202, 210, 220, 224, 231–32, 233, 240, 241–42, 250, 253, Tunisia, changes in CSP, 205, 207–8, 211–14, 227–28, 230, 261

Peteet, J., 9

Petroleum, 100

Phosphates, 33, 35

PI (Parti Istiqlalien), Morocco, 36, 37, 41, 43, 44, 46, 49, 51, 61

Pinochet, Augusto, 18, 20

Plan of Action, 216

PLO (Palestine Liberation Organization), 99, 100, 107, 112, 190

Portraits de Femmes (publication), 53

Pluralism, 110, 185, 187, 198, 201, 232, 238, 243, 245, 254, 255, 260, 264

Poland: abortion rights, 14–16; Catholic Church, 14–15, 16; Democratic Left Alliance, 16; parliament (Sejm), women's presence in, 15; Peasant Party, 16; Solidarity, 14–15, 16

Political liberalization, see Liberalization

Political transitions, 8, 12, 252, 253, 254, 256, 257

Polygamy, 10, 59, 122, 132, 166, 178, 194, 195, 205, 208, 213, 231, 250

PPS (Parti du Progrés et du Socialisme), Morocco, 36, 43, 44, 49, 51, 80, 83

Press, 99, 114, 196; see also Media

Princess Basma Women's Resource Center (PBWRC), 162, 164

Prison conditions, 37; see also Amnesty International

Progressive Democratic Alliance, Jordan, 113

Przeworski, 3
PSD (Parti Socialiste Destourien),
    Tunisia, 178, 182, 185, 186, 187,
    188, 194, 195, 204, 221, 230, 235,
    250
PSP (Social Party for Progress),
    Tunisia, 193
PVOs, 64

QAF (Queen Alia Fund for Social
    Development), 144, 158, 159, 160,
    162, 163, 171
Qa'war, Fakhri, 108
Al-Qidha, Nuh, 147–48
Qirrish, Ya'qub, 110
Queen Alia Fund for Social
    Development (QAF), see QAF
Queen Zein al-Sharaf Complex for
    Development, 162

Rabat, 33, 40; pro-Iraq demonstration
    in, 54
Rabitat, see Alliances
Al-Ra'i (publication), 146
Ramadan, 73, 179, 188
Rand, Jordan, 151, 162, 170
Rape, 78, 82; see also Violence, against
    women
Rashdan, Na'ila, 135–36, 154, 155,
    169
Al-Rayah (publication), 71, 72
Al-Razzaz, Mu'nis, 153
RCD (Rassemblement Constitutionnel
    Démocratique), Tunisia, 182, 194,
    195, 197, 199, 215, 236, 237, 242,
    260
Reform and Renewal Movement
    (Harakat al-Islah w-al-Tajdid),
    Morocco, 55, 71, 72, 80
Regimes, authoritarian, 7, 19, 20;
    changes in, 2, 3, 7; communist, 13;
    conservatism, relationship between,
    252; martial law, 96, 99, 101, 103,
    104, 107, 149

Religion, 10, 72, 234; Catholic
    Church, 14–15, 17, 18, 19, 263,
    264; Christian, 96; fundamentalism,
    xiv, 183; habous (religious endow-
    ments), 178; ijtihad, 57, 72, 178;
    Islam, 74, 91, 192; Protestantism,
    264; Russian Orthodox Church,
    16–17
Reproductive rights, 13; see also
    Abortion; Contraception
Revolution, 2; women's activity in, 2
Al-Rifa'i, Zayd, 101, 105, 110
Rihana, 243
RNI (Rassemblement National des
    Independants), Morocco, 60
Romania, 7; abortion rights, 14
RONGOs, 171, 219
Royal Jordanian Airlines, 103
RSP (Progressive Socialist Assembly),
    Tunisia, 193
Russia: abortion, 16–17; Perestroika;
    16; Russian Orthodox Church,
    16–17; women's political
    representation, 16

Sa'id, Hamza, 195
Sahara, 39
Al-Sahwah (publication), 72
Sarney, José, 19
Sarvath, Princess, 158
Saudia Arabia, 40, 106, 182, 197
Secularism, 9, 178–79, 192, 194, 233
SERNAM (the National Women's
    Service), Chile, 20
Sexism, 19
Sex segregation, 106, 110, 111, 114,
    156, 157, 173, 195, 247
Sexual harassment, 260
Sfar, Rachid, 190
Al-Shabibah al-Islamiyyah, Morocco,
    36
Al-Shabibah al-Tunisiyyah, 204
Shamaylah, 'Abdallah, 147
Shanqiti, Shaykh Mahmud, 147

Sharaf, Layla, 101, 104, 134, 147, 169
Sharaf, Princess Zayn, 120
Shari'a, 50, 52, 57, 58, 61, 71, 72, 81,
    105, 106, 110, 146, 149, 180, 210,
    231, 244
Shraydeh, 'Abd al-Majid, 150, 151–52
Shubaylat, Layth, 110
Sisters of Purity, Morocco, 46
Society of the Jordanian Women's
    Federation, 120
Spain, 32
Sqalli, Badia, 61–62, 65, 84–85, 86
State, defined, 6
State feminism, 10, 11, 25, 170, 205,
    222, 263 268n28
State/regime, 3
Strasbourg Center (France), 64
Sudan, 11
Suez Canal Company, 99
Syria, 98, 100

Tahar Haddad Club, 221
Al-Tahawwul (le changement), 191–
    199, 229, 232, 236, 239
Talal, Crown Prince, 120
Talib, Hadi Abu, 87
Taliban, 2
Tarawineh, Ahmad, 136
Thabit, Hadj Mohammed Mustapha,
    78
Thabit Affair ("Thabitgate"), 78–81,
    82

Transjordanians, see Jordan
Treaty of Rome, 37
Transjordan, 96; see also Jordan
Tunis, University of, 179
Tunisia, 7, 11; Algieria, relationship
    with, 182, 183, 194; Alliances
    (rabitat), 226, 227, 236, 237; al-
    Tahawwul (le changement), 191–199,
    229, 232, 236, 239; Association for
    Preserving the Qur'an (Association
    pour la Sauvegarde du Coran), 179;
    civil society organizations, 179;

constitution, 184, 192; contraception, 180, 209, 211, 221, 249;
criminal code, 210, 213, 224; CSP
(Code du Statut Personnel), 178,
180, 189, 192, 194, 202, 210, 220,
224, 230, 231–32, 233, 240, 241–
42, 250, 253; CSP, changes in, 205,
207–8, 211–14, 227–28, 230, 261;
divorce and alimony, 178, 194, 205,
208, 211, 212, 213, 231; economy,
181–82, 184–85, 191, 197, 200,
231; education, 180, 195, 205, 209,
211, 213, 218, 241, 249; elections,
185, 186, 188–89, 194, 195, 196,
200, 215, 234, 242; external factors,
role of, 182–83, 255; external
funders, 214–218; Guide Juridique,
215; Gulf crisis, 182, 196; habous
(religious endowments), 178;
human rights, 197, 199, 200, 216,
218, 239, 255; infitah, 181;
inheritance laws, 210–11, 228;
Islamists, 185, 188, 189, 190, 191–
92, 193–94, 195, 200, 213, 228,
232, 241, 244; Islamization of state
discourse, 192, 233; jihad, 179;
labor, women in, 197, 209–102,
211, 213, 223; legal rights of
women, 207–11, 218, 241; legislation, 178, 204; liberalization in,
183–88, 199–200, 228, 230, 248,
249, 261; Libya, relationship with,
182; media, 196, 197, 198, 200,
228, 239; Ministry of the Family
and the Promotion of Women, 190,
207, 229; multi-partyism, 187;
mutiny, 186; National Council on
Public Liberties, 185; National
Pact, 193, 194, 233, 234, 239, 241,
245; nationality, 210, 213; organizations, licensing of, 187, 193, 197,
203, 238, 239, 258; pluralism, 185,
187, 198, 232, 238, 243, 245, 254,
255, 260; Political Party Law, 193;

political system in, 177–81, 211; reciprocity, 212; secularism, 178–79, 192, 194, 233; sex segregation, 195; state feminism, 10, 11, 180, 205; strikes and rioting, 181, 186, 188, 189, 194, 195, 198, 224; Tripoli, relationship with, 182; United States, relationship with, 183; women's movement, 202–7, 220–25; women's rights and status in, 180, 204, 213–14, 233, 239, 240, 241, 249
Turkey, state feminism, 10
Tutor (*wali*), 57, 59, 70, 76, 212

UAF (Union de l'Action Féminine), Morocco, 52, 69–71, 72, 76, 79, 82, 83, 87, 251, 256
UDU (Unitary Democratic Union), Tunisia, 193
UFT (Union des Femmes de Tunisie), 203
UGTT, (Union Générale de Travailleurs Tunisiens), 177, 185–86, 187, 188–90, 199, 223–24, 233
Ulama (religious scholars), 32, 47, 49, 58, 71, 72, 179, 252
UMFT (Union Musulmane des Femmes de Tunisie), 202
UMT (Union Marocaine de Travail), 47, 71
UNAT (Union Nationale d'Agricoles Tunisiens), 177, 187
UN Conference on Women, 206
UN Decade on Women, 48, 50, 124, 126, 130, 229
UNEM (Union Nationale Estudiantine Marocaine), 50
UNFM (Union Nationale des Femmes Marocaines), 47, 56, 75, 88
UNFT (Union Nationale de la Femme Tunisienne), 177, 187, 189, 203, 204–7, 215, 218, 219, 221, 225, 226–27, 231, 233, 235–38

Union des Jeunes Filles de Tunisie, 203
Union Nationale des Forces Populaires, Morocco, 48
United Nations Fund for Population, 158
United States Agency for International Development (USAID), see USAID
United States government, 64–65, 97, 183
United States Information Service (USIS), see USIS
Universal Declaration on Human Rights, 35, 37
UNRWA (United Relief and Works Agency for Palestine Refugees), 164
UPFM (Union Progressiste des Femmes Marocaines), 47
USAID (United States Agency for International Development), 64, 140–41, 159, 214–16
USFP (Union Socialiste des Forces Populaires), Morocco, 36, 37, 41, 44, 48, 49, 61, 71, 84
USIS (United States Information Service), 64–65, 66, 216–27
UTICA (Union Tunisienne de l'Industrie, du Commerce et de l'Artisanat), 178, 187
Utilité publique, 47, 55, 67

Veil, wearing of, 50
Vengeance killing, 138; see also Honor crimes
Violence, against women, Argentina, 20; Jordan, 137, 138, 166; Morocco, 54, 63, 66, 82–83, 260; Tunisia, 194, 213, 234, 240
Violence Free Society, Jordan, 138

West Bank, see Jordan
Western Sahara, 35; war in, 33
WFJ (Society of the Women's Federation in Jordan), 124–25, 129, 150, 279n17

Who's Who, Jordanian parliament, 143
WID (Women in Development), 140–
41, 144
Women, see Jordan; Morocco; Personal
status laws; Tunisia; Women's
organizations
Women in Development (WID), see
WID
Women's Day (Tunisia), 207–8, 212,
221, 241
Women's Decade, see UN Decade on
Women
Women's League in Jordan (al-Rabitah
al-Nisa'iyyah f-il-Urdunn), 126
Women's organizations, 18, 19, 56–57,
90, 187, 203, 257, 258–59, 260;
Argentine, 18; Chilean, 20; limitations to women's participation, 56–
57; Jordanian, 120, 121–23, 124–25,
126–27, 128, 129–30, 134, 136, 137,
138, 140, 141, 144, 149, 150, 151,
155, 158–63, 164, 264–67, 168, 169,
170, 172, 238, 251, 260, 262,
279n17; Moroccan, 46, 48, 49, 50,

51–52, 54, 55, 56, 63, 69–71, 72, 73,
76, 79, 80, 82, 83, 87, 88, 251, 256;
Tunisian, 177, 187, 189, 202, 203,
204–7, 215, 218, 219, 221, 225,
226–27, 231, 233, 235–38
"Women question," 9, 180, 203, 207
Women's Research Center, Jordan,
149
Women's Social Solidarity Society,
Jordan, 120
Women's Status Committee of the
Jordanian Lawyers Union, 134

Yaacoubi, Souad, 229, 230
Yacine, 'Abd al-Salam, 54, 55
Yarmouk University, student
demonstrations, 100
Yeltsin, Boris, 17

Za'im (political boss) syndrome, 261
Zarrouk, Neziha, 242
Zionism, 122
Zitouna University, 179, 185, 192, 195
Zumaylah, Mahdiyyah, 153–54